Michael Jackson

VISUAL DOCUMENTARY BY ADRIAN GRA

Dedicated to Michael, and all the fans around the world...
DON'T STOP 'TIL YOU GET ENOUGH!

Copyright © 1994 Omnibus Press
This edition Copyright © 2005 Omnibus Press
(A Division of Music Sales Limited)

Research by:
ADRIAN GRANT, JAYNE ROSS, GLORIA HAYDOCK,
CHRIS CADMAN, LISA CAMBELL, SHONA CARPENTER, ANGELIKA MEISEL

Cover and Book Design by:
ADRIAN GRANT

Picture Research by:
ADRIAN GRANT
NIKKI LLYOD, SARAH BACON

For more information on Michael Jackson please visit: www.mjworld.net

ISBN 1.84449.432.2
Order No. OP50325

Exclusive Distributors:
MUSIC SALES LIMITED
8/9 Frith Street,
London W1D 3JB, UK.

MUSIC SALES CORPORATION
257 Park Avenue South,
New York, NY 10010, USA.

MACMILLAN DISTRIBUTION SERVICES
53 Park West Drive,
Derrimut, Vic 3030,
Australia.

To the Music Trade only:
MUSIC SALES LIMITED
8/9 Frith Street,
London W1D 3JB, UK.

Picture credits:
Front Cover : Jonathan Exley, MJJ Productions
Back Cover: All London Features International
Barry Plummer: All pictures on pages 122-123
Disney Publicity: 98a&b
Motown Records: 11, 18a-c, 33
Epic Records: 34a&b, 102a, 103b, 146c
Popperfoto/Reuters: 213
Shannon Morgan: 229b
Michael Jackson with son, Prince Michael Jr., pictures courtesy of OK! magazine.
Rex Features: 29a, 48b, 50a, 52a, 56a, 57a, 61b, 65a&b, 68b, 69a-c, 70, 71, 76a, 78a, 79a, 82b,84, 87,
94, 109, 11b, 115, 116, 118b, 119b, 133, 136, 146b, 147a&b, 154, 157, 161a&b, 164a&c, 172, 173a&b, 174, 203, 206, 208-9
MJJ Productions: 4b, 5a, 108, 120a&b, 121, 126, 135, 142a, 148b, 150a, 152, 155, 160, 164b, 165, 169, 198, 201, 223
London Features International: 1, 3, 12, 14b, 26a, 28a&b, 36, 43, 45a, 47a, 53a, 56b-d, 58b-d, 59, 62b, 63a-c, 64, 66a,
68a, 72, 74, 75a, 79b, 81, 85s-d, 91b, 92b, 95, 96a&b, 96c, 97b, 99a, 101a, 104, 105, 106c, 107, 110a&b, 111a, 112, 119a&c,
120c, 123a&b, 124b, 125a, 128a, 129a&b 130b,131b&c, 137, 138a, 143b, 151a-d, 159, 161c&d, 200a, 205a, 207, 210, 212,
214, 215, 216, 217, 218, 219, 221, 222, 224, 225, 226, 227, 228, 229a, 230, 231, 233, 234, 236, 237, 238, 240, 242, 243

Every effort has been made to trace the copyright holders of the photographs in this book but one or two were unreachable.
We would be grateful if the photographers concerned would contact us.

Printed in Singapore

A catalogue record for this book is available from the British Library.

Visit Omnibus Press on the web at www.omnibuspress.com

AUTHOR'S NOTE

The first time Michael Jackson really grabbed my attention was shortly after 'Thriller' had been released. Although I had previously enjoyed older Jackson tracks, I had been unaware of Michael's individual talent. As my admiration for Michael grew, so did my love for entertainment.

In 1988 I was fortunate enough to be able to combine these two passions with the publication of OFF THE WALL magazine, a Michael Jackson fanzine and fan club I had created. Through OFF THE WALL I was able to experience the wonderful world of Michael Jackson at first hand.

Although I have now met Michael on many different occasions, the most memorable will always be the first when, on behalf of the readers of OFF THE WALL, I presented an Appreciation Award to him at Record One Studios, where he was recording new tracks for the album 'Dangerous'.

I don't know why but I felt very relaxed before being introduced to Michael. Maybe I was in a daze and floating on the fact that I was about to meet the world's biggest superstar! Having been ushered into the non-descript Studio, situated in urban L.A, I waited in a chic lounge, with Michael's photographer Sam Emerson. He chatted casually about this famous person and that, and then all of a sudden I heard an amazing vocal being sung around the corner. The voice grew louder and more beautiful as it got nearer, until Michael entered the room smiling and singing. Oh wow! You can hear him sing on stage and on record, but nothing can compare to hearing him sing unaccompanied right next to you! His electric charismatic presence illuminated the room and I couldn't help but steer at his distinguished appearance and gazelle-like movements.

Mr. Bob Jones, Vice President of MJJ Productions, introduced me to Michael and left me to make the presentation of the award. He absolutely loved the accolade, which was an amazing 6x3 foot oil painting depicting Michael's illustrious career, created by British artist Vincent McKoy. The painting really touched Michael, as did the messages from the readers of OFF THE WALL.

The rest of the day just got better and better, as Michael made me feel right at home. I've met many celebrities and I really don't know any as giving as Michael Jackson. He really does think about and care for his fans. Firstly he phoned Vincent to thank him for the painting. He then played me an exclusive track he had recorded and posed for a few photographs for my magazine. But to top it all he invited me to his house for lunch! Things don't get much better than that...

As time went on, my magazine spread around the world, reaching readers all over Europe and as far afield as Australia, Africa, America and Asia. I came into contact with many devoted fans, who had been enthralled, not just by Michael's music and dance, but also by his humanatarian efforts which had touched many less fortunate lives.

The VISUAL DOCUMENTARY is for the fans, and I am glad that upon writing this fourth edition it has been acknowledged by many, including Michael, as the essential guide to The King of Pop. I would just like to say a BIG THANK YOU to the following for helping me to compile this book:

Jayne Ross, Chris Cadman, Lisa Campbell and Gloria Haydock
(Your research, time & effort was invaluable)

Shona Carpenter, Paulette Murray, Angelika Meisel, Emine Dayioglu, Pamela Phelps, Jeff Beasley, Helen Brown, Justin Travill, Sadie Parsons, Bob Jones, Kimberly Ingram, Evvy Tavaasci, Deborah Dannelly, Chris Charlesworth and names not listed here whom have helped in some way, you are not forgotten!

Adrian Grant – January 2005

(Note: As Michael's career started in the US, most of the chart information contained within is US based, unless otherwise stated.)

Author, Adrian Grant, with Michael Jackson, Los Angeles, 1990.

Michael Joseph Jackson was born on August 29, 1958 in the small steel town of Gary in Indiana in America's north east. He was the fifth son and seventh of nine children born to Joseph and Katherine Jackson who, following a whirlwind courtship, were married in 1949.

The Jackson family's rise to success is the epitome of the all-American dream but as Katherine admitted in the early part of 1994, the dream has become a nightmare. Her comments, unsurprisingly, were swiftly tempered by the Jackson's spokesman, her ever-watchful son Jermaine. Spearheading a family reunion show, at a time when Michael faced allegations of child abuse and the Jacksons required all their inner strength, Jermaine was close at hand to promote – however unconvincingly – the unity of the Jackson family.

Talk of child molestation is inappropriate in a book about the life and career of the man who many regard as the world's greatest all-round entertainer. Michael's career is unparalleled in the history of music business – and so too is the media's unrelenting hunger for gossip about him.

Michael's accomplishments in the Eighties made him the most influential musician of the decade, a living legend, recognised the world over. From his groundbreaking videos, innovative dance routines, countless hit records and breathtaking live performances to his humanitarian activities spanning two decades and culminating in the launch of his own children's charity – the Heal The World Foundation – Michael Jackson's name has become synonymous with all that is good and pure in the world of entertainment. He even rubbed shoulders with three Presidents.

It all seemed too good to be true; too much for one man to have the world at his feet, to be equipped with a voice that could touch millions, irrespective of creed or colour. It seemed almost as if someone, somewhere became intolerant with the ever-increasing power and influence which Michael enjoyed, and planned for it to end in the most cruel manner imaginable.

Michael Jackson
INTRODUCTION

And so it was that on Monday, August 23, 1993, while Michael was on tour in Bangkok about to thrill hundreds of thousands of adoring fans with his electrifying stage presence, the scandal-hungry gutter press finally had their day. Allegations of child abuse! The story of the century! With little regard for the truth or for the consequences, the race for sensational headlines to boost tabloid sales and TV ratings began. At last the media pack had something with which to damage and perhaps destroy Michael's untainted image. The very same medium which had helped to catapult Michael's career to the dizzy heights of mega-stardom – the likes of which are unlikely ever again to be equalled – was now plotting his downfall.

The reporting in the tabloid press was cold-blooded and malicious. For years Michael's relationship with the press had been on a downward slide, accelerated by his refusal to give any interview whatsoever. Now it was time for the backlash. With each passing day the stories became more and more outrageous. Like snowballs increasing in size as they gather speed, the stories about Michael and the damage to his reputation grew and grew. After all, 'mud sticks' they would write – over and over again. Uncorroborated statements from so-called witnesses willing to 'tell all' – for the right price, of course – were dished out daily.

The louder the cries from these 'witnesses', the more the voices of the quiet masses – Michael's fans – were drowned. With a press unwilling to print any positive statements about Michael or even cover his defence, millions of tormented admirers were forced to witness Jackson-bashing at fever pitch. Compelled to stand by helplessly, they tried to comprehend what was happening in a world they no longer understood. How could a star which had once shone so brightly be dimmed so mercilessly.

With the final chapter of Michael Jackson's career still unwritten, it would be unwise to dwell too long on this unfortunate period in his life. But it is worth mentioning that while the investigation against Michael Jackson continues, over one hundred thousand children from the New York metro area voted to honour Michael at their Second Annual Children's Choice Awards by presenting him with a 'Caring For Kids' award. Regardless of the vindictive

publicity, he remains, in their eyes, the voice of the voiceless, the world's most caring star.

When the furore abates and the history books are written, Michael will be remembered mostly for the immense pleasure he has given to millions of people around the world over three decades through his music, his unique dancing style, his pioneering music videos and, last but certainly not least, for the barriers he broke down in opening doors for other Black entertainers. 'Billie Jean,' lest we forget, became the first video by a Black artist to be added to MTV's playlist in America.

In compiling a documentary of this kind, it is inevitable that events which Michael himself would prefer remain forgotten are nevertheless chronicled. In the early Seventies, when Berry Gordy was masterminding the explosion of the Jackson 5 onto the music scene, the media was much easier to control. Indeed, everything was easier to control. Berry was dealing with five young boys between the ages of 11 and 18, who were inexperienced in the music business. They saw Berry as their mentor and were willing to do everything exactly as they were instructed. They gave Berry the same respect previously reserved for their father who, after accepting that he would never be a successful musician himself, decided to realise his ambition through his talented offspring.

It seems, however, that the respect Joe earned from his sons grew out of fear. Joe Jackson was a man possessed with the desire to succeed – at any cost. Here was a man who transformed his boys into virtual dancing machines, rehearsing them day after day, hour upon hour, denying them the basic right 'to play' and to interact with their peers. In years to come, it would be virtually all that Michael could recall of his childhood, a childhood filled with fear so intense that he would regurgitate at the mere sight of his father, even into adolescence, a childhood consisting of work, work and more work.

To the world outside the family, the Jacksons' success story unfolds like a fairy tale. After a hard day's work at the Inland Steel Mill, Joseph comes home to discover his sacred guitar – Joe had been a member of a local group called The Falcons – had a broken string. On discovering the culprit, and after calming his fury, he demanded of Tito: "Let me see what you can do!" Tito's sneak exercises had paid off and he impressed his father, as did Jackie and Jermaine. And so it was that in that year, 1961, the Jacksons took their first steps on the road to stardom.

It would be a couple of years before Michael would join his brothers singing and playing bongos. That year, cute, loveable, little Michael took centre stage at Garnett Elementary School for a rousing a cappella version of 'Climb Every Mountain.' His performance received a thunderous applause from the audience, bringing tears to the eyes of his mother and his teachers. At just five years of age his raw talent was awesome. The same charisma which captivated that audience would be refined and cultivated over many years and would ultimately lead to a kind of stardom undreamt of in Hollywood, let alone Gary, Indiana.

By this time, 2300 Jackson Street - named after President Andrew Jackson - was beginning to resemble a recording studio with all types of musical equipment crammed into a two-bedroomed home which housed eleven people! Joe prepared his boys relentlessly for one talent show after another, and Michael can recall stern punishments from his father. "If you messed up, you got hit, sometimes with a belt, sometimes with a switch (tree branch). My father was real strict with us – real strict," says Michael. Although the smallest, Michael would rebel more than his brothers, and once threatened never to sing again if his father were to hit him. Fortunately, Michael continued to sing and the gruelling practice sessions began to pay off as the group won prize after prize.

It was not long before this success led to their first record on a small label called Steeltown. 'Big Boy' led to greater things for the Jackson 5, who actually numbered six, with Johnny Jackson (no relation) playing drums. In 1967 the Jackson 5 took part in a talent show at New York's legendary Apollo Theatre. Also performing that night were Gladys Knight & The Pips, and James Brown. Michael's insatiable desire to learn, coupled with a capacity to absorb and imitate, was cultivated as he watched James Brown's every move on stage, his young inquisitive mind taking in the master's steps, grunts, spins and turns. To this day, Michael has never outgrown this unquenchable thirst for knowledge, and he is said to read a book each day.

Some consider Michael Jackson to be the last great legend, for he has lived through a period rich in great musical performers. Michael has said that many of the world's greatest thinkers were self-taught. Likewise, Michael has taught himself, largely from observing the great talents of the entertainment world, Sammy Davis Jr., Jackie Wilson, Elizabeth Taylor, Frank Sinatra, Liza Minnelli, Diana Ross, Charlie Chaplin and, perhaps his greatest idol of all, to whom he dedicated his autobiography *Moonwalk*, Fred Astaire. These are not only great performers in their field, but also survivors in the fickle world of show business. Michael has learned to cultivate his own extraordinary God-given talents by combining them with the knowledge and experience of other successful artists, and has created for himself a truly unique, electric-charged presence.

When Berry Gordy signed the Jackson 5 to Motown in 1968, he said he would make them the biggest group in the world. Berry was a clever, calculated businessman, who not only knew how to make hits but also how to control the media. The Jacksons' talent made his premonition come true, but at what cost? Somewhere along the line something got lost. As Michael Jackson's talents have continued to grow, so too has his stardom and the Jackson empire. As a boy, Michael was told what to do. As a man, Michael was led by an inner 'force' to the point where his creative energy was way ahead of its time. 'Thriller' earned him megastar status and its current world sales of 51 million can surely never be beaten, not even by Michael himself. As a child, Michael said, "I'd watch everything. They couldn't get away with nothing without me seeing." As a man, Michael Jackson's kingdom has simply become too big for him to watch over. Are Michael's 'minders' protecting him too much? Is he being shielded too much from the outside world? Has he, as is so often asserted, lost touch with the real world?

When Michael agreed to be interviewed by Oprah Winfrey in 1993, more than a hundred million people around the world became privy to the fantasy of Neverland, his California pleasuredome. The interview was dissected globally as the public tried hard to understand more about this illusive, reclusive 'manchild'. In *Q* magazine, Paul Du Noyer wrote in 1987: "There is a blankness to Michael Jackson's public face. A man with no age, no race, no sex, no opinions." But Michael Jackson does have opinions, as we would learn in this interview. More importantly, he truly does have God-given talents. Michael's short a cappella version of 'Who Is It' became the highlight of the interview, so much so that a special version of the song including this passage was rush marketed in the US. This was Michael doing what he does best. The 'force' which drives Michael to sing comes from within. Michael Jackson himself is the force.

It is time to stop digging at the superficial surface we see and read about in the tabloids, whose only concern is to sell newsprint. It is also time that the industry refrain from treating him like a 'Dancing Machine' – a clockwork toy, lest we lose this precious, magical force altogether.

This Visual Documentary is a book for the fans and admirers of this wondrous superstar, for whom all superlatives seem inadequate. You will find no new scandalous gossip about the undisputed King of Pop, Rock and Soul here. Neither will you discover what Michael eats for breakfast or whether he sleeps with his animals at night. What you will find is simply the most comprehensive, chronological guide to the life and career of the world's greatest-ever entertainer. Enjoy.

With respect...

Adrian Grant, May 1994

The Jackson Family Tree

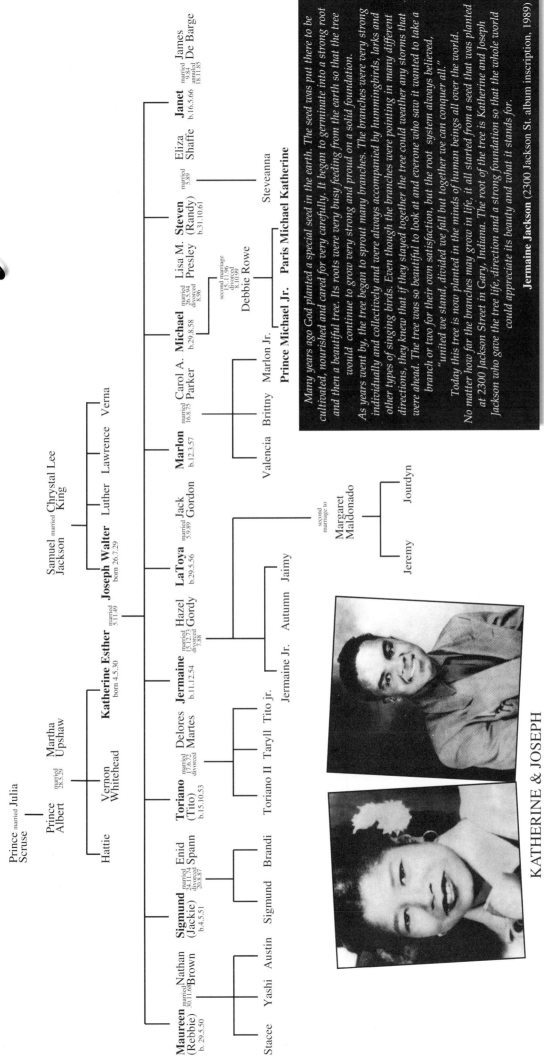

Prince married Julia Scruse

Samuel married Chrystal Lee Jackson King

Prince Albert married 28.5.29 Martha Upshaw

Joseph Walter born 26.7.29 married 5.11.49 Katherine Esther born 4.5.30

Vernon Whitehead

Hattie

Verma

Luther Lawrence

Maureen (Rebbie) b. 29.5.50 married 30.11.68 Nathan Brown

Sigmund (Jackie) b.4.5.51 married 24.11.74 divorced 20.8.87 Enid Spann

Toriano (Tito) b.15.10.53 married divorced Delores Martes

Jermaine b.11.12.54 married 15.12.73 divorced 7.88 Hazel Gordy

second marriage to Margaret Maldonado

LaToya b.29.5.56 married 5.9.89 Jack Gordon

Marlon b.12.3.57 married 16.8.75 Carol A. Parker

Michael b.29.8.58 married 26.5.94 divorced 8.96 Lisa M. Presley

second marriage 15.11.96 divorced 8.10.99 Debbie Rowe

Steven (Randy) b.31.10.61 married 5.89 Eliza Shaffe

Janet b.16.5.66 married 9.84 annuled 18.11.85 James De Barge

Stacee Yashi Austin Sigmund Brandi

Toriano II Taryll Tito jr.

Jermaine Jr. Autumn Jaimy

Jeremy Jourdyn

Valencia Brittny Marlon Jr.

Prince Michael Jr. Paris Michael Katherine

Prince Michael Jr. Paris Michael Katherine

Steveanna

KATHERINE & JOSEPH

REBBIE *Maureen Reilette*

JACKIE *Sigmund Esco*

TITO *Toriano Adaryll*

JERMAINE *Lajaun*

LATOYA *Yvonne*

MARLON *David*

MICHAEL *Joseph*

RANDY *Steven Randall*

JANET *Damita Jo*

1958

1958
August 29

Michael Joseph Jackson is the seventh child born to Katherine and Joe Jackson in Gary, Indiana.

1959

Michael begins to show the first signs of musical interest in the Jackson family's traditional sing-alongs that are led by mother Katherine's renditions of songs like, 'You Are My Sunshine,' 'Cotton Fields,' 'She'll Be Coming Round The Mountain' and 'Wabash Cannonball.' This tradition began in 1955 when the family TV set broke.

1960

Father Joe begins coaching Jermaine, Tito and Jackie in his spare time and they are soon joined by Marlon and Michael. Joe later recruits drummer Johnny Jackson.

1963
Autumn

Michael starts Kindergarten at Garnett Elementary School in Gary and, at the age of five, participates in a school pageant, singing an a cappella version of 'Climb Every Mountain' taken from the film *The Sound of Music*.

His emotional delivery brings his teacher and his mother to tears. This is Michael's first public performance.

Shortly afterwards, Michael takes over from Jermaine as lead vocalist in the group.

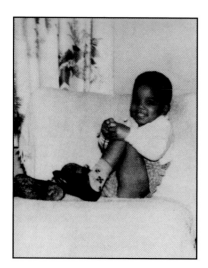

This Page: Young, cute and full of charisma, Michael recalls singing at a very early age.

This Page: The Jackson 5 and Johnny Jackson (on drums) in an early publicity photograph.

1965

The brothers' first invitation to perform comes courtesy of a children's fashion show in Glen Park. Having until then performed as the Jackson Family and the Jackson Brothers, it is here that the name The Jackson 5 is born, in preference to the Jackson Brothers Five suggested by show organiser, Evelyn Leahy. They perform three numbers, one being a current hit by The Larks, 'Doin' The Jerk.' Michael takes his position on the bongos.

After a suggestion from Joe's sister-in-law, Bobbie Rose Jackson, The Jackson 5, comprising Michael, Marlon, Jermaine, Jackie and Tito, enter and win the Roosevelt High School talent show. They succeed with a rendition of The Temptations' hit, 'My Girl,' with Michael and Jermaine alternating verses, and an original piece which enables each member of the group to be introduced and gives Michael an opportunity to show off his already amazing footwork.

Two months later, The Jackson 5 win the Annual Talent Search at Gilroy Stadium. Michael steals the show with his rendition of the Robert Parker hit, 'Barefootin''. The Jackson 5 also receive their first ever press in the *Gary Post Tribune*.

To further their musical education and strengthen the reputation they are building, Joseph Jackson books The Jackson 5 into Mr. Lucky's, a nightclub in Gary. They earn $8 a night for five sets, six or sometimes even seven days a week. They prove popular

with the customers who show their appreciation by throwing money onto the stage, amounting to well above their nightly fee.

Joseph Jackson sends Motown founder, Berry Gordy, a tape of The Jackson 5. Three months later, it is returned with no offer.

1967

The Jackson 5 win first prize in an amateur talent show at Gary's Memorial Auditorium.

Joseph Jackson enters The Jackson 5 in the Sunday Night Amateur Talent show at the Regal Theater, Chicago where they become three-time winners. Their victory not only earns them the right to appear with other multiple show winners, but also the chance to share the bill with a top established star or act.

The Jackson 5 win the Regal Theater's Multiple Winners Super Talent night and are placed on the same bill as top R&B act of 1967, Gladys Knight & The Pips. With their reputation preceding them, The Jackson 5 are entered straight into the 'Super Dogs' final at Harlem's legendary Apollo Theater and bring the house down with their polished performance. This proves to be the launching pad of their professional career. As winners, they receive an invitation to come back as paid performers. Appearing at the Apollo and other well-known theatres, Michael gets to watch and study his favourite performers, including James Brown.

Michael will soon adopt some of Brown's moves into his own choreography. New York lawyer, Richard Arons, agrees to help Joe to secure a contract with a major record label. He begins by booking gigs in several States which sees The Jackson 5 team up with other young acts, such as The Delfonics, The Emotions, The O'Jays and The Vibrations. During this time, they play in cities such as St. Louis, Philadelphia, Kansas City, Washington and New York.

1968
January

The Jackson 5 release the single 'Big Boy' on Steeltown Records, Gary, courtesy of a colleague and mutual music-loving friend of their father's, Mr. Keith. The single receives its radio début on an American station called WWCA and, although The Jackson 5 are delighted, it does not get picked up by enough radio stations to become a chart hit.

Needless to say, this single is now a much sought-after collectors' item, reportedly fetching up to $1,000.

Steeltown Records is headed by Ben Brown who will go on to work for the Jacksons in their home studio and with Joe Jackson's Jackson Records.

Spring

The Jackson 5 record their second single for Steeltown, 'You Don't Have To Be Over 21 (To Fall In Love)'/'Jam Session,' which eventually sees the light of day in 1971.

April

The Jackson 5 perform at a campaign rally for Richard Hatcher in Gary. The bill includes close friend Bobby Taylor, and Diana Ross & The Supremes also perform. This is the occasion Motown publicists later use to suggest that Diana Ross 'discovered' the group.

July 12

Bobby Taylor & The Vancouvers perform with The Jackson 5 at the Regal Theater in Chicago. Group member, Thomas Chong, later claims that it was during these performances that they 'discovered' the group.

August

The Jackson 5 are invited to appear on the David Frost Show in New York, after the producer is suitably impressed by their act.

Winter

The Jackson 5's TV début is shelved as they get their biggest break to date when they are asked to audition for Berry Gordy, founder and President of Motown Records in Detroit. One of the songs the group perform is 'Who's Loving You' but as Gordy cannot be present for the audition, it is video-taped for him. The Jackson 5 are subsequently signed to Motown Records.

Motown immediately begin to groom The Jackson 5 for public appearances and move the boys to Los Angeles in southern California to prepare for their first recording. Motown is also in the process of moving its headquarters to LA.

1968

This Page: The boys get used to smiling for the camera at an early age.

1968

This Page: Before Motown there was Steeltown, a small independent label which realised The Jackson 5 talent in 1968.

The Jackson 5, father Joe and his assistant Jack Richardson are temporarily accommodated at the Hollywood Hills homes of Berry Gordy and Diana Ross.

The Jackson 5 perform at a party at Berry Gordy's home with many of Motown's established stars welcoming them: The Four Tops, Stevie Wonder, The Temptations, Diana Ross and Smokey Robinson.

1969
August 11

Diana Ross invites Hollywood's media to come and meet Motown's newest act - The Jackson 5 - between 6.30 p.m. and 9.30 p.m. at Daisy's Disco, 326 Rodeo Drive, Beverly Hills. Berry Gordy boldly predicts that The Jackson 5's first three singles will be number one hit singles and that they will become one of the biggest-selling acts of the decade.

The Jackson 5's early months in southern California are spent camped in the Hitsville studio with Bobby Taylor, acknowledged as the man who took The Jackson 5 to Motown, and writers/producers Freddie Perren, Deke Richards and Fonce Mizell - collectively known as 'The Corporation.'

The Jackson 5 perform 'It's Your Thing' as they make their first TV appearance on the 1969 *Miss Black America Pageant*.

A young Motown executive, Suzanne de Passe, becomes a major influence in moulding The Jackson

5's public image for the media, providing them with the right answers to the questions the press will be asking, changing their hairstyles, helping with choreography, stage numbers and outfits.

October

'I Want You Back'/'Who's Loving You,' The Jackson 5's début single is released on Motown Records and sells two million copies in six weeks. This is the group's first Gold record but, because Motown is not a member of the RIAA, it is not certified as such.

October 18

Diana Ross & The Supremes introduce the Jackson 5 on ABC-TV's *The Hollywood Palace Special*, where they perform 'I Want You Back' and 'Can You Remember?'

November 15

'I Want You Back' enters the Pop singles chart at number 90.

November 22

'I Want You Back' enters the Black singles chart. It peaks at number 1 holding its position for four weeks and remains on the charts for eighteen weeks.

December 14

The Jackson 5 appear on *The Ed Sullivan Show* and perform 'I Want You Back' and 'Who's Loving You.' Later, they also appear on

The Johnny Carson Show and *Soul Träin*.

December 18

'Diana Ross Presents The Jackson 5' (LP), The Jackson 5's first album for Motown produced by Bobby Taylor, is released.

This Page: The Jackson 5 in an early Motown pose.

1970

DIANA ROSS PRESENTS THE JACKSON 5

The Jackson 5
Motown MS-700
Motown STML 11142

Side One
1. Zip A Dee Doo Dah
2. Nobody
3. I Want You Back
4. Can You Remember
5. Standing In The Shadows Of Love
6. You've Changed

Side Two
1. My Cherie Armour
2. Who's Loving You
3. Chained
4. (I Know) I'm Losing You
5. Stand
6. Born To Love You

This Page: The Jackson 5 in a promotional shot for 'ABC,' their second number one single.

Page Opposite: The Jackson 5 at home in Encino, California.

January

The Jackson 5 receive their first Image Award from the NAACP for Best Singing Group of the Year.

The Jackson 5 receive *Sixteen* and *Spec* magazines' awards for Best Group of the Year and Best Single of the Year for 'I'll Be There.'

January 17

'Diana Ross Presents The Jackson 5' (LP) enters both the Black and Pop albums charts peaking at number 1, holding its position for nine and five weeks respectively. The LP spends a total of 32 weeks on the Pop charts.

January 31

'I Want You Back'/'Who's Loving You' by The Jackson 5 enters the Top 50 singles chart in Britain peaking at number 2 and remains on the charts for 13 weeks, selling over 250,000 copies.

'I Want You Back' hits number 1 on both the Pop and Black singles charts, holding its position for one and four weeks respectively and remains on the Pop charts for nineteen weeks.

To promote 'ABC', The Jackson 5 appear on *American Bandstand* where they also perform 'I Want You Back' and receive personal Gold discs for the sales of their number one hit.

March 6

'Motown At The Hollywood Palace' (LP) containing live recordings of The Jackson 5 from ABC-TV's special of the previous October is released.

March 21

'ABC'/'The Young Folks' by The Jackson 5, released on February 24, enters the Black singles chart. It peaks at number 1 holding its position for two weeks and remains on the charts for four weeks.

The single, originally titled '1-2-3,' sells over two million copies in three weeks.

'Diana Ross Presents The Jackson Five' (LP) is released in Britain peaking at number 16 and remains in the Top 75 for four weeks.

April 25

'ABC' hits number 1 on the Pop singles chart, replacing The Beatles' 'Let It Be,' holding its position for two weeks and remains on the charts for thirteen weeks.

'ABC' hits number 1 on the Black singles chart holding its position for four weeks and remains on the charts for twelve weeks.

May 16

'ABC'/'The Young Folks' by The Jackson 5 enters the Top 50 singles chart in Britain peaking at number 8 and remains on the charts for 11 weeks.

May 19

The Jackson 5 hold their first major concert as Motown artists at the Los Angeles Forum playing before an audience of

ABC

The Jackson 5
Motown MS-709
Motown STML 11156

Side One
1. The Love You Save
2. One More Chance
3. ABC
4. 2-4-6-8
5. (Come Round Here) I'm The One You Need
6. Don't Know Why I Love You

Side Two
1. Never Had A Dream Come True
2. True Love Can Be Beautiful
3. La-La Means I Love You
4. I'll Bet You
5. I Found That Girl
6. The Young Folks

18,000 and bringing in receipts of $100,000. At one point in the show, teenage girls invade the stage, forcing the group to run for safety until order is restored.

May 30
'The Love You Save'/'I Found That Girl' by The Jackson 5, released on May 13 by Motown Records, enters the Pop singles chart. It goes on to sell over two million copies.

June 1

The Jackson 5 are on the front cover of *Soul* magazine.

June 4
'The Love You Save' enters the Black singles chart. It peaks at number 1 holding its position for six weeks

and remains on the charts for fourteen weeks.

June 6
'ABC' (LP), The Jackson 5's second album released on May 8 by Motown Records, enters both the Black and Pop albums charts where it peaks at numbers 1 and 4 respectively. It holds its number 1 position on the Black charts for twelve of its twenty-five week residence and remains on the Pop charts for fifty weeks. The LP spawns two hit singles for The Jackson 5.

June 27
'The Love You Save' hits number 1 on the Pop singles chart, replacing The Beatles' 'The Long And Winding Road.' It holds its position for two weeks and remains on the charts for thirteen weeks. The Jackson 5 become the first act of the rock era to have their first three releases go to number one, thereby fulfilling Gordy's prediction for the group's success.

July 24

'The Love You Save'/'I Found That Girl' is released in Britain peaking at number 7 and remains in the Top 50 for nine weeks.

August 15

'ABC' (LP) enters the Top 75 albums chart in Britain peaking at number 22 and remains on the charts for six weeks.

The Jackson 5 perform 'I'll Be There' on *The Jim Nabors Hour*.

September 26

'I'll Be There'/'One More Chance' by The Jackson 5,

released in August by Motown Records, enters the Black singles chart. It peaks at number 1 holding its position for six weeks and remains on the charts for thirteen weeks.

The Jackson 5 reach sales of ten million worldwide for the singles 'I Want You Back,' 'ABC' and 'The Love You Save' during a nine-month period - a record unsurpassed in such a time period.

'Third Album' (LP) by The Jackson 5, released on September 15 by Motown Records, enters the Pop albums chart peaking at number 4 and remains on the charts for fifty weeks.

The Jackson 5 sing the National Anthem at the opening game of the 1970 World Series at Riverfront Stadium, Cincinnati, Ohio.

October 3

'Third Album' (LP) enters the Black albums chart peaking at number 1 and holds its position for ten weeks.

October 9
The Jackson 5 embark on their first national tour playing shows in Boston, Cincinnati, Tennessee and New York City. There are incidents during these shows of teenage girls fainting, and trying to mount the stage. Whilst on tour, The Jackson 5 are accompanied by a private tutor, Rose Fine.

October 15
'The Jackson 5 Christmas Album' (LP) is released on Motown.

October 17

'I'll Be There,' which entered the Pop singles chart at number 40 on September 19, hits number 1, holds its position for five weeks and remains on the charts for sixteen weeks. It also hits number 1 on the Black singles chart holding its position at the top for six weeks. The Jackson 5's career now reaches new record-breaking heights as they become the first act of the rock era to have their first FOUR consecutive singles hit the number one spot. And although The Jackson 5 are a tight family unit, there is no doubt that they are at the top because their lead singer performs with the maturity of an old professional and sings with a soulful voice evident only among Motown's top stars.

November

'Santa Claus Is Coming To Town'/'Christmas Won't Be The Same This Year' by The Jackson 5 is released on Motown.

The Jackson 5 appear before a sell-out crowd at New York City's Madison Square Garden.

'I'll Be There' becomes Motown's third biggest-selling single in history after Marvin Gaye's 'I Heard It Through The Grapevine' and Diana Ross and Lionel Richie's 'Endless Love.'

November 21

'I'll Be There'/'One More Chance' enters the Top 50 singles chart in Britain peaking at number 4 and remains on the charts for seventeen weeks.

Late November

The Jackson 5 concert scheduled to take place in Buffalo, New York is cancelled following threats on Michael's life made by teenage gangs in phone calls to the group's hotel room. Refunds are given to over 9,000 fans who had hoped to see the show.

November 28

The Jackson 5 perform at the War Memorial Auditorium in Rochester, New York.

Three concerts in Texas are cancelled after the Southern Christian Leadership Council Operation Breadbasket complain that Motown should have hired a Black promoter to handle the dates.

The Jacksons move to their parents' first home in Encino, California.

December

'Diana Ross Presents The Jackson 5' (LP) has sold a million copies. This is the group's first Gold album but, because Motown is not an affiliated member of the RIAA, it is not certified as such. The albums 'ABC' and 'Third Album' are also reported to have sold over a million copies.

'The Jackson 5 Christmas Album' (LP) is released in Britain but does not chart.

1970 US TOUR

December 27

The Jackson 5 perform in concert in Charlotte, North Carolina.

December 28

The Jackson 5 perform in concert in Greensboro, North Carolina, playing to a record crowd of 12,275.

December 29

The Jackson 5 perform in concert in Nashville, Tennessee.

December 30

The Jackson 5 perform in concert in Jacksonville, Florida.

The Jackson 5 tour continues with dates in Miami Beach, Florida and Mobile in Alabama.

Late 1970

Billboard magazine's end of year chart shows all four Jackson 5 singles ranking in the Top 20 Best Selling Singles of the Year: 'I Want You Back' (19), 'The Love You Save' (14) 'ABC' (13) and 'I'll Be There' (2).

THE JACKSON 5
CHRISTMAS ALBUM

The Jackson 5

Motown MS-713
Motown STML 11168

Side One
1. **Have Yourself A Merry Little Christmas**
2. **Santa Claus Is Coming To Town**
3. **The Christmas Song**
4. **Up On The Housetop**
5. **Frosty The Snowman**

Side Two
1. **The Little Drummer Boy**
2. **Rudolph The Red-Nosed Reindeer**
3. **Christmas Won't Be The Same This Year**
4. **Give Love On Christmas Day**
5. **Someday At Christmas**
6. **I Saw Mommy Kissing Santa Claus**

This Page: The Jackson 5 in one of their first concerts.

Page Opposite: Michael - on the wall.

1971

THIRD ALBUM

The Jackson 5

Motown MS-718
Motown STML 11174

Side One
1. I'll Be There
2. Ready Or Not Here I Come
3. Oh How Happy
4. Bridge Over Troubled Water
5. Can I See You In The Morning

Side Two
1. Goin' Back To Indiana
2. How Funky Is Your Chicken
3. Mama's Pearl
4. Reach In
5. The Love I Saw In You Was Just A Mirage
6. Darling Dear

This Page: The Jackson 5 arrive back in Indiana for a reunion show.

1971

'We Don't Have To Be Over 21 (To Fall In Love)'/'Jam Session' by The Jackson 5 is released on Steeltown Records more than three years after it was recorded. The Jackson 5 are, at this time, signed to Motown Records.

Steeltown also releases 'Let Me Carry Your Schoolbooks'/'I Never Had A Girl' by The Ripples And Waves Plus Michael, which Steeltown actually deny as being The Jackson 5.

The Jackson Five by Ellen Motoviloff, the first book ever on The Jackson 5, is published by Scholastic Books, New York.

January

The Jackson 5 are awarded the NAACP's Image Award for Best Singing Group Of The Year for the second successive year.

Early 1971
'I'll Be There' has sold over 250,000 copies in Britain.

January 30
'Mama's Pearl'/'Darling Dear' by The Jackson 5, released on January 7 by Motown Records, enters the Pop singles chart peaking at number 2 and remains on the charts for ten weeks. 'Mama's Pearl' was originally titled, 'Who's Been Making Whoopie With My Girlfriend.'

January 31
The Jackson 5 return home for the first time since moving to California. They play two benefit concerts for Mayor Richard Hatcher's re-election campaign at Westside High School and receive the Key to the City.

Jackson Street is renamed 'Jackson 5 Boulevard' for the week January 25-31 in a proclamation by Richard Hatcher, Mayor of Gary, Indiana. A ceremony is held outside their former home at 2300 Jackson Street where a sign reads, 'Welcome Home Jackson Five - Keepers of the Dream.' In addition, a plaque is dedicated in their name at Indiana University stating The Jackson 5 gave 'Hope to the Young.' They are also presented by their Congressman with the flag that flew on top of the State Capitol. The event is filmed and eventually used in a TV special called *Goin' Back To Indiana*.

February

'Third Album' (LP) by The Jackson 5 is released in Britain but does not reach the Top 50.

'The Motown Story' (LP) is released. The album includes 'I Want You Back' and Michael talking about his life as a member of The Jackson 5.

February 6
'Mama's Pearl' enters the Black singles chart peaking at number 2 and remains on the charts for eleven weeks.

March

Motown announces that 'Mama's Pearl'/'Darling Dear' by The Jackson 5 has sold a million copies since January.

March 16
At the Grammy Awards show held at the Hollywood Palladium, 'ABC' is nominated for an award in the category Best Pop Song, but does not win.

March 29
'Diana' (LP), Diana Ross' TV soundtrack album containing The Jackson 5 medleys 'Mama's Pearl'/'Walk On By'/'The Love You Save' and 'I'll Be There'/'Feelin' Alright' is released on Motown.

The Jackson 5 appear on *The Stephanie Edwards Show* to chat and listen to their next single, 'Never Can Say Goodbye.'

April

Michael appears on the cover of *Soul Illustrated*.

April 2
'Mama's Pearl'/'Darling Dear' is released in Britain peaking at number 25 and remains in the Top 50 for seven weeks.

April 3
'Never Can Say Goodbye'/'She's Good' by

The Jackson 5, released in March by Motown, enters the Pop singles chart peaking at number 2 and remains on the charts for twelve weeks.

April 10
'Never Can Say Goodbye' enters the Black singles chart. It peaks at number 1 holding its position for three weeks and remains on the charts for thirteen weeks.

April 18
The Jackson 5 appear with Diana Ross on her first solo TV Special. They perform 'The Love You Save' and Michael also appears in a couple of comedy sketches with a tongue-in-cheek impersonation of Frank Sinatra to 'It Was A Very Good Year.'

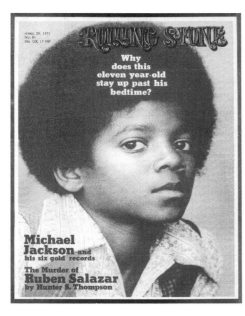

April 29
Michael Jackson appears on the cover of *Rolling Stone* magazine.

May
'Feelin' Alright' by Diana Ross and The Jackson 5, a promotional record taken from the album 'Diana,' is released on Motown.

Two albums released by Motown Records 'Motown Chartbusters Vol. 3' and 'Motown Chartbusters Vol. 4' contain songs by The Jackson 5.

May 1
'Maybe Tomorrow' (LP), released on April 12 by Motown Records, enters both the Black and Pop albums charts peaking at number 1 on the Black charts where it holds its position for six weeks, and number 11 on the Pop charts during its forty-one week run.

Summer
The Jackson 5 embark on their second tour playing some 40 dates with concerts in cities including Philadelphia, New York and Milwaukee. The opening act is an up-and-coming group from Tuskegee, Alabama called The Commodores featuring lead singer Lionel Richie. The tour ends on September 12 in Honolulu. For security on this tour, a former Los Angeles police officer is hired as Security Chief. Bill Bray will go on to work for the Jacksons and subsequently for Michael.

July 10
'Maybe Tomorrow'/'I Will Find A Way' by The Jackson 5, released in June on Motown Records, enters the Pop singles chart peaking at number 20 and remains on the charts for nine weeks.

July 17
'Never Can Say

Goodbye'/'She's Good' enters the Top 50 singles chart in Britain peaking at number 33 and remains on the charts for seven weeks.

July 23
The Jackson 5 play before an audience of 80,000 at the Lake Michigan Summer Festival.

July 24
'Maybe Tomorrow' enters the Black singles chart peaking at number 3 and remains on the charts for eight weeks.

September
Ebony, *Life* and *Creem* magazines carry cover stories on Michael and The Jackson 5.

The Jackson 5 are guests on *The Flip Wilson Show*.

September 9
The Jackson 5 perform at the Michigan State Fair.

September 11
An animated cartoon series based on The Jackson 5 débuts on ABC-TV. Their speaking voices are not used although their songs are, with 'Mama's Pearl' being the theme tune.

MAYBE TOMORROW

The Jackson 5
Motown MS-735
Motown STML 11188

Side One
1. Maybe Tomorrow
2. She's Good
3. Never Can Say Goodbye
4. The Wall
5. Petals

Side Two
1. 16 Candles
2. (We've Got) Blue Skies
3. My Little Baby
4. It's Great To Be Here
5. Honey Chile
6. I Will Find A Way

This Page Left: The first ever Jackson 5 Tour Programme.

Below: A still from The Jackson 5 Cartoon series.

1971

> "I don't know what I could do besides sing but I'm not worried because I figure I've got the rest of my life to find out!"
>
> **Michael Jackson - October 1971**

GOIN' BACK TO INDIANA

The Jackson 5
Motown M742L

Side One
1. I Want You Back
2. Maybe Tomorrow
3. The Day Basketball Was Saved

Side Two
1. Stand
2. I Want To Take You Higher
3. Feelin' Alright
4. Medley: Walk On - The Love You Save
5. Goin' Back To Indiana

This Page: Scenes from The Jackson 5's TV special, *Goin' Back To Indiana*.

September 19
Goin' Back To Indiana, their first TV special for ABC-TV airs, featuring guests Bill Cosby and The Smothers Brothers. The special includes the group performing their hits, acting in skits, and footage of the celebration filmed in their hometown of Gary back in January.

September 20
A special commendation for the Jackson 5 appears in the US Congressional Record for their contribution to music, stating that the group has "become a symbol of pride among black youth."

September 24
The Jackson 5 are on the front cover of *Life*.

October
'Maybe Tomorrow' (LP) is released in Britain but fails to enter the Top 50.

'Rock Gospel - The Key To The Kingdom' (LP) is released on Motown and includes The Jackson 5's version of 'Bridge Over Troubled Water.'

The Jackson 5 are on the cover of the very first issue of *Right On!* magazine.

October 9
'Goin' Back To Indiana' (LP), released on September 7 by Motown, enters the Pop albums chart. It peaks at number 16 and remains on the charts for twenty-six weeks.

October 16
'Goin' Back To Indiana' (LP) enters the Black albums chart and peaks at number 5.

October 30
'Got To Be There'/'Maria (You Were The Only One)' by Michael Jackson, released on October 7 by Motown Records, enters the Black and Pop singles charts peaking at number 4 on both. Michael's solo career begins with this, his first solo single.

Late 1971
The Jackson 5 tour the US performing in fifty cities.

December
The Jackson 5 are on the cover of *Right On!*

December 11
'Sugar Daddy'/'I'm So Happy' by The Jackson 5, released in November by Motown Records, enters the Pop singles chart peaking at 10 and remains on the charts for ten weeks.

December 18
'Sugar Daddy' enters the Black singles chart. It peaks at number 3 and remains on the charts for eleven weeks.

1972

Michael spends time visiting Diana Ross on the set of her movie, *Lady Sings The Blues.*

The Jackson 5 embark on their first international tour.

Save The Children, a film documentary, features an appearance by The Jackson 5. Their song, 'I Wanna Be Where You Are,' is featured in the soundtrack.

A book entitled *The Jackson Five* is published in Britain by New English Library.

January

The Jackson 5 receive the NAACP's Image Award for Male Vocal Group of the Year.

January 1

The Jackson 5 perform at Nashville's Municipal Auditorium.

'Greatest Hits' (LP) by The Jackson 5, released on December 9 by Motown Records, enters the Pop albums chart peaking at number 12 and remains on the charts for forty-one weeks.

January 7

'Got To Be There' / 'Maria (You Were The Only One)' is released in Britain peaking at number 5 and remains in the Top 50 for eleven weeks.

January 8

'Greatest Hits' (LP) by The Jackson 5 enters the Black albums chart and peaks at number 2.

The Jackson 5 are on the cover of *Right On!* magazine. The magazine will includes stories on Michael and The Jackson 5 in its next six issues February to July.

January 18

The Jackson 5 headline the first annual Martin Luther King Birthday Commemoration Concert the Metropolitan Auditorium in Atlanta.

February 12

The Jackson 5 perform at the Kiel Auditorium in St. Louis.

February 19

'Got To Be There' (LP) by Michael Jackson (LP), released on January 24 by Motown Records, enters the Black and Pop albums charts peaking at numbers 3 and 14 respectively and remains on the Pop charts for twenty-three weeks. This is Michael's first solo album.

February 26

Michael Jackson is voted Best Male Singer Of The Year by *16* magazine.

March

'Sugar Daddy' / 'I'm So Happy' is released in Britain but fails to reach the Top 50 singles chart.

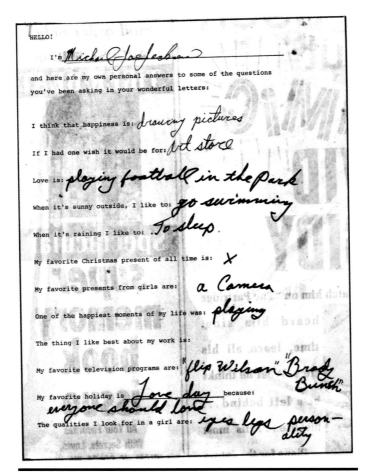

"I like all our fans, even the ones who keep calling me 'cute.' But I'm getting bigger every day so they'll have to call me something else."

Michael Jackson - January 1972

This Page: Michael personally answers some fan questions which appeared in *Right On!* magazine. Note the 'x' by Christmas presents.

Below: A newspaper advert promoting a Jackson 5 performance to commemorate the birthday of Martin Luther King, Jr.

1972

This Page: Michael and The Jackson 5 pose for Motown publicity photographs. Michael has just embarked on his own solo career.

March 1

The Jackson 5 take part in ABC-TV's comedy special, *Hellzapoppin*, singing 'Sugar Daddy' and 'Got To Be There.'

March 11

'Rockin' Robin'/'Love Is Here And Now You're Gone,' released in February on Motown Records, enters the Black and Pop singles charts peaking at number 2 on both and remains on the Pop charts for thirteen weeks. This is Michael's second solo single and is a remake of Bobby Day's 1958 hit.

March 18

'Rockin' Robin' enters the Black singles chart. It peaks at number 2 remaining on the charts for nine weeks.

March 30

Michael reveals that he gets $5 per week allowance and spends it on art supplies.

April 16

The Jackson 5 are on the cover of *Spec* magazine.

April 29

'Little Bitty Pretty One'/'If I Have To Move A Mountain' by The Jackson 5, released this month by Motown Records, hits both the Black and Pop singles charts peaking at numbers 8 and 13 respectively and remains on the Pop charts for nine weeks. This is the group's ninth single and is a cover version of the Thurston Harris hit.

May 20

'Rockin' Robin'/'Love Is Here And Now You're Gone' by Michael Jackson enters the Top 50 singles chart in Britain peaking at number 3 and remains on the charts for fourteen weeks.

May 27

'I Wanna Be Where You Are'/'We've Got A Good Thing Going' by Michael Jackson, released this month by Motown Records, enters the Pop singles chart peaking at number 16 and remains on the charts for eleven weeks. This is Michael's third solo single.

June 3

'I Wanna Be Where You Are' enters the Black singles chart. It peaks at number 2 and remains on the charts for twelve weeks.

'Lookin' Through The Windows' (LP) by The Jackson 5, released on May 17 by Motown Records, enters the Pop albums chart peaking at number 7 and remains on the charts for thirty-three weeks.

'Got To Be There' (LP) enters the Top 50 albums chart in Britain peaking at number 37 and remains on the charts for five weeks.

June 10

'Lookin' Through The Windows' (LP) enters the Black albums chart peaking at number 3 and remains on the charts for twenty-nine weeks.

July

'Ben,' the theme song for a film of the same name, is released on Motown. The song is a ballad of friendship between a boy and a rat (*Ben* is the follow-up to the 1971 film, *Willard*). The song will later win a presti-gious Golden Globe Award.

July 15

'Lookin' Through The Windows'/'Love Song' by The Jackson 5, released in June by Motown Records, enters the Pop singles chart peaking at number 16 and remains on the charts for ten weeks.

July 22

'Lookin' Through The Windows' enters the Black singles chart peaking at number 5 and remains on the charts for eleven weeks.

August

'That's How Love Goes' by Jermaine Jackson, a single released in July from his new LP, features backing vocals by The Jackson 5. It peaks at number 46 on the Pop singles chart.

August 4

'Ben' (LP) by Michael Jackson is released. The album's original cover features a horde of rats super-imposed on the bottom of Michael's picture. This is soon withdrawn after complaints that children find the rats disturbing. Today, the withdrawn 'Rats Cover' is a much sought-after collectors' item.

August 5

'Ben'/'You Can Cry On My Shoulder' by Michael Jackson, released in July by Motown Records, enters the Pop singles chart and peaks at number 1, becoming Michael's first solo number one hit, selling over 1 million copies.

August 19

'Ain't No Sunshine'/'I Wanna Be Where You Are,'

1972

LOOKIN' THROUGH THE WINDOWS

The Jackson 5
Motown M 750L
Motown STML 11214

Side One
1. Ain't Nothing Like The Real Thing
2. Lookin' Through The Windows
3. Don't Let Your Baby Catch You
4. To Know
5. Doctor My Eyes

Side Two
1. Little Bitty Pretty One
2. E-Ne-Me-Ne-Mi-Ne-Moe
3. If I Have To Move A Mountain
4. Don't Want To See Tomorrow
5. Children Of The Light
6. I Can Only Give You Love

BEN

Michael Jackson
Motown 755L
Motown STML 11220

Side One
1. Ben
2. The Greatest Show On Earth
3. People Make The World Go Round
4. We've Got A Good Thing Going
5. Everybody's Somebody's Fool

Side Two
1. My Girl
2. What Goes Around Comes Around
3. In Our Small Way
4. Shoo Be Doo Be Doo Da Day
5. You Can Cry On My Shoulder

1972

released only in Britain, enters the Top 50 singles chart peaking at number 8 and remains on the charts for eleven weeks.

August 19
'Ben' by Michael Jackson enters the Black singles chart. It peaks at number 4 and remains on the charts for fourteen weeks.

August 26
'Ben' (LP) enters the Pop albums chart peaking at number 5 and remains on the charts for thirty-two weeks.

September

Michael Jackson appears on the TV show, *The Dating Game* and picks Latany Simmons for his 'date.'

The Jackson 5 receive special commendations from the US Congress for providing positive role models for youths.

'Little Bitty Pretty One'/'Maybe Tomorrow' is released in Britain but fails to enter the charts.

Michael makes his first solo appearance on *American Bandstand* performing 'Ben.'

September 7
'Greatest Hits' (LP) by The Jackson 5 enters the Top 50 albums chart in Britain peaking at number 26 and remains on the charts for fourteen weeks.

October

The Jackson 5 appear on several TV shows, including *The Sonny and Cher Comedy Hour* and a special called *One More Time*, where they sing with The Mills Brothers and Pat Boone.

October 28
'Corner Of The Sky'/'To Know' by The Jackson 5, a track from the Broadway

musical *Pippin* released this month by Motown Records, enters the Pop singles chart peaking at number 18 and remains on the charts for twelve weeks.

The Jackson 5 tour Europe with concerts in Amsterdam, Brussels, Frankfurt, Munich, Paris and four cities in Britain.

November

The Jackson 5 arrive in Britain as part of their first ever tour of Europe, scheduled for twelve days. Scenes at Heathrow Airport are reminiscent of Beatlemania, as security struggle to protect the group.

Whilst in Britain, The Jackson 5 break the Liverpool Empire's record attendance, which was previously held by The Beatles, as well as playing other shows in Birmingham, Manchester and London. They also play a Royal Command performance in the presence of the Queen Mother. The rest of the tour takes in Amsterdam, Brussels, Frankfurt and Paris.

November 5
The Jackson 5 Show, the group's second TV special, airs on CBS-TV whilst they are touring Europe.

Jackson Five

5 ARE COMING

ODEON THEATRE
BIRMINGHAM
THE JACKSON FIVE
1st PERFORMANCE 6-30 p.m.
THURSDAY
NOVEMBER **9**
CENTRE STALLS
£1·50
N11
No ticket exchanged nor money refunded
THIS PORTION TO BE RETAINED [P.T.O.

Appearing at:

November 9th Odeon, Birmingham
November 10th Belle Vue, Manchester
November 11th Empire, Liverpool
November 12th Empire Pool, Wembley

see them on
The Royal Variety Performance
November 5th and on
Top of the Pops
November 9th
also on the tour 'Sisters Love'.
Their new single 'Mr. Fix It Man' TMG 828
is now available

Lookin' Through The Windows
STML 11214

Greatest Hits
STML 11212

Got To Be There
(Michael Jackson) STML 11205

Also Available
Diana Ross Presents The Jackson Five
STML 11142
A.B.C.
STML 11156
Jackson Five Christmas Album
STML 11168
Third Album
STML 11174
Maybe Tomorrow
STML 11188
Available on Cassette and Cartridge

Released on October 27th
Jackson Five…Lookin' Through The Windows TMG833

and Released on November 10th.
Michael Jackson…Ben TMG 834

EMI   Tamla Motown

November 9
The Jackson 5 appear on the British TV pop programme, *Top Of The Pops*, where they perform 'Lookin' Through The Windows.'

November 11
'Corner Of The Sky' enters the Black singles chart peaking at number 9 and remains on the charts for eleven weeks.

'Lookin' Through The Windows'/'Love Song' enters the Top 50 singles chart in Britain peaking at number 9.

November 18
The Jackson 5 perform at an NAACP fund-raising dinner in Hollywood.

'Lookin' Through The Windows' (LP) enters the Top 50 albums chart in Britain peaking at number 16.

This Page: An advert from the *New Musical Express* promoting The Jackson 5's first ever UK tour.

The Jackson 5 in action.

Page Opposite: The Jackson 5 go shopping in Paris with Security Chief, Bill Bray.

1972

November 20
'I Want You Back'/'ABC' and 'The Love You Save'/'I'll Be There' are re-issued on Motown's Yesteryear label.

November 25
'Ben'/'You Can Cry On My Shoulder' by Michael Jackson enters the Top 50 singles chart in Britain peaking at number 7 and remains on the charts for fourteen weeks, selling over 250,000 copies.

December

Billboard magazine names Michael Jackson as Top Singles Artist and Top Singles Male Vocalist of the year.

'That's How Love Goes' by Jermaine Jackson, which includes backing vocals by The Jackson 5, is released in Britain.

December 23
'Santa Claus Is Coming To Town'/'Someday At Christmas'/'Christmas Won't Be The Same This Year' enters the Top 50 singles chart in Britain peaking at number 43 and remains on the charts for three weeks.

Michael Jackson appears at the Watts Christmas parade in Los Angeles.

1973
January

Michael Jackson receives a Gold Record for the single 'Ben.'

The Jackson 5 are on the cover of *Right On!*

January 13

'Ben' (LP), Michael's second solo LP, enters the Top 50 albums chart in Britain peaking at number 17 and remains on the charts for seven weeks.

February 17

'Doctor My Eyes'/'My Little Baby' enters the Top 50 singles chart in Britain peaking at number 9 and remains on the charts for ten weeks.

March

Michael receives a nomination for Best Song for 'Ben' at the Academy Awards (the Oscars) and performs the song at the presentation ceremonies. The song, however, does not win.

The Jackson 5 perform concerts in Oklahoma, Monroe in Louisiana and Houston in Texas.

March 17

'You Made Me What I Am'/'Hallelujah Day' by The Jackson 5, released in February by Motown Records, enters the Pop singles chart peaking at number 28 and remains on the charts for ten weeks. NB: 'Hallelujah Day' is the single which charts.

'Hallelujah Day' enters the Black singles chart peaking at number 10 and remains on the charts for eight weeks.

April 14

'Skywriter' (LP) by The Jackson 5, released on March 29 by Motown Records, enters the Pop albums chart peaking at number 44 and remains on the charts for sixteen weeks. It proves to be their least successful album to date.

April 22-May 3

The Jackson 5 tour Japan. Whilst in Japan, they take time to visit Buddhist temples, art museums and the Oriental Gardens of the Takanawa Prince Hotel. Amongst their dates the group play Tokyo's Annual Music Festival at the Imperial Palace as well as Osaka and Hiroshima.

April 28

'Skywriter' (LP) enters the Black albums chart and peaks at number 15.

May 5

'Music & Me' (LP) by Michael Jackson, released on April 13 by Motown Records, enters both the Black and Pop albums charts peaking at numbers 24 and 92 respectively and remains on the Pop charts for twelve weeks.

'With A Child's Heart'/'Morning Glow' by

Michael Jackson, released in April by Motown Records, enters the Pop singles chart peaking at number 50 and remains on the charts for seven weeks. This is the only single released from the LP 'Music & Me' and Michael does not release another single for the label for almost two years.

The Jackson 5 perform in concert in Portland, Oregon.

May 6

The Jackson 5 perform in concert in Seattle, Washington.

May 12

'With A Child's Heart' enters the Black singles chart peaking at number 14 and remains on the charts for ten weeks.

1973

SKYWRITER

The Jackson 5
Motown M761L
Motown STML 11231

Side One
1. Skywriter
2. Hallelujah Day
3. The Boogie Man
4. Touch
5. Corner Of The Sky

Side Two
1. I Can't Quit Your Love
2. Uppermost
3. World Of Sunshine
4. Ooh I'd Love To Be With You
5. You Made Me What I Am

This Page: The Jackson Five say farewell to Japan.

Left: Michael gets his first taste of commercial endorsements with Alphabits cereal.

1973

MUSIC AND ME

Michael Jackson

Motown 767L
Motown STML 11235

Side One
1. With A Child's Heart
2. Johnny Raven
3. Up Again
4. All The Things You Are
5. Happy
6. Too Young

Side Two
1. Doggin' Around
2. Euphoria
3. Morning Glow
4. Music And Me

This Page: The Jackson 5 in concert.

May 18
The Jackson 5 hold concerts in Philadelphia, Pennsylvania.

May 19
The Jackson 5 hold concerts in Dayton, Ohio.

May 20
The Jackson 5 hold concerts in Columbus, Ohio.

June 9
'Hallelujah Day'/'To Know' enters the Top 50 singles chart in Britain peaking at number 20 and remains on the charts for nine weeks.

June 18
'Mama's Pearl'/'Never Can Say Goodbye', 'Maybe Tomorrow'/'Sugar Daddy' by The Jackson 5 and 'Got

To Be There'/'Rockin' Robin' by Michael Jackson are released on Motown's Yesteryear label.

Late June/Early July
The Jackson 5 are the first Black group ever to tour Australia, giving concerts in Adelaide, Brisbane, Melbourne, Perth and Sydney. They also hold concerts in Christchurch and Wellington in New Zealand, where they are presented with Gold discs for the sales of a single not released anywhere else, 'I Saw Mommy Kissing Santa Claus.' Over two million people see the Australian-New Zealand tour.

July
The Jackson 5's 'Skywriter' (LP) and Michael's 'Music

& Me' (LP) are released in Britain but neither reaches the Top 50.

'Morning Glow'/'My Girl' by Michael Jackson is released in Britain but does not reach the Top 50.

July 20
The Jackson 5 perform in concert in Pittsburgh, Pennsylvania.

July 21
The Jackson 5 perform in concert in Poconos, Pennsylvania.

July 22
The Jackson 5 perform in concert in New York City.

July 24/25
The Jackson 5 perform in concert in Chicago.

July 27
The Jackson 5 perform in concert in Cleveland, Ohio.

July 28
The Jackson 5 perform in concert in Detroit, Michigan.

July 29
The Jackson 5 perform in concert in Indianapolis in Indiana, their home State.

August 3
The Jackson 5 perform in concert in Richmond, Virginia.

August 4
The Jackson 5 perform in concert in Hampton, Virginia.

August 5
The Jackson 5 perform in concert in Baltimore, Maryland.

August 6
The Jackson 5 are on the cover of *Soul* magazine.

August 7
The Jackson 5 perform in concert in Greensboro, North Carolina.

August 8
The Jackson 5 perform in concert in Nashville, Tennessee.

August 10
The Jackson 5 perform in concert in Columbia, South Carolina.

August 11
The Jackson 5 perform in concert in Atlanta, Georgia.

August 12
The Jackson 5 perform in concert in Miami, Florida.

August 17
The Jackson 5 perform in concert in Memphis, Tennessee.

August 18
The Jackson 5 perform in concert in St. Louis, Missouri.

August 21
The Jackson 5 perform in concert in New Orleans, Louisiana.

August 22
The Jackson 5 perform in concert in Dallas, Texas.

August 24
The Jackson 5 perform in concert in San Francisco, California.

August 25
The Jackson 5 perform in concert in Los Angeles, California.

'Get It Together'/'Touch' by The Jackson 5, released in August by Motown Records, enters the Black singles chart peaking at number 2 and remains on the charts for eighteen weeks.

August 26
The Jackson 5 perform in concert in Las Vegas, Nevada.

September
'Skywriter'/'Ain't Nothin' Like The Real Thing' is released in Britain but fails to reach the Top 50 singles chart.

September 1
'Get It Together' enters the Pop singles chart peaking at number 28 and remains on the charts for thirteen weeks.

September 2
The Jackson 5 perform in concert in Honolulu, Hawaii.

September 25
'A Motown Christmas' (LP), a compilation featuring six tracks by The Jackson 5 and 'Little Christmas Tree' by Michael Jackson, is released on Motown.

September 29
'Get It Together' (LP), a disco-style album by The Jackson 5 released on September 12 by Motown Records, enters the Black albums chart peaking at number 4 and remains on the charts for nineteen weeks.

October 6
'Get It Together' (LP) enters the Pop albums chart but never makes it past number 100 in its twenty-nine week stay in the charts.

November
'Get It Together'/'Touch' is released in Britain but fails to reach the Top 50.

'Get It Together' (LP) is released in Britain but fails to reach the Top 50.

'Season's Greetings From Motown Records,' a Christmas record to radio stations and record distributors featuring short messages from Michael and his brothers, is issued by Motown Records.

December
Michael Jackson and The Jackson 5 have appeared on the front cover of every issue of *Right On!* magazine this year.

GET IT TOGETHER
The Jackson 5
Motown M 783 V1
Motown STML 11275

Side One
1. **Get It Together**
2. **Don't Say Goodbye Again**
3. **Reflections**
4. **Hum Along And Dance**

Side Two
1. **Mama I Gotta Brand New Thing (Don't Say No)**
2. **It's Too Late To Change The Time**
3. **You Need Love Like I Do (Don't You?)**
4. **Dancing Machine**

This Page: Young Michael in a thoughtful mood.

1974

The Jackson 5 appear on the *Sonny & Cher* show where they perform 'Dancing Machine.'

Michael appears at the American Music Awards to present awards with Donny Osmond for Favourite Soul Group to The Temptations, and with Donny Osmond, Ricky Segal and Ricky Allen Rippy for Favourite Pop Group to The Carpenters.

Two Motown albums, 'Maybe Tomorrow' and 'Stand' (Motown's 'Goin' Back To Indiana') are reissued by Pickwick Records.

The Jackson 5 receive the Key to the City of Buffalo from Mayor Stanley Makowski.

January 10
One More Time, a TV special featuring The Jackson 5, is aired on CBS-TV.

January 29
The Jackson 5 and entourage board PanAm flight 184 for their African tour.

The Jackson 5 land in Dakar at Yoff Airport in Senegal and are greeted by a posse of dancers and drummers playing the African rhythms. After holding a press conference with Senegalise radio, the group check in to the Taranga Hotel near Independence Square.

The Jackson 5 perform at Demba Drop Stadium, Dakar in Senegal, opening with 'Get It Together.' During their one week stay they receive an award from

the Organisation for African Unity for strengthening the status of Afro-Americans.

The Jackson 5 visit Goree Island and learn about its history, experiencing firsthand the poverty suffered by the inhabitants. During their trip, they shoot a film called *Isomin Cross And Son*, which tells of a family crossing the US in 1860 and the problems they encounter.

The Jackson 5 play two nights at the Theatre National Daniel Sorano.

February 22
The Jackson 5 perform at the Astrodome in Houston, Texas. A week later, Elvis performs at the same venue.

March
The Jackson 5 appear on the cover of *Blues & Soul* magazine, with a feature covering their African trip.

March 2
The Jackson 5 present Gladys Knight & The Pips with a Grammy for Best Rhythm & Blues Vocal Performance By A Duo,

Group or Chorus for 'Midnight Train To Georgia.'

March 9
'Dancing Machine'/'It's Too Late To Change The Time' by The Jackson 5, released in February by Motown Records, enters the Black singles chart peaking at number 1, where it holds for one week, and remains on the charts for twenty weeks. This is the first time they have topped the Black charts since 'Never Can Say Goodbye' in May '71.

March 11
A TV special called *Free To Be... You And Me* featuring Michael Jackson is aired on ABC-TV.

March 16
'Dancing Machine' enters the Pop singles chart peaking at number 2 and remains on the charts for twenty-two weeks.

April
'The Boogie Man'/'Don't Let Your Baby Catch You,' a single shelved in America in March 1973, is released in Britain but fails to reach the Top 50.

Page Opposite: The Jackson 5 perform on the Sonny & Cher show.

This Page: Michael finds some time to put his feet up and relax.

1974

This Page: The Jackson Family backstage after one of their sell-out Vegas shows.

'Save The Children' (LP) featuring 'I Wanna Be Where You Are' by The Jackson 5 is released on Motown.

Early April
Motown announces that 'Dancing Machine' by The Jackson 5 has sold over a million copies in less than a month.

April 9-24
Joe Jackson arranges for the whole family, including sisters Rebbie, LaToya and Janet, to play the cabaret circuit at the MGM Grand Hotel, Las Vegas. The shows are a big hit with fans, breaking attendance records, but receive a critical pounding.

April 26
'Little Bitty Pretty One'/'Lookin' Through The Windows,' 'Corner Of The Sky'/'Hallelujah Day,' and Michael's 'Ben'/'I Wanna Be Where You Are' are re-issued on Motown's Yesteryear label.

May
The Jackson 5 give concerts in Las Vegas, Chicago and Los Angeles as well as a number of European venues.

'Music And Me'/'Johnny Raven' is released in Britain but does not reach the Top 50.

ABC-TV's special *Free To Be... You And Me* featuring

Michael wins an Emmy as Best Children's Special.

June
A proposed tour of Britain by The Jackson 5 is cancelled after a girl dies at a David Cassidy concert on May 24. The question of security and safety causes many anxious parents to return Jackson 5 tickets.

'Dancing Machine'/'It's Too Late To Change The Time' is released in Britain but does not reach the Top 50.

July 15
'Fulfillingness First Finale' (LP) by Stevie Wonder is released featuring 'You

Haven't Done Nothin'', with backing vocals by the Jackson 5.

July 19
The Jackson 5 appear in concert in Pittsburgh, Pennsylvania.

July 21
The Jackson 5 appear in concert in Richmond, Virginia.

July 26
The Jackson 5 appear in concert in Buffalo, New York.

July 27
The Jackson 5 perform at Madison Square Garden in New York City.

August 6
The Jackson 5 appear in concert in Huntsville, Alabama.

August 7
The Jackson 5 appear in concert in New Orleans, Louisiana.

August 10
The Jackson 5 appear in concert in St. Louis, Missouri.

August 11
The Jackson 5 appear in concert in Kansas City, Missouri.

August 16
The Jackson 5 appear in concert in St. Paul, Minnesota.

August 17
The Jackson 5 are featured at the World Expo in Spokane, Washington.

August 21-Sept. 3
The Jackson 5 return to the MGM Grand Hotel for another series of shows.

September
'You Haven't Done Nothin'' by Stevie Wonder is released on the Tamla label. The single features backing vocals by The Jackson 5.

'Fulfillingness First Finale' (LP) by Stevie Wonder featuring 'You Haven't Done Nothin'', with backing vocals by the Jackson 5 is released in Britain.

September 4-October 1
The Jackson 5 tour South America with concerts in Panama, Venezuela and Brazil amongst others.

October
'You Haven't Done Nothin'' by Stevie Wonder featuring backing vocals by The Jackson 5 is released in Britain.

October 5
'Dancing Machine' (LP) by The Jackson 5, released on September 5 by Motown Records, hits the Pop albums chart peaking at number 16 and remains on the charts for twenty-one weeks. Surprisingly, the LP does not enter the Black charts. An interesting fact is that songs written and produced specifically by Stevie Wonder for The Jackson 5 were not included on the final selection.

October 4-6
The Jackson 5 move their cabaret set to Sahara Tahoe in Nevada.

October 7-November 1
The Jackson 5 tour the Far East with concerts in Japan, Hong Kong, Australia and the Philippines amongst others.

October 26
'Whatever You Got, I Want'/'I Can't Quit Your Love' by The Jackson 5, released this month by Motown Records, hits both the Black and Pop singles charts peaking at numbers 3 and 38 respectively and remains on the Pop charts for eleven weeks.

November
'The Life Of The Party'/'Whatever You Got, I Want' is released in Britain but fails to reach the Top 50.

'Dancing Machine' (LP) is released in Britain but fails to reach the Top 50.

November 20-December 3
The Jackson 5 return to the MGM Grand Hotel for a further run of shows with their cabaret set.

1974

DANCING MACHINE

The Jackson 5
Motown M6-780S1
Motown STML 11275

Side One
1. I Am Love
2. Whatever You Got, I Want
3. She's A Rhythm Child
4. Dancing Machine

Side Two
1. The Life Of The Party
2. What You Don't Know
3. If I Don't Love You This Way
4. It All Begins And Ends With Love
5. The Mirrors Of My Mind

This Page: The Jackson 5 live in Las Vegas.

1975

FOREVER, MICHAEL

Michael Jackson
Motown M6-825S1
Motown STMA 8022

Side One
1. We're Almost There
2. Take Me Back
3. One Day In Your Life
4. Cinderella Stay Awhile
5. We've Got Forever

Side Two
1. Just A Little Bit Of You
2. You Are There
3. Dapper-Dan
4. Dear Michael
5. I'll Come Home To You

MOVING VIOLATION

Jackson 5
Motown M6-829S1
Motown STML 11290

Side One
1. Forever Came Today
2. Moving Violation
3. (You Were Made)
   Especially For Me
4. Honey Love

Side Two
1. Body Language (Do The
   Love Dance)
2. All I Do Is Think Of You
3. Breezy
4. Call Of The Wild
5. Time Explosion

1975

The Jackson 5 are made Honorary Members of the Congressional Black Caucus.

January

The Jackson 5 tour the West Indies.

Michael and The Jackson 5 are featured in six *Right On!* issues this year: January, February, April, July, August and October.

Michael Jackson accepts the Favourite Soul Female award on behalf of Diana Ross at the American Music Awards. With sister Janet, he also presents the award for Favourite Soul Group to Gladys Knight & The Pips.

January 18

'I Am Love (Part 1)'/'I Am Love (Part 2)' by The Jackson 5, released in December by Motown Records, enters the Pop singles chart peaking at number 15 and remains on the charts for fourteen weeks.

January 25

'I Am Love (Parts 1 and 2)' by The Jackson 5 enters the Black singles chart peaking at number 5 and remains on the charts for twelve weeks.

February 7

The Jackson 5 perform in concert at Radio City Music Hall in New York City.

February 8

'Forever, Michael' (LP), released on January 16, enters the Black albums chart and is very successful, peaking at number 10.

February 15

'Forever, Michael' (LP) enters the Pop albums chart remaining on the charts for nine weeks but never climbs higher than number 101.

Mid-February

The Jackson 5 return to Britain for a concert tour, supported by the group The Real Thing.

March

'Forever, Michael' (LP) is released in Britain but fails to reach the Top 50.

March 1

'We're Almost There'/'Take Me Back' by Michael Jackson, released in February by Motown Records, enters both the Black and Pop singles charts peaking at numbers 7 and 54 respectively and remains on the Pop charts for eight weeks.

March 3

'I Am Love (Parts 1 and 2)' is released in Britain but fails to reach the Top 50.

April

'One Day In Your Life'/'With A Child's Heart' is released in Britain but does not reach the Top 50.

April 18

'Dancing Machine'/'Get It Together' by The Jackson 5 is re-issued on Motown's Yesteryear label.

May

'Disc-O-Tech #1' (LP) and 'Disc-O-Tech #2' (LP), both containing a Jackson 5 song, are released on Motown's Various Artists packages.

May 24

'Just A Little Bit Of You'/'Dear Michael,' released in April by Motown Records, enters the Black singles chart peaking at number 4 and remains on the charts for fifteen weeks. This is Michael's seventh single for the label.

May 28

The Jackson 5 sign a new contract with CBS Records' Epic Records to begin with the expiry of their current contract with Motown in March, 1976. They cite low royalty payments and lack of artistic control among some of the problems with Motown. Brother Jermaine, who recently married Motown founder Berry Gordy's daughter, Hazel, is replaced by Randy, and remains with Motown to pursue a solo career.

June 7

'Just A Little Bit Of You' enters the Pop singles chart peaking at number 23 and remains on the charts for twelve weeks.

June 14

'Moving Violation' by The Jackson 5, released on May 15 during a period of discontent in the Jackson family towards Motown, enters both the Black and Pop albums charts peaking at numbers 6 and 36 respectively. It remains on the Pop charts for fifteen weeks. This will be the last Jackson 5 album released by Motown - all subsequent releases are compilations of earlier recordings.

June 28

'Forever Came Today'/'All

I Do Is Think Of You' by The Jackson 5, released in June by Motown Records, enters the Black singles chart peaking at number 6 and remains on the charts for thirteen weeks. This is the only single released from the LP 'Moving Violation' and will be their last single for Motown.

June 30

Joseph Jackson calls a press conference at the Rainbow Grill in Manhattan to announce that The Jackson 5 will not be renewing their contract with Motown when it expires in 1976. The group are to re-sign with CBS who promise them more artistic freedom (writing and producing) than Motown will allow. Following the press conference, Joseph Jackson is informed by Motown Vice Chairman, Michael Roshkind, that the Jackson 5 name is owned by the company, not the group. The logo and the name had apparently been registered by Berry Gordy on March 7, 1973. The group is subsequently renamed 'The Jacksons.'

Motown Executive, Tony Jones contacts Joseph Jackson demanding that The Jackson 5 record another album for the company in order to see through their contractual obligations. Michael is in favour of honouring his contract but Joseph Jackson refuses to comply.

July

'Moving Violation' (LP) is released in Britain.

The Jackson 5 appear on *The Carol Burnett Show* to perform 'Forever Came

Today' with an absent Jermaine.

July 5

'Forever Came Today' hits the Pop singles chart peaking at number 60 and remains on the charts for nine weeks.

September

'Forever Came Today'/'I Can't Quit Your Love' is released in Britain but does not reach the Top 50.

'The Best Of Michael Jackson' (LP) is released in Britain but does not reach the Top 60.

'Body Language'/'Call Of The Wild (Do The Love Dance),' the next proposed

single by The Jackson 5, is withdrawn.

September 27

'The Best Of Michael Jackson' (LP), released on August 28 by Motown Records, enters the Pop albums chart peaking at an abysmal number 156 and remains on the charts for just five weeks.

October

'Just A Little Bit Of You'/'Dear Michael' is released in Britain but fails to reach the Top 60.

October 11

'The Best Of Michael Jackson' (LP) peaks at number 44 on the Black albums chart.

This Page: Michael plus Afro.

1976
January

Motown begin court proceedings over The Jackson 5's departure to CBS. Depositions are filed with Motown seeking $20 million damages.

Steve Manning, a friend of the Jacksons and president of their fan club, publishes a book on the family titled, *The Jacksons*.

Michael Jackson accepts the award for Best Soul Group on behalf of Gladys Knight & The Pips at the American Music Awards show. He also presents, together with David Soul, the award for Favourite Soul Female to Aretha Franklin.

'Star Trackin' 76' (LP) is issued on the Ronco label and features 'Dancing Machine' by The Jackson 5.

'Disc-O-Tech #3' (LP) containing 'Forever Came Today' by The Jackson 5 is issued on Motown's Various Artists package.

March

An official announcement is made confirming that the Jacksons' contract with Motown will not be renewed.

March 10

The Jackson 5's recording contract with Motown Records expires and they are free to move to CBS Records. A legal battle ensues between Motown and Epic and The Jacksons which will take some five years to settle. From 1969-1976, The Jackson 5 and Michael alone recorded eleven albums and sold

This Page: The Jacksons in new promotional poses for Epic Records..

over ten million records with Motown.

April

'Motown's Original Versions' (LP) featuring 'Never Can Say Goodbye' by The Jackson 5 is released on Motown.

May

An 'Earth News' album which includes an interview with Michael Jackson is issued for radio broadcast.

June

Michael is featured on four of the seven issues of *Right On!* magazine published in the second half of the year: June, September, November and December.

June 16

The Jacksons star in their own variety series which airs on CBS called *The Jacksons*. The show, which was first announced in January 1973, is based on their successful Las Vegas shows and features the whole family with songs from the Motown era as well as new material. Michael, however, hates doing the series each week!

July 10

'The Jackson 5 Anthology' (LP), released on June 15 by Motown Records, enters the Black albums chart peaking at number 32.

July 17

'The Jackson 5 Anthology' (LP) enters the Pop albums chart peaking at number 84 and remains on the charts for nine weeks.

October 16

'Enjoy Yourself'/'Style Of Life' written by Michael and Tito, The Jacksons' début single on CBS and a big hit for the group, enters the Black singles chart peaking at number 2 and remains on the charts for twenty weeks.

October 26

'Joyful Jukebox Music' (LP) by The Jackson 5 is released on Motown just prior to the group's début single with CBS. It becomes the first Jackson 5 release not to enter the Top 200 albums chart.

'Enjoy Yourself' is released in Britain but fails to reach the Top 60.

November

The Jacksons are on the cover of *Rock & Soul* magazine.

'The Jacksons' (LP) by The Jacksons, their first album for Epic, is released and is much more successful than their last releases from Motown. It contains two self-penned compositions: 'Style Of Life' and 'Blues Away,' a song written by Michael about a man coming out of a depression.

'The Jacksons' (LP) is released in Britain.

November 13

'Enjoy Yourself' enters the Pop singles chart peaking at number 6 and remains on the charts for twenty-one weeks.

December

'Joyful Jukebox Music' (LP) is released in Britain.

December 4

'The Jacksons' (LP) enters both the Black and Pop albums charts peaking at numbers 6 and 36 respectively. It spends a total of twenty-seven weeks on the Pop charts.

December 20

The Jacksons are on the cover of *Soul* magazine.

1976

THE JACKSONS

The Jacksons
Epic PE-34229
Epic EPC 86009

Side One
1. **Enjoy Yourself**
2. **Think Happy**
3. **Good Times**
4. **Keep On Dancing**
5. **Blues Away**

Side Two
1. **Show You The Way To Go**
2. **Living Together**
3. **Strength Of One Man**
4. **Dreamer**
5. **Style Of Life**

This Page: The Jacksons in performance at the Circle Star Theater in San Carlos, California, on December 18, 1976.

1977

This Page: Michael Jackson aged 18 years.

1977

Joe Jackson hires the management team of Weisner/DeMann as partners in managing The Jacksons. Freddy DeMann and Ron Weisner will manage The Jacksons, and later Michael, for several years.

January

'The Jackson 5 Anthology' (LP) is released in Britain but does not reach the Top 60.

The Jacksons begin a second series of their TV show for CBS.

The Jacksons perform 'Good Times' at the American Music Awards.

February 10

'Enjoy Yourself' by The Jacksons becomes their first official Gold record certified by the RIAA.

February 19

At the Hollywood Palladium, The Jacksons present Natalie Cole with Best R&B Vocal Female.

March

Michael is on the cover of *Rock & Soul* magazine.

Michael and The Jacksons appear on the cover of four issues of *Right On!* magazine this year: March, June, July and October.

'Motown's Preferred Stock: Stock Option No. 2' (LP), a Motown's Various Artists compilation including five Jackson 5/Michael Jackson songs, is released.

A collection of Jackson 5 songs is released entitled 'Motown Special - The Jackson 5.'

April 1

'We're Almost There'/'Just A Little Bit Of You' by Michael Jackson is re-issued on Motown's Yesteryear label.

April 2

'Show You The Way To Go'/'Blues Away' by The Jacksons, the group's second single for their new label, hits the Black singles chart peaking at number 6 and remains on the chart for fourteen weeks.

April 5

'The Jacksons' (LP), the group's début album on CBS, is certified Gold.

April 9

'Enjoy Yourself'/'Style Of Life' by The Jacksons, re-issued by Epic in Britain, enters the Top 50 singles chart. It peaks at number

42 and remains on the charts for four weeks.

May

The Jacksons play a two-and-a-half week tour of Europe, the highlight of which is the Royal Command Performance at King's Hall, Glasgow as part of Queen Elizabeth's Silver Jubilee celebrations. Michael describes this as being one of the greatest honours of his life. Other dates include Amsterdam, Bremen and Paris.

May 7

'Show You The Way To Go' hits the Pop singles chart peaking at number 28 and remains on the charts for ten weeks.

June 20

Michael attends a Studio 54 party for the stage show *Beatlemania*.

June 25

'Show You The Way To Go'/'Blues Away' which entered the Top 50 singles chart on June 4, hits number 1 in Britain holding for one week and remains on the charts for ten weeks. This is the boys' first ever number one record in Britain.

July

Michael takes his sister LaToya with him for company when he moves to New York for six months to begin rehearsals and filming for his first movie role in Universal Pictures' film, *The Wiz,* a remake of The Wizard Of Oz. The film features an all-Black cast with Michael playing The Scarecrow opposite good friend Diana Ross, cast as Dorothy and film heavyweight Richard Pryor as The Wiz.

July 4

During an outing to Coney Island whilst visiting brother Jermaine's home, Michael suffers an attack of pneumothorax and is rushed to hospital. This condition, which causes acute loss of breath, was further aggravated by mild pleurisy, something not so uncommon in slim people.

July 16

'The Jacksons' (LP) enters the Top 60 albums chart in Britain for the first time since its release in November 1976.

Whilst working on *The Wiz*, Michael meets Quincy Jones.

This Page: The Jacksons backstage at the King's Hall, where they took part in the Royal Command Performance, May 1977.

1977

"When I get onstage, I don't know what happens. It feels so good, it's like it's the safest place in the world for me... I was raised on stage.

Certain people were created for certain things, and I think our job is to entertain the world. I don't see no other thing that I could be doing.

...I've seen the very rich and the very poor, but I'm mainly interested in the poor... I want to appreciate what I have, and try to help others.

When I go to other countries, I wish to see the 'poorer' parts. I want to see what it's really like to starve. I don't want to hear it, or read it. I want to see it.

It's a whole different thing when you see it! All the things I've read in my schoolbooks about England and the Queen were okay, but my eyes are the greatest book in the world. When we did the Royal Command Performance, and then after it I actually looked into the Queen's eyes, it was the greatest thing! And it's the same with starvation, when you see it, you just receive a little more...

Michael Jackson - August 1977

August

'Skywriter' is re-released by Motown in Britain but this time the single includes 'I Want You Back' and 'The Love You Save.' The three-track single, however, does not reach the Top 50.

Michael visits Studio 54 accompanied by his sisters LaToya and Janet.

August 13

'Dreamer'/'Good Times' enters the Top 50 singles chart in Britain peaking at number 22 and remains on the charts for nine weeks.

August 16

Michael is featured on the cover of *Jet* magazine.

September

Michael is on the cover of *Soul* magazine with an exclusive interview. He says: "I'm different from most people my age."

'Great Interpretations' (LP), a Various Artists package including Michael's rendition of 'My Girl,' is released on Motown's Natural Resources label.

Universal Pictures hold a press conference at Astoria Studios in Queens, New York to announce the making of *The Wiz*. Michael Jackson attends the conference along with Diana Ross, Nipsey Russell and Tony Award-winning actor, Ted Ross.

'Show Tunes' (LP) featuring 'Corner Of The Sky' by The Jackson 5 is released on Motown's Natural Resources label.

'Enjoy Yourself'/'Do What You Wanna' is released on Epic's Memory Lane label.

October-December

Filming on *The Wiz* begins at the Astoria Studios and on location in New York. Michael will call the experience one of his greatest to date.

At this time, Michael, aged 19, accompanies his father to a meeting with Ron Alexenburg, President of Epic Records. Michael convinces Alexenburg to allow The Jacksons to write and produce their entire next LP. Alexenburg agrees, appointing two executive producers, Bobby Colomby and Mike Atkinson, to oversee their work.

October 8

'Goin' Places'/'Do What You Wanna' by The Jacksons, released this month in the US and Britain on Epic, hits both the Black and Pop singles charts peaking at numbers 8 and 52 respectively. It remains on the charts for fifteen and seven weeks respectively.

October 25

The cast of *The Wiz* hold a party at Studio 54 in Michael Jackson's honour.

October 29

'Goin' Places' (LP) by The Jacksons, released this month on Epic both in the US and Britain, enters the Pop albums chart peaking at number 63 and remains on the charts for eleven weeks. Two songs on the album are again written and produced by The Jacksons: 'Different Kind of Lady' and 'Do You Wanna.'

November

Michael appears on the cover of *Rock & Soul*.

November 5

'Goin' Places' (LP) enters the Black albums chart peaking at number 11 and remains on the charts for thirteen weeks.

'Goin' Places'/'Do What You Wanna' enters the Top 50 singles chart in Britain peaking at number 26 and remains on the charts for seven weeks.

December 3

'Goin' Places' (LP) enters the Top 60 albums chart in Britain peaking at number 45 and remains on the charts for one week.

1977

GOIN' PLACES

The Jacksons
Epic PE-34835
EPC 86035

Side One
1. Music's Takin' Over
2. Goin' Places
3. Different Kind Of Lady
4. Even Though You're Gone

Side Two
1. Jump For Joy
2. Heaven Knows I Love You Girl
3. Man Of War
4. Do What You Wanna
5. Find Me A Girl

This Page: Michael as the Scarecrow in *The Wiz*.

1978

1978

Michael meets Paul McCartney twice: once at a function on board the Queen Mary and a second time at a Beverly Hills party, where they discuss a collaboration.

'A Very Special Musical Interview Feature With The Stars Of The Wiz,' a radio broadcast two-record set featuring an interview with Michael Jackson, is released by Backstage Productions Inc. of Los Angeles.

Michael Jackson appears on the cover of *Right On!* magazine in six issues this year: January, March, June, September, October and December.

January 22

The Jacksons begin a world concert tour, including the US and Europe.

February 4

'Different Kind Of Lady'/'Find Me A Girl' by The Jacksons, released this month on Epic, enters the Black singles chart peaking at number 38 and remains

on the charts for twelve weeks. This single, which uses the B-side as the chart entry, does not enter the Pop singles chart.

February 11

'Even Though You're Gone'/'Different Kind Of Lady' enters the Top 50 singles chart in Britain peaking at number 31 and remains on the charts for four weeks.

March

'Music's Taking Over'/'Man Of War' is released in Britain but fails to reach the Top 50.

March 10

The Jacksons attend the First Annual Rock 'N' Roll Sports Classic.

May 13

The Jacksons' live performance at the Dodger Stadium, Los Angeles, is later released as the picture disc album, 'Ten Q Radio 1020 - Jacksons Dodgers Teen Night, May 13, 1978' (LP) or simply referred to as the 'Goin' Places Picture Disc.'

August

A twenty-year-old Michael Jackson purchases his first Rolls Royce.

August 12

'Blame It On The Boogie'/'Do What You Wanna' by The Jacksons enters the Pop singles chart peaking at number 54 and remains on the charts for six weeks.

September 2

'Blame It On The Boogie' enters the Black singles chart peaking at number 3 and remains on the charts for sixteen weeks. There is a video to accompany the song.

September 9

'Ease On Down The Road'/'Poppy Girls' by Michael Jackson and Diana Ross, released this month by MCA Records, hits the Black singles chart peaking at number 41 and remains on the charts for nine weeks. The single - released just prior to *The Wiz* film release - is taken from the film, but Michael sings on the A-side only.

This Page: The Jacksons in the UK for a date at London's Odeon Hammersmith.

September 16

'Ease On Down The Road' enters the Pop singles chart peaking at number 17.

September 23

'Blame It On The Boogie'/'Do What You Wanna' enters the new Top 75 singles chart in Britain peaking at number 8 and remains on the charts for twelve weeks.

October

'The Wiz' (LP) soundtrack is released in Britain but does not enter the charts.

October 21

'The Wiz' (LP), the original motion picture soundtrack album featuring Michael on six tracks - 'Ease On Down The Road,' 3 versions, 'Brand New Day,' 'Be A Lion' and 'A Brand New Day' - enters the Black and Pop albums charts peaking at numbers 17 and 40 respectively and remains on the Pop charts for seventeen weeks.

October 23

Michael Jackson visits famed toy store F.A.O. Schwartz in Manhattan, New York.

October 25

The film, *The Wiz* premières at the Pitt's Century Plaza Theater in Century City, Los Angeles with tickets selling at $150 each.

Michael attends the opening night party.

The Wiz is severely slated by many American film critics, contributing to slow ticket sales. Michael, however, wins the praise of most critics and the public alike for his demanding

role, with their predictions of a glittering film career for him. With these favourable reviews come rumours of Michael being offered several other parts, including *A Chorus Line*, *Summer Stock* and *The Story Of Bill Robinson - 'Mr. Bojangles.'*

November 18

'Ease On Down The Road'/'Poppy Girls' released by MCA enters the Top 75 singles chart in Britain peaking at number 45 and remains on the charts for four weeks.

Billboard magazine contains a 10-page anniversary supplement dedicated to The Jacksons.

Late 1978

A music video to the song 'Blame It On The Boogie' is released by The Jacksons.

December

The Jacksons launch their first production company, Peacock Productions. The idea for the name comes when Michael reads about the bird's characteristics in a newspaper article, which explains how the colours of its wing span integrate when the bird is in love. This epitomises just how Michael wants his music to be perceived: to appeal to all races and sects.

'Destiny' (LP) by The Jacksons is released on Epic. This is the first

album for which the Jacksons have total creative control and is a major success. With the exception of 'Blame It On The Boogie,' all the songs on the LP are written by the group.

'We Wish You A Merry Christmas' (LP), a Various Artists album including 'Give Love On Christmas Day' and 'The Christmas Song' by The Jackson 5, is released on Motown's Natural Resources label.

'Destiny'/'That's What You Get (For Being Polite)' is released in Britain.

'Destiny' (LP) is released in Britain.

December 9

'Destiny' (LP) enters the Black albums chart peaking at number 3 and remains on the charts for sixteen weeks.

December 16

'Destiny' (LP) enters the Pop albums chart peaking at number 12 and remains on the charts for forty-one weeks.

The Jacksons perform 'Shake Your Body (Down To The Ground)' on *American Bandstand*.

DESTINY

The Jacksons
Epic JE-35552
EPC 83200

Side One
1. **Blame It On The Boogie**
2. **Push Me Away**
3. **Things I Do For You**
4. **Shake Your Body (Down To The Ground)**

Side Two
1. **Destiny**
2. **Bless His Soul**
3. **All Night Dancin'**
4. **That's What You Get (For Being Polite)**

1979

1979

Videos to the songs 'Don't Stop 'Til You Get Enough' and 'Rock With You' are released by Michael Jackson.

Peter Pan tops a list of Michael's favourite books submitted to the Chicago Public Library's Young Adult Services section. He also promotes book reading through a library programme called 'Boogie To The Book Beat.'

The Jacksons are honoured at a party in Beverly Hills hosted by Mayor Tom Bradley, who declares it 'Jackson Day.' Michael's date for the evening is Tatum O'Neal.

Early 1979

During a thirteen-day tour of Britain, The Jacksons fly to Switzerland for two days to film a TV special.

Seven concerts have to be cancelled due to Michael's strained voice.

The film, *The Wiz*, premières in London.

January

'Boogie' (LP) by The Jackson 5 comprising mainly of previously unreleased material is issued on Motown's Natural Resources label. It does not enter the charts and only a limited number of albums are released. It is now a very much sought-after collectors' item!

Michael is featured on the cover of *Rock & Soul* magazine, which runs a special feature on *The Wiz*.

'Earth News' (LP), 'Record

Report With Robert W. Morgan' (LP) and Westwood One's 'Star Trak' (LP), three radio broadcast records featuring interviews with Michael are issued for airplay.

Pickwick Records issue 'Zip-A-Dee-Doo-Dah,' a compilation of Jackson 5 songs.

January 20

'You Can't Win (Part 1)'/'You Can't Win (Part 2)' by Michael Jackson, released this month as a solo single by Motown Records, enters the Black singles chart peaking at number 42 and remains on the charts for ten weeks.

January 22

The Jacksons begin a world tour to promote the 'Destiny' album with their opening concert in Bremen. Countries to be visited include Britain, Holland, France and Kenya with concerts in Madrid, Amsterdam, Geneva, London, Brighton, Preston, Sheffield, Glasgow, Manchester, Birmingham, Halifax, Leicester, Cardiff, Bournemouth, Paris and Nairobi, amongst others.

January 27

'Shake Your Body (Down To The Ground)'/'That's What You Get (For Being Polite)' by The Jacksons, released this month on Epic, enters the Black singles chart peaking at number 3 and remains on the charts for twenty-three weeks. It goes on to become their first multi-platinum single and the biggest-selling hit single The Jacksons ever record, with over 2.5 million copies sold.

February 1

The Jacksons are on the cover of *Jet*.

February 3

'Destiny'/'That's What You Get (For Being Polite)' enters the Top 75 singles chart in Britain peaking at number 39 and remains on the charts for six weeks.

February 17

'Shake Your Body (Down To The Ground)' hits the Pop singles chart peaking at number 7 and remains on the charts for twenty-two weeks.

February 24

'You Can't Win' enters the Pop singles chart peaking at number 81 and remains on the charts for three weeks.

The Jacksons are on the cover of *Right On!*

March 13

'Destiny' (LP) is certified Gold.

March 24

'Shake Your Body (Down To The Ground)'/'All Night Dancin'' enters the Top 75 singles chart in Britain peaking at number 4 and remains on the charts for twelve weeks.

Spring

The Jacksons perform

Page Opposite: The Jacksons in concert 1979.

1979

concerts in Britain, although some are cancelled due to Michael suffering a bad bout of flu.

During their British dates, The Jacksons fly to Switzerland for two days to film two numbers for an Abba special: 'Shake Your Body Down To The Ground' and 'Blame It On The Boogie.'

The Jacksons are asked to tour South Africa, but before they formally accept they are threatened with a boycott of their albums and concerts worldwide by an organisation called the African Jazz Art Societies & Studios (AJASS). In an effort not to offend AJASS and other groups that support the AJASS stand, The Jacksons decide against the proposed tour.

April 12

'Shake Your Body (Down To The Ground)' is certified Gold.

April 14-15
The Jacksons perform in concert in Cleveland, Ohio.

April 19-22
The Jacksons perform in concert at the Valley Forge Music Fair, Valley Forge, Pennsylvania.

April 25-29
The Jacksons perform in concert in Chicago, Illinois.

May

'You Can't Win (Part 1)'/'You Can't Win (Part 2)' is released in Britain but does not chart. A 7" picture disc is also released.

May 3
The Jacksons perform in concert in St. Petersburg, Florida.

May 5
'Destiny' (LP) enters the Top 60 albums chart in Britain - some six months after its release - peaking at number 33 and remains on the charts for seven weeks.

May 6
The Jacksons perform in concert in Jacksonville, Florida.

May 8
'Destiny' (LP) is certified Platinum.

May 10-12
The Jacksons perform in concert in Houston, Texas.

May 13
The Jacksons perform in

concert in Baton Rouge, Louisiana.

May 16
The Jacksons perform in concert in Birmingham, Alabama.

May 17
The Jacksons perform in concert in Columbus, Georgia.

May 18
The Jacksons perform in concert in Nashville, Tennessee.

May 19
The Jacksons perform in concert in Atlanta, Georgia.

May 20
The Jacksons perform in concert in Memphis, Tennessee.

May 24
The Jacksons perform in concert in Pine Bluff, Arkansas.

May 26
The Jacksons perform in concert in Kansas City, Missouri.

May 27
The Jacksons perform in concert in Oklahoma City, Oklahoma.

May 30
The Jacksons perform in concert in Shreveport, Louisiana.

June

Michael is set to star in the film translation of *A Chorus Line* - cast as the dancer who gets his start as a female impersonator. At first, Michael has reservations, saying, "If I do it, people will link me with the part. Because of my voice, some people already

the night is actress, Tatum O'Neal.

July 28

'Don't Stop 'Til You Get Enough'/'I Can't Help It' by Michael Jackson, the first single from his début solo album, 'Off The Wall,' released for CBS/Epic this month, enters the Pop singles chart at number 87.

> "'Triumph' will be much better, much more creative than 'Destiny,' we've learned a lot since we made that. We didn't have a chance to be as creative on it as we would have liked. We were rushed. We were pressured. It was the first album we wrote - and we had to prove to the Epic people we could write. Now the pressure is off. We don't have to prove anything any more."

Michael Jackson, June 24, 1979

OFF THE WALL

Michael Jackson

Epic FE 35745
EPC 83468

Side One
1. Don't Stop 'Til You Get Enough
2. Rock With You
3. Working Day And Night
4. Get On The Floor

Side Two
1. Off The Wall
2. Girlfriend
3. She's Out Of My Life
4. I Can't Help It
5. It's The Falling In Love
6. Burn This Disco Out

think I'm that way - homo. Though I'm actually not at all." He later says, "I saw *A Chorus Line* again and I love the part. It's dramatic, emotional - and if you have any feelings at all, it has to touch you."

June 1
The Jacksons perform in concert in Norfolk, Virginia.

June 3
The Jacksons perform in concert in Columbia, South Carolina.

June 8
The Jacksons perform in concert in Charlotte, North Carolina.

June 9
The Jacksons perform in concert in Washington DC.

June 11
'Shake Your Body (Down To The Ground)' is certified Platinum.

Late June
The Jacksons begin recording the 'Triumph' LP.

July
Mayor Tom Bradley declares 'Jackson Day' in Los Angeles in honour of the group's Gold and Platinum achievements. Some 300 guests attend a party in the City National Bank Vault in Beverly Hills, which is equipped with a special dance floor. The Jacksons receive a Platinum Record for their 'Destiny' album as well as other Gold and Silver records. Michael's date for

August
'Off The Wall' (LP) by Michael Jackson is released. Mixing pop, R&B and jazz, the LP is produced by Quincy Jones with Michael co-producing the three songs which he wrote. 'Off The Wall' breaks new ground vocally for Michael, with his most adventurous and mature vocals to date. It breaks music industry records by being the first album ever to spawn four Top Ten singles in the US, two of which become number 1 hits and are certified Gold. In Britain, for the first time in music history, a record five hit singles are released from one album, 'Girlfriend,' written by Paul McCartney, being one of them.

This Page: Michael shows off his friendship with actress, Tatum O'Neal, at a Hollywood party.

1979

The album exceeds all expectations and is hugely successful on both the Pop and Black albums charts, eventually selling over twelve million copies worldwide. Some of the early copies of 'Off The Wall' feature a free 7" picture disc of 'You Can't Win.' With the release of this album, the world sees a new Michael Jackson. His voice has deepened and his nose, once broad, is definitely thinner.

'Motown's Love Songs' (LP) featuring 'Never Can Say Goodbye' is released on Motown's Natural Resources label.

August 16
Michael Jackson is on the cover of *Jet* magazine, which includes an interview.

August 20
Michael is on the cover of *Soul* magazine, 'Michael Jackson at 21,' which includes an exclusive interview.

August 29
Michael is 21 years old today and celebrates his birthday at Studio 54 in New York City.

Michael's contract with his father Joe Jackson expires and he now takes control of his own career.

September

Motown continue to release their product on the back of new Jackson material by issuing '20 Golden Greats' (LP) in Britain. Needless to say, the LP does not chart.

The Jacksons are on the cover of *Ebony* magazine with a feature titled, 'No Longer Little Boys.'

'Off The Wall' by Michael Jackson enters both the Black and Pop albums charts peaking at numbers 1 and 3 respectively and remains on the Pop charts for a mammoth eighty-four weeks. It holds its position at number 1 on the Black charts for a lengthy sixteen weeks during a sixty-one week residence.

September 15
'Don't Stop 'Til You Get Enough'/'I Can't Help It,' released in Britain in August, enters the Top 75 singles chart peaking at number 3 and remains on the charts for twelve weeks.

September 29
'Off the Wall' (LP) enters the Top 60 albums chart in Britain peaking at number 5 and remains on the charts for an astounding one hundred and seventy-three weeks.

October

The Jacksons' 'Destiny' World Tour begins in New Orleans, Louisiana. They will visit eighty cities.

'Hot Nights & City Lights' (LP), a Various Artists anthology including 'Shake Your Body (Down To The Ground),' is released on the K-Tel International label.

Michael and The Jacksons are the cover story of *Rock & Soul* magazine for the third time this year.

'Keep The Fire' (LP) by Kenny Loggins, which

includes Michael singing harmony vocals on the track 'Who's Right, Who's Wrong,' is released on the Columbia label.

October 13
'Don't Stop 'Til You Get Enough' hits number 1 on the Pop and Black singles charts holding its position for one and five weeks respectively and remains on the charts for twenty-one and twenty weeks respectively. A music video released to promote the single features Michael in a tuxedo and showcases his advancing dance steps.

October 31
Michael attends his friend Jane Fonda's Halloween disco party at the Hollywood Palace.

November

'Off The Wall'/'Working Day And Night' enters the Top 75 singles chart in Britain peaking at number 7 and remains on the charts for ten weeks.

November 3
'Rock With You'/'Working

Day And Night' by Michael Jackson, released this month on Epic, enters the Black singles chart peaking at number 1 and remains on the charts for twenty-five weeks. There is an accompanying video directed by Bruce Gowers featuring Michael dressed in a silver sequinned suit with matching boots.

November 8
The Jacksons appear in concert at Nassau Coliseum in Hampstead, New York.

November 27
Michael's publicity agency, Norman Winter Associates, approaches America's prestigious magazine, *Rolling Stone*, to see if they are interested in doing a cover story on Michael Jackson. They receive the following reply:

"Michael Jackson has, in fact, been on the cover of Rolling Stone, contrary to your statement in your recent letter to me. We would very much like to do a major piece on Michael Jackson, but feel it is not a cover story."

Jann S. Wenner

This letter proves quite significant in years to come.

November 29
'Don't Stop 'Til You Get Enough' is certified Gold.

December 10
'Off The Wall' (LP) is certified Gold and Platinum. The album will go on to sell twelve million worldwide.

1979

1980

1980

Michael spends several weeks in New Hampshire on the set of *On Golden Pond,* visiting with friend Jane Fonda. While there, he forms friendships with the movie's other stars, Henry Fonda and Katharine Hepburn. The experience deepens Michael's love of movies and his desire to work more in films.

'Winners' (LP), the Various Artists compilation including the special disco version of 'Shake Your Body (Down To The Ground),' is released by I&M Teleproducts.

Cashbox magazine names 'Off The Wall' the Most Popular Soul Album Of The Year.

Michael performs 'Don't Stop 'Til You Get Enough' at a UNICEF benefit concert.

'Old Crest On A New Wave' (LP) by Dave Mason featuring background vocals by Michael Jackson on the track 'Save Me' is released by Columbia Records.

The Jacksons receive the NAACP's Image Award for Best Singing Group Of The Year.

The 'Triumph' video is released by the Jacksons.

Michael Jackson releases a video for 'She's Out Of My Life.'

'Hitline' (LP) and 'Wings Of Sound' (LP), two Various Artists albums both featuring 'Don't Stop 'Til You Get Enough,' are released by K-Tel International. 'Rock With You' is also included on 'Hitline.'

January

Michael does an interview with Silvya Chase for ABC-

TV's *20/20* programme which profiles The Jacksons. Michael responds to statements that he has not had to deal with the real world, saying that it is difficult for him because people see him differently and don't treat him like they would a neighbour. Interviews become increasingly rare for Michael Jackson.

January 18

Michael Jackson wins three American Music Awards in the soul category: from Andy Gibb and Dionne Warwick he accepts Favourite Soul Single - 'Don't Stop 'Til You Get Enough,' from Chuck Berry and Lief Garrett he accepts Favourite Soul Album - 'Off The Wall' and from Bonny Pointer and Dave Mason he accepts Favourite Soul Male. Michael attends the ceremony dressed in his then trademark tuxedo with a silver sequinned shirt.

This Page: The Jacksons looking fresh and ready for more success.

Michael shows off one of his 1980 American Music Awards with actress Nicolette Larson.

1980

"*I love the whole world of dance, because dancing is really the emotions through bodily movement. And however you feel, you just bring out that inner feeling through your mood. A lot of people don't think about the importance of it, but there's a whole psychological thing to just letting everything loose. Dancing is important, like laughing, to back off tension. Escapism... it's great.*

I really believe that each person has a destiny from the day he's born, and certain people have a thing that they're meant to do. There's a reason why the Japanese are better at technology, and a reason why the Negro race are more into music - you go back to Africa and the tribes and the beating of the drums...

I love Studio 54 in New York, it's so theatrical and dramatic. People come there as characters, and it's like going to a play. You make yourself up to be this thing and just go crazy with the lights and the music, and you're in another world. It's very escapist...

Escapism and wonder is influence. It makes you feel good, and that allows you to do things. You just keep on moving ahead, and you say, 'God, is this wonderful - do I appreciate it.'

Michael Jackson, March 1980

This Page: John Travolta and Michael Jackson exchange moves.

remains on the charts for nine weeks.

February 14
'Rock With You' is certified Gold.

February 16
'Off The Wall'/'Get On The Floor' by Michael Jackson, released this month on Epic, enters the Pop singles chart peaking at number 10 and remains on the charts for seventeen weeks.

February 23
'Off The Wall' enters the Black singles chart peaking at number 5 and remains on the charts for thirteen weeks.

February 27
At The Shrine Auditorium in Los Angeles Michael Jackson is awarded his first Grammy as a solo performer in the category Best R&B Vocal Performance - Male for 'Don't Stop 'Til You Get Enough'. Michael boycotts the event in disgust at being pigeon-holed into only R&B soul categories and is disappointed that 'Off The Wall' was overlooked for Best Album. He vows his next album won't be ignored. It is widely accepted that the awards do not do justice to the hugely successful LP.

March

'20/20: Twenty No. 1 Hits From Twenty Years at Motown' (LP) including three Jackson 5 songs and 'Ben' by Michael is released on Motown.

March 1
Michael appears on the cover of *Melody Maker*, with an exclusive interview: 'Michael In Wonderland.'

Michael, together with Nicolette Larson, also presents an award for Favourite Pop Album to The Bee Gees for 'Spirits Having Flown,' which is accepted by Andy Gibb.

January 19
'Rock With You' hits number 1 on the Pop singles chart holding its position for four weeks and remains on the charts for twenty-four weeks.

February 9

'Rock With You'/'Get On The Floor' by Michael Jackson enters the Top 75 singles chart in Britain peaking at number 7 and

'Ben' by Michael Jackson with 'Abraham, Martin And John,' the Marvin Gaye classic on the B-side, is re-released in Britain on the Motown label.

April 19

'She's Out Of My Life'/ 'Get On The Floor' by Michael Jackson, released this month on Epic, enters the Pop singles chart peaking at number 10 and remains on the charts for sixteen weeks. It is Michael's second single of the year and the fourth Top Ten hit from one album. A touching ballad, which brings Michael to tears at the end, it has an accompanying video, again directed by Bruce Gowers.

Michael Jackson becomes the first solo artist in America to chart four Top 10 singles from one album, equalling a feat only previously accomplished by the group, Fleetwood Mac, for their 'Rumours' LP, and the soundtracks 'Saturday Night Fever' and 'Grease.'

May 3

'She's Out Of My Life' enters the Black singles chart peaking at number 43 and remains on the charts for eight weeks.

'She's Out Of My Life'/'Push Me Away' enters the Top 75 singles chart in Britain peaking at number 3 and remains on the charts for nine weeks.

Michael Jackson's 'Off The Wall' (LP) reports sales of over five million in America alone and is certified Triple Platinum in Britain, Seven Times Platinum in Australia,

Triple Platinum in Canada and Gold in Holland.

Dave Mason's LP including the song 'Save Me,' featuring Michael on backing vocals, is released in Britain.

July

Michael Jackson becomes the first artist in Britain to release five singles from an album when 'Girlfriend'/ 'Bless His Soul' is released. It peaks at number 41 on the Top 75 singles chart and remains on the charts for five weeks. This single is not released in America.

July 31

Michael Jackson in on the cover of *Jet* magazine, with sister LaToya.

August

'Love Lives Forever' (LP) by Minnie Riperton featuring 'I'm In Love Again,' with vocals by Michael Jackson, is released.

'The Robert W. Morgan Special Of The Week - The Jacksons' (LP), a radio broadcast record including an interview with The Jacksons, is released.

August 15

'Michael Jackson - Superstar Series Vol. 7' (LP) is released on Motown.

September

'Night Time Lover' by LaToya Jackson, co-written by Michael and LaToya, is released on Polydor. Michael arranges and produces this song for his sister. It is originally titled 'Fire Is The Feeling' and was written with Donna Summer in mind.

'LaToya Jackson' (LP), which includes the song 'Night Time Lover,' co-written, arranged and produced by Michael, is released on Polydor.

Motown re-releases four Jackson 5 singles in Britain with new B-sides: 'Got To Be There'/'I Miss You Baby,' 'I Want You Back'/'The Love You Save,' 'I'll Be There'/'ABC,' and 'Lookin' Through The Windows'/'Doctor My Eyes.'

September 3

In recognition of their contribution to music, the Hollywood Chamber of Commerce honour The Jacksons with a Star on Hollywood Boulevard's 'Walk of Fame.'

September 9

'The Jackson 5 - Superstar Series Vol. 12' (LP) is released on Motown.

Sept. 18, 19, 25, 26

The Jacksons perform at The Forum, Los Angeles.

September 27

'Lovely One'/'Bless His Soul' by The Jacksons, released this month on Epic, enters the Pop and Black singles charts peaking at numbers 12 and 2 respectively and remains on the Pop charts for eighteen weeks. It's their seventh single for the label and the first from the 'Triumph' LP.

October

Michael appears in *Gentleman's Quarterly*, with a minor interview.

'Hotter Than July' (LP) by Stevie Wonder featuring

TRIUMPH

The Jacksons

Epic FE 36424
EPC 86112

Side One
1. **Can You Feel It**
2. **Lovely One**
3. **Your Ways**
4. **Everybody**

Side Two
1. **Heartbreak Hotel**
2. **Time Waits For No One**
3. **Walk Right Now**
4. **Give It Up**
5. **Wondering Who**

1980

'All I Do' with backing vocals by Michael Jackson, is released on Motown's Tamla label.

'Love Lives Forever' (LP) by Minnie Riperton featuring 'I'm In Love Again' with vocals by Michael Jackson is released in Britain.

Motown Records releases Michael and Jackson 5 as A and AA sides. 'Got To Be There' is coupled with Marv Johnson's 'How I Miss You.'

Three Jackson 5 double AA classics are issued: 'I Want You Back'/'The Love You Save,' 'I'll Be There'/'ABC' and 'Lookin' Through The Window'/'Doctor My Eyes.'

October 4
'Another One Bites The Dust' by Queen hits number 1 on Billboard's Hot 100 – a song suggested for release by Michael.

October 11
'Triumph' (LP) enters the Top 60 albums chart in Britain peaking at number 13 and remains on the charts for sixteen weeks.

October 18
'Triumph' (LP) by The Jacksons, who once again have complete creative control of this album released in September, enters both the Black and Pop albums charts peaking at numbers 1 and 10 respectively and remains on both charts for twenty-nine weeks.

October 25
'Lovely One'/'Things I Do For You' enters the Top 75 singles chart in Britain

peaking at number 29 and remains on the charts for six weeks.

November
'Hotter Than July' (LP) by Stevie Wonder featuring 'All I Do' with backing vocals by Michael Jackson is released in Britain.

December
LaToya Jackson's self-named LP is released in Britain featuring 'Night Time Lover' by brother Michael.

Billboard magazine ranks Michael Jackson, his 'Off The Wall' album, and his singles on six of their year end charts. Michael takes the most coveted place as number 1 Top Black Artist Of The Year, with 'Off The Wall' ranking as number 1 Black Album Of The Year. Other rankings are: number 2 Top Pop Male Artist Of The Year, number 3 Top Pop Album Of The Year ('Off The Wall'), number 2 Top Black Single Of The Year ('Rock With You') and number 4 Top Pop Single Of The Year ('Rock With You').

'Don't Stop 'Til You Get Enough'/'Shake Your Body (Down To The Ground)' is released on Epic's Memory Lane label.

December 6
'Heartbreak Hotel'/'Things I Do For You' by The Jacksons, their eighth single released this month for Epic, enters both the Pop and Black singles charts peaking at numbers 22 and 2 respectively and remains on the charts for sixteen and seventeen weeks respectively.

The single begins with a blood-curdling scream, courtesy of sister LaToya. Because of the confusion with the Elvis Presley hit of the same name, The Jacksons' single is renamed 'This Place Hotel' in 1984.

December 10
'Triumph' (LP) is certified Gold and Platinum.

December 13
'Heartbreak Hotel'/'Different Kind Of Lady' enters the Top 75 singles chart in Britain peaking at number 44 and remains on the charts for six weeks.

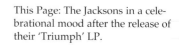

This Page: The Jacksons in a celebrational mood after the release of their 'Triumph' LP.

1981

Michael appears in media adverts for Suzuki in Japan.

Michael is a guest on Diana Ross's TV special, *Diana* and performs 'Rock With You.' He also steps onto stage at a live Diana Ross concert to join in with her hit, 'Upside Down.' A segment where Diana talks to Michael in between clips of 'Ease On Down The Road,' which they perform in look-alike tuxedos, and 'Rock With You Duet With Diana,' is also specially filmed for her TV special.

The special is re-broadcast in 1984 during the height of 'Michaelmania.'

Cashbox magazine chooses 'Off the Wall' as Soul Album Of The Year.

'Share Your Love' (LP) by Kenny Rogers featuring 'Goin' Back To Alabama' with backing vocals by Michael Jackson and Lionel Richie is released.

January

The Jacksons receive the NAACP's Image Award for Best Singing Group Of The Year for the second successive year.

January 30

At the American Music Awards ceremony, Michael Jackson accepts the award for Favourite Soul Album – 'Off the Wall' – from Peaches and Herb along with Larry Grant. He also accepts the award for Favourite Soul Male from Bonny Pointer and sister, LaToya. At this event, he also pays tribute to Chuck Berry along with his fellow artists.

'The Dude' (LP) by Quincy Jones, which acknowledges a guest appearance by Michael, is released on A&M Records. However, Michael's specific contribution is unknown although both 'Turn On The Action' and 'Somethin' Special' sound like him.

February 28

'Can You Feel It'/'Wondering Who,' released in Britain this month, enters the Top 75 singles chart peaking at number 6 and remains on the charts for fifteen weeks.

March

Michael Jackson gives what turns out to be his last interview for many years to come to Danny Baker of Britain's *New Musical Express*. Baker flies to Los Angeles to meet Michael and conducts the interview over a three week period.

March 9

Epic Records begin distribution of the promo single 'Can You Feel It' written by Michael and Jackie Jackson.

Michael Jackson is on the cover of *Jet* magazine.

Spring

The Triumph, the promotional film conceived, written and produced by Michael for the single, 'Can You Feel It,' which contains amazing special effects, is released.

April

'One Day In Your Life' is re-released by Motown in Britain but this time with 'Take Me Back' on the B-side.

'Sometimes Late At Night' (LP) by Carole Bayer Sager featuring 'Just Friends' with backing vocals by Michael Jackson is released by Boardwalk Records. This song is produced by Michael and Burt Bacharach.

April 4

Michael appears on the cover of Britain's *NME*, which includes an exclusive interview with Danny Baker.

April 11

'Can You Feel It'/ 'Wondering Who' by The Jacksons, their ninth for

1981

This Page: Michael shows off one of his 1981 American Music Awards with good friend, Diana Ross.

Epic released this month, enters the Black singles chart peaking at number 30 and remains on the charts for nine weeks.

April 18
'One Day In Your Life'/'Take Me Back' by Michael Jackson, released in March by Motown Records, enters the Pop singles chart peaking at only number 55 and remains on the charts for seven weeks.

April 25
'One Day In Your Life' enters the Black singles chart peaking at number 42 and remains on the charts for ten weeks.

'One Day In Your Life' (LP) by Michael Jackson, released on March 25 by Motown Records, enters the Pop albums chart but, containing only old material, it peaks at number 144 and remains on the charts for ten weeks.

May 2
'One Day In Your Life' (LP) enters the Black albums chart peaking at number 41 and remains on the charts for ten weeks.

'Can You Feel It' enters the Pop singles chart peaking at number 77 and remains on the charts for five weeks.

June
'Walk Right Now'/'Your Ways' is released in Britain.

'Lovely One'/'She's Out Of My Life' and 'Off The Wall'/'Rock With You' are issued on Epic's Memory Lane label.

June 10
Motown re-issues five Jackson-related albums: 'Diana Ross Presents The Jackson 5' (LP), 'ABC' (LP), 'Third Album' (LP), 'Got To Be There' (LP) and 'Ben' (LP).

June 27
'Walk Right Now'/'Your Ways' by The Jacksons, their tenth single for Epic released this month, enters both the Pop and Black singles charts peaking at numbers 73 and 50 respectively and remains on the charts for four and ten weeks respectively.

'One Day In Your Life' becomes Michael's first solo number 1 hit in Britain, holding its position for two weeks and remaining on the charts for fourteen weeks.

July 9
The Jacksons' Triumph World Tour begins in Memphis, Tennessee and concludes in Los Angeles, California. Concerts in Florida and Alabama are cancelled after Michael collapses from exhaustion. *Rolling Stone* magazine will later cite The Jackson's 1981 World Tour as one of 'the greatest live performances of the Seventies and Eighties.'

July 18
'One Day In Your Life' (LP), released this month in Britain, enters the Top 75 albums chart peaking at number 29 and remains on the charts for eight weeks.

July 22
The Jacksons give a special benefit concert for the Atlanta Children's

Foundation at the Omni Auditorium in Atlanta, Georgia and raise $100,000 for the charity. The Foundation is established in response to a series of kidnappings which had been occurring in Atlanta.

August
'The Artists & Music That Started It All' (LP), a promotional six record set including four Jackson 5 songs, is released on Motown.

August 1
'We're Almost There'/'We've Got A Good Thing Going,' released in July in Britain, enters the Top 75 singles chart peaking at number 46 and remains on the charts for four weeks.

September
Michael visits Katharine Hepburn in her Manhattan home. She attends a Jacksons concert at Madison Square Garden.

'Time Waits For No One'/'Give It Up' is released in Britain.

'Elite' (LP), the Various Artists anthology which includes Michael's 'Rock With You,' is released by K-Tel International.

September 15
Two more Jackson-related albums, 'Greatest Hits' (LP) and 'The Best Of Michael Jackson' (LP) are released on Motown.

This Page: Michael appears in promotional adverts for Suzuki in Japan.

The Jacksons 1981 World Tour Programme.

Page Opposite: Michael sings 'Ease On Down The Road' with Diana Ross on her TV special, *Diana.*

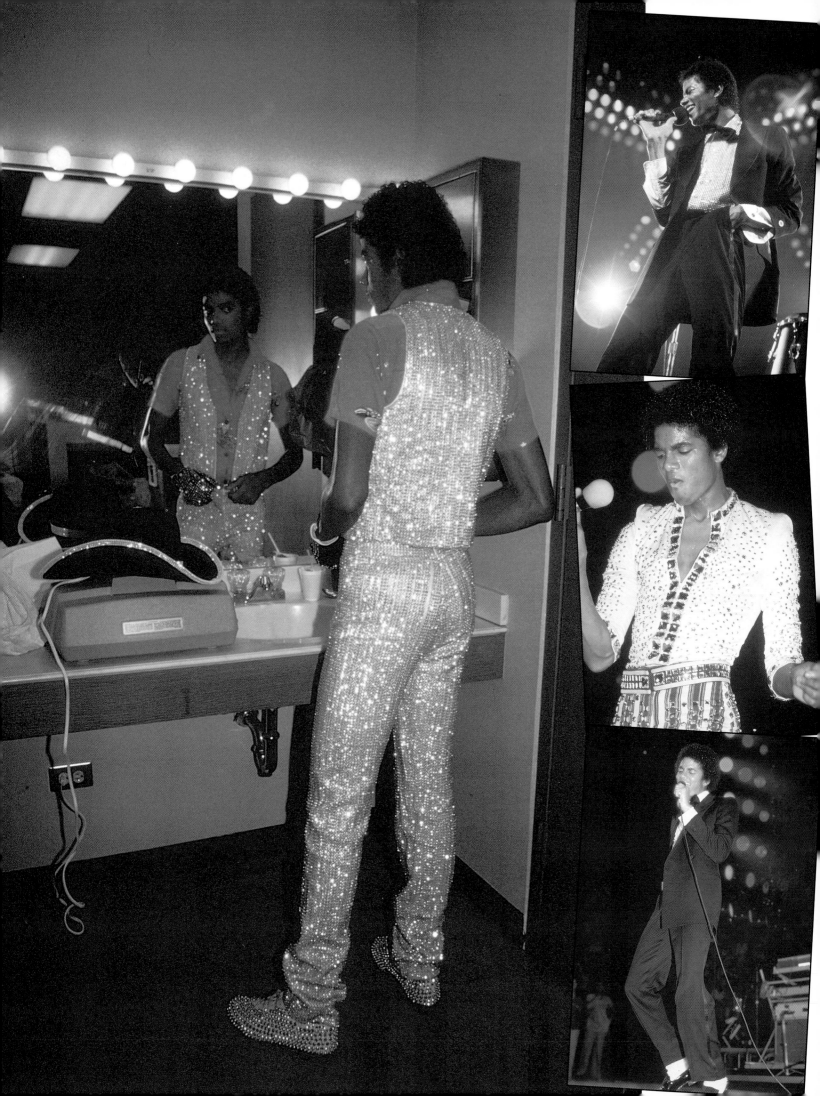

1981

This Page: Michael at Studio 55 with singer Joe Carrasco.

Below: The Jacksons backstage with Don Dempsey of Epic Records.

Other Shots Pages 56-59 Michael performing on The Triumph Tour.

October

The Jacksons are on the cover of *Ebony* magazine.

October 16

While at Studio 55 in Los Angeles, Michael lends his vocal talents to singer Joe 'King' Carrasco for his new album. Michael sings backing vocals on the song 'Don't Let A Woman Make A Fool Out Of You.'

'Things I Do For You'/'Don't Stop 'Til You Get Enough' is released in Britain.

November 5

Michael appears on the cover of *Jet* magazine, in which he is voted Most Popular Male Entertainer.

November 28

'Jacksons Live' (LP), based on tour concerts given earlier in the year released by Epic in the US and Britain this month, enters the Pop and Black albums charts peaking at numbers 30 and 10 respectively and remaining on the charts for seventeen and twenty-two weeks respectively.

December 12

'Jacksons Live' (LP) enters the Top 100 albums chart in Britain peaking at number 53 and remains on the charts for nine weeks.

Billboard magazine's end of year chart shows The Jacksons ranking in four categories: number 10 Top Black Album ('Triumph'), number 10 Top Black Artist, number 4 Top Dance Artist and number 4 Top Audience Response for the hit Single ('Can You Feel It').

1982

1982

'Donna Summer' (LP) by Donna Summer, which includes backing vocals by Michael on the song 'State Of Independence,' is released.

'The Jacksons In Concert,' a commercial video recording is made in the UK.

'Synapse Gap (Mundo Total)' by Joe 'King' Carrasco including backing vocals by Michael on the song 'Don't Let A Woman Make A Fool Out Of You' is released by MCA Records.

January

'That Girl'/'All I Do' by Stevie Wonder, featuring Michael Jackson on the B-side, is released on the Tamla label.

January 14

'Maybe Tomorrow' (LP) is re-issued by Motown.

March

Paul McCartney records 'The Girl Is Mine' with Michael in a Los Angeles studio.

A special 'Best Of Michael Jackson' issue of *Right On!* is published.

April

'Off The Wall'/'Don't Stop 'Til You Get Enough' is released in Britain.

'Jane Fonda's Workout Record' (LP), including 'Can You Feel It' by The Jacksons, is released by Columbia Records.

'Stevie Wonder's Original Musiquarium I' (LP), which includes 'You Haven't Done Nothin'' featuring The Jackson 5 on backing vocals is released on Motown.

Summer

Both Pepsi and Coca Cola turn down sponsorship deal proposals put forward by Jay Coleman, president of Rockbill, who were contacted by Michael Jackson's managers.

July

Motown Records issue two Flip Hits cassette singles by Michael and The Jackson 5: 'One Day In Your Life'/ 'Got To Be There'/ 'Ben'/'Ain't No Sunshine' by Michael Jackson and 'I Want You Back'/'I'll Be There'/'Lookin' Through The Windows'/'ABC' by The Jackson 5.

July 9

'Goin' Back To Indiana' (LP) by The Jackson 5 is re-issued on Motown.

July 26

'Christmas Album' (LP) by The Jackson 5 is re-issued on Motown.

August

Michael Jackson and Quincy Jones begin work on the 'Thriller' album.

'Michael Jackson's Greatest Original Hits' (EP) is released by Epic on cassette in Britain: 'Can You Feel It'/'Shake Your Body'/ 'Show You The Way To Go'/'Blame It On The Boogie.'

August 20

Whilst Michael is recording an exclusive interview for the October issue of Andy Warhol's publication *Interview*, Warhol calls Michael and takes part in the interview.

September

'Silk Electric' (LP) by Diana Ross featuring a song Michael wrote for her titled 'Muscles' is released on RCA along with the single 'Muscles'/'I Am Me.'

September 24

'12 No. 1 Hits From The 70's' (LP), the Various Artists package with three Jackson-related songs, is released on Motown.

'Lookin' Through The Windows' (LP) is re-issued by Motown.

Autumn

Michael and Quincy Jones begin work on the 'E.T.: The Extra-Terrestrial' storybook album.

October

'The Jackson 5' (LP) is issued in Britain on the Pickwick label.

October 2

'Muscles,' the Diana Ross song written and produced by Michael Jackson, enters the Pop singles chart at number 61, peaking at number 10, and the Black singles chart at number 33. It remains on the Pop charts for ten weeks. The single, named after Michael's pet snake, earns a Grammy nomination.

October 23

'Muscles' enters the Top 75 singles chart in Britain peaking at number 15 and remains on the charts for nine weeks.

'The Girl Is Mine' is released as a one-sided single by Epic.

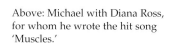

Above: Michael with Diana Ross, for whom he wrote the hit song 'Muscles.'

Below: Michael with Paul McCartney.

November

'E.T.: The Extra-Terrestrial' (LP) is released by MCA Records. The children's storybook album telling the story of *E.T.* is narrated by Michael and contains one song, 'Someone In The Dark.' A legal battle immediately ensues over the release of the album. CBS Records, Michael's record company, claim that MCA violated their agreement by releasing the storybook album before the end of the year, thereby conflicting with Michael's solo album. A New York Supreme Court judge prohibits further sales of the album. The release of 'Someone In The Dark' as a single is also prohibited.

'Michael Jackson's Greatest Original Hits' (EP) is released by Epic: 'Don't Stop'/'Rock With You'/ 'She's Out Of My Life'/ 'Off The Wall.'

November 6

'The Girl Is Mine,' the duet by Michael and Paul McCartney with 'Can't Get Outta The Rain' on the B-side, released on October 25 on Epic, enters the Pop singles chart peaking at number 2 and remains on the charts for eighteen weeks.

'The Girl Is Mine'/'Can't Get Outta The Rain,' released on October 29 in Britain, enters the Top 75 singles chart peaking at number 8 and remains on the charts for ten weeks. A 7" picture disc is also issued.

November 13

'The Girl Is Mine' hits the Black singles chart peaking at number 1. It holds its position for three weeks and remains on the charts for twenty weeks.

December

Michael and 'E.T.' are on the cover of *Ebony* magazine.

Michael razes and rebuilds the Encino family home as a gift to his mother, Katherine.

A planned Michael Jackson single from the 'E.T.: The Extra-Terrestrial' album, 'Someone In The Dark' goes unreleased by MCA Records, although some promotional copies are distributed.

December 1

'Thriller' (LP) is released and ensures that Michael Jackson will never again be seen as just another Jackson. A masterpiece of brilliant songwriting, it sports an impressive collection of musicians that span the pop, R&B, rock and jazz genres: Greg Phillinganes, Eddie Van Halen, Steve Lukather, Louis Johnson, Steve Porcaro and Vincent Price, to name but a few. 'Thriller' will go on to become the most successful album of all time, selling over 51 million copies worldwide and will provide seven hit singles, including four of Michael's own songs. It is certified Platinum in fifteen countries and Gold in four others, and receives seven Grammy

Awards. Three promotional videos are released.

'The Girl Is Mine' is the first single released in Israel since 1977. It is issued on coloured vinyl in various colours including yellow and orange.

December 11

'Thriller' (LP), released on December 6 in Britain, enters the Top 100 albums chart and peaks at number 1. It dominates the number 1 spot for eight weeks in four different periods and remains on the charts for a total of one hundred and sixty-eight weeks. On its release, some record shops give away 'The Girl Is Mine' picture disc with early copies of the LP.

December 25

'Thriller' (LP) by Michael Jackson hits the number one spot on both the Pop and Black albums charts and holds its position on the Pop charts for a massive thirty-seven weeks during a one hundred and twenty-two week residency.

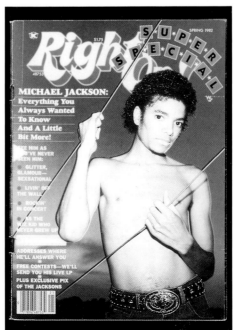

THRILLER

Michael Jackson
Epic QE 38112
EPC 85930

Side One
1. **Wanna Be Startin' Somethin'**
2. **Baby Be Mine**
3. **The Girl Is Mine**
4. **Thriller**

Side Two
1. **Beat It**
2. **Billie Jean**
3. **Human Nature**
4. **Pretty Young Thing (P.Y.T)**
5. **The Lady In My Life**

1983

1983

There is no disputing that musically, this year belongs to Michael Jackson. Nothing could have prepared anyone for what was about to happen to Michael's career in 1983, because no-one could have anticipated the amazing events that would catapult 'Thriller' to where no album had ever gone before – or has been since. At this stage, Michael Jackson's 'Thriller' has earned around 130 gold and platinum awards around the world.

'Dick Clark's Rock, Roll & Remember,' the Various Artists three-album set including 'I'll Be There' is released on the Heartland label.

Papa Joe's Boys: The Jacksons' Story by Leonard Pitts is published by Starbooks in Cresskill, New Jersey.

January

'E.T.: The Extra-Terrestrial' (LP) is released in Britain.

January 8
Michael and Diana Ross appear on the cover of *Black Echoes*.

Michael appears on the cover of *Disco 45* poster magazine.

January 13
'The Girl Is Mine' by Michael and Paul McCartney is certified Gold.

January 22
'Billie Jean'/'Can't Get Outta The Rain,' which

This Page: Michael celebrates his 'Thriller' LP going Double Platinum.

was originally titled 'Not My Lover' released on Epic this month, enters the new British Gallup Top 100 singles chart at number 47.

January 29
'Billie Jean' hits the Black singles chart peaking at number 1. It holds its position for nine weeks and remains on the charts for twenty-three weeks.

Michael becomes the first artist to reach the top of the Black singles chart in only three weeks since he and his brothers achieved the feat in 1970 with 'ABC,' 'The Love You Save' and 'I'll Be There.'

'Billie Jean'/'It's The Falling In Love,' released this month in Britain, enters the Top 100 singles chart.

January 31
'Thriller' (LP) is certified Gold and Platinum.

February

'Billie Jean' is released as a one-sided single by Epic.

Michael attends the British Record Industry Awards in London to accept an award on behalf of Barbra Streisand.

During his stay in Britain, Michael and Paul McCartney work on two new songs, 'Say, Say, Say' and 'The Man.'

A strike by London water workers, and the possibility of a contaminated water supply, cause Michael to arrange for Perrier water to be delivered to his hotel suite each day. The tabloids have a field day as they report that Michael drinks, cooks, shaves and even bathes in bottled water.

February 8
Michael and Paul McCartney appear on the cover of *Rolling Stone* magazine, 'Michael Jackson and Paul McCartney Team Up For TV.'

February 12
'E.T.: The Extra-Terrestrial' (LP) enters the Top 100 albums chart in Britain peaking at number 82 and remains on the charts for two weeks.

February 17
Michael appears on the cover of *Rolling Stone* magazine, 'Michael Jackson: Life As A Man,' who they dub as 'The Prince Of Pop' in an interview by Gerri Hirshey.

February 25
At a CBS Records press conference Jane Fonda presents Michael with a Double Platinum certification for 'Thriller' (LP).

February 26
'Beat It' released this month on Epic, enters the Pop singles chart.

Michael is on the cover of *Record Mirror*.

March

The Jacksons part company with co-managers Freddy DeMann and Ron Weisner after a five year association. Joe Jackson takes over as sole manager.

Costing over a quarter of a million dollars to make, Michael's video for 'Billie Jean,' which showcases his amazing dancing ability, is added to MTV's playlist, as is 'Beat It' a month later. This is seen as a major breakthrough for a Black artist, who had previously been largely ignored by the channel.

Michael is on the cover of *Rock & Soul* magazine.

March 5

'Thriller' (LP) hits number 1 on the Top 100 albums chart in Britain, which marks the first time in music history that an artist has simultaneously held the number one spot on the albums chart in both Britain and America.

'Billie Jean' reaches number 1 on the Top 100 singles chart in Britain holding its position for 1 week and remains on the charts for fifteen weeks.

'Billie Jean' hits number 1 on the Pop singles chart holding its position for 7 weeks and remains on the charts for twenty-four weeks.

March 7

Michael Jackson is the first artist to simultaneously hold the number one spot on Billboard's rock albums and rock singles charts, as well as the R&B albums and singles charts.

March 9

On Skid Row, east of Hollywood, Michael begins filming a video for 'Beat It' in which he unites two rival gangs through song and dance.

The video is directed by Bob Giraldi and choreographed by Michael Peters, who also appears in the video alongside 25 dancers and 50 actual Los Angeles gang members to give the video an authentic look. The cost of the video is estimated at $150,000.

March 20

Michael attends the opening night party of the stage show, *Dreamgirls*.

March 25

Rehearsals for *Motown's 25th Anniversary Show* begin.

April

The Jacksons meet with several promoters to plan their proposed 1984 tour.

This Page: Michael in the video for 'Billie Jean.'

Above: Michael rehearses for *Motown's 25th Anniversary Show* at the Pasadena Civic Auditorium.

Left: Michael with dancers on the 'Beat It' set. To the right of Michael is Jeffrey Daniels who will dance again with Michael in the 1987 promo for 'Bad.'

1983

'Beat It', the video, is added to MTV's playlist.

'25 No. 1 Hits From 25 Years' (LP), a compilation album featuring songs by The Jackson 5, is released on Motown. It is later re-issued on compact disc.

'We're Almost There'/ 'We've Got A Good Thing Going' is released in Britain.

'Billie Jean'/'Can't Get Outta The Rain' is issued on Epic's Instant Classics label.

April 2
'Beat It' enters the Black singles chart. It peaks at number 1 holding its position for one week and remains on the charts for nineteen weeks.

April 6
Michael attends a post-concert party for Liza Minnelli at the New Universal Amphitheater, Hollywood.

April 9
All the Jackson brothers,

including Jermaine, rehearse and tape their segment of the *Motown 25* TV special at the Pasadena Civic Auditorium.

'Beat It'/'Burn This Disco Out,' released in March in Britain, enters the Top 100 singles chart peaking at number 3 and remains on the charts for twelve weeks.

Melody Maker magazine in Britain reports that negotiations are underway for Michael, Lionel Richie and Diana Ross to perform together in concert at London's Royal Albert Hall. Promoter Ken Beecham says in a statement that contracts are very close to completion and that the concert will be broadcast around the world. However, this concert never takes place.

April 13
'25 No. 1 Hits From 25 Years' (LP), featuring three Jackson-related songs, is released on Motown.

April 14
'Billie Jean' is certified Gold.

April 16
Michael and Samir Kamoun don Charlie Chaplin outfits to pay tribute to Chaplin on his birthday.

Michael becomes the first artist of the Eighties to hold two chart positions in Billboard's Top Five with 'Beat It' and 'Billie Jean.'

April 25
Michael appears on the cover of *Jet* magazine.

April 30
'Beat It' hits number 1 on the Pop singles chart holding its position for 3 weeks and remains on the charts for twenty-five weeks. 'Beat It' recaptured the top spot just one week after 'Billie Jean' had been replaced by Dexy's Midnight Runners' 'Come On Eileen.' This equalled the feat accomplished by Hall & Oates some twelve months earlier, placing a

Page Opposite: Michael in a thoughtful mood after filming the 'Beat It' video.

This Page: Michael and dancers in action for the 'Beat It' video.

Michael and Samir Kamoun pay tribute to Charlie Chaplin.

A Michael sketch of his hero Chaplin.

This Page: The Jacksons reunite for an unforgettable performance at Motown's 25th Anniversary.

A ticket from the evening.

song either side of Olivia Newton-John's 'Physical.' The Beatles still hold the record of replacing their own hits - 'I Want To Hold Your Hand' was removed by 'She Loves You' which, in turn, was replaced by 'Can't Buy Me Love.'

May 9
'Beat It' is certified Gold.

May 13
'Motown Superstars Sing Motown Superstars' (LP), which includes the previously unreleased Jackson 5 song, 'Ask The Lonely,' is released.

May 16
Just as it seems that sales of 'Thriller' are about to slow down, over forty-seven million Americans watch Michael moonwalk across the stage during his first ever solo performance of 'Billie Jean' at the Pasadena Civic Auditorium when NBC broadcast the two-hour TV special, *Motown 25: Yesterday, Today, Forever.* It reunites many former Motown groups including The Jackson 5. Michael joins his brothers

in a medley of their early hits, they then depart, leaving the stage to Michael for four spellbinding minutes of inspired song and dance. His performance of 'Billie Jean' is entertainment at its most powerful and showcases his first ever public performance of the moonwalk.

The next day he is congratulated by Fred Astaire who says, "You're a hell of a mover. Man you really put them on their asses last night. You're an angry dancer. I'm the same way. I used to do the same thing with my cane... You're a hell of a mover!"

Michael's electrifying performance remains in the minds of fans and non-fans alike as sales of the album soar again the very next day. The enormity of Michael's talent and originality becomes apparent when he discloses that on the evening prior to the show, he had no idea what he was going to do. He relates how he went to the kitchen and played the song loudly.

Michael says, "I pretty much stood there and let the song tell me what to do. I kind of let the dance create itself. I really let it talk to me."

Michael also acknowledges that three kids taught him the basics of the now legendary 'moonwalk,' to which he added other steps before performing it on the *Motown 25* show.

May 25
'The Motown Story: The First 25 Years' (LP), which includes 'Dancing Machine' by The Jackson 5, is released on Motown.

May 28
'Wanna Be Startin' Somethin'' / 'Wanna Be Startin' Somethin' (2)' by Michael Jackson, released this month on Epic, enters the Pop singles chart peaking at number 5 and remains on the charts for fifteen weeks. There is no video to accompany this single.

June
Michael is on the cover of *Creem* magazine.

Members of The Jacksons World Fan Club receive a special 7" single featuring an on-the-spot improvised tune, called the 'Surprise Song,' and an interview with the brothers.

Management contracts with Freddy DeMann and Ron Weisner expire and are not renewed. The management contract between Joseph Jackson and Michael also expires. This is also not renewed and from this time forth Joe Jackson will no longer represent Michael Jackson.

June 4
'Wanna Be Startin' Somethin'' enters the Black singles chart peaking at number 5 and remains on the charts for seventeen weeks.

June 11
'Wanna Be Startin' Somethin''/'Rock With You,' released this month in Britain, enters the Top 100 singles chart peaking at number 8 and remains on the charts for nine weeks.

June 21
Reports claim that 'Thriller' is helping the music business out of a difficult recession with over 10 million worldwide sales since its late December release. 7.2 million have been sold in America alone and it is top of the charts in many other countries, including Australia, Britain, France, Germany, Holland and Canada.

Bitter exchanges between Joe Jackson and the co-management team of Freddy DeMann and Ron Weisner appear in *Billboard* magazine.

July
In the Annual Awards Special Edition of *Cashbox* magazine, Michael is voted number one in eight different categories: Top Male Artist, Top Pop Single ('Billie Jean'), Top Male Singles Artist, Top Black Album ('Thriller'), Top Pop Album ('Thriller'), Top Black Male Artist, Top Black Male Singles Artist and Top Black Single ('Billie Jean').

Rumours abound that Michael will write and produce the soundtrack for a proposed Steven Spielberg film, *Peter Pan*, in which he is interested in the lead role.

'18 Greatest Hits Of Michael Jackson And The Jackson 5' (LP) is released in Britain on Motown.

'Westwood One Concerts & Specials' (LP), the radio broadcast album featuring the songs from the 'Jacksons Live' album from 1981, is issued by Westwood One.

Black Radio Exclusive present Michael Jackson with their Artist Of The Year award.

July 9
Michael appears on the cover of the teenage magazine *Tops*.

July 16
'Happy (Love Theme From 'Lady Sings The Blues')'/'We're Almost There,' re-released on July 1 by Motown, enters the Top 100 singles chart in Britain peaking at number 52 and remains on the charts for four weeks. The song is

also released as a 7" poster and a 7" picture disc.

July 23
'Human Nature'/'Baby Be Mine' by Michael Jackson, released this month on Epic, enters the Pop singles chart peaking at number 7 and remains on the charts for fourteen weeks. There is no video to accompany the single, which is the fifth Top Ten hit from 'Thriller.'

'Club House - Do It Again Billie Jean,' a medley including Michael's song, enters the Top 100 singles chart in Britain peaking at number 11 and remains on the charts for six weeks.

July 30
'Human Nature' enters the Black singles chart peaking at number 27 and remains on the charts for twelve weeks.

August
Michael appears on the front cover of *Best* magazine in France.

'Beat It'/'Get On The Floor' is released on Epic's Instant Classics label.

August 14
'18 Greatest Hits' (LP), a TV-advertised Michael Jackson/Jackson 5 compilation, hits number 1 on the Top 100 albums chart in Britain holding its position for three weeks and remains on the charts for fifty-five weeks.

August 25
'Michael Jackson & The Jackson 5 - Great Songs And Performances That Inspired The Motown 25th

1983

1983

Anniversary Television Special' (LP) featuring ten tracks from The Jackson 5 era is released on Motown.

September

It is announced that The Jacksons will tour the US in 1984.

Michael is on the cover of *US* and *Black Beat* magazines.

At this point, 12 million copies of 'Thriller' have been sold as well as 12 million copies of the singles, 4 million in America alone. The LP is certified Platinum in fifteen countries: US (8x), Canada (4x), UK, Holland, Australia and New Zealand (3x), Japan, Germany, France, Sweden, Belgium, Switzerland, Spain, Greece and South Africa (1x), Gold in three countries: Denmark, Italy and Israel, and Silver in Norway. The LP has received some 37 awards and has reached number 1 in eight different countries. The singles 'Billie Jean' and 'Beat It' have reached number 1 in nine and seven countries respectively.

September 17

'Superstar,' a female reply to Michael's 'Billie Jean,' enters the Top 100 singles chart in Britain peaking at number 14 and remains on the charts for ten weeks.

September 25

Michael's 'Billie Jean' performance from the *Motown 25* TV special is shown on the Emmy Awards presentation broadcast, where it has received a nomination for Best Individual Performance On A Variety Or Music Programme.

This Page: Michael in costume for the 'Say Say Say' video.

Although Michael loses the Emmy to Leontyne Price for *Live From Lincoln Centre,* the TV special itself does win an Emmy.

Autumn

Promoter Don King advises Jay Coleman of Rockbill to seek a multi-million dollar sponsorship deal from a soft drinks company. After initial rejections by Coke and Pepsi, King pushes Coleman to try again, and in doing so secures a $5 million contract with Pepsi.

September 30

The Jacksons sign boxing tycoon, Don King, as promoter of their forthcoming tour.

October

Michael is on the cover of *People*, *Interview*, *Globe*, and *Rock & Soul* magazines.

Michael and Diana Ross are on the cover of *Ebony* magazine.

'Got To Be There'/'Ben' (LP), a double-album Michael Jackson cassette, is issued by Motown.

October 3

'Say, Say, Say,' the Jackson/McCartney duet, is released as a 7" and 12" single by Parlophone in Britain and carries 'Ode To A Koala Bear' on the B-side.

'Say, Say, Say'/'Ode To A Koala Bear' is released in the US by Columbia Records.

October 4

Shooting of the 'Say, Say, Say' promotional film begins. It casts Michael and Paul McCartney as

travelling conmen and has cameo appearances by Linda McCartney and LaToya Jackson. The video is filmed in Santa Ynez Valley, California, where Michael will one day own Neverland Valley Ranch.

October 8

'P.Y.T. (Pretty Young Thing)' by Michael Jackson backed with The Jacksons' 'Working Day And Night' released this month by Epic Records, enters the Pop singles chart peaking at number 10 and remains on the charts for sixteen weeks. There is no video to accompany the single.

'Ashaye - Michael Jackson Medley' enters the Top 100 singles chart in Britain peaking at number 45 and remains on the charts for four weeks.

October 12

A 12" version of 'Say, Say, Say'/'Ode To A Koala Bear' is released by Columbia Records.

'Say, Say, Say' enters the Top 100 singles chart in Britain peaking at number 2 and remains on the charts for fifteen weeks.

October 22

'Say, Say, Say' enters the Black singles chart peaking at number 2 and remains on the charts for twenty weeks.

October 29

'P.Y.T. (Pretty Young Thing)' enters the Black singles chart peaking at number 46 and remains on the charts for eight weeks.

October 31

'Pipes Of Peace' by Paul McCartney, which

includes a guest appearance by Michael duetting with Paul on 'Say, Say, Say' and 'The Man,' is released by Parlophone in Britain and Columbia in the US.

November

'Michael Jackson 9 Singles Pack' is released on red vinyl in Britain.

'Michael Jackson - 14 Original Greatest Hits With The Jackson 5' (LP) is released by K-Tel Records.

Michael and Diana Ross are on the cover of *Ebony* magazine.

'Thriller'/'Things I Do For You' is released in Britain.

The Jacksons become interested in a sponsorship deal with Quaker Oats for the Victory tour. However, the deal - which would have been worth 40% more to The Jacksons - cannot be negotiated because Don King has given exclusive sponsorship rights to Pepsi-Cola. This is the start of many disagreements in the Jackson camp which continue up to the opening night, and beyond.

November 6

Michael is approached to appear at the Royal Variety Performance but has to decline due to other commitments.

November 11

A $5 million endorsement contract is signed between Michael Jackson, The Jacksons and Pepsi-Cola, involving sponsorship of the Victory tour and two TV commercials.

November 19

'Thriller' enters the Top 100 singles chart in Britain peaking at number 10 and remains on the charts for twenty-five weeks.

November 30

The Jacksons and promoter Don King hold a press conference at New York's Tavern on the Green to announce plans for The Jacksons' forthcoming Victory tour which will reunite Michael with his brothers, including Jermaine. All the brothers attend the press conference and all wear sunglasses. Don King does most of the talking with Michael only introducing his parents and

sisters who are in the audience. Pepsi's sponsorship of the tour is also announced and Michael promises Roger Enrico of Pepsi that he will "make Coke wish they were Pepsi."

December

'Beat It' by Michael Jackson wins in five categories at the Billboard Music Video Awards held in Pasadena, California: Best Video, Best Male Performance, Best Use of Video to Enhance the Artist's Image, Best Use of Video to Enhance a Song and Best Choreography.

The 'Michael Jackson Suite' at the Hotel Royal Plaza in Florida's Disney World opens. The suite, which can be rented if not occupied by Michael himself, houses many of his awards, including Grammys and American Music Awards. Michael says: "I'm honoured to share what is mine with the world. I am here for the people, and what better place to display my personal memorabilia (which is so special to me) than Disney World, where children of

This Page: Michael finds some escapism at home in Encino, California via reading, his animals and the comforts of the Jacksons' own movie theater.

1983

all ages can share my joy and deep appreciation."

The Making Of Michael Jackson's Thriller, the video-cassette has accumulated record advance orders of over 100,000. It will eventually become the biggest-selling music video in history with sales in excess of one million copies worldwide, over 130,000 of

time still a practising Jehovah's Witness, the video carries the following disclaimer from Michael: "Due to my strong personal convictions, I wish to stress that this film in no way endorses a belief in the occult." The reaction to the video is instantaneous and unparalleled. In the three months following its release, aided by the

December 8
Michael Jackson leaves for New York to promote his new video, 'Thriller.'

December 10
'Say, Say, Say,' the Jackson/McCartney duet which entered the Pop singles chart at number 26 on October 15, hits number 1 holding its position for six weeks and remains on the charts for twenty-two weeks. This single becomes Michael's seventh Top Ten hit of the year, setting a record for the most Top Ten hits in a single year by one artist, a record previously held by Elvis Presley and The Beatles.

"Due to my strong personal convictions, I wish to stress that this film in no way endorses a belief in the occult."
Michael Jackson, December 1983

---

which are sold in the UK alone. The video showcases the 'Thriller' video itself along with a behind-the-scenes look at the special effects used in the film, dance rehearsals, and the impressive make-up artistry used to turn Michael Jackson into a werewolf.

Michael is on the cover of *Right On!*, *Rolling Stone* and *The National Leader*.

December 2
A year and a day following the release of the 'Thriller' album, MTV débuts the 'Thriller' video, a 14-minute short film of the LP's title track which outshines even the brilliance and excitement of 'Billie Jean' and 'Beat It.' At a cost of $800,000, 18 dancers, who have had years of professional training are recruited for the video but, according to choreographer Michael Peters, Michael is better than any of them. At this

unprecedented music awards it wins in the following two months, the 'Thriller' LP sells an additional 7.5 million copies in America alone.

December 3
A nine-pack collection of Michael's best-selling Epic singles, pressed onto red vinyl, enters the Top 100 albums chart in Britain peaking at number 66 and remains on the charts for three weeks.

Michael appears on the front cover of *Record Mirror* and *Rolling Stone* magazine in a drawing with Paul McCartney.

The Tube, a British music TV programme, shows a special screening of Michael Jackson's million dollar epic, 'Thriller' at one o'clock in the morning. The exclusive proves so popular that public demand forces *The Tube* to repeat it the following late evening.

December 12
'Say, Say, Say' is certified Gold.

December 14
The Making of Michael Jackson's Thriller is released, selling over 500,000 copies in its first month.

Billboard magazine's end of year chart shows four Michael Jackson songs ranking in the Top 20 Best Selling Singles of the Year: 'Billie Jean' (2), 'Say, Say, Say' (4), 'Beat It' (8) and 'The Girl Is Mine' (20). Michael achieved this feat with his brothers in 1970 when their first four releases ranked in *Billboard's* Top 20 year end charts.

Michael Jackson ends the year by holding the number one spots on both the Pop singles and Pop albums charts with 'Say, Say, Say' and 'Thriller.' In America, Michael is also the first act of the Eighties to have had three records hit number one during one calendar year.

This Page: Michael waves to fans after leaving a private screening of *The Making of Thriller.*

He has also had seven Top Ten hits in one calendar year, a record second only to The Beatles, who logged eleven Top Ten hits in 1964.

'Thriller' spends all 52 weeks of 1983 in the Top Ten of the Pop albums chart, 37 weeks of which are spent at number 1. It also becomes the first album in the history of recorded music to start a year at number 1 and end the same year at number 1.

In Britain, Michael has three entries on the year's British Best Sellers Charts with 'Thriller' at number 1 and The Jackson 5's '18 Greatest Hits' at number 10 on the albums chart, and 'Billie Jean' at number 17 on the singles chart.

Michael's dominance of the music industry this year around the world also becomes apparent with a long list of honours, including: 'Best Artist,' 'Best Male Vocalist' and 'Album Of The Year' in Japan, 'Album Of The Year' and 'Single Of The Year' in Australia, 'Artist Of The Year' in Italy, 'Record Of The Year' in Greece, 'Album Of The Year' in Holland, 'Most Important Foreign Album' in Spain and 'International Artist Of The Year' in Brazil. The Brazilian fans also named a dance after him, called 'Funk Jackson.'

Billboard magazine's end of year chart shows Michael Jackson ranking top in thirteen categories! They are:

Pop Artist Of The Year
Black Artist Of The Year
Pop Album: Thriller
Pop Album Artist
Pop Singles Artist
Pop Male Album Artist
Pop Male Singles Artist
Black Album Artist
Black Album: Thriller
Black Singles Artist
Dance/Disco Artist
Dance/Disco 12" LP Cut: Billie Jean (tie)
Dance/Disco 12" LP Cut: Beat It (tie)

Michael also receives honours for his 'Beat It' promo, in the Billboard Video Awards:

Best Overall Video Clip
Best Performance By A Male Artist
Best Choreography
Best Use Of Video To Enhance A Song
Best Use Of Video To Enhance An Artist's Image

This Page: Pretty Young Thing - Michael Jackson.

1984

Dear Michael,

I was pleased to learn that you were not seriously hurt in your recent accident. I know from experience that these things can happen on the set – no matter how much caution is exercised.

All over America, millions of people look up to you as an example. Your deep faith in God and adherence to traditional values are an inspiration to all of us, especially young people searching for something real to believe in.

You've gained quite a number of fans along the road since I Want You Back, and Nancy and I are among them.

Keep up the good work, Michael. We're very happy for you.

Sincerely,

**Ronald Reagan
February 1, 1984**

This Page: Michael is accompanied by Brooke Shields to the 1985 American Music Awards.

1984

There is a wealth of books and magazine specials published on Michael this year.

'Dear Michael'/'Dear Michael (Part 2),' a tribute to Michael Jackson by actress Kim Fields, is released on the Critique label.

Michael appears on the cover of France's *Paris Match* magazine.

Motown releases five more compilation albums containing one or more Jackson 5 tracks: 'Every Great Motown Song' (LP) and four different 'Top 10 With A Bullet' (LP) anthologies.

Michael wins four Canadian Black Music awards in the categories Top International Album ('Thriller'), Top International Single ('Billie Jean'), Top Male Vocalist, and Entertainer Of The Year.

'Somebody's Watching Me' by Rockwell, whose real name is Kennedy Gordy, son of Berry Gordy, featuring Michael Jackson is released on Motown.

Michael appears on the cover of *US* magazine.

'Spotlight Specials - Michael Jackson' (LP), a radio broadcast album containing an interview with Michael, is issued.

Michael devises the themes and settings for the Victory tour and he and his brothers begin visiting companies capable of producing the stage from his designs.

'Letter To Michael' by Leslie is released on Stonehenge Records.

January 7

Michael is on the cover of Britain's *Black Echoes*.

'Let's Beat It' (LP), a charity album is released, with the monies raised being donated to The Music And Entertainments Industry's own charity, 'The T. J. Martell Foundation For Leukaemia And Cancer Research.'

January 10

Michael Jackson visits the Burn Centre at Brotman Memorial Hospital in Los Angeles.

January 11

At the first annual Black Gold Awards, produced by Dick Clark, Michael Jackson wins in four categories: Top Male Vocalist, Best Video Performance ('Beat It'), Best Single Record Of The Year ('Billie Jean') and Best Album Of The Year ('Thriller').

January 16

Michael wins an unprecedented eight awards at the 11th American Music Awards, broadcast live from the Shrine Auditorium in Los Angeles, which he attends in the company of Brooke Shields. At the age of only 25, Michael is the youngest recipient of the special Award of Merit. Michael also wins: Favourite Pop Album, Favourite Soul Album ('Thriller'), Favourite Pop Single ('Billie Jean'), Favourite Pop Video, Favourite Soul Video ('Beat It'), Favourite Pop/Rock Male Artist, and Favourite Soul Male Vocalist.

The show is viewed by over sixty million people and in the week following Michael's swoop in capturing 39% of the evening's awards, 'Thriller' sells a further one million copies in America.

January 22

'Thriller' (LP) hits number 1 on the Top 100 albums chart in Britain.

January 24

Shooting of the first Pepsi commercial begins with Alfonso Ribeiro, the 12 year old star of the Broadway show *The Tap Dance Kid*, starring alongside Michael who, together with Pepsi, reworks the lyrics of 'Billie Jean.'

January 26

'Somebody's Watching Me' (LP) by Rockwell featuring Michael on the title track is released on Motown.

January 27

The New York publishing house, Doubleday & Co. announces it will publish Michael Jackson's autobiography to be edited by Jacqueline Onassis.

During the filming of a second Pepsi commercial, Michael suffers second and third degree scalp burns and is rushed to Cedar Sinai Medical Center, where his arrival causes a media frenzy. He is later moved to Brotman Memorial Hospital for treatment - the Burns Centre to which he had paid a courtesy call only two weeks earlier.

January 28

Michael is released from hospital but before leaving, visits other burn patients, some of whom he had visited earlier in the month.

Following Michael's injury, 700,000 extra copies of 'Thriller' are sold in America.

'The Man,' a duet featuring Michael Jackson, from Paul McCartney's 'Pipes Of Peace' LP, is scheduled to be released by Parlophone Records, but is cancelled.

February

Michael receives a Crystal Globe Award for record sales exceeding five million outside the US. Michael's companion at the ceremony is Brooke Shields.

'Eat It'/'That Boy Could Dance' by 'Weird Al' Yankovic with parody lyrics based on Michael's 'Beat It' is released. Michael gives permission for the hilarious reworking of his lyrics, and enjoys it.

Construction of the Victory tour stage begins.

'Thriller'/'Can't Get Outta The Rain' is released on Epic.

'The Happy Chipmunks Sing Michael Jackson's Greatest Hits' (LP) is released by Audiofidelity Enterprises.

'P.Y.T. (Pretty Young Thing)'/'Working Day And Night,' 'The Girl Is Mine'/'Can't Get Outta The Rain' and 'Wanna Be Startin' Somethin''/'Wanna Be Startin' Somethin' (2)' are released on Epic's Instant Classics label.

February 1
Michael receives an official letter from President

Reagan wishing him a speedy recovery from his burn injury.

February 4
'Somebody's Watching Me' by Rockwell enters the Top 100 singles chart in Britain peaking at number 6 and remains on the charts for eleven weeks.

February 5
'One Day In Your Life' (LP) by Michael Jackson is re-issued on Motown.

Michael makes his first public appearance since his burn injury on January 27 when he visits the Los Angeles zoo in the company of Emmanuel Lewis, star of the TV series, *Webster*.

February 6
Michael and Emmanuel Lewis are on the cover of *Jet* magazine.

February 7
Michael, along with 15,000 invited guests, attends the New York Metropolitan Museum of Natural History to receive awards from CBS and *The Guinness Book Of World Records*. To date, 'Thriller' has sold over 25 million copies worldwide - more than any other album in recording history. Michael is presented with the first edition of the 1984 paperback version of *The Guinness Book Of World Records*, which he receives from Norris McWhirter.

For the first time ever, Bantam Books halt the presses between January 20 and 23 so that two new entries can be added to the book at the last minute announcing 'Thriller' as the

"I've always wanted to do great things and achieve many things, but for the first time in my entire career, I feel like I have accomplished something because I'm in The Guinness Book Of Records!"
**Michael Jackson
February 7,1984**

largest-selling album of all time and the album with the most Top Ten singles (six).

Despite below-freezing temperatures more than 1,000 fans wait patiently for a mere glimpse of Michael. The invitation itself was unique, printed on a single white cloth glove. Amongst the celebrities attending are Cyndi Lauper, Mary Tyler Moore, Carly Simon, Calvin Klein, Andy Warhol, Sean Lennon, Robin Williams and Gloria Gaynor.

Allen Davis, President of CBS Records International says: "Tonight Michael...

This Page: Michael in a buoyant mood after receiving awards from CBS and *The Guinness Book Of World Records*.

This Page: Michael celebrates unprecedented Grammy success with ace producer, Quincy Jones.

your milestones for the album 'Thriller' are a total of 67 Gold and 58 Platinum awards in 28 countries on six continents. And the singles, with 9 million sales have earned fifteen more awards, bringing the total to 140 Gold and Platinum awards.

Michael's date for the night is again Brooke Shields.

February 11
'Thriller' by Michael Jackson débuts at number 20 on the Pop singles chart peaking at number 4 and remains on the chart for fourteen weeks.

February 12
Michael appears on the cover of *The News Of The World's* Colour Supplement in Britain.

February 18
'Thriller' enters the Top Ten in its second week on the charts - the first single to achieve this feat since John Lennon's 'Imagine' hit the Top Ten in its second

week in 1971. It is also the highest débuting single (20) since Lennon's 'Imagine.' 'Thriller' is also the fifth Top Five single and seventh Top Ten single from the album of the same name making Michael the first artist in music history to achieve seven Top Ten singles from one album. The previous record was four Top Ten singles. 'Thriller' peaks on the Pop singles chart at number 3.

'Thriller' enters the Black singles chart peaking at number 3 and remains on the charts for fourteen weeks.

February 23
'Compact Command Performances - 18 Greatest Hits' by Michael Jackson and The Jackson 5 is released on CD by Motown.

February 26
Michael attends the première of Pepsi's Jacksons commercials at a black-tie event for 1,000 bottlers at

New York City's Lincoln Center.

February 27
The Jacksons' Pepsi commercials are previewed on MTV as part of a 28-minute Bob Giraldi documentary. MTV broadcast the two 60-second commercials free of charge.

Michael and Brooke Shields are on the cover of *Jet* magazine.

February 28
In the company of Brooke Shields and Emmanuel Lewis, Michael attends the 26th annual Grammy Award ceremonies broadcast from the Shrine Auditorium in Los Angeles.

Michael wins eight Grammys in ten categories: Album Of The Year ('Thriller'), Best Pop Male Vocal ('Thriller' LP), Record Of The Year ('Beat It'), Best Rock Male Vocal ('Beat It'), Best R&B Male Vocal ('Billie Jean'), Best New Song Of The Year ('Billie Jean'), Producer Of The Year (with Quincy Jones) and Best Children's Recording ('E.T.: The Extra Terrestrial' with narration by Michael Jackson).

The Jacksons' Pepsi commercials are aired during the telecast and are amongst the most successful and most popular ads ever, and the first and only set of advertisements ever to be included in the weekly *TV Guide* listings.

Michael appears on many covers this month including *Creem, Blues & Soul, People, US, Sun, The Star, National Enquirer, Number One* and *The Globe*.

Michael receives twenty-four nominations in eight categories for the 2nd annual American Video Awards. He wins in four of the eight categories.

Michael wins The People's Choice Award for Best All-round Male Entertainer and 'Thriller' is Favourite Video. Michael does not attend the presentation.

March

Gerald Jaccover representing Fred Sandford issues a Writ against CBS in a copyright infringement case over, 'The Girl Is Mine.' He claims it has been plagiarised from his song, 'Please Love Me Now,' which he submitted to CBS in 1981. James Klenk representing CBS says that the suit is without foundation, and the case is put back to December 1984.

March 14

News reports appear about a student protest at Bound Brook High School in New Jersey; the protesters have been banned from wearing their white Michael Jackson gloves in school.

March 15

Sales continue to rise for the 'Thriller' album, already the world's biggest-selling album, which has now passed the 30 million mark. The 'Victory' album by The Jacksons is shelved until sales of 'Thriller' begin to fall off.

Michael is *Rolling Stone* magazine's cover story, with a letter from Jackson to Don King in which King was officially instructed: 'Not to communicate with anyone on Michael Jackson's behalf without

prior permission.'
'That all monies paid to Michael Jackson for his participation in the tour would be collected by Michael Jackson's personal representatives, not by Don King.'
'That King did not have permission to approach any promoters, sponsors, or any other persons on Michael's behalf.'
'That King was not to hire any personnel, any local promoters, book any halls, or for that matter, do ANY-THING without Michael Jackson's prior personal approval.'

March 17

'Eat It' by 'Weird Al' Yankovic enters the Pop singles chart peaking at number 12 and remains on the charts for seven weeks.

March 19

Michael is on the cover of *Time* magazine, with a nine page article on the star.

March 20

Michael Jackson hires Frank Dileo, Vice President of Promotions at Epic Records, as his manager. Dileo, was instrumental in the success of 'Thriller.'

March 23

I Love Quincy, broadcast by Channel Four TV in Britain, includes segments of Michael rehearsing for the 'Thriller' video and shows footage of a rare interview with Michael.

Michael appears on the cover of *Jet* magazine.

March 29

The Jackson family selects Frank Russo to run the Victory tour in association with Danny O'Donovan.

March 30

The Making of Michael Jackson's Thriller is released in Britain. The video sells 100,000 copies in only three days and becomes the biggest-selling video ever for several years to come.

March 31

'P.Y.T. (Pretty Young Thing)'/'Heartbreak Hotel,' released in February in Britain, enters the Top 100 singles chart peaking at number 11 and remains on the charts for eight weeks.

April

Michael's 'Thriller' has spent a record-breaking 37 weeks at number one, surpassing the previous record of 31 weeks held by Harry Belafonte's 'Calypso' and Fleetwood Mac's 'Rumours' on the Pop contemporary chart. There are only two albums that have outperformed 'Thriller' - both soundtrack collections: 'West Side Story' (54 weeks) and 'The Broadway Cast Album For South Pacific' (69 weeks). 'Thriller' has also spent 71 consecutive weeks in Billboard's Top Five, surpassed only by one other album, 'The Sound Of Music.'

Michael appears on the cover of *Right On!* magazine - 'Michael's Clean Sweep.'

Leaders of Michael's church, the Jehovah's Witnesses, censor him for wearing make-up, an image they do not like projected by their followers.

Rumours appear in *Record Mirror* regarding a new up-

1984

1984

tempo, self-penned Michael Jackson composition called, 'Buffalo Bill.'

'Michael Jackson And The Jackson 5 - 18 Greatest Hits' (LP) is released by Motown.

Pepsi publicises the times and dates for the airing of The Jacksons' commercials in 317 US newspapers.

'Jermaine Jackson' (LP), Jermaine's first album for Arista, contains a duet with Michael on 'Tell Me I'm Not Dreaming,' and features The Jacksons on 'Escape From The Planet Of The Ape Men.' Epic do not give permission to Arista Records to release the duet as a single, forcing frustrated Michael fans to buy the album. 'Jermaine Jackson' is certified Gold within three weeks.

Michael appears on many covers this month, including *USA Today*, *Sun*, *Cable Vision*, *Rock & Folk*, *Pop Giants*, *The Globe* (2x), the *National Enquirer* (3x) and the *Star* (4x).

Liza Minnelli accompanies Michael to Swifty Lazar's Oscar night party. After a short stay they go on to visit Liza's father, director Vincente Minnelli.

April 9
David Smithee, a 14-year-old sufferer from cystic fibrosis, is invited to visit Michael at the Encino family home. David's last wish is to meet Michael. David dies seven weeks later.

April 12
Beverly Paige, from the firm handling publicity for the concerts, announces the

tour will include only twelve cities, instead of the original thirty.

It is reported that the Hip-Hop junior shops of all John Wanamaker stores will start selling Michael Jackson inspired jackets, pants, skirts and tops from May onwards. Some outfits will come with a glitter glove or a pair of socks.

April 14
Michael Jackson endows a nineteen-bed unit at the Mount Sinai New York Medical Center. The centre is a division of the T. J. Martell Foundation for Leukaemia and Cancer Research.

Mid-April
Promoter Frank Russo is removed as tour manager after only three weeks.

April 17
Michael undergoes reconstructive scalp surgery at Brotman Memorial Hospital. Plastic surgeon, Dr. Steven Hoefflin, performs revolutionary laser surgery on Michael to repair damage he suffered to his scalp during the filming of a Pepsi commercial.
After the surgery, Hoefflin says: "Michael is doing fine. We were able to cover the area using his own hair, he did not need any implants or transplants. He really needs to rest, and this will provide him with that opportunity. He jumps back very rapidly, but we would like him to stay here several days.
This has been quite traumatic, physically and emotionally for him. The operation was very important to him, to have a full head of hair without the neces-

sity of wigs or other hair coverings. He wanted to get it over with." Whilst at the hospital, Michael receives over 5,000 telephone calls from his fans.

Richard Hack, a contributor to the news magazine *Breakaway*, reports that Michael is working on a new project called 'Tingle.' It is said to involve an album, a film, and three videocassettes, one of which has Michael on fire while wearing a purple dress! The next day Hack admits his report was false due to a spoof article which had been printed in *On Cable* magazine.

April 21
In Britain, *Melody Maker* magazine puts Michael's name on its list of 'Ten Fruitcakes,' citing accounts that Michael bathes in Perrier water and talks to inflatable geese as the basis for this rather dubious distinction.

April 26
Michael Jackson wins the NARM Gift of Music Award for the Best Selling Album ('Thriller') and Best Selling Single ('Billie Jean'). It is the first time in the history of the awards that this has happened.

April 29
Michael appears on the cover of *The News Of The World's* colour supplement, 'The World's Hottest Property.'

Late April
Musicians for the Victory tour are hired and rehearsals begin.

Rolling Stone magazine's Readers' Poll nominate

This Page: The Jacksons in the first of their Pepsi Commercials.

Page Opposite: Michael with President Reagan at the White House.

Michael with Shirley Maclaine backstage at her Broadway show.

Michael as their Number 1 Artist, Number 1 Soul Artist, Number 1 Producer (with Quincy Jones), and choose 'Beat It' as their Number 1 Video. The Critics' Poll votes him: Number 1 Artist, Number 1 Male Vocalist, Number 1 Soul Artist and choose 'Billie Jean' as their Number 1 Video.

May

Michael and two companies licensed by him, Entertainers Merchandise Management Corp. and MJJ Productions, file a civil suit in New York City over unauthorised Jackson memorabilia. An estimated $50 million worth of bogus Michael Jackson memorabilia is in the marketplace. Stephen Huff, Michael's New York lawyer says Michael, "is concerned that the public doesn't get cheap, inferior goods."

During a stay at Helmsley Palace Hotel in New York City, Michael expresses his liking for the uniform worn by elevator operator, Hector Carmona, who

gives him one of his spares. Michael later wears the jacket to the White House.

Michael is on many covers this month, including *Ebony* magazine, which names him one of the 100 Most Influential Black Americans.

Although no contract was signed, Frank Russo files a $20 million lawsuit against the Jacksons for going back on their verbal agreement to make him manager of the Victory tour.

Two 'Thriller' 3-D viewers are released in Britain, one of which is musical.

May 5
Katherine Jackson receives a £75,000 Rolls Royce covered in ribbons and flowers from her sons for her 56th birthday. Although the gift is Jermaine's idea, news reports attribute only Michael with giving his mother the elaborate gift.

May 11
Michael attends a Kool and The Gang concert at Radio City Music Hall in New

York City accompanied by Tatum O'Neal. Michael is heavily disguised in a beard and an Afro wig.

Agents for Michael begin confiscating unauthorised Jackson memorabilia.

May 12
Michael visits Shirley Maclaine backstage after her performance in *Shirley Maclaine on Broadway*.

May 14
President Reagan presents a Special Achievement Award to Michael in a garden ceremony at the White House in recognition of his contribution to the nation's advertising campaign aimed at discouraging young people from drinking and driving. Michael's song 'Beat It' was used by the Transportation Department in the campaign.

The inscription on the plaque reads: "To Michael Jackson with appreciation for the outstanding example you have set for the youth of America and the world. Your historic

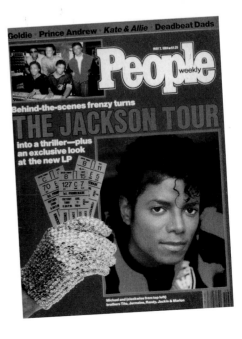

1984

record-breaking achievements and your pre-eminence in popular music are a tribute to your creativity, dedication, and great ability. The generous contribution of your time and talent to the National Campaign Against Teenage Drunk Driving will help millions of young Americans learn that drinking and driving can kill a friendship."

Mid-May

Michael purchases a $10,000 professional make-up kit from Rick Baker, who worked with him on the 'Thriller' video.

May 15

Thriller, the stage show production featuring Michael Jackson imitators, opens in Philadelphia.

Despite President Reagan's request that the Victory tour stops in Washington DC, The Jacksons' personal manager announces that city is not on the list of twelve, which will be released gradually to help build excitement.

May 17

'Farewell My Summer Love 1984' (LP), containing nine unreleased Jackson tracks recorded in the early Seventies, is distributed to radio stations. The track is part of a 40-song collection thought lost after Motown moved from Detroit to Los Angeles. The album meets with much negative criticism and the '1984' is dropped from the title of later pressings.

The Fashion Foundation Of America's 43rd annual survey of custom tailors and designers name Michael Jackson, President Reagan

and The Archbishop of New York as America's best-dressed men.

May 22

Awake, a Jehovah's Witnesses publication, quotes Michael as saying that he will never do a video like 'Thriller' again because of feelings that it has offended many people. It also states that he has blocked further distribution of the film.

It is announced that only Jacksons' merchandise will be available at Victory concerts, and not Michael Jackson merchandise.

May 23

Willie Nelson announces on NBC's *Today* show that he may record a duet with Michael.

May 24

'Michael Jackson & The Jackson 5 - 14 Greatest Hits' (LP) and 'Michael Jackson & The Jackson 5 - 16 Greatest Hits' (LP) are released on Motown.

Motown re-issues seven Jackson-related albums: 'Skywriter' (LP), 'Dancing Machine' (LP), 'Get It Together' (LP), 'Moving Violation' (LP), 'Joyful Jukebox Music' (LP), 'Forever Michael' (LP) and 'Music & Me' (LP).

May 26

'Farewell My Summer Love'/'Call On Me' by Michael Jackson, released this month by Motown Records, enters the Pop singles chart peaking at number 38 and remains on the charts for twelve weeks. This is only the third commercially released Jacksons' single from Motown issued with a picture sleeve.

May 27

The Victory tour stage, which took four months to construct, is completed.

June

Michael's 'Thriller' (LP) has sold over 30 million copies worldwide, as follows: America (20m), Canada (2.2m), Britain (2m), France (1.8m), Germany (0.8m) and Japan (0.7m). *The Making Of Michael Jackson's Thriller* video is also confirmed as the biggest-selling video on both sides of the Atlantic. Current sales in Britain stand at 130,000; expected sales of a music video are around 4,000.

Michael is on the cover of *People*, *National Enquirer*, *Modern Screen*, *US*, *Black Beat* and *Right On!*

Two books, *Michael Jackson*, by Stewart Regan and *Papa Joe's Boys'* by Leonard Pitt are published in Britain.

Michael Jackson meets with other supporters of Camp Good Times in Malibu, a charity dedicated to young cancer patients by MacDonald's. Others present are Dustin Hoffman, David Soul, Neil Diamond and Richard Chamberlain.

A Michael Jackson telephone hotline is set up in San Francisco and soon spreads to six other cities.

June 2

'Farewell My Summer Love' (LP) enters the Pop and Black albums charts peaking at numbers 46 and 31 respectively and remains on both charts for fifteen weeks.

'Farewell My Summer Love'/'Call On Me' by

Michael Jackson, released in May in Britain, enters the Top 100 singles chart peaking at number 7 and remains on the charts for twelve weeks.

June 5
The Victory tour contract is signed by boxing promoter Don King, football promoter, Chuck Sullivan and Joe and Katherine Jackson. Sullivan pays $38.5 million to become tour promoter, of which $12.5 million is paid up front.

June 9
'Farewell My Summer Love' enters the Black singles chart peaking at number 37 and remains on the charts for ten weeks.

Michael attends briefly the unveiling of a wax likeness of himself at The Guinness Museum of World Records in San Francisco. A crowd of about 2,000 fans gathers to watch.

'Farewell My Summer Love' (LP) enters the Top 100 albums chart in Britain peaking at number 9 and remains on the charts for fourteen weeks.

June 13
Contracts are signed for Victory tour dates in Birmingham, Kansas City, Dallas and Jacksonville. 'State Of Shock,' the Jackson/Jagger duet and the first single from The Jacksons' 'Victory' album, is aired on radio stations.

KIQQ FM go Jackson crazy by playing 'State Of Shock' around the clock. DJs act as though nothing unusual is happening and inform listeners they had just heard Bruce Springsteen,

Cyndi Lauper and others, when they had been listening to The Jacksons for nearly twenty-four hours!

June 15
Chuck Sullivan announces the first three venues for the Victory tour in Kansas City, Irving and Jacksonville, with the opening concerts scheduled for July 6-8 at Arrowhead Stadium in Kansas City, Missouri.

June 19
Fans besiege Post Offices in Kansas City to buy money orders for the purchase of Victory tour tickets. Likewise, early editions of the *Kansas City Times* are snapped up so they can clip the coupon ads and purchase their tickets to the Victory tour concert. An extra 20,000 copies of the paper are printed to satisfy the expected demand.

Bob Chapman of KVLL, a Dallas radio station, accuses The Jacksons' promoters of 'overriding arrogance' regarding their attitude towards the distribution of tickets.

Reverend Al Sharpton of The National Youth Movement points to a media blitz against The Jacksons, and states that they (The Jacksons) are being punished for "not staying in the plantation of the music business."

Michael is denounced by the Kremlin as a singer who has sold his Black soul for White profit. They see him as a tool of the Reagan administration, helping to keep the US public's mind off the country's real problems.

June 20
Governor Edwin Edwards of Louisiana says that he will not repeal the amusement tax for The Jacksons' appearance at the New Orleans Superdome, as they have requested.

June 21
The manager of Washington DC's RFK Stadium announces that The Jacksons will give concerts on July 28-30 but this is not confirmed by the tour's publicists.

June 22
It is confirmed that the Jacksons will bank all the money orders sent in for concert tickets and collect the interest.

It is announced that due to knee surgery, Jackie will not be performing with his brothers on the tour.

June 23
'Michael Jackson & The Jackson 5 - 14 Greatest Hits' (LP) enters the Pop albums chart peaking at number 168 and remains on the charts for seven weeks.

'Every Great Motown Song' (LP), a Various Artists compilation including 'Never Can Say Goodbye' and 'Ben' is released.

'The Great Love Songs Of Michael Jackson' (LP) and 'The Great Love Songs Of The Jackson 5' (LP) is released on Motown.

June 26
Michael and his brothers arrive in Birmingham for secret pre-tour rehearsals at the Birmingham-Jefferson Civic Center.

1984

This Page: The Jacksons with promoter Don King, announce Victory tour dates. Michael is accompanied by Emmanuel Lewis.

1984

Officials for Arrowhead Stadium in Kansas City, Missouri say they have already received more ticket requests than there are tickets available for the three Jacksons concerts.

June 27
Elaborate ticket-purchasing guidelines for the Victory tour are announced in New York City.

June 28
Michael attends a screening of Prince's *Purple Rain* at the Warner Bros. lot in Burbank, California.

June 29
During Victory tour rehearsals in Atlanta, Michael and his brothers greet a crowd of several thousand fans who have gathered outside their hotel.

June 30
'State Of Shock,' the Jackson/Jagger duet released this month, enters both the Pop and Black singles charts peaking at numbers 3 and 4 respectively and remains on the charts for fifteen and fourteen weeks respectively.

July
Michael appears on the cover of many magazines this month, including: *Teen Bag*, *Bop*, *People*, *Teen Set*, *Movie Mirror*, *Tiger Beat*, *16*, *Right On!*, *Musician*, *Black Beat*, *Newsweek*, *Time*, and *Billboard*.

The Guinness World Records Museum in Gatlingburg, Tennessee unveils its wax statue of Michael (a second of which

is housed in the Guinness museum in San Francisco).

'Centipede (Part 1)'/ 'Centipede (Part 2)' by Rebbie Jackson is released on Columbia Records. The song is written and produced by Michael who also sings backing vocals. The single peaks at number 24 on the Pop singles chart.

'Jane Fonda's Workout Record – New And Improved' (LP) including 'Wanna Be Startin' Somethin'' by Michael Jackson is issued by Columbia Records.

'Victory' (LP) is released in the US and Britain and, for the first time in music history, ships double Platinum.

To date, The Jacksons have sold over 100 million records, a figure surpassed only by The Beatles. The LP is released as a record album, a cassette, a CD and a special picture disc with the science fiction cover portrait of The Jacksons pressed into clear plastic for serious collectors.

The sleeve of the LP is designed by Michael Whelan, who created the book cover of *Foundations Edge*, by Isaac Asimov. All the Jacksons, with the exception of Michael, pose for the cover. Whelan has to work from photos of Michael, which are changed four times during the process.

'Show You The Way To Go'/'Blame It On The Boogie' is released in Britain.
'Disconet Program Service,

Volume 6, Program 3' (LP) including an extended edit version of 'Can You Feel It' is released.

In Sevran, France, a 17 year old commits suicide after his parents refuse to pay for plastic surgery to make him look like Michael Jackson. Identified only as Eugene, his mother says: "he had become obsessed."

While on the road with the Victory tour, Michael and Tito accept the NAACP's Dr. H. Claude Hudson Medal of Freedom Award and the 1984 Olympic Medal of Friendship Award on behalf of the entire Jackson family.

July 1
According to a local limousine service owner, Michael Jackson dons a disguise and hands out Jehovah's Witness literature door to door in Birmingham, Alabama.

July 4
The NAACP announces that Michael Jackson and his brothers have been named honorary co-chairmen of the civil rights organisation's National Voter Registration Drive. Registration booths will be set up outside Arrowhead Stadium in Kansas City, venue of the tour's opening concert.

July 5
After receiving a letter from an eleven-year-old fan, Ladonna Jones, in which she accuses the Jacksons and the promoters of being 'selfish and just out for money,' Michael Jackson holds a major press conference to announce

VICTORY

The Jacksons
Epic QE-38946
EPC 86303

Side One
1. **Torture**
2. **Wait**
3. **One More Chance**
4. **Be Not Always**

Side Two
1. **State Of Shock**
2. **We Can Change The World**
3. **The Hurt**
4. **Body**

This Page: All the Jackson brothers together again for the 'Victory' LP.

changes in the tour's organisation and also to announce that the whole of his share of the proceeds from the Victory tour will be donated to charity. Michael's tour profits will be split between three charities: The United Negro College Fund, Camp Good Times, and the T. J. Martell Foundation for Leukaemia and Cancer Research.

Ladonna Jones, later receives VIP treatment to a concert in Dallas.

July 6-8

The Victory tour's opening concerts are performed at Arrowhead Stadium, Kansas City, Missouri. The Jacksons draw 135,000 fans over the three sell-out shows, breaking the previous record of nearly 58,000 established in 1977. The Victory tour, with 55 concerts, reportedly grosses $90 million and sets a new record for the largest grossing tour.

July 6

At 9.45 p.m. it is dark enough for the opening show in Kansas to begin. This sees Jermaine together with his brothers on stage for the first time in over eight years. This show does not include Michael's hit, 'Thriller' and although it is suggested that it is omitted due to pressures from the Jehovah's Witnesses who complain that it glorifies Satanic worship, the occult and evil in general, aides insist that it is because Michael is not yet satisfied with the live set.

At a press conference following the opening night's concert, Chuck Sullivan announces that local Black

promoters will be affiliated with local White stadium managers in each future venue, to assure total racial harmony and promotional saturation in each city's local community.

A Mount Vernon man makes bootleg videos of the opening concert at Arrowhead Stadium by tapping into the transmitted closed-circuit multi-camera signal from the video feed to the giant screen above the stage. He is later arrested for selling the bootlegs in the State of New York.

July 7

'State Of Shock'/'Your Ways,' released in June in Britain, enters the Top 100 singles chart peaking at number 14 and remains on the charts for ten weeks. The song, written by Michael and Randy Hamen, was originally to be sung with Freddie Mercury. A special limited edition of 2,000 is also issued.

July 8

Rev. Jesse Jackson, in Kansas City to address the African Methodist Episcopal Church Convention, visits The Jacksons at their hotel and attends the concert at the Arrowhead Stadium.

July 10

KLSI radio station announces that during their less than two hours on stage, The Jacksons made $1 million per hour, and a total of $6 million during their three-day stay in Kansas. It is also estimated that The Jacksons' concerts generated approx-

"We're beginning our tour tomorrow and I wanted to talk to you about something of great concern to me. We've worked a long time to make this show the best it can be. But we know a lot of kids are having trouble getting tickets. The other day I got a letter from a girl in Texas named Ladonna Jones. She'd been saving her money from odd jobs to buy a ticket, but with the current tour system, she'd have to buy four tickets and she couldn't afford that. So, I've asked our promoter to work out a new way of distributing tickets, a way that no longer requires a $120.00 money order. There has also been a lot of talk about the promoter holding money for tickets that didn't sell. I've asked our promoter to end the mail order ticket system as soon as possible so that no one will pay money unless they get a ticket. Finally, and most importantly, there's something else I am going to announce today. I want you to know that when I first agreed to tour, I decided to donate all the money I make from our performances to charity."

Michael Jackson, July 5, 1984

imately $26 million for the city and local businesses.

July 13-15
The Jacksons perform concerts at Texas Stadium in Dallas, Texas. They donate 1,200 tickets to underprivileged children, while their sponsors, Pepsi-Cola, donate an additional 1,300 tickets, valued at $39,000. Security for these shows is three times that usually required for a Dallas Cowboys game, with 340 security officers on duty that night. At this 'Friday, the thirteenth' concert the stadium is full of celebrities, including Dave Lee Roth, Emmanuel Lewis and Prince.

July 14
Eddie Van Halen, in Dallas for his own concert, joins Michael on stage for a 'Beat It' guest appearance playing electric guitar.

July 16
Michael Jackson is on the cover of *Newsweek*.

July 20
Publicity of The Michael Jackson doll begins. There are six different outfits available for the miniature figure. Retailing at $13.00, the doll is officially approved by Michael.

July 21-23
The Jacksons perform in concert to three sell-out audiences of over 135,000 at the Gator Bowl in Jacksonville, Florida. This is a record, surpassing attendance records for previous rock events set by The Rolling Stones in 1975 (75,000), The Beatles in 1964 (20,000) and The Who in 1976 (15,000).

After the first concert, Michael meets eight children suffering from incurable diseases backstage. Fourteen year old Malanda Cooper, who has only a short time to live, wrote to Jake Godbold, Mayor of Jacksonville, informing him of her wish to meet her idol. Godbold wrote to Michael, who despite a very busy schedule, makes the time to see this little girl. 700 disadvantaged or handicapped children are also treated to the thrill of their lives, as special guests of Michael.

July 21

Billboard magazine's special issue devoted to Michael with a twenty-eight page pullout and photos from his personal collection, is due to hit the streets. Release is delayed, however.

Michael appears on the cover of *Paris Match* and *Record Mirror* with articles on the Victory tour.

'Victory' (LP) enters the Top 100 albums chart in Britain peaking at number 3 and remains on the charts for thirteen weeks. The album is later released as a limited edition picture disc with a chance to see Michael Jackson in concert.

'Victory' (LP) enters the Pop and Black albums charts peaking at numbers 4 and 3 respectively and remains on the charts for thirty and twenty-eight weeks respectively.

'Ease On Down The Road' is re-issued in Britain and re-enters the Top 100 singles chart peaking at number 83 and remains on the charts for three weeks.

July 22

Ticket sales set an all-time record, with 165,000 tickets selling in less than nine hours, when it is announced that The Jacksons will appear in New York at Giants Stadium on July 29-31, and at Madison Square Garden on August 4-5.

July 29-31

The Jacksons perform in concert at Giants Stadium in East Rutherford, New Jersey. Amongst the celebrities at the first show are Katherine and Janet Jackson, actor Eric Estrada, Yoko Ono, Sean Lennon, and director Bob Giraldi.

August

Special Michael Jackson issues of *Bop* and *Modern Screen Special* are published, and Michael is also on the cover of *16*, *Super-pop*, *Rock & Soul*, *Blues & Soul*, *Day Time TV*, and *Right On!* magazines. Since January, Michael has been on the covers of over 170 magazines this year.

'Touch The One You Love'/'Girl You're So Together' by Michael Jackson is released in the US and Britain by Motown.

'Motown Love Collection' (LP), a Various Artists compilation featuring three Jackson 5 songs and 'Let's Beat It,' the charity compilation album organised by Michael for cancer research, are released by K-Tel International.

'Torture'/'Torture (Part 2)' by The Jacksons is released on Epic.

'An Appreciation To Michael Jackson' hosted by

Paul Gambaccini is aired on Radio One in Britain.

K-Tel International release 'Let's Beat It' (LP), a compilation of songs from various artists, including two from Michael, 'Say, Say, Say' and 'Human Nature.' All profits from sales are to be donated to the T. J. Martell Foundation. It is reported that Michael is largely instrumental in the album's release.

The Jehovah's Witnesses debate Michael's Superstar pop image which conflicts with many of their beliefs.

August 4

Less than a month into the Victory tour, 700,000 tickets have been sold for Jacksons concerts in five cities, a feat that would normally take a major act some thirty-five concerts to achieve.

'Victory' (LP) has sold over 3.5 million copies worldwide to date.

August 4-5

The Jacksons perform in concert in New York City; thousands of people who could not get tickets stand outside in the hope of getting a glimpse of Michael Jackson as he arrives at Madison Square Garden.

More than 2,000 uniformed, plainclothed and mounted New York City Police officers are on duty at a cost to the city of $678,000. These precautions are taken to prevent muggings which occurred at previous rock concerts.

Celebrities at the New York concerts include Andy Warhol, Mayor Koch, Cyndi Lauper, Pia Zadora,

1984

This Page and Opposite: The Jacksons in action on the Victory tour.

1984

Bette Midler, John Denver, Neil Sedaka, Peter Frampton, Brooke Shields and Emmanuel Lewis.

During his stay in New York, Michael has dinner with Katharine Hepburn at her city townhouse.

The Jacksons stay at the New York Penta Hotel which displays six 40 foot busts of The Jacksons and a banner reading 'Pepsi Presents The Jacksons.'

August 7-9

Death threats against Michael received by *The Knoxville News Sentinel* - which print them word for word - have created chaos in ticket sales for the Knoxville concerts scheduled for these dates.

The FBI are called in to analyse the threats which state that Michael will be assassinated on stage with many of his fans perishing along with him. Although the FBI deem the threats to be unfounded, security in all forms is tightened.

With death threats and heavy rain, this is the first Victory show which is not a sell-out. However, with 48,783 tickets sold, it is the largest audience of the tour to date and all three shows are a roaring success with Saturday and Sunday's shows both sell-outs with 50,239 and 49,485 tickets sold respectively.

August 9

By 4.00 a.m., 3,000 fans have gathered in the parking lot of Detroit's Pontiac Silverdome to purchase Victory tour tickets. By midday, the crowd has grown to 10,000.

August 11

'Girl You're So Together' enters the Top 100 singles chart in Britain peaking at number 33 and remains on the charts for nine weeks.

August 12

Michael appears on the cover of *The News Of The World's* colour supplement, 'Victory Tour.'

August 13

In New York City, The Jacksons are scheduled to begin shooting the 'Torture' video, directed by Jeff Stein.

August 17-19

The Jacksons perform in concert at the Pontiac Silverdome in Detroit, Michigan. Michael shouts, "We love you Motown" to the crowd in 'Motor City' where he recorded his first number 1 hit fifteen years earlier, and is so exuberant at the end of the show that he throws his black sequined jacket to a lucky fan in the audience.

During the three Detroit dates, The Jacksons sell 145,000 tickets grossing $4,350,030. The last show is a sell-out with an audience of 49,200 - even the 'obstructed view' seats which only go on sale that day, sell out.

As negotiations to play in Gary, The Jacksons' home town, broke down, the group pay all expenses for forty disadvantaged children from The Thelma Marshall Children's Home for orphans, foster children and abandoned children, The Hoosier Boys Home and The Donzels Work-Study Program for high school students working

toward a college education, to attend the third date in Detroit. Michael is staying with his friend, former child star Spanky McFarland of the *Our Gang* movies.

Michael films a 'home video' at Pontiac City Hall, Michigan with a troop of police officers, all donning sunglasses!

August 18

The Jackson brothers have three hits on the Pop singles chart this week: 'State Of Shock' by The Jacksons (3), 'Dynamite' by Jermaine (24) and 'Torture' by The Jacksons débuting at number 48. There are also four Jackson LPs on the Pop albums chart: The Jacksons' 'Victory' (4), and Michael's 'Thriller' (31), 'Farewell My Summer Love' (105) and 'Off The Wall' (111).

'Torture' enters the Pop singles chart peaking at number 17 and remains on the charts for twelve weeks.

Michael appears on the cover of Britain's *Woman* magazine.

August 22

Reports appear in the *New York Daily News* about problems which occur during production of the 'Torture' video at the Kaufman Astoria Studios in Queens, New York. An argument apparently breaks out between Michael and his brothers, resulting in neither Michael nor Jermaine participating in the video. Stand-ins perform Michael's dance sequences, and a wax figure is used for close-ups.

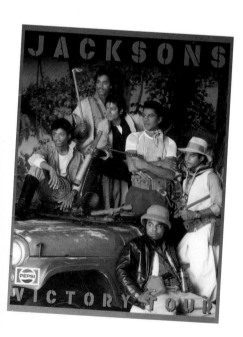

This Page: The Jacksons Victory Tour Programme.

Page Opposite: Michael and Marlon in action on The Victory Tour.

Michael is said to be so upset over the incident that he takes a break from the tour and visits Disney World.

It is announced that the tour will play Philadelphia on Labor Day weekend – September 1, 2 and 3. Despite unsold tickets, Stadium management Corporation do not advertise the concerts at all. Instead, as has been the policy throughout the tour, they rely - unwisely - on word of mouth publicity to spread the news of Michael's arrival at each venue. This results in many unsold tickets, and the possibility of third shows in Buffalo and Denver do not materialise due to poor initial sales.

Michael's career suffers a backlash as only three days before the opening Buffalo concert 38,000 tickets remain unsold. Whilst he is recognised as a highly talented and creative individual, the public respond negatively to bad organisation. Last minute tour planning which announces the Buffalo dates only one week before they are to take place and a false announcement about a third concert that week leaves some people feeling they are being manipulated and causes others to boycott the concerts altogether. Despite this, some fans camp out for over 25 hours to obtain their choice seats. By the time the concerts open at the weekend each show has sold just over 47,000 tickets for the capacity 48,200 stadium. However, merchandise sales are the best to date, according to Chuck Sullivan.

1984

August 25-26
The Jacksons perform in concert at Rich Stadium in Buffalo, New York.

August 25
'Torture' enters the Black singles chart peaking at number 12 and remains on the charts for thirteen weeks.

August 26
The Detroit Free Press reports that Michael Jackson albums are selling for around a hundred roubles ($130) on the black market in the Soviet Union.

A record 1.1 million tickets have been sold for the Victory tour in only two months.

August 29
It is Michael's 26th birthday today, but in keeping with his religion, he does not celebrate. The only acknowledgement is from his fans holding 'Happy Birthday Michael' banners in Detroit and Buffalo.

August 31
Reports appear that some members of the Jehovah's Witnesses now believe that Michael is the returned Messiah as foretold in a Bible passage about the raising up of the Archangel Michael, a symbol for the resurrected Christ.

September

Michael is on the cover of *Life, Black Beat, Creem, Closeup, Cracked, Rock Post Cards, Right On! Focus, Horoscope* and *Rock & Soul* magazines.

Madame Tussaud's of London approach Frank Dileo with a request to produce a wax figure of Michael Jackson.

'Centipede' (LP) by Rebbie Jackson including the song 'Centipede,' written and produced by Michael and 'Come Alive It's Saturday Night,' written by Michael and three other Jackson brothers, is released by Columbia.

'A Special Part Of Me' (LP) by Johnny Mathis featuring 'Love Never Felt So Good,' co-written by Michael Jackson, Paul Anka and Kathy Wakefield, is released in Britain.

September 1-2
The Jacksons perform in concert at JFK Stadium in Philadelphia, Pennsylvania. This show attracts one of the largest audiences of the entire show with 60,000 fans packed into the stadium. Amongst the celebrity guests are Sly Stone and Bruce Springsteen. Andy Hernandez (aka Coati Mundi) of the rock group Kid Creole & The Coconuts visits the show and says of Michael: "As a performer who believes in injecting high energy into a show, I can appreciate more than most what goes into the making of a Michael Jackson performance. The dictionary should contain another word that means 'great, superb, professional, energetic, entertaining,' and that word should be 'michael-jackson.'"

September 3
The third Philadelphia Victory tour concert is rained out. It is rescheduled for September 28, with an additional concert set for September 29. This 'rained out' concert causes Senator Lloyd to introduce a Bill requiring all outdoor concerts to have 'rain dates' scheduled in future.

'Torture' video débuts on MTV with the two lead vocalists - Michael and Jermaine - absent!

According to the manufacturers of View-Master 3-D viewers, Michael Jackson has eclipsed E.T. as the public's favourite subject.

September 5
A press conference is held to dispel rumours about Michael's sex life, plastic surgery and reports that he takes female hormones to keep his high voice. Although not present in person, Michael's two-page, self-penned statement – to set the record straight 'once and for all' – is read out by his personal manager, Frank Dileo.

September 7
Neither Michael nor any other member of the Jackson family attend the marriage of Janet to James DeBarge of the Motown group, DeBarge, who are married in secret in Grand Rapids, Michigan. The marriage will be annulled in four months' time.

September 7-8
The Jacksons perform in concert at Mile High Stadium in Denver, Colorado. Michael visits with Elton John, who is giving his own concert at McNichols Arena, Denver. The Jacksons play to a sell-out crowd of 53,678 while Elton John and James Taylor, also in concert that weekend, play to capacity crowds of 14,000 and 9,000 respectively.

This is the 25th and final concert in America – the tour now moves on to Canada.

September 8

'Torture,' released in August in Britain, enters the Top 100 singles chart peaking at number 26 and remains on the charts for six weeks.

September 14

At the first annual MTV Video Awards show, Michael Jackson's 'Thriller' video wins awards in three separate categories including Best Overall Performance, Best Choreography and the highly coveted Viewer's Choice Award. Michael does not attend the presentation.

September 15

Michael, accompanied by Quincy Jones and four bodyguards, goes on a small shopping spree at the Paragraph Bookstore in Montreal, Canada. Michael buys: *Costume Cavalcade, The History Of Costume, Scene Design* and *Stravinsky In The Theater*.

'Jacksons Live' (LP) re-enters the Pop albums chart peaking at number 191 and remains on the charts for two weeks.

September 16

Michael attends Sunday service at the Snowdon Kingdom Hall of the Jehovah's Witnesses in Montreal, Canada. He is accompanied by a body-guard and a secretary.

September 17-18

The Jacksons play to audiences of more than 116,540 in two sell-out dates at Montreal's Olympic Stadium in Quebec. During the finale, Jackie hobbles on stage to join The Jacksons for 'Shake Your Body (Down To The Ground)', which sees all six brothers together and in costume for the first time during the tour.

September 21-22

The Jacksons perform to capacity audiences of 90,000 at two concerts at RFK Stadium, Washington DC. The tickets sell out in just three days. At the first show - the twenty-ninth of the tour - the first acknow-ledgement of the album after which the tour is named is made when the 'Torture' video is played on the screen above the stage. Amongst celebrities attending are Mike Love of The Beach Boys, Peaches of Peaches & Herb, Eva Gabor and Ethel Kennedy.

The Jacksons stay at the Regent Hotel in George-town, where Michael meets three winners of an anti-drunk-driving writing competition at a dinner held in their honour.

Michael also goes book-shopping again, buying a photo book on Judy Garland and Liza Minnelli.

Whilst in Washington, Michael visits the Kennedy Center Opera House to see Anthony Quinn and Lila Kedrova in the touring pro-duction of *Zorba*. He sits in the Presidential Box with Presidential Counsellor, Ed Meese. Although Michael tries to remain incognito, the cast know of his arrival, saying: "Okay, get out the white gloves for the open-ing number."

"For some time now, I have been searching my conscience as to whether or not I should publicly react to the many falsehoods that have been spread about me. I have decided to make this statement based on the injustice of these allegations and the far-reaching trauma those who feel close to me are suffering. I feel very fortunate to have been blessed with recognition for my efforts. This recognition also brings with it a responsibility to one's admirers through-out the world. Performers should always serve as role models who set an example for young people. It saddens me that many may actually believe the present flurry of false accusations. To this end, and I do mean END: No, I've never taken hormones to maintain my high voice! No, I've never had my cheekbones altered in any way! No, I've never had cosmetic surgery on my eyes! Yes, one day in the future I plan to get married and have a family. Any state-ments to the contrary are simply untrue. I have advised my attorneys of my will-ingness to institute legal action and sub-sequently prosecute all guilty to the fullest extent of the law. As noted ear-lier, I love children. We all know that kids are very impressionable and there-fore susceptible to such stories. I'm cer-tain that some have already been hurt by this terrible slander. In addition to their admiration, I would like to keep their respect."

Michael Jackson's Statement read by manager, Frank Dileo, on September 5, 1984

1984

September 28-29
The Jacksons perform in concert in Philadelphia, Pennsylvania. This is the rescheduled concert of September 3. Fans who cannot attend do not get a refund!

October

Michael appears on the cover of many magazines including *Song Hits*, *Right On!*, *Cracked*, *Focus* and *Record Collector*.

The Michael Jackson Fact File from Omnibus Press is published in Britain.

Reports appear in *Melody Maker* and *NME*, that Michael is considering an offer from Geffen to star in a full-length feature film, *Street Dandy*.

'Body'/'Body (instrumental)' by The Jacksons is released on Epic peaking at number 47 on the Pop singles charts. Michael does not appear in the video.

Calibre records in Britain release 'I'm In Love With Michael Jackson's Answerphone' by 'Julie.'

October 5-7
The Jacksons perform in concert at the Canadian National Exhibition Stadium in Toronto.

This Page: A Victory tour ticket.

October 6
'Got To Be There' (LP) and 'Ben' (LP), are released on a special 'Twinpax Cassette' by Motown.

October 12-14
The Jacksons perform in concert at Comiskey Park in Chicago, Illinois.

October 19-20
The Jacksons perform in concert at Municipal Stadium in Cleveland, Ohio.

October 26-27
The Jacksons perform in concert at Fulton County Stadium in Atlanta, Georgia.

November

People magazine publish *People Extra*, the first issue ever devoted entirely to one person - Michael Jackson.

'Love Never Felt So Good' by Johnny Mathis, co-written by Michael, Paul Anka and Kathy Wakefield, is released in Britain.

The Jacksons are on the cover of *Black Beat*.

Early November
Michael Jackson sits for Madame Tussaud's sculptor, Jim Mathieson, in Houston, Texas. Mathieson makes drawings and

takes photographs for creation of the clay model which will form the basis of Michael's wax likeness.

November 2-3
The Jacksons perform in concert at the Orange Bowl in Miami, Florida.

November 9-10
The Jacksons perform in concert at the Astrodome in Houston, Texas.

November 16-18
The Jacksons perform in concert at Place Stadium in Vancouver, Canada, donating hundreds of tickets to the needy and underprivileged.

November 18
Michael Jackson is made an honorary member of the New Westminster Police Department while in British Columbia, Canada. Appointed PC 49, he swears as a police constable to 'serve the Queen and cause the peace to be kept and preserved.'

November 20
5,000 fans turn out to see Michael at the unveiling of his Hollywood Boulevard star, No. 1,793 on the 'Walk Of Fame,' which is located in front of Mann's Chinese Theater between the stars of country singer Lefty Frizzell and actress Lupe Velez. He has to abandon his speech, fearing serious injury to many youngsters fighting to catch a glimpse of him.

Michael becomes the first celebrity to have two different stars dedicated to him, having first received one as a member of The Jacksons in the '70s.

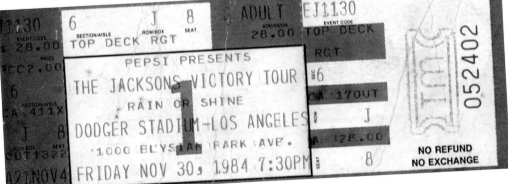

November 27

The Jacksons are sued for $50 million by designers Sandra Simone and Donn Greer of Cinema City Studios. It is claimed that the group used their concepts, including musical instruments and costume 'light-up' boots, without payment or credit.

November 30-Dec. 2

The Jacksons perform in concert in Dodger Stadium, Los Angeles, California.

December

Michael Jackson is voted 1984's 'Hero Of Young America' by a poll of 4,000 teenagers which gains him an entry in *The World Almanac And Book Of Facts 1985*.

Michael is on the cover of *Ebony*, *Black Beat* and *US* magazines.

Michael wins three polls in the British newspaper, *The Sun* for: Best Male Singer, Best Video ('Thriller') and Best Album.

Rock's Thriller, a 90-minute special on Michael Jackson is aired on Britain's Radio One.

LA Is My Lady, a video with music produced by Quincy Jones for Frank Sinatra, and featuring brief appearances by Michael and LaToya, is released.

December 4

Although nearing its close, there are still many internal wranglings between the promoters and Jackson representatives. A dispute over gate receipts sees a short suspension in ticket sales, and fears of cancellation grow.

December 6

Michael Jackson is in Chicago to testify in court that he wrote 'The Girl Is Mine.' His testimony is part of CBS's rebuttal to the $5 million suit filed by Fred Sanford, who claims it is his song, 'Please Love Me Now,' submitted to CBS in March 1982.

In his court testimony, Michael states that he has written and recorded many, many unreleased songs saying he has simply lost count, and names as examples, 'Why Can't I Be,' 'Thank You For Life' and 'The Toy,' written but not used for the Richard Pryor movie. Michael uses a look-alike as a decoy in order to get into the court.

December 7-9

The Jacksons play their last Victory tour concerts at Dodger Stadium in Los Angeles, California. Over two million people came to see The Jacksons during the fifty-five-concert, five-month tour, which crisscrossed America and Canada with the most ambitious design and execution ever created for the concert stage.
During 'Shake Your Body,' Michael announces his split from The Jacksons.
The tour grossed a record $75 million and, thanks to Michael Jackson, for the first time Pepsi-Cola overtake their arch-rivals, Coca Cola. However, there are a number of law suits involving the tour pending.

Jonathan King says of the tour: "What you saw on stage at the Jackson's tour was the Michael Jackson of the single glove, the interesting hat, the moonwalk-ing and all that. What you didn't see was Michael Jackson, the real performer.
I think Michael should go out on stage with a small backing band and do a show where he just performs his excellent numbers on his own. ...Michael Jackson is extraordinarily talented; he is backed up by brothers who are not particularly talented and to cover that over, they do a lot of spectacle and pantomime and special effects.
Also, it was booked by people who don't normally book tours out. So, it did several venues in each place and sometimes not the right venues with the result that it did not always sell out."

December 13

Michael returns to Brotman Memorial Hospital, where he underwent treatment for a burn injury in April. He donates $1.5 million, monies received as compensation from Pepsi, to set up the Michael Jackson Burn Unit to help child victims.

December 14

The jury in the Fred Sanford lawsuit against CBS Inc. finds the Corporation innocent of plagiarising Sanford's song, 'Please Love Me Now,' as the basis for Michael's song, 'The Girl Is Mine.'

Billboard magazine's year end charts rank Michael in the following categories: number 1 Pop Album ('Thriller'), number 2 Black Album, number 2 Top Pop Artist, number 3 Most Successful Single ('Say, Say, Say') and number 6 Top Black Artist.

1984

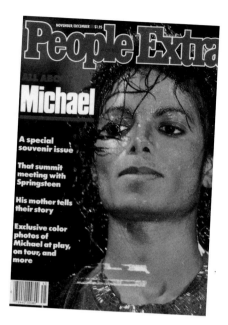

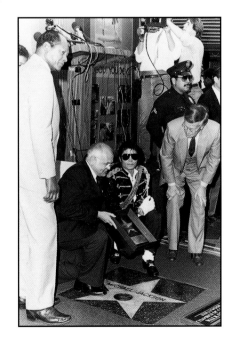

This Page: Michael receives his star on Hollywood Boulevard.

1985

Michael saves a chimp from a cancer research centre in Texas. Bubbles becomes a close companion of Michael's and is taught several tricks including his own version of the moonwalk.

Bubbles also has a budding acting career, appearing in *Back To School*, with Rodney Dangerfield. He also co-stars in *The Entertainers*, a TV movie with Bob Newhart.

Curly, a book about one of the Three Stooges by Joan Mauer Howard, daughter of Stooge, Moe Howard, is published by Citadel Press. The book contains a foreword by one of Curly's biggest fans - Michael Jackson. In the foreword, Michael reveals he once wrote a song about Curly.

The Jacksons - Their History In Collectors Stamps, an 18-page booklet edited by Tito Jackson and Mark Miller, is issued by the Kellogg Company as part of the post-Victory tour promotion.

'Philly Ballads Vol. 2,' a Various Artists compilation featuring 'Find Me A Girl' by The Jacksons, is released on the Philadelphia International label.

Plans are announced for *La-La Means I'm Hungry: Also Known As The Michael Jackson Diet* by Joi Fondakinadee to be published by Carlton Press in 1986.

January

Michael is on the cover of *Right On!* magazine.

January 15-23

Michael Jackson and Lionel Richie work together to compose a song for African famine relief. Paired by Quincy Jones, Michael comes up with basic music for 'We Are The World.' Recording of the instrumental track is made at Lion's Shario Studio in Los Angeles, where final changes are made to the lyrics.

January 24

Demo Cassettes of 'We Are The World' are sent to all artists involved in the recording.

January 28

Michael Jackson receives four nominations at the 12th annual American Music Awards for Favourite Black Male Vocalist, Favourite Album and Favourite Black Album ('Thriller'), and The Jacksons are nominated for Favourite Group. Michael does not win in any of the categories and does not attend the presentation.

Two hours after the American Music Award ceremony, Michael and 44 other artists gather secretly for ten hours at A&M Recording Studios in Los Angeles to record 'We Are The World,' co-written by Michael and Lionel Richie. With this recording, USA For Africa is born to fight the epidemic of starvation in Africa, following on from the initiative started by Bob Geldof with Band Aid in Britain.

Geldof just back from Ethiopia says, "... I think it is best to remember that the price of a life this year is a piece of plastic, seven inches wide with a hole in the middle... I don't know if we in particular can conceive of nothing. But nothing is not having a cardboard box to sleep under in minus ten degrees; nothing is not having any drink to get drunk, it's not having water. And you walk into one of the corrugated iron huts and you see meningitis and malaria and typhoid buzzing around in the air; and you see dead bodies lying side by side with the live ones. And, on a good day, you can only see 120 people die slowly in front of you. In some camps you see 15 bags of flour for 27,000 people and that's what we're here for."

February

'Pulse' (LP) by Greg Phillinganes featuring 'Behind The Mask,' a song written by Michael, Chris Mosdell and Ryuichi Sakamoto is released. It is also released as a Planet Records single.

'Do What You Do' by Jermaine Jackson featuring 'Tell Me I'm Not Dreamin'' on the B-side is released in the US and Britain.

'Wait' by The Jacksons, the third single from the 'Victory' LP featuring a live version of Michael's 'She's Out Of My Life' on the B-side, is released.

February 14

Michael helps with the delivery of a baby deer born to his pet deers Prince and Princess. The birth of Valentino, born on Valentine's Day, is videotaped.

February 23

Michael Jackson appears on the cover of *TV Guide* for the first time.

February 26

At the 27th annual Grammy Awards held at the Shrine Auditorium in Los Angeles, Michael wins in the category Best Video Album for *The Making Of Michael Jackson's Thriller* video. Michael does not attend the presentations.

March

The Making Of Michael Jackson's Thriller wins two awards at the 3rd annual American Video Awards in the categories: Best Long Form Video and Best Home Video. Rebbie Jackson accepts the awards on Michael's behalf.

Michael is on the cover of *Rock & Soul*, *Beatbox*, *Look In* and *Right On!* magazines.

March 26

Michael arrives at London Heathrow Airport on the supersonic Concorde and is subjected to an half-hour body and baggage search.

March 27

Michael attends the futuristic musical *Starlight Express* at the Apollo Theatre, Victoria in London and meets the cast backstage.

March 28

Michael arrives at a besieged Madame Tussaud's wax museum for the unveiling of his wax model, his first public visit to England since The Jacksons' tour in 1979. London is brought to a standstill as 8,000 fans clamour for a glimpse of their hero. On leaving, Michael leaps onto the roof of his chauffeured car to wave to his adoring fans. He will later be billed

£2,000 to cover the cost of damage to the paintwork!

'We Are The World' (LP) is released by Columbia.

March 29

Michael Jackson leaves the Montcalm Hotel to visit a London Hospital, where he views the skeleton of John Merrick, the Elephant Man. At Marylebone Police Station in the afternoon, he is treated to a police drill and presented with a police badge and helmet. And finally, at an evening reception and party in his honour, CBS Records present him with an 8x Platinum wall-mounted plaque.

We Are The World: The Video Event is released on video and becomes the ninth best-selling video of 1985.

April

Michael Jackson and seven members of USA For Africa are on the cover of *Life* magazine, the only press allowed to photograph and report on the all-night recording session.

Michael and Elizabeth Taylor go to see their friend, Liza Minnelli's 'Comeback' tour.

The proposed May release of a British Virgin Islands postage stamp which puts Michael's image together with that of the Queen is withdrawn by the Palace, who state: "The Queen will not appear on any stamp which portrays a living person." Nevertheless, a limited number of the British Virgin Islands stamps are printed before being withdrawn and are now valuable collectors'

Page Opposite: Michael unveils himself at Madame Tussaud's in London, amid mass fan hysteria.

1985

items, fetching up to £250 each. The Caribbean island of St. Vincent later issues a set of stamps showing Michael in eight different poses.

April 1
Michael flies home aboard a Concorde, which departs from London Airport.

April 4
Reports appear that 'We Are The World' (LP) was certified Gold (500,000 copies) within forty-eight hours of release, and that the single has sold over 4 million, accruing $8 million for USA For Africa.

April 5
Good Friday, and 'We Are The World' is broadcast simultaneously by over 8,000 radio stations around the world.

April 8
Michael and Lionel Richie are on the cover of *Jet* magazine.

April 13
'We Are The World' with Quincy Jones' tune 'Grace' on the B-side, released on March 7, hits number 1 on the Pop singles chart holding its position for four weeks.

'We Are The World' enters the Top 100 singles chart in Britain. It peaks at number

This Page: Michael on the set of *Captain EO* with Francis Ford Coppola and George Lucas.

1 holding its position for two weeks and remains on the charts for nine weeks.

April 18
'Got To Be There' is re-issued in Britain by Motown, with the popular 'Rockin' Robin' on the B-side.

Julian Shapiro, Michael Jackson's aide, says that Michael will appear in a new full-length feature film, *Peter Pan,* with creative input and an album release.

May 1
The Story Of 'We Are The World', a documentary film on the recording session, premières on the Home Box Office cable network.

Michael is featured on the cover of *National Lampoon.*

May 10
Michael Jackson visits the Brandywine River Museum's exhibit of paintings by N. C. Wyeth.

May 14
It is reported that Michael receives a royalty cheque from Epic Records for $53 million, for sales of the 'Thriller' LP.

May 17
'We Are The World' creates recording history by becoming the first ever Multi-Platinum single and being certified in all categories (Gold, Platinum, Multi-Platinum) within the space of a month. The single is the industry's first ever Multi-Platinum single.

'Motown Legends - Michael Jackson' (LP), 'Motown Legends - The Jackson 5 Featuring

Michael Jackson' (LP) and 'Motown Legends - Love Songs' (LP) are released.

July
'State Of Shock'/'Torture' is released on Epic's Memory Lane label.

Michael is on the cover of *Black Beat* magazine.

July 9
Court proceedings commence in Paris, France to establish whether a section of 'Wanna Be Startin' Somethin'' has been taken from Manuy Dibango's song, 'Soul Makossa.'

The NAACP criticises Michael Jackson, among other Black celebrities, for not hiring more Blacks to work for him. However, this statement is not accepted by all the organisation's members.

July 12
Figures are published that 'We Are The World' (LP) has sold three million, and 'Off The Wall' (LP) has sold five million copies to date.

July 24
It is announced that Michael Jackson will star in a 3-D science-fiction musical film, *Captain EO,* to be shown exclusively at Disneyland and Disney World; Francis Ford Coppola will direct, and George Lucas will produce the film.

July 30
Michael severely sprains his right hand during the filming of *Captain EO* for Walt Disney Productions. He is treated at the Brotman Memorial

Hospital, where he also visits a sick fan.

August

'Eaten Alive' by Diana Ross and co-written by Michael with Barry and Maurice Gibb is released on RCA.

'Say You Love Me' (LP) by Jennifer Holliday featuring 'You're The One,' a song co-written with Buz Kohan and produced by Michael is released.

Mid-August

After ten months of negotiations, Michael Jackson purchases the ATV back catalogue from Australian multi-millionaire, Robert Holmes, for $47.5 million. Columbia Records, a division of CBS Records, are reported to have financed the deal. The catalogue, comprising over 4,000 compositions, includes 251 songs by The Beatles as well as hits by Pat Benatar, Little Richard, The Pointer Sisters and The Pretenders. Michael already owns the publishing rights to the Sly Stone collection as well as a collection of 60s hits. For their help in negotiating the 'Beatles' deal, Michael rewards attorney John Branca and manager Frank Dileo each with a Rolls Royce.

September

'20 Greatest Songs In Motown History' (LP) featuring 'Never Can Say Goodbye' is released on CD by Motown.

'Eaten Alive' (LP) by Diana Ross including 'Eaten Alive,' the song co-written by Michael with Barry and Maurice Gibb, is released by RCA Records. The back cover contains a handwritten note to Diana from Michael, "You are truly supreme, good to be with you again. I love you, Michael 1998."

Michael sends a constant stream of flowers and fresh fruit to Los Angeles Cedar Sinai Hospital after hearing of Little Richard's car accident.

'Eaten Alive' enters the Top 100 singles chart in Britain peaking at number 71 and remains on the charts for three weeks.

October

Michael Jackson and Prince are on the cover of *Rock & Soul* magazine.

October 21

Michael Jackson visits the Cohuna Wildlife Sanctuary in Perth, Australia.

December

Michael Jackson tops the 1985 'Bozo Awards' (named after the renowned Bozo The Clown), for 'single-handedly reviving the glove industry.'

Reports appear that Y&M Associates are to release a line of stuffed animals based on Michael's own private zoo. An animated cartoon show featuring the animals is also planned.

In *Billboard's* annual listing of America's Top Ten videos, Michael Jackson again dominates the chart with videos which are now two years old! 'Thriller' (1), 'Beat It' (2) and 'Billie Jean' (6).

This Page: Michael with Kenny Loggins and Steve Perry at the recording of 'We Are The World.'

1986

1986

It is rumoured that Michael Jackson is to make an appearance in the US drama, *The Colbys.*

The British group, Five Star, have reportedly been invited to record with Michael in America.

January 25-26

'Dick Clark's Rock Roll & Remember' (LP), a Various Artists radio broadcast recording featuring sixteen group and solo songs by

Tokyo, The Beatles In The Magical Mystery Tour and *The Beatles At Shea Stadium.*

Michael Jackson and the surviving Beatles join forces for the first time to protect the work of The Beatles as Michael Jackson successfully obtains a court order barring sales of three bootleg movies which have found their way onto the market: *The Beatles In*

Michael and The Jacksons as well as a seven-part interview with Michael, is aired.

January 27

Michael Jackson arrives half-way through the 13th annual American Music Awards ceremonies in the company of Elizabeth Taylor, where he, Quincy Jones, Lionel Richie and promoter Ken Kragen receive awards for 'We Are The World.' At the show's conclusion, they join with many celebrities to sing the award-winning song.

February

Reports circulate that Michael Jackson is to be best man at Diana Ross's wedding, but he cancels at the last minute. In October 1985, Diana and Arne Naess, a Norwegian millionaire, were married in a private ceremony in New York but they marry publicly this month in Switzerland.

February 2

A profile about Quincy Jones is aired on the CBS *60 Minutes* programme, which includes a five-minute interview with Michael Jackson, who speaks only about Quincy.

February 18

Fourteen-year old heart transplant patient, Donna Ashlock from Patterson in California, receives a call from Michael Jackson after he learns she is a devoted fan. Michael wishes her well and invites her to visit him at the Encino family home once she is feeling better.

February 25

Michael and Lionel Richie attend the 28th annual Grammy Awards. 'We Are The World' wins four of its six nominations for Song Of The Year, Record Of The Year, Best Pop Performance By A Duo Or Group, and Best Music Video (Short Form).

March

Former Victory tour promoter Frank Russo loses his claim over a breach of contract against the Jacksons. Nevertheless, he continues to pursue compensation for a three-week managerial stint.

This Page: Michael attends the American Music Awards with good friend, Elizabeth Taylor.

Below: Michael at the Grammy Awards with Stevie Wonder, Quincy Jones, Dionne Warwick and Lionel Richie.

An $18 million contract is signed between Michael Jackson and Entertainment Properties Inc., which will manufacture a line of clothing for children using Michael's name.

Michael is on the cover of *Right On!* magazine.

March 8
Heart transplant recipient Donna Ashlock visits Michael Jackson at his home in Encino, California. She stays for lunch and watches a movie with Michael.

March 11
'We Are The World' wins the 1985 People's Choice Award as 'Favourite New Song.' Neither Michael Jackson nor Lionel Richie attend the presentation, which is aired on CBS-TV. USA For Africa member, Kenny Rogers, accepts the award on their behalf.

April
Good Friday, and 'We Are The World' is again broadcast simultaneously by radio stations around the world.

'Hands Across America'/ 'We Are The World' is released in support of the Hands Across America project sponsored by USA For Africa. 'We Are The World,' credited to Voices Of America on early issues of the record, is later correctly credited to USA For Africa.

Michael accompanies Elizabeth Taylor to the opening of the Hollywood Park Race Track in Inglewood.

The administration of Michael Jackson's song catalogue, ATV Music, is moved from EMI Music Publishing to MCA Music Publishing.

George Michael states during an interview that he is to record with Michael Jackson in June, with the proceeds of the song going to the African Relief Fund.

May
St. Vincent, a Caribbean island north of Grenada in the Grenadines chain, begins to issue postage stamps bearing the likeness of Michael Jackson. (Not to be confused with the abortive stamp issue by the British Virgin Islands.)

May 5
It is reported that Michael is to film another three commercials for Pepsi for a record-breaking fee of $15 million. Pepsi later denies the fee is that large.

May 9
Michael with Emmanuel Lewis and aides stay at the Helmsley Palace Hotel. They later go on a shopping spree at Video Shack.

May 10
Michael attends the Sunday matinèe of Broadway's *Big Deal* with Emmanuel Lewis. He later

sees *Jo Jo Dancer, Your Life Is Calling,* starring Richard Pryor, at the Coronet Theater.

May 11
On another visit to Video Shack, Michael buys *The Goonies* for Emmanuel's viewing.

May 12
A press conference is held at New York's Red Parrot, announcing the new PepsiCo contract with Michael Jackson.

In one of the ballrooms at the Helmsley Palace Hotel, Michael receives a Guinness Book of World Records plaque for having received the largest fee ever paid for a product endorsement, a reported $15 million from Pepsi Cola.

May 13
On their last evening in New York, Michael, Emmanuel Lewis and their bodyguards watch *The Little Shop Of Horrors* in New York's East Village.

May 19
'Looking Back To Yesterday - Never Before Released Masters' (LP), an anthology of early Michael Jackson/Jackson 5 songs is released on Motown.

June
Michael's pet boa constrictor, Muscles, dies. His new friend is an 18-foot, 300 pound python named Crusher. Michael also adds a giraffe to his private zoo. Mahali is purchased for $15,000 from the Sedgewick County Zoo in Wichita, Kansas.

1986

This Page: The Michael Jackson Virgin Islands stamp not issued.

Michael is acknowledged by *The Guinness Book Of Records* as having the largest endorsement agreement in history between an individual and a major corporation (Pepsi).

Michael attends the races with Elizabeth Taylor and George Hamilton.

During a visit to Disneyland, Michael Jackson dons a surgical mask, sunglasses, black fedora and is transported around in a wheelchair. Apparently a ploy to attract less attention, this does quite the opposite.

July

Michael is on the front cover of *Right On!* magazine.

July 30

Michael Jackson attends the funeral of film director, Vincent Minnelli, Liza Minnelli's father, held at Forest Lawn in Glendale, California.

August

A range of Jackson 5 CDs are released by Motown. Most notable of these new collections of old songs is 'The Michael Jackson Anthology.'

August 26

Michael appears on the cover of *Celebrity* magazine.

September

Michael attends the concert of the Norwegian group, A-Ha, in Hollywood. He is accompanied by Sophia Loren and arrives in a surgical mask.

A library in the town of Ojai, Hollywood says it will ignore overdue book fines from Michael, if he agrees to sign them on return.

September 12

Captain EO, Michael's 17-minute space fantasy, 3-D movie premières at Epcot Center in Disney World, Florida. The film is a collaboration between George

Lucas, Francis Coppola and Michael and, at an estimated cost of $30 million, is the most expensive film - minute-for-minute - ever made. Michael stars in the title role alongside Anjelica Huston, and two new songs by Michael are featured: 'Another Part Of Me' and 'We Are Here To Change The World.'

September 13

Captain EO premières at Disneyland in Pasadena, California.

September 16

Michael appears on the cover of the *National Enquirer* in an oxygen chamber. Frank Dileo, and Michael's personal doctor, Steve Hoefflin are rumoured to have said that Michael's wishes to purchase such a chamber as he believes it will help him to live longer.

September 29

A new line of Michael Jackson children's clothes is launched at the Palladium nightclub in New York. Manufactured by Entertainment Properties Inc. all the clothes carry the MJ monogram.

October

Former Victory tour promoter Frank Russo's claims over a three-week managerial stint are finally settled out of court.

It is reported that following two years of talks and negotiations over a film script for Geffen Productions, the idea is scrapped due to Michael's dissatisfaction with the project.

It is rumoured that Michael has refused any further use of Beatle songs for the London musical *Lennon*. Promoters had hoped to take the show on a fifteen-city tour.

November

Michael and Elizabeth Taylor attend a Liza Minnelli concert at the Universal Amphitheater in Hollywood.

It is announced that *Motown On Showtime,* a Showtime cable TV series devoted to Motown performers, will focus on The Jackson 5. The hour-long special, due to air in March 1987, will highlight the careers of The Jacksons and Michael.

The British music press report that Michael is to release a single and an album in January and February, 1987. It is stated that he has recorded enough material for three albums, and a duet with George Michael is

1986

Page Opposite: Michael in *Captain EO.*

This Page: Michael attends the funeral of Vincent Minnelli with his daughter, Liza, and widow, Lee.

Left: The rare 3-D *Captain EO* Comic.

1986

favourite to be included. Another report states that Michael is to record a duet with Barbra Streisand for the forthcoming LP.

Michael is on the cover of *Black Beat* magazine.

Magic Beat perfume is marketed by Michael Jackson. There are three fragrances, 'Wildfire,' 'Unwind' and 'Heartbeat.'

'Michael's Pets' are marketed. The stuffed animal line is modelled after his own pet zoo with one character, Cool Bear, being based on Michael himself. The rest of the line includes Jabbar (giraffe), Louie (llama), Muscles (snake), Bubbles (chimp), Uncle Tookie (frog - Michael's nick-name for Frank Dileo), Spanky and Mr. Bill (dog), Suzy (rabbit) and Jeannine (ostrich).

This Page: Michael with his pet snake Muscles. Inset is the stuffed animal of the same name, a new line in Michael's Pets. Michael requests that from each purchase, one dollar should be donated to a children's charity.

Michael Jackson's affection for children and animals is the inspiration for **MICHAEL'S PETS**, a line of designer plush toys resembling his very own personal menagerie. Michael has asked the distributors, Y&M Associates, to donate one dollar from the purchase of each stuffed animal to a children's charity.

TOP: The superstar is pictured with one of his resident pets, **MUSCLES THE BOA CONSTRICTOR**.

BOTTOM: The stuffed counterparts, which will be available in the Fall wherever quality toys are sold.

Norman Winter / Associates / Public Relations
1020 Carol Drive, West Hollywood, CA 90069 (213) 858-1182

November 6

Rolling Stone reports that Michael is working with rap team Run-DMC on an anti-drug song for his forthcoming album. Martin Scorsese is said to be directing the accompanying video. They also state that, according to Rick Rubin of Def Jam Recordings, Michael denied The Beastie Boys permission to record The Beatles' 'I'm Down' with new lyrics, which were described as too 'salacious.'

November 9

Michael appears on the cover of *The News Of The World's* colour supplement.

November 12

In a list of *People* magazine's most popular ever editions, an issue published on February 13, 1984 is third. It carried Michael on the front cover and sold 3.45 million copies. Inside was an article on his burn injuries.

November 15

'Their Very Best - Back To Back' featuring Motown's four biggest recording artists, Michael, Diana Ross, Gladys Knight and Stevie Wonder, enters the Top 100 albums chart in Britain peaking at number 21 and remains on the charts for ten weeks.

November 18

The Making Of Disney's 'Captain EO' is premièred on cable TV's Disney Channel.

November 19

Boys at Masters School in Dobbs Ferry, a tiny hamlet in upstate New York, are given the day off after a record company request

extras for a pop video. It is only on arrival that they learn they are to take part in a Michael Jackson video. Scenes are also filmed on a commuter train and in a subway station in the Bronx. Martin Scorsese directs Michael's first video for his upcoming LP, a 16-minute piece called 'Bad.' The song and video tell the story of Daryl, a Black youth from the ghetto, who returns home from his private prep school to discover that he no longer quite fits in with his friends from the neighbourhood. The video is based loosely around a true story.

December

Billboard magazine ranks *Motown 25: Yesterday, Today, and Forever* as the number 2 Top Music Video of the year.

Rumours circulate that Michael is in love with a blonde twenty-five year old named Karen Faye. It is later established that Faye is already happily attached and is, in fact, Michael's make-up artist who he met whilst working on the *Captain EO* video.

December 10

Michael Jackson withdraws from the board of directors of USA For Africa. Although the reasons are unclear, it is believed to be related to a disagreement over using 'We Are The World' as the B-side on 'Hands Across America.'

Michael attends a presentation by the American Friends Of The Hebrew University where Steven Spielberg receives the coveted Scopus Award.

1987

Kenny Rogers publishes a book of photographs of celebrities titled, *Your Friends and Mine*. The first person photographed and the inspiration for the book is Michael Jackson. The black and white photograph of Michael, with Bubbles, is the first photograph in the book.

'Time Out For The Burglar' by The Jacksons, a song from the Whoopi Goldberg film, is released by MCA. The single does not feature Michael.

January 17

Michael attends The American Cinema Awards with Sophia Loren and Sylvester Stallone.

'Behind The Mask,' a version by Eric Clapton, enters the Top 100 singles chart in Britain peaking at number 15 and remains on the charts for eleven weeks.

The song was originally recorded by Michael's keyboard player Greg Phillinganes, and was written by Michael Jackson, Chris Mosdell and Ryuichi Sakamoto. However, Michael is strangely not credited on Clapton's version.

Press reports suggest that Steven Spielberg is planning to cast Michael in the lead role of *Phantom Of The Opera*.

Motown executives dismiss rumours that Michael is planning to buy Motown Records.

January 26

The release date of Michael's new single passes with reports that he is not yet totally satisfied with his new recordings.

Number One magazine prints exclusive photos from the new video 'Bad.'

February

Photos from Michael's new Pepsi adverts appear in *Number One* magazine with news of the accompanying song, apparently titled 'The Price Of Fame.'

Michael begins filming a second video for his upcoming LP. Colin Chilvers (Academy Award winner for special effect direction *Superman, The Movie*) directs 'Smooth Criminal.'

March

Michael is on the cover of *Right On!* magazine.

The release date for Michael's first single and the new album is now scheduled for April. The album is said to include tracks titled 'Bad' and 'Pyramid Girl,' later confirmed to be 'Liberian Girl.'

March 14

Michael and Paul McCartney appear on the cover of *The Sun* newspaper in Britain after giving permission for 'Let It Be' to be recorded for the Zeebrugge Tragedy Fund.

March 15

Michael appears on the cover of *The News Of The World's* colour supplement, 'The High Price Of Michael Jackson's Smile.'

In America, fans of The Beatles jam the phonelines of a New York radio station objecting to Michael's plans to use the Fab Four's songs for jingles in commercials.

April

Michael withdraws from the Jehovah's Witnesses.

1987

This Page: Michael attends the American Cinema Awards with Sophia Loren.

1987

William Van De Wall, a spokesman of the Brooklyn headquarters of the Jehovah's Witnesses, tells the press, "He took the initiative. We didn't take any action. We were informed of his wishes."

May

First reports surface that Michael is supposedly offering over £1 million to purchase the bones of John Merrick, The Elephant Man, which are held at the London Hospital's Medical College. It is later reported that the offer is rejected.

Michael and Prince have a 'face to face' meeting in Los Angeles, which is orchestrated by Quincy Jones. Michael's 'Bad' was written as a duet with Prince in mind. The meeting concludes after 30 minutes with Prince rejecting the idea but conceding, however, that the song will be a hit, with or without his participation.

It is announced that a world tour is scheduled to commence in Japan in September and to arrive in Britain in the summer of 1988.

June

Michael is on the cover of *Spin* magazine, 'Michael Jackson Running Scared.'

Two anthology CD albums on Michael and The Jackson 5 are released by Motown.

June 1

Sales of 'Thriller' now stand at just over 38.5 million worldwide, with the US accounting for a little more than half that total.

July

The first world tour dates of Michael's first ever solo tour, beginning in Tokyo on September 12, are announced. Australia and New Zealand shows are scheduled for November and December. America, the UK and Europe will follow in 1988.

July 13

Twenty-five CBS Records' executives and representatives from record chains across the country are invited to a dinner party at Michael Jackson's Encino home in California. They are treated to a preview of the 'Bad' album and the 'Bad' video. Dinner is prepared by celebrity chef, Wolfgang Puck.

Epic announces that Michael Jackson's new album, 'Bad,' has been completed and will be released on August 31 in all configurations, album, cassette and CD. Eight of the ten songs on the LP as well as the CD bonus track, 'Leave Me Alone,' are penned by Michael. All lead and background vocals are sung by Michael except on three songs: 'Just Good Friend,' a duet with Stevie Wonder, 'I Just Can't Stop Loving You,' a duet with Siedah Garrett, and 'Man In The Mirror,' the gospel song featuring Andrae Crouch and the Andrae Crouch Choir, the Winans and Siedah Garrett.

Other musicians include: Greg Phillinganes, Steve Porcaro, David Paich, Paulinho da Costa, Michael Boddicker, Jimmy Smith, Larry Williams, John Barnes, and Billy Idol band

guitarist, Steve Stevens, is the featured soloist on 'Dirty Diana.' The album is produced by Quincy Jones, co-produced by Michael Jackson and digitally recorded and mixed by Bruce Swedien, the same team responsible for 'Off the Wall' and 'Thriller.'

The original album cover, which showed a close-up of Michael's face covered with a patterned lace net, was rejected by Walter Yetnikoff, President of CBS Records. The eventual cover was photographed during a 15-minute break from the 'Bad' video shoot.

July 15

Britain's Radio One premières 'I Just Can't Stop Loving You' on the Gary Davis Lunchtime Show.

July 22

The first single, 'I Just Can't Stop Loving You,' officially goes to radio in the US.

July 27

'I Just Can't Stop Loving You' is released worldwide. There is no video to accompany this, the first single from Michael's eagerly-awaited follow-up album to 'Thriller.'

August 8

'I Just Can't Stop Loving You' enters the Top 100 singles chart in Britain at number 5.

'I Just Can't Stop Loving You' enters the Pop and Black singles charts.

Michael appears on the cover of *Number One* magazine.

This Page: Michael records 'I Just Can't Stop Loving You' with Siedah Garrett.

Mid-August

Eleven of the fourteen Japanese shows are already sold-out - three each in Tokyo and Osaka and five in Yokohama. With total attendance expected to be more than 300,000, this is unprecedented in Japanese concert history.

August 15

'I Just Can't Stop Loving You' hits number 1 on the Top 100 singles chart in Britain in only its second week. It holds its position for two weeks and remains on the charts for nine weeks.

It is reported in the press that Michael is considering playing the lead role in a Johnny Appleseed film about a man who plants apple trees all over America and becomes a folk hero. The idea of Michael accepting the lead role upsets the Black Workers' League, who object to a Black man playing a White man's role.

Michael counters that the story appeals to all races.

Michael appears on the cover of *News Weekly*.

Britain's Radio One DJ, Mike Smith, announces that he will première Michael's new album on Thursday, August 27.

August 27

Mike Smith is prevented from playing tracks from the 'Bad' album after CBS serve a court injunction on him. He is only allowed to play two songs, 'I Just Can't Stop Loving You' and the title track. Smith tells disappointed listeners that he will find another dependable force to allow him to première the album on his Bank Holiday Monday show.

An Illinois woman, Billie Jean Jackson, files a $100 million law suit against Michael, claiming that he is the father of her three children.

August 31

'Bad' (LP) is released worldwide except in England, where August 31 is a Bank holiday.

Michael Jackson: The Magic Returns, a TV special premières worldwide, marking the release of the 'Bad' album. The 30-minute special includes a chronology of Michael's career and the full 17-minute version of his 'Bad' mini-feature. In America, *Michael Jackson: The Magic Returns* is the sixth highest-rated show of the week with 30% of 85 million TV households tuning in to see Michael Jackson.

Mike Smith premières Michael Jackson's album, 'Bad' on his Radio One morning show after obtaining an advance copy from an unknown source.

September

Michael is on the cover of *Ebony* magazine.

BAD

Michael Jackson
Epic OE 40600
EPC 83468

Side One
1. Bad
2. The Way You Make Me Feel
3. Speed Demon
4. Liberian Girl
5. Just Good Friends

Side Two
1. Another Part Of Me
2. Man In The Mirror
3. I Just Can't Stop Loving You
4. Dirty Diana
5. Smooth Criminal

1987

Forbes magazine lists Michael Jackson as the ninth highest-paid entertainer with two-year estimated earnings of $43 million.

In response to a story on plastic surgery airing on *20/20* in which Michael

Jackson is referred to as 'a plastic surgery addict,' Michael phones host Barbara Walters. He tells Walters that he has had his nose cosmetically altered twice and a cleft added to his chin but has had no other plastic surgery. He explains that his change in appearance is also due to

This Page and Opposite: Michael on the 'Bad' Tour in Japan.

his change in diet over the years, having become a vegetarian. He explains that many conclusions about his 'extensive' plastic surgery are based on comparison of photos of him when he was very young to photos of him now.

September 1
'Bad' (LP) is released in Britain with copies leaving the record shops faster than assistants can fill the shelves. A limited edition picture disc is soon to be released.

Reports abound in Britain of the opening day siege on record shops to purchase the 'Bad' album. Tower Records in London sell 200 copies in the first hour of trading while CBS estimate that some 150,000 copies will be sold at the end of the first day's trading. In America, fans queue outside shops from New York to Los Angeles and extra staff are hired to cope with the demand.

September 7
'Bad' enters the Top 100 albums chart in Britain at number 1 holding its position for five weeks and remains on the charts for 109 weeks consecutively. In the first five days of trading, 'Bad' sells over 350,000 copies - the highest ever sales of an album in Britain at this time. 'Bad' outsells the number 2 album, 'Hits 6' by ten-to-one in the first week and its sales are greater than the rest of the entire Top 40. Throughout the first week, every one in four albums sold in Britain is Michael Jackson's 'Bad.'
'Bad' (LP) also sells over 40,000 copies on CD, yet

another record, possibly enhanced by the CD's extra track, 'Leave Me Alone.' In America, 2,250,000 copies of 'Bad' are shipped to record stores, while Britain and Japan have pre-orders of 600,000 and 400,000 copies respectively 'Bad' also breaks all existing shipping records to Germany, France and Holland.

'Bad' (LP) enters the Pop and Black albums charts at number 1, holding its position for six and eighteen weeks respectively and remains on the Pop charts for eighty-seven weeks, 38 of which are spent in the Top Five. This breaks a record of 26 weeks in the Top Five set by The Eagles' 'Hotel California.'

September 9
Michael arrives at Naritas Airport in Japan, where he is besieged by fans. The airport is cordoned off to prevent him from being mobbed.

Whilst in Japan, Michael stays on the 10th floor of the Capitol Hotel, which renames its top floor of rooms, The Michael Jackson Suite.

Michael's pet chimp, Bubbles, accepts a ceremonial sword from the Japanese Prime Minister Nakasone.

September 10
Michael visits Korakuen Amusement Park, located next to the stadium where he will open his 'Bad' tour.

September 12
Michael, dubbed 'Typhoon Michael' by the Japanese, kicks off his first ever solo

tour with the first of fourteen sell-out concerts at the Korakuen Stadium, Yokohama.

Costumes for the 'Bad' tour, which at this point includes only two songs from the new album - 'I Just Can't Stop Loving You' and the title track - had to be hastily tailored in two months, due to the long delay in release. A team of fifty dressmakers and five Los Angeles shops fit out the seven piece band and quartet of dancers.

Nippon TV films one of the shows for a documentary with behind-the-scenes footage of Michael at a giant toy store and in Disneyland, Tokyo. Over 100 journalists from around the world attend the opening show, with ten from Britain alone.

The Japanese leg of the 'Bad' tour lasts for one month with Michael playing to 450,000 people at 14 concerts in three cities.

A special evening edition of *Good Morning America* which includes a live interview with Quincy Jones in Japan, is broadcast a few hours before Michael's opening concert. Jones says that Michael Jackson is not the strange being the press make him out to be.

'Thriller' and 'Off The Wall' re-enter the Top 100 albums chart in Britain peaking at numbers 15 and 36 respectively and remain on the charts for thirty-four and fifteen weeks respectively.

September 13
Michael supports a cam-

paign to stamp out racism by lending his name to the NAACP's endeavour to challenge widespread discrimination against Black artists.

September 14
Michael is on the cover of *People* magazine, 'Is This Guy Weird Or What?' In the article, Frank Dileo states that stories that Michael sleeps in a hyper-

baric chamber and tried to buy The Elephant Man's bones are untrue. He also describes stories of Michael purposely lightening his skin as preposterous.

While in Osaka, Michael is presented with the Key to the City by Mayor Oshima at a formal tea ceremony. Michael is accompanied by Bubbles.

September 19
'I Just Can't Stop Loving You' reaches number 1 on the Pop singles chart holding its position for one week and remains on the charts for fourteen weeks. The single will also rise to number 1 on the Black singles chart.

'Bad,' the second single from the album, enters the Pop singles chart at number 40. It also enters the Black singles chart.

September 24
Michael, in the form of a caricature, is on the cover of *Rolling Stone* magazine.

September 26
'Bad' enters the Top 100 singles chart in Britain

> *"If you want to make the world a better place take a look at yourself and then make that change. I am never totally satisfied. I always wish the world could be a better place. Hopefully, you know, that what I do with my music, brings happiness to people."*
> **Michael Jackson on Ebony/Jet Showcase, September 1987**

peaking at number 3 and remains on the charts for fourteen weeks. A limited edition red vinyl 12" is also released.

Michael appears on the cover of *Number One* magazine.

During one of the Japanese concerts, Michael dedicates 'I Just Can't Stop Loving You' and the remaining dates of his Japanese tour to the memory of Yoshiaki Ogiwara, a five-year-old boy who was kidnapped and horrifically murdered.

He says that the young boy's life is a tragic loss and, also donates $20,000 to the child's family.

1987

Michael receives favourable reviews in Britain for the opening night concert:

'No Pets, No Plastic, Just Raw Sex'
Today

'Japs Go Whacko Over Raunchy Jacko'
News Of The World

'100m Bonanza As World Rushes To See Bad Jacko'
The Sun

'The Greatest Show On Earth'
Daily Mirror

'Magical Michael Has His Fans In A Spell'
Daily Express

Whilst in Japan, Michael grants an exclusive interview to Mollie Mildrew for Australian TV. Mollie had interviewed Michael some ten years earlier.

Ebony/Jet Showcase airs an interview with Darryl Dennard where Michael talks about his new album and the crazy tabloid stories which often surround him.

like the old Indian proverb SAYS Do not judge a man until you've walked 2 moons in his Moccosins.
Most people don't know me, that is why they write such ~~--~~ things in wich Most is not TRUE I cry very very often Because it Hurts and I wory about the children all my children all over the World, I live for them.
If a man could say nothing AgAinsT a character but what he can prove, History could not Be written.
Animals sTrike, not from Malice, But because they want To live, it is the same with those who CRiTisize, they desire our Blood, not our pain. But still I must achieve I must seek Truth in all things. I must endure for the power I was sent forth, for the world for the children BuT Have Mercy, for I've been Bleeding a long Time now. MJ.

October
Michael closes his Japanese tour by donating 30 personal items to the United Nations Educational Scientific and Cultural Organisation for a charity auction to raise funds for educating children in developing countries.

October 11
Michael Jackson is on the cover of the *LA Times* mag-

azine with an article titled, 'The Marketing Of An Eccentric.'

October 12
Michael plays his last Japanese concert at Nishinomya Stadium in Osaka. It is reported that during his one month tour, Michael has earned over £14 million from the sale of concert tickets and merchandise.

Michael is on the cover of *People* magazine, which includes an interview with Todd Gold. In response to the adverse publicity he has been receiving since the release of 'Bad' and the outrageous rumours circulating about him, Michael makes an emotional plea in the form of a hand-written note sent to the press, which *People* magazine publish. Much of the bad publicity has upset his mother, Katherine, more than anyone and she pleads with him to fight back.

October 17
Michael is on the cover of *Fresh magazine*, 'Michael Mania Again.'

October 18
Michael is on the cover of *News Of The World's* colour supplement, 'Secret Double Life - The Real Michael Jackson Revealed.'

October 24
'Bad' reaches number 1 on the Pop and Black singles charts. It holds its position on the Pop charts for two weeks remaining on the charts for fourteen weeks.

Late October
Michael visits Ocean Park in Hong Kong.

October 31
MTV débuts Michael's video for 'The Way You Make Me Feel' featuring Tatiana Thumbtzen. When filming the final scene, in which he closely hugs Tatiana, Michael requests the set be cleared of anyone who is not necessary to the filming. The video, in which LaToya makes her second cameo appearance, is directed by Joe Pytka and choreographed by Michael and Vince Patterson.

'Love Songs' by Diana Ross and Michael Jackson enters the Top 100 albums chart in Britain peaking at number 12 and remains on the charts for twenty-six weeks.

November
Michael appears on the cover of Britain's *Q* magazine, 'Everybody Say 'AAOW' - Michael Jackson Tours - World Surrenders.'

November 11
Michael arrives in Sydney, Australia and takes an onward flight to Melbourne for the start of the Australian leg of the tour where he will play five sold-out shows to audiences totalling 135,000. Michael, dubbed 'Crocodile Jackson' by Australians, is greeted by hundreds of

screaming fans on his arrival in Melbourne. Dressed in a black and red military-style jacket, he emerges from a special exit on the plane to be greeted by aboriginal dancers.

November 12
Michael visits a children's hospital whilst in Australia.

November 13
Michael kicks off the Australian leg of the 'Bad' tour with a concert at the Olympic Park in Melbourne.

November 20, 21
Michael performs to capacity audiences at two concerts at the Paramatta Stadium in Sydney. Stevie Wonder sings on stage with Michael at one of the shows.

November 21
'The Way You Make Me Feel' enters both the Pop and Black singles charts.

November 23
'The Way You Make Me Feel' is released in Britain.

November 25, 28
Michael performs to capacity audiences of 135,000 at two concerts at Brisbane's Entertainment Centre, an indoor venue.

Concerts in Perth and Adelaide and a planned tour of New Zealand are cancelled when the Cricket Association refuse permission for chairs to be placed on the playing fields.

November 29
Tickets for Michael's first ever solo tour of Britain go on sale around the country for July 14 and 15, 1988.

It is reported that the 144,000 tickets for Michael Jackson's first two Wembley Stadium concerts sell out within three hours. Over 6,000 people queue outside Wembley's Box Office, many camping out overnight despite below-freezing temperatures. Earnings on the tickets is reported to be in the region of £2.5 million.

Michael donates £10,000 to the Children In Need Appeal in Britain.

November 30
Michael leaves Australia for the USA.

In New York, reports begin to surface that Michael Jackson and Lionel Richie are being sued for over £300 million in a copyright infringement suit. A former Jackson 5 member,

Reynaud Jones, claims that he handed over tapes of 'The Girl Is Mine,' 'Thriller' and 'We Are The World' to Joe Jackson but that he never received the £10,000 in payment.

1987

'The Way You Make Me Feel' is released as a 7" single with a competition leaflet to see Michael in concert.

'The Way You Make Me Feel' is released as a 12" single with four different mixes.

December
'Bad' is voted Best Album and Video by *Smash Hits* readers and Michael is voted Best Male Vocalist.

Page Opposite: The hand-written note from Michael published in *People* magazine, October 1987.

Michael finds some time to reflect while on tour in Japan.

This Page: Michael visits sick children in hospital.

Michael is greeted by Aboriginal dancers when he arrives in Melbourne.

'Bad,' released only four months before year's end, is the best-selling album of 1987 in Britain and the USA, with nearly two million albums sold in Britain. The album also sets a record by reaching number 1 in 25 countries around the world.

Billboard magazine's year end charts rank Michael Jackson as the ninth Top Hot Crossover Artist of 1987.

Michael is voted Best Vocal Artist of 1987 by readers of *Aftonbladet*, one of Sweden's largest newspapers. The only award of its kind in Scandinavia, this highly coveted honour has been presented to stars such as Bruce Springsteen, David Bowie and Prince.

December 5
'The Way You Make Me Feel' enters the Top 100 singles chart in Britain peaking at number 3 and remains on the charts for ten weeks.

'I Saw Mommy Kissing Santa Clause'/'Frosty The Snowman'/'Santa Claus Is Coming To Town'/'Up On The House Top' by Michael Jackson and The Jackson 5, released by Motown Records, enters the Top 100 singles chart in Britain peaking at number 91 and remains on the charts for four weeks.

December 26
'Michael Jackson Mix' (LP) released by Stylas enters the Top 100 albums chart in Britain peaking at number 27 and remains on the charts for twenty-five weeks.

1988

Fred Astaire: His Friends Talk by Sarah Giles is published. The book contains remembrances and thoughts about Fred Astaire. Among the many people making contributions to the book is Michael Jackson, who writes of his admiration for Astaire's perfectionism.

Two men from Gary, Indiana, Robert Smith and Reynaud Jones, and a third man from Chicago, Clifford Rubin file a $400 million lawsuit against Michael Jackson, Lionel Richie, Quincy Jones, Joseph Jackson and Rod Temperton, claiming their songs were used to create 'Thriller,' 'The Girl Is Mine' and 'We Are The World.' The suit will not be settled until 1994.

January

MTV airs *From Motown To Your Town*, a special including footage of Michael Jackson's career and the 'Bad' tour.

Michael Jackson wins one of his two nominations at the 15th annual American Music Awards for Best Soul/R&B Single ('Bad'). He loses to Paul Simon in the category for Best Pop/Rock Male Vocalist. Michael does not attend the award presentation.

Michael visits magicians Siegfried and Roy's *Beyond Belief Show* in Las Vegas. He had invited them to create illusions for his 'Bad' tour and, in return, wrote a special number to open their show at the Mirage Hotel in Las Vegas, 'Might In The Magic.'

The two world-famous, German-born illusionists are Las Vegas' number one entertainment attraction. Since its opening in 1981, Siegfried and Roy's spectacular illusion show has never played to a single empty seat!

A judge drops a $150 million paternity suit against Michael Jackson brought by Lavon Powlis, who calls herself 'Billie Jean Jackson.' Powlis claims Michael is the father of her three children, and she continually harasses Michael. Violating a restraining order forcing her to keep 100 yards from Michael's Encino estate, she is sentenced to two and a half years in jail. It is learned that Michael Jackson is not the only celebrity she has claimed as the father of her children.

The newest members of the Rock & Roll Hall Of Fame are inducted. Among the inductees is Motown Records founder, Berry Gordy. In accepting the honour, Gordy reads a congratulatory telegram he has received, "Congratulations. You deserve it. You are the father of fine music. Love Always. Your son, Michael Jackson."

January 23

'The Way You Make Me Feel' reaches number 1 on the Pop and Black singles charts holding its position for one and four weeks respectively and remains on the charts for eighteen and thirteen weeks respectively.

This is Michael's third number one record from a single album and it is the first time ever that he has achieved this feat, which also distinguishes him as one of only four male vocalists in the rock era to have had three consecutive number one singles.

This is also Michael's ninth solo number one record in America which places him in joint fourth position of artists with the most number ones, behind The Beatles (20), Elvis Presley (17) and The Supremes (12).

'The Way You Make Me Feel' is Michael's seventh number one solo hit of the '80s, breaking a three-way tie between himself, Madonna and Whitney Houston. He now holds the record for the most number one hits of the '80s.

February

'The Original Soul Of Michael Jackson' (LP) is released in Britain by Motown, but does not chart.

Tour rehearsals are held in Pensacola, Florida at the Pensacola Civic Center. *Entertainment Tonight's* co-host Mary Hart is very impressed with what she sees when she visits the rehearsals. "It's a pretty awesome experience to watch him rehearse," she says. "He knows exactly what he wants and how to get it. He's very much in charge!"

While in Florida, Michael is invited to an antique bookstore and is offered a first edition of *The Elephant Man* by Frederick Treves, the doctor who befriended John Merrick, The Elephant Man.

Page Opposite: Michael on the Bad tour.

This Page: Michael meets magicians Siegfried and Roy (either side of Michael) with manager, Frank Dileo.

1988

This Page: Michael greets the winners of Pepsi's BAD Campaign (Be Against Drugs) at a specially arranged Press Conference on March 1, 1988.

Michael gets closer than close to dancer Tatiana Thumbtzen in a sizzling performance of 'The Way You Make Me Feel' at New York's Madison Square Garden.

February 6

'Man In The Mirror' enters the Pop and Black singles charts. The video for the single is a compilation of footage depicting starving children, the homeless, and some of the people who have made a difference. Michael's royalties from the single are donated to Camp Ronald McDonald For Good Times, a camp for children with cancer.

February 8

Michael Jackson is named Best International Solo Artist at the 7th Annual British Phonographic Industry Awards (The Brits) in London.

February 20

'Man In The Mirror,' released in Britain on February 8, enters the Top 100 singles chart peaking at number 21 and remains on the charts for five weeks. The song is also issued as a square picture disc.

February 23, 24

Michael kicks off his first ever solo tour of America in Kansas City performing to an audience of 33,918 during two sell-out shows at the Kemper Arena. The standing room only concerts bring in some $700,000, $200,000 more than any other artist has ever achieved at the venue, including Elvis Presley.

Early 1988

Michael, accompanied by Bubbles attends the wedding of his attorney, John Branca to Julie McArthur.

March 1

Michael attends a specially arranged Press Conference with Pepsi to preview the new four-part Pepsi ads and to present a $600,000 cheque to The United Negro College Fund, monies earned from ticket sales for his March 3 Madison Square Garden concert. Pepsi link the conference via satellite from Manhattan's 1018 Club to journalists across the world, in the hope that Michael will take part in a question and answer session. However, all they get is a 15-word 'Thankyou' speech.

March 2

At the 30th Annual Grammy Awards at Radio City Music Hall in New York City, Michael brings the house down in one of his rare, live television appearances with a spellbinding performance of 'The Way You Make Me Feel' and 'Man In The Mirror.' Although 'Bad' is the world's best-selling album of 1987 and has reached number one in over twenty-five countries, he wins in only one of his four nominated categories for Best Engineered Recording.

In the weeks following the Grammy telecast, *Billboard* magazine reports that sales of 'Bad' rise higher than those of U2's 'The Joshua Tree,' the LP which *did* win the 1988 Album of the Year Grammy!

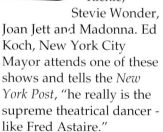

The Grammy telecast premières another set of innovative Pepsi commercials by Michael Jackson. The commercials are so popular, they are requested specifically by Soviet officials to be aired on Soviet television. They are the first American ads to air in the Soviet Union, and are seen by an estimated 150 million Soviets.

March 3, 4, 5

Michael performs to a capacity audience of 57,000 at three sell-out shows at Madison Square Garden, New York. During one of these shows, Michael hits the headlines for kissing Tatiana Thumbtzen on stage during 'The Way You Make Me Feel.' Amongst celebrity guests for these shows are Brooke Shields, Quincy Jones, Prince, Lionel Richie, Stevie Wonder, Joan Jett and Madonna. Ed Koch, New York City Mayor attends one of these shows and tells the *New York Post*, "he really is the supreme theatrical dancer - like Fred Astaire."

Concerts scheduled for St. Louis, Missouri, the tour's next stop, are cancelled due to Michael's cold and laryngitis.

March 8

It's *Michael Jackson Weekend* on MTV in America. The

1988

video network features Michael's videos, specials and concert reports throughout the weekend.

March 10

Michael is honoured by the United Negro College Fund as one of their highest contributors at the 44th annual anniversary dinner held at the Sheraton Hotel in New York. He receives their highest honour, the Frederick D. Patterson Award for his continued efforts towards alleviating world hunger, helping terminally ill children and for his inspirational example to the youth of America. This is a special moment for Michael with his Michael Jackson Scholarship Fund, set up in 1984, having provided 97 scholarship awards. Michael scholars have been enrolled in almost every one of UNCF's 42 schools.

At the 2nd annual Soul Train Awards, Michael wins two of his three nominations for Best Single, Male ('Bad') and Best Album, Male ('Bad'). 'The Way You Make Me Feel' loses in the category Best Video to Janet's 'Control' video. Neither Michael nor Janet attend the presentation ceremonies.

Michael agrees to a charity auction being held at his Encino home. The auction raises some $2 million which are donated to the South African Council of Churches for housing, clothing and medical supplies. Whoopi Goldberg hosts the auction.

March 12, 13

Michael performs to capacity audiences of 36,000 at two shows at The Arena, St. Louis in Missouri.

March 12

The US cable network, Showtime, airs *Motown on Showtime: Michael Jackson... The Legend Continues*. Michael is one of the executive producers of the programme, which includes footage from his entire career. The special is nominated for a Cable Ace Award for Outstanding Musical Special along with *From Your Town to Motown*. The award goes to Billy Joel. *Michael Jackson... The Legend Continues* receives the ACE Award for Outstanding Editing in a Musical Special.

"I would like to say this about the United Negro College Fund. An education opens a person's mind to the entire world, and there is nothing more important than to make sure everyone has the opportunity for an education. To want to learn, to have the capacity to learn and not to be able to is a tragedy. I am honoured to be associated with an evening that says this will never happen."

Michael Jackson, March 10, 1988

March 14

Michael cancels a third concert at The Arena due to illness.

March 18, 19

Michael performs two concerts at the Market Square Arena in Indianapolis, Indiana.

This Page: Michael is honoured by The UNCF, with good friends Quincy Jones and Whitney Houston amongst those who also pay respect.

Michael in one of the new Pepsi commercials.

1988

March 20
Michael performs in concert at Freedom Hall, Louisville, Kentucky.

Michael is on the cover of *Jet* magazine.

March 23, 24
Michael performs to capacity audiences of 40,251 at two shows at McNichols Arena in Denver, Colorado.

March 26
'Man In The Mirror' reaches number 1 on the Pop and Black singles charts. It holds its position for two weeks and one week respectively remaining on the charts for seventeen and fourteen weeks respectively.

With 'Man In The Mirror' reaching number one, Michael is now the first artist ever to have four number one singles from one album. 'Bad' is only the second album to have spawned four top charting singles, the other being the soundtrack to *Saturday Night Fever*.

Michael also becomes the first artist to have four consecutive number one singles as a member of a group and as a solo artist. He is also the first artist to have four Top Ten hits from three consecutive albums.

Billboard magazine names Michael Jackson as the third most successful songwriter of the year. Michael has written three number one singles this year: 'I Just Can't Stop Loving You,' 'Bad' and 'The

Way You Make Me Feel.' Whilst in New York, . Michael escorts Liza Minnelli to Broadway's top stage hit, *Phantom Of The Opera,* where they meet the show's stars, Michael Crawford and Sarah Brightman, backstage.

Two more additional Wembley dates are announced for Michael's 'Bad' tour of Britain for July 26 and 27. This brings the total number of concerts to seven making him the first artist ever to perform so many concerts at Wembley during one tour.

It is reported that the 'Bad' album has sold 1,850,000 copies in Britain since September 1987.

March 30, 31, April 1
Michael performs to capacity audiences of 45,188 at three shows at the Civic Center in Hartford, Connecticut.

April
'Fat' by 'Weird Al' Yankovic is released from his album, 'Even Worse.' 'Fat' is another parody by Yankovic of Michael Jackson, this time reworking the lyrics and video to 'Bad.' Michael, who again gives permission to Yankovic to use his music, reportedly loves the hilarious result.

Friday Night Videos is dedicated entirely to Michael Jackson videos. It is the first time the video programme has ever been devoted to just one artist.

At a pop auction at Philips in London, a pair of purple stage shoes (glass studded)

and a stage shirt worn by Michael Jackson are bought by the Hard Rock Café for £4,400. The *Daily Star* newspaper purchases Michael's silver lamé stage costume, a pair of stage shoes, a personally signed photograph and a Motown album signed by The Jackson 5.

April 8, 9, 10
Michael performs in concert at The Summit in Houston, Texas.

April 13, 14, 15
Michael performs in concert at The Omni in Atlanta, Georgia where tickets are given to the children's charity for terminally ill children, Make A Wish Foundation.

April 14
The video for 'Dirty Diana' premières on MTV. It is Michael's first performance video, filmed in Long Beach, California.

April 16
'I Want You Back ('88 Remix)' released on Motown enters the Top 100 singles chart in Britain peaking at number 8 and remains on the charts for nine weeks. The accompanying video comprises a compilation from The Jackson 5's Cartoon Show.

April 19, 20, 21
Michael performs to capacity audiences at three dates at The Rosemont Horizon in Chicago, Illinois, where he is presented with the Key to the City by Mayor Eugene Sawyer.

April 20
Moonwalk, Michael Jackson's long-awaited autobiography, which has

been edited by Jacqueline Onassis, is published by Doubleday. Within two weeks, *Moonwalk* is top of the Best Sellers List in Britain with the first 70,000 print run having sold out. A reprint of 12,500 is ordered, followed by a second reprint of 30,500 a week later.

In America, *Moonwalk* enters the Best Sellers' Lists of the *Los Angeles Times* at number one and the *New York Times* at number two, moving up to the number one position in its second week on the chart. These two book charts are considered the most important in the publishing industry. Within a few months, it is announced that *Moonwalk* has sold in excess of 450,000 copies in fourteen countries around the world.

Michael dedicates *Moonwalk* to one of his all-time idols, the late, great, Fred Astaire.

April 23
'Get It' enters the Black singles chart peaking at number 4 and remains on the charts for eleven weeks.

April 25, 26, 27
Michael performs in concert at The Reunion Arena in Dallas, Texas.

April 30
'Dirty Diana' enters the Black singles chart peaking at number 5 and remains on the charts for thirteen weeks.

People magazine airs a TV special featuring The Jacksons. Joseph Jackson denies Michael's claims of child abuse made in *Moonwalk*, describing beat-ings as 'little spankings.' In an interview, Marlon agrees with Michael, saying they were hit - and often.

May
Michael Jackson moves out of Hayvenhurst, the family's Encino home, to his recently purchased ranch in the Santa Ynez Valley about 100 miles north of Los Angeles. The 2,700 acre Sycamore Valley Ranch is soon renamed Neverland Valley Ranch from Michael's favourite book, *Peter Pan*, the boy from Never Never Land. The purchase price is widely reported at $28 million, though other sources say the actual price is $17 million.

Another date is added to the already lengthy British tour schedule. Michael will perform at the famous Aintree Racecourse in Liverpool - home of his heroes, The Beatles.

May 4, 5, 6
Michael performs to capacity audiences of 50,662 at three concerts at the Metropolitan Center, Minneapolis, Minn.

These are the last of thirty concerts on the first leg of the US tour, during which half a million Americans came to see Michael performing live.

May 7
'Get It' enters the Pop singles chart peaking at number 80 and remains on the charts for six weeks.

May 16
Michael is on the cover of *Jet* magazine.

May 18
Michael's *Moonwalker* is previewed at the Cannes Film Festival in the South of France. The film is scheduled for a Christmas release.

May 19
Michael arrives at Leonardo Da Vinci Airport, Rome in Italy in preparation for the opening night concert of the European leg of his 'Bad' world tour. He is escorted twelve miles into the city. Whilst in Rome, Michael stays at the luxury Lord Byron Hotel.

May 21
Michael visits the Sistine Chapel in the Vatican where Michelangelo masterpieces have been carefully restored. Michael is accompanied by US Ambassador Maxwell Rabb.

It is reported that Michael plans to meet with the Pope in the Vatican during his visit to Rome.

May 22
Michael visits sick children aged five to twelve in two wards at the Bambin Gesu Children's Hospital in Rome. He signs autographs and hands out candy, albums and tapes to the children, promising to donate £100,000 to the hospital.

May 23
Michael kicks off the European leg of his 'Bad' tour with the first of two concerts at the Flaminio Stadio in Rome, where he plays to audiences of 70,000. Although suffering from laryngitis, Michael refuses to disappoint his Roman fans and the show

1988

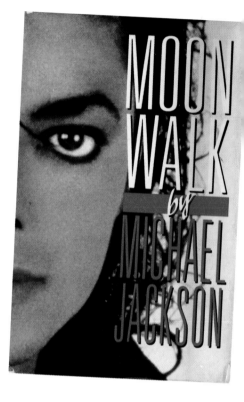

1988

goes ahead as planned. Two of the celebrity guests at this show are Sophia Loren and Gina Lollobrigida, who have not spoken to each other for years until Michael brings them together for a photo.

An after-show party is held at the 16th Century Palazzo Taverna. Michael makes a brief appearance and is greeted by guests Sophia Loren, Gina Lollobrigida, Federico Fellini and Georgio Armani.

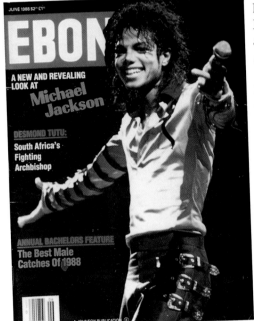

It is announced that Pepsi is to donate over 4,000 tickets from his UK concerts to ITV's Telethon, which will raise some £200,000 for Great Ormond Street Children's Hospital.

May 24
Michael performs his second concert at the Flaminio Stadio in Rome.

May 25
The Pope is unable to meet Michael due to a backlog of engagements which has built up during the Pope's visit to South America.

Michael is the guest of honour at a party at the house of film director, Franco Zeffirelli.

May 28
'Get It' by Stevie Wonder and Michael Jackson enters the Top 100 singles chart in Britain peaking at number 37 and remains on the charts for four weeks. The

song is taken from 'Characters' (LP) by Stevie Wonder.

May 29
Michael performs in concert to an audience of 53,600 in Turin, Italy.

Michael's Italian concerts reportedly produce two bootleg CDs, 'My Way,' a taping of a show on May 23 and 'Michael Jackson Live,' the taping of a concert on May 29.

May 30
A concert in Lyon, France, is cancelled after only half of the 30,000 tickets are sold.

Captain EO Backstage is aired in America, hosted by Whoopi Goldberg. The TV special goes behind the scenes of *Captain EO*, showing dance rehearsals, make-up and special effects.

June
Memorabilia from music stars is auctioned off with the proceeds being donated to the T. J. Martell Foundation For Leukemia, Cancer, and AIDS Research. A black fedora signed by Michael Jackson brings a winning bid of $4,125.

The Inland Revenue agree to drop a £3 million claim against Michael before his tour arrives in Britain. Michael's promoters find a loophole in the tax laws which prevent their client from paying the 25% earnings demand that is usually paid before a final assessment is made.

Michael is on the cover of *Ebony* magazine.

June 1
Michael sets another record as the first artist ever to have three albums with US sales of more than six million copies each. On June 1, both 'Bad' and 'Off the Wall' simultaneously pass the benchmark figure, with total worldwide sales of each album now at 15 and 9 million respectively. Michael's 'Thriller' is still the best-selling album of all time, with global sales of over 40 million units.

June 2
Michael performs to a capacity audience of 55,000 at a sell-out concert at the Prater Stadium in Vienna, Austria.

June 3
'Michael Jackson: The Legend Continues...' is released by Motown Video and within days becomes Britain's fastest-selling video.

June 5, 6, 7
Michael performs to capacity audiences of 145,200 at three concerts at the Feyenoord Stadium in Rotterdam, Holland.

June 11, 12
Michael performs to capacity audiences of 106,000 at two concerts in Gothenburg, Sweden.

June 16
Michael performs before a capacity audience of 50,000 at a sell-out concert at St. Jakobe Stadium in Basel, Switzerland. Amongst celebrities at this show are Elizabeth Taylor and Bob Dylan.

While in Basel, Michael meets Mrs. Oona Chaplin, the widow of one of his heroes, Charlie Chaplin.

Page Opposite: Michael giving it all he's got on the 'Bad' 1988 tour.

June 19

Michael performs to an audience of 50,000 at the Berlin Wall, West Germany where clashes with police break out as they charge into thousands of young East German fans. The East Germans gather at the Brandenburg Gate to listen to Michael's concert being held at the Reichstag in the West. Just hours before Michael's 'Bad' concert is due to begin, the East Germans try to upstage his arrival by presenting their own concert, which is MC'd by Katarina Witt, the East German World Ice Skating Champion. Among the artists performing are Bryan Adams and Big Country.

Unfortunately, it is the Brandenburg Gate violence which headlines in the tabloids and not Michael's music, which is usually synonymous with bringing people of all nations and races together.

June 27, 28

Michael performs to capacity audiences of 128,000 at two concerts at the Parc de Prince in Paris, France. Amongst the celebrities at this show are Grace Jones and designer, Patrick Kelly.

Whilst in France, Mayor Chirac presents Michael with La Grande Medaille de la Ville de Paris, an honour usually given only to heads of state.

Tickets go on sale for the second US leg of the 'Bad' tour, four to six months in advance of the show's scheduled dates. Tickets sell out quickly, with three shows scheduled in most cities.

July 1

The first ever issue of *Off The Wall* magazine is published by Adrian Grant, who names the fanzine after his favourite Michael Jackson LP. Only 200 copies of the first issue are ever available, but it isn't long before readership grows around the world, being read not only by Michael's fans, but also by the man himself!

Michael performs to an audience of 50,000 at the Volkspark Stadium in Hamburg, Germany, which Opera star Placido Domingo attends.

Michael is on the cover of *News Weekly*.

Within ten minutes of 'Bad' concert tickets going on sale for the Milton Keynes Bowl show on September 10, the city's telephone network is jammed with calls from fans wanting to purchase tickets.

Whilst on tour in Germany, Michael falls in love with the 19th Century Carousel at Phantasialand in Cologne and it is reported that he offers the Park owners, Richard Schmidt and Gottlieb Löffelhardt a healthy profit on the £160,000 they paid for the Italian-built roundabout.

Also in Cologne, Michael purchases two lifelike dolls called Kasimir and Frederike for £650.

Marcelle Avron, Managing Director of Mama Concerts, the promoters of his European tour, reveals that Michael is earning over £3,425 a minute for his European shows. Michael has negotiated a deal worth £20 million, of which he receives 90% of the proceeds from all concert projects. After paying his entourage of 140, he is left with profits of around £400,000 per show.

July 2

'Dirty Diana,' which entered the chart on May 7, reaches number 1 on the Pop singles chart holding its position for one week and remains on the charts for fourteen weeks. The record reaches number 5 on the Black singles chart.

With 'Dirty Diana' reaching number one on the Pop singles chart, Michael Jackson becomes the first artist to have five or more Top Ten hits from two consecutive albums; 'Thriller' enjoyed seven Top Ten hits, and 'Dirty Diana' is the fifth Top Ten hit from the 'Bad' album.

July 3

Michael performs to a capacity audience of 70,000 at Müngersdorfer Stadium in Cologne, Germany.

July 8

Michael performs to a capacity audience of 72,000 at a sell-out concert at the Olympic Stadium in Munich, Germany.

July 10

Michael performs to a capacity audience of 70,000 at a sell-out concert at the Müngersdorfer Stadium in Cologne, Germany.

July 11

Michael arrives, two hours late, at London's Heathrow Airport where the rooftop is lined with thousands of fans, hoping for a glimpse of the superstar. Transport is brought to a standstill in London as Michael leaves to check in to the Mayfair Hotel, where he has a suite of rooms on the 7th floor. Among his road crew of 120, are Michael's personal entourage of 20, including his doctor, dentist, throat specialist, manicurist, chiropodist, masseur, hairdresser, two secretaries, chef and seven minders.

Michael is unable to bring his pet chimpanzee, Bubbles, into the country because of Britain's strict anti-rabies laws forcing any animal to be quarantined for six months.

July 12

Michael visits Hamley's toy store in London.

July 13

Michael visits children at Great Ormond Street Hospital, London while his fans camp out all night at Wembley in order to secure front row positions at the opening concert.

July 14-16, 22, 23

At 8.20 p.m. on a damp and otherwise nondescript night, Michael sets Wembley alight when he opens his show to a thunderous reception from 72,000 fans at the first of five sell-out concerts at the Stadium. Opening for Michael on his European dates is MCA recording star, Kim Wilde. Amongst the celebrities at the opening night are Jack Nicholson, Terence Trent D'Arby, Dead or Alive, Billy Connelly, Adam Faith, Russ Abbott, Jane Seymour, John Peel, Valerie Singleton, Shirley Bassey, George Lucas, Harrison Ford and Frank Bruno.

July 16

Prince Charles and Princess Diana attend the third Wembley concert of the 'Bad' tour. Michael meets the Prince and Princess of Wales backstage before the show. He presents the Royal couple with specially-made tour jackets for Prince William and Prince Harry, and a special presentation collection of his recordings. Michael also presents a cheque for £150,000 for the Prince's Trust and another for £100,000 to Great Ormond Street Children's Hospital.

'Dirty Diana' enters the Top 100 singles chart in Britain peaking at number 4 and remains on the charts for eight weeks.

'Fat' by 'Weird Al' Yankovic, the tongue-in-cheek version of Michael's 'Bad' song enters the Top 100 singles chart in Britain peaking at number 80 and remains on the charts for four weeks.

July 18

Michael spends the day with his companion, Jimmy Safechuck, seeing the sights of London by car. Before returning to the hotel in the early hours of the morning, they visit Elstree Studios where his friend, Steven Spielberg, is directing his latest film, *Indiana Jones And The Last Crusade*, and both meet Harrison Ford.

July 20

Michael visits Great Ormond Street Hospital and meets many of Britain's terminally ill children. On one of the wards where the children are less critical, he spends time telling them a story.

In the evening, a banquet is held in Michael's honour at the Guildhall, London, to celebrate the British leg of the tour.

July 22

Mickey Mouse and Donald Duck characters present Michael with a pair of specially engraved ice skates backstage before his concert.

July 23

Michael is on the cover *Hello!* magazine.

July 26

Michael performs to a capacity audience of 55,000 at a concert at Cardiff Arms Park in Wales, where he is dubbed, 'The Prince Of Wails' by the crowd.

'Another Part Of Me,' taken from the score of *Captain EO*, enters the Pop and Black singles charts peaking at numbers 11 and 1 respectively and remains on the Pop charts for thirteen weeks.

By peaking at number 11, the single breaks a string of Top Ten hits for Michael of 17 songs. However, it becomes the album's fifth number one hit on the Black singles chart, tying a record for the most number one hits from the same album with Janet, who had five number one hits on the Black charts from her album, 'Control.'

'Another Part Of Me' is Michael's ninth number one hit on the Black singles chart, making him the artist with the most number one hits ever on this chart.

July 30, 31

Michael performs to capacity audiences of 120,000 at two concerts in Cork, Eire, despite suffering from a sore ankle, an injury sustained during the Welsh Cardiff Arms Park concert.

July 30

Michael is on the cover of *Number One* magazine.

'Michael Jackson And The Jackson 5 18 Greatest Hits' re-enters the Top 100 albums chart in Britain peaking at number 85 and remains on the charts for three weeks.

'Bad Souvenir Singles Pack,' a special collection of six square picture discs released to commemorate the 'Bad' tour, enters the Top 100 albums chart in Britain peaking at number 91 and remains on the charts for one week.

Michael Jackson: Around The World, a 90-minute Michael Jackson special featuring concert footage of the 'Bad' tour airs. 'Another Part Of

Cynthia Horner has known Michael ever since she became Editor of *Right On!* when Michael was 18. She is honoured to learn that she is the first and only media person to be invited by Michael to stay at his hotel. The band and most members of his organisation are checked in to another hotel a few streets away from the Mayfair.

Horner reports on her experience at Wembley, saying: *"Once we arrived at Wembley Stadium, I was immediately escorted to Michael's private dressing room where a shivering Michael smiled and teased me as he waited to meet a few contest winners. Unlike other performers, Michael doesn't like to have a lot of people around him prior to a show. He spends most of his time getting ready and meeting selected guests."*

Horner, who has had plenty of opportunity to observe his behaviour around other people, says: *"He's usually quiet and rather humble. However, it may sound strange to say but people feel energy drawing from him, almost as though he's endowed with superhuman powers. People are usually so struck by him that they cannot even speak. Indeed, Michael weaves a magic spell over his fans. Michael seems to be more open and outgoing around children, especially those he knows well."*

Her overall comment on Michael's performance: *"Michael Jackson on stage is as good as it gets!"*

Page Opposite: Michael on the 'Bad' tour.

1988

Me' is also premièred. It is the highest-rated summer special ever in America in its 11.30 p.m. time slot, with 27% of the television audience tuning in.

August

Frank Dileo holds a press conference to announce that the 'Bad' tour will be Michael Jackson's last.

August 5

Michael performs to a capacity audience of 28,000 at a concert in Marbella, Spain.

Whilst in Spain, Michael hires the Incosol Health Farm at a cost of £50,000 per week.

August 7

Michael performs to a capacity audience of 60,000 at a concert at Vicente Calderón in Madrid, Spain.

Whilst in Spain, Michael is presented with a quad-ruple Platinum Award for 'Bad' before his concert.

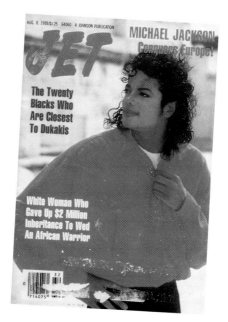

August 8

Michael is on the cover of *Jet* magazine.

August 9

Michael performs in concert at Nou Camp in Barcelona, Spain.

August 21

Michael performs to a capacity audience of 43,000 at a concert at Talavera Wiesen in Würzburg, Germany.

August 23

Michael performs to a capacity audience of 55,000 at a concert in Werchter, near Brussels in Belgium.

This Page: It's not a ghost, it's not a plane, it is indeed, Michael Jackson

August 26, 27

On the first evening of his last two appearances at Wembley Stadium Michael asks the crowd to pray for Elizabeth Taylor, who is suffering from a painful illness. He dedicates 'I Just Can't Stop Loving You' to his close friend, saying:

"I have a very important message to make. Can I have everybody's attention. A very, very dear friend of mine is very, very sick tonight and the pain that she is experiencing is unbearable. So I ask that everyone in the Stadium tonight just bow their heads for five seconds to Elizabeth Taylor. And Elizabeth. I dedicate this song to Elizabeth. Thank you very much."

Earlier in the day, Michael returns to Madame Tussaud's for a private visit with his mother, Katherine.

August 29

Michael performs to a capacity audience at a concert at Roundhay Park in Leeds, England. Michael is 30 years old today and following his performance of 'Heartbreak Hotel,' 90,000 voices unite to sing 'Happy Birthday.' His mother, Katherine and sister, Janet are in Britain to congratulate him. The concert is a benefit for the British charity, Give For Life. The organisation's goal is to raise £1 million towards immunising children. Michael donates £65,000 to the charity.

Earlier in the day, Michael greets fans from his hotel balcony in his own inimitable way - wrapped in a net curtain - and throws heart-rending messages of affection to his loyal following gathered at the hotel to wish him a happy birthday. One of these messages reads: "You all have really proved your loyalty to me. I wish I could truly look you in the eyes and talk to you all, but I'm too shy. It sounds silly but it's true. I truly love all of you very much."

On another note, Michael writes: "Don't believe all the strange stories that people make up about me. Sometimes I cry, but it's fans like you that make me endure."

A party is held by CBS Records at London's Guildhall to celebrate Michael's birthday and to recognise the success of the 'Bad' album and tour.

September

The Flintstone Kids airs. The cartoon featuring young Fred, Barney, Wilma and Betty, have the kids earning extra money to attend the Michael Jackstone concert. Michael lends his song 'Beat It' to the cartoon, allowing the song to be re-worked with new lyrics encouraging kids to stay away from drugs.

September 2

Michael performs in concert at the Niedersachsen Stadium in Hannover, Germany. However, due to bad weather conditions, instead of flying, Michael decides to take the ferry to Hannover. Unbeknown to 2,000 holiday-makers, he travels from Dover to Calais on P&O's flagship, Pride Of Dover - but remains in a limousine with darkened windows.

September 4
Michael performs to an audience of 52,000 at the Park Stadium in Gelsenkirchen, Germany.

September 6
Michael performs in concert in Linz, Austria.

September 7
Michael Jackson receives the MTV Video Vanguard Award from 1987's recipient, Peter Gabriel. Following the presentation, a specially taped performance of 'Bad' from Wembley is aired.

September 8
Michael is presented with an award by Wembley

European concert to a capacity audience of 125,000 at Aintree Racecourse in Liverpool - the largest concert audience ever at the racetrack.

In a rush to the front, some fans are injured when they are crushed against the stage.

The 'Bad' tour is the largest tour ever in Britain, playing to over 800,000 fans and grossing over £13 million.

Stadium Management for setting a new record for playing more dates at Wembley Stadium than any other artist. Michael's seven sell-out concerts were attended by 504,000 people. His achievement also gains him another entry in *The Guinness Book Of World Records*.

September 10
Michael performs to a capacity audience of 60,000 at a concert at The Bowl in Milton Keynes.

September 11
Michael performs his final

Autumn
Bubbles is a guest on *Dick Clark Live!*, bringing a note from his master, which reads: "Dear Dick, I am giving Bubbles the night off so he can come play on your show. Sincerely, Michael Jackson." Bubbles performs some of his tricks on the show, including the moonwalk!

September 12
Michael leaves Britain at the end of his massively successful European tour to begin the second leg of his American tour.

Forbes magazine lists Michael Jackson as the number one highest-paid entertainer with two-year estimated earnings of $97 million.

'Live' (LP) by Michael Jackson and The Jackson 5

is released by Motown but it does not enter the charts.

September 19
MTV presents a Michael Jackson Marathon, airing back-to-back Michael Jackson specials: *From Motown To Your Town*, *Another Part Of Me* and *The Making Of Michael Jackson's Thriller*.

September 22
As the 'Bad' tour comes to town in Pittsburg, Pennsylvania - Frank Dileo's hometown - it is declared 'Frank Dileo Day.'

September 26, 27, 28
Michael performs his opening concerts in America to a capacity audience of 48,694 at three sell-out shows at the Civic Arena in Pittsburg, PA.

October 3, 4, 5
Michael performs to capacity audiences of 61,061 at three concerts at East Meadowland Arena in Rutherford, New Jersey.

October 10, 11
Michael performs to

This Page: Michael brings the excitement of his videos to the stage on his 'Bad' tour.

Michael receives the MTV Video Vanguard Award from Peter Gabriel.

Michael shares his emotions on stage.

This Page and Opposite: Michael in the 'Smooth Criminal' video.

Michael with Frank Dileo, on the set of *Moonwalker*.

capacity audiences of 38,000 at two concerts at the Coliseum in Richfield, Ohio.

October 11
British fans are given first chance of seeing the Michael Jackson *Moonwalker* movie at a special screening in London, thanks to *Off The Wall* and *Time Out* magazines.

October 13, 17-19
Michael performs to capacity audiences of 69,883 at four concerts at the Capitol Center Landover in Washington.

October 13
MTV premières the video for 'Smooth Criminal.'

October 23
In a brief ceremony outside the old Motown recording studio, Michael Jackson presents Esther Edwards and Berry Gordy with a cheque for the sum of $125,000 for the Motown Museum Historical Foundation. Michael also donates a black fedora, one of his famous rhinestone gloves and a costume he wore on American Bandstand in 1972 when he performed 'Ben.'

October 24-26
Michael performs to an audience of over 50,000 at three concerts at the Palace of Auburn in Rochester, Minn. The first concert is a benefit for the Motown Museum.

Late October
Moonwalker makes its début in Japanese theatres.

October 31-Nov. 2
Michael cancels three concerts scheduled to take place at the Dome in Tacoma, Washington when his vocal cords become swollen. The concerts, which were sold out, are not rescheduled.

November
Michael Jackson is named as an honouree in the music category of the American Black Achievement Awards.

Ebony magazine names Michael Jackson as one of the '20 People to Watch in 1989.'

The Winter 1988 issue of *Right On!* magazine is a special collectors edition devoted entirely to Michael Jackson.

Los Angeles Mayor, Tom Bradley, declares November to be 'Michael Jackson Month.'

November 7-9
Michael performs to capacity audiences of 45,000 at three concerts in Irvine Meadows, Laguna Hills, California. When tickets for these shows went on sale, the first two shows sold out in a record 47 minutes. Within another hour, tickets for the remaining show were also sold out.

November 12
'Smooth Criminal' enters the Pop and Black singles charts peaking at numbers 7 and 2 respectively and remains on the both charts for fifteen weeks.

November 13
Michael performs to a capacity audience of 18,000 at a concert at the Sports Arena in Los Angeles, California.

Nov. 14, 15, 20-22
Michael cancels five further concerts, scheduled to take place at the Sports Arena, due to illness. These dates are rescheduled for January, 1989.

November 18
Billboard magazine celebrates the 101st anniversary of CBS Records. Included in the salute to the record company is a full-page congratulatory ad from the company's biggest-selling artist:

"The joy of music... to inspire the young and the old... To make the world a better place.

Michael Jackson Congratulations."

November 21
A 'Smooth Criminal' limited edition souvenir pack is issued including four colour postcards from *Moonwalker*.

November 26
'Smooth Criminal' released on November 14 enters the Top 100 singles chart in Britain at number 12, peaking the following week at number 8 and remains on the charts for ten weeks.

Michael Jackson's album 'Bad' is now the first in chart history to yield seven Top 40 singles in Britain.

November 28
A limited edition 12" Avant calendar single is issued in a gatefold sleeve. In all, 'Smooth Criminal' is issued in six formats: 2 x 7", 3 x 12" and CD.

December
Michael is voted Best Male Vocalist at the *Smash Hits* Poll Winners' Party for the second consecutive year, and accepts his award via satellite.

Friday Night Videos is devoted entirely to Michael Jackson videos, for the second time. The show is hosted by Ahmad Rashad.

Dec. 9-11/17-19/24-26
Michael begins the second leg of his Japanese tour with nine sell-out dates at the Tokyo Dome, formerly Korakuen Stadium, now roofed and renamed. Attendance figures are said to be four times greater than for any other tour.

December 11
Frank Dileo arrives in Britain to promote *Moonwalker*, along with the young star who performs 'Bad' in the film, Brandon Adams.

December 26
Moonwalker is rush-released at cinemas across Britain, with long queues being reported all over the country. Described as a 'magical musical journey into the world of Michael Jackson,' it tells the story of good overcoming evil.

Michael performs his last concert of the Japanese leg of the tour with Frank Dileo announcing that this will be Michael's last world tour.

Late December
Reports appear in the press that Michael has been making compassionate visits to the bedside of David Rothenburg, a 12-year-old who was hospitalised after his father set him alight in an act of revenge against his estranged wife. David was only seven years old when he suffered the cruel attack.

'Bad' is the biggest-selling album of the year again in America, and it is also the year's biggest-selling album in Great Britain.

MTV counts down the Top 100 videos of 1988 with Michael Jackson having the most entries on the chart with 'Another Part Of Me,' 'Smooth Criminal,' 'The Way You Make Me Feel,' 'Dirty Diana' and 'Man In The Mirror.' The latter ranked as the fifth video of the year, is Michael's highest placing.

Blues & Soul magazine Readers' Poll names Michael Jackson as the 1988 Outstanding Artist of the Year. The 'Bad' tour is voted as the Best Live Show of 1988.

Record Mirror votes Michael Jackson Artist Of The Year.

It is reported that throughout 1988, Michael Jackson has appeared on the covers of over one hundred magazines.

A Gallup Poll taken in Great Britain shows that the members of the Royal Family are the nation's most popular personalities. Respondents to the Poll under the age of 25, however, name Michael Jackson as their number one choice.

Video Storyboard Tests conduct a survey to determine the Top Ten Outstanding TV Campaigns. Diet Pepsi ads featuring actor, Michael J. Fox and *The Chase*, starring Michael Jackson, are rated number one.

1989

1989

The first week of the year shows Michael with three entries in the Top 100 albums chart in Britain: 'Thriller' at 79, 'Love Songs, Michael Jackson and Diana Ross' at 66 and 'Bad' at 9.

'Say Yes To A Youngster's Future' programme honours Michael Jackson for his role in encouraging elementary school children to study mathematics and science, by presenting him with the National Urban Coalition Artist/ Humanitarian Of The Year Award.

In *The Sun* newspaper's Readers' Poll in Britain, Michael is voted Top International Male with 2,782 votes against runner-up, Prince, with 892 votes.

Rolling Stone magazine, which generally caters to hard rock bands and their fans, publishes the results of its 1988 Readers' Poll with disappointing results for Michael Jackson. He is voted the number one Worst Male Singer, Most Unwelcome Comeback, and Worst Dressed Male Singer. 'Bad' is voted as the number four Worst Album, and the number four Worst Album Cover. 'Bad' is chosen as the number three Worst Video, with 'Smooth Criminal' at number five. The Poll ranks the 'Bad' tour as the second Worst Tour of the Year.

US magazine's Readers' Poll isn't any better with Michael voted as the Most Unwelcome Comeback, 'Bad' is chosen as the Worst Album and 'Bad' is ranked as the number two Worst Single.

Ebony magazine's Readers' Poll has much different results with 'Thriller' being voted the readers' Favourite Video Of All Time.

January

The highest-rated show in America, *The Cosby Show*, has the Huxtable family attending a Michael Jackson concert.

January 2

MTV premières the video for 'Leave Me Alone.' The song is not officially released as a single in America, although it, and the video, do receive considerable airplay. The video features a unique blend of animation and live action and shows Michael's humourous side while addressing some of the ridiculous rumours still being circulated about him.

January 8

MTV declares it Michael Jackson Sunday. Michael Jackson videos, specials and concert footage is featured throughout the day.

January 10

Moonwalker is released on video in America, with 300,000 copies being shipped out – the largest first shipment ever for a home video. In just over a month, it will sell 600,000 units in the States.

The video cassette features a review of Michael's career, videos, a special 42 minute mini movie of 'Smooth Criminal' and a special live performance of The Beatles' 'Come Together.'

Moonwalker débuts at number one on Billboard's Top Music Video Cassette chart and stays there for 22 weeks before being replaced by himself, with *Michael Jackson: The Legend Continues.*

January 15

Record Mirror this week shows 'Bad' as a NINE-times platinum seller in Britain (2.7 million). The album rises to number 4 on the Top 100 albums chart in its 72nd consecutive week. 'Thriller' is at number 65 and is also a nine-times platinum seller, having spent 256 weeks in total on the charts.

January 16-18, 26, 27

Michael begins the third and final leg of the American tour performing five sell-out shows to audiences of 86,882 at the Sports Arena in Los Angeles.
  Among the celebrities who turn out to see Michael in Los Angeles are Gregory Peck, Barbra Streisand, Sylvester Stallone, Sidney Poitier, Elizabeth Taylor, Whitney Houston, Berry Gordy, Sean Lennon, Yoko Ono, Katherine and Joe Jackson and sisters Janet and Rebbie. Close friend, Liza Minnelli attends every one of the five concerts.

These are the rescheduled dates which were cancelled due to illness in November. The proceeds from one of the LA shows are donated to Childhelp USA, the largest non-profit child abuse prevention organisation in America. In recognition of Michael's contribution, Childhelp USA establishes the 'Michael

Jackson International Institute For Research On Child Abuse,' which is based in south California.

January 21
Michael is on the cover of *TV Guide* along with Elvis Presley, Bruce Springsteen and Madonna. The cover story is about the greatest live TV performances and two of Michael's TV performances are chosen amongst the best ever.

His performance of 'Billie Jean' from *Motown 25: Yesterday, Today, and Forever*, is described as 'the flashiest TV performance ever,' and as 'his most unforgettable moment on TV.' Michael Jackson's performance of 'Man In The Mirror' from the 1988 Grammys is chosen as the 'most spirited' TV performance.

January 24
After only two weeks on release, *Moonwalker* is reported to have outsold *Making Michael Jackson's Thriller*, giving Michael Jackson the top two best-selling music video cassettes in America.

Announced as the 'farewell concert,' Michael Jackson plays the 123rd and final show at the Los Angeles Sports Arena and ends his 'Bad' tour with arms outstretched and his gaze firmly fixed towards the sky. Mayor Tom Bradley declares it 'Michael Jackson Day' and presents Michael with the proclamation.

The third leg of the US tour saw Michael playing to almost a quarter of a million Americans. The Bad World Tour attendance figures total 4.4 million,

making Michael's sixteen month tour, which played in fifteen countries, the largest in history. Michael Jackson's 1987-1989 Bad World Tour is also the highest grossing concert

tour, grossing over $125 million, more than any other entertainer has ever grossed on a single tour.

At most stops, Michael showed his concern for underprivileged children by inviting them to concerts as his personal guests and by contributing to hospitals, orphanages and other charities.

January 30
At the 16th American Music Awards, held at the Shrine Auditorium in Los Angeles, Michael Jackson is presented with two special honours, the American Music Award Of Achievement and the Video Pioneer Award, presented by friend Eddie Murphy, who also narrates a four-

teen-minute film tribute to Michael. The inscription on the Award Of Achievement reads:

"Because his album, 'Bad,' is the first ever to generate five number one singles, because it has been a number one best seller in a record-breaking twenty-five countries around the world, and because it has been the largest international seller in each of the last two years, the American Music Award Of Achievement is presented to Michael Jackson on January 30, 1989."

February 7
Michael Jackson visits the Cleveland Elementary School in Stockton, California. A few weeks earlier, Patrick Purdy (25) had opened fire on the school's playground killing five children and wounding 39 others before turning the gun on himself.

Michael hands out signed albums and videos and speaks to the parents and children with many of them saying that Michael's visit helped them to feel safe again and to understand that the world does care and that not every adult is out to hurt them.

February 13
Michael wins two awards at the 8th British Record Industry Awards (Brits) for Best Music Video – 'Smooth Criminal' and Best International Male Artist. Michael accepts his awards via satellite.

"For his pioneering efforts in the field of music videos epitomised by 'The Triumph,' a pre-1980s breakthrough in concept and special effects, and 'Thriller,' an innovative combination of drama, music and dance. This Video Pioneer Award is given to Michael Jackson on the occasion of his new feature-length film anthology, Moonwalker becoming the largest-selling music home video of all time."

American Music Awards, 1989

This Page: Michael receives the American Music Award Of Achievement from Eddie Murphy.

1989

This Page: Michael takes 200 disadvantaged children to the circus.

February 14

After four years of phenomenal success, which began with 'Thriller,' Lee Solters, Michael Jackson's publicist, announces that Michael and his manager, Frank Dileo, are to part company.

It is described as an amiable split and in a brief statement read by Solters, Michael says: "I thank Frank for his contribution on my behalf during the past several years."

No real reason is given for the abrupt split, leaving the media to speculate about possible causes suggesting that Dileo was trying to be bigger than Michael, that his managing technique was too flamboyant and that he tried to promote him as a wacky person.

Nevertheless, Dileo's record for successfully managing Michael's career over the period has proved to be unchallenged.

February 18

'Leave Me Alone' enters the Top 100 singles chart in Britain peaking at number 2 and remains on the charts for nine weeks. The 7" single is also issued as a limited edition pop-up sleeve.

Music Week write: Entering the charts at number 4, 'Leave Me Alone' is the highest-débuting single of the week. However, as the track does not appear on either the LP or cassette version of 'Bad,' it's a matter of interpretation whether the album has now surrendered seven or eight hits. If it's the former, 'Bad' still shares the honour for most Top 75 hits off an album with

Janet Jackson and Luther Vandross. If the latter, it is the first album ever to yield eight hit singles. 'Leave Me Alone' becomes the first single by an American act to make its chart début in the British Top 10 since 'Bad' itself did it, entering at number five on September 26, 1987.

In all its forms, 'Bad' is now Britain's third best-selling album, behind Jackson's previous album, 'Thriller,' and 'Brothers In Arms' by Dire Straits. 'Thriller' has sold over 2.9 million copies in Britain, but 'Bad' is only 150,000 behind, and with sales of nearly 10,000 a week, is expected to top the three million mark shortly before 'Thriller.'

February 25

At the 31st annual Grammy Awards held at the Shrine Auditorium in Los Angeles, Michael Jackson's 'Man In The Mirror' does not win its nomination for Record Of The Year, which goes to Bobby McFerrin's, 'Don't Worry, Be Happy.' The Grammy for Best Concept Recording goes to 'Weird Al' Yankovic for 'Fat,' his parody of 'Bad.' Michael does not attend the ceremony.

February 27

Michael is on the cover of *Jet* magazine.

March

'Smooth Criminal' is voted Favourite Music Video at the People's Choice Awards.

The Black Radio Exclusive Humanitarian Award is

presented to Michael Jackson at the Universal Amphitheater in Universal City, California.

LaToya Jackson is featured in a semi-nude photo layout for *Playboy* magazine, 'Michael's Sister In A Thriller Pictorial.'

March 5

Michael Jackson takes 200 disadvantaged children from St. Vincent's Home For Dysfunctional Children and from Big Brothers and Big Sisters to Circus Vargas in Santa Barbara, California. He waves, jokes, laughs and generally clowns around, enjoying the circus as much as his guests before taking them back to his ranch to see his own private zoo.

American Top Forty counts down the Top 40 Dance Hits Of The '80s. Michael Jackson has four entries. 'Wanna Be Startin' Somethin'' is at number 40, 'Bad' – 7, 'Beat It' – 3 and the number 1 dance hit of the decade is 'Billie Jean.'

Berry Gordy offers for sale Jobete Music, the music publishing division of Motown Records. Interested parties are reported to include Sony, Warner Communications and Michael Jackson.

Enjoying tremendous success with her album, 'Janet Jackson's Rhythm Nation 1814,' Janet tells *Rolling Stone* magazine that her biggest inspiration is her brother, Michael.

April

Michael is on the cover of *Ebony* magazine.

Filming begins in Los Angeles for the video for 'Liberian Girl.' The video includes appearances by over forty friends and celebrities, including Paula Abdul, Debbie Gibson, Dan Aykroyd, Quincy Jones, Steve Guttenberg, Olivia Newton-John, Rosanna Arquette, John Travolta, Steven Spielberg, Whoopi Goldberg and Bubbles. Michael dedicates the video to his close friend, Liz Taylor. The single is released only in Britain.

April 12
Michael attends the 3rd annual Soul Train Awards at the Shrine Auditorium in Los Angeles where he has three nominations. Michael wins in the categories for Best R&B Urban Contemporary Single By A Male ('Man In The Mirror') and Best R&B Urban Contemporary Music Video ('Man In The Mirror'), and also receives two special awards.

To celebrate his 20th year in show business, he is the third recipient of the prestigious Heritage Award for career achievement, and the first ever recipient of the Sammy Davis Jr. Award for outstanding stage performance.

Eddie Murphy and Elizabeth Taylor present the awards following a tribute to Michael and a taped congratulatory message from Sammy Davis Jr. One of his other awards is presented to Michael by Mike Tyson, who calls him 'The Greatest.'

This Page: Michael at the 1989 Soul Train Awards.

April 14
At the 2nd World Music Awards, Michael Jackson receives The Philips Hall Of Fame Award For Special Achievement In Video and the award for Number One Video In The World ('Dirty Diana'). Michael accepts both awards from Whitney Houston via satellite from his ranch.

April 15
Moonwalker is broadcast on the cable channel, Showtime.

The 1988 Bad World tour is nominated for Tour Of The Year at the first International Rock Awards but the award goes to Amnesty International. Michael does not attend the presentations.

May
Michael's 'Thriller' video is voted top of *Ebony* magazine's Video Poll.

May 2
'Nothin'', by The Jacksons, which does not include Michael, is released. The 12" includes Michael's live version of 'Heartbreak Hotel.'

May 3
Michael Jackson: The Legend Continues is released on video cassette in America.

Michael Jackson is seized by armed police after being mistaken for a robber whilst shopping in disguise at Zales jewellers in Simi Valley. A phone call brings three LA patrol cars and eight burly police officers racing to the shop, after the assistants report that Michael and his young companion are acting suspiciously.

Michael, dressed in a red baseball cap, red shirt and blue trousers but also wearing an Afro wig, buck teeth and a false moustache, explains that he donned the disguise so he wouldn't get mobbed by fans. Michael had already told manageress, Celeste Marsh, the same story but she said: "He looked so odd, I thought the guy had got off an elevator between floors."

Police describe Michael, who was shopping for rings with a 12 year old boy, as 'very co-operative.' No charges are filed and after Michael produces his Driving Licence, and signs a few autographs, they are allowed to leave.

June

A lawsuit is filed against Michael Jackson by George Mollases and John Griffen claiming the 'Man In The Mirror' video infringes on their 1986 video 'All Over The World.'

June 1
BET, The Black Entertainment Television channel in America, features only Jackson videos on its Video Soul programme. While videos from all family members are shown, the bulk of the show comprises videos by Michael and Janet.

June 13
Michael gives a second sitting to sculptor, David Goode, in Los Angeles for the latest Madame Tussaud's wax figure.

Michael has a giraffe shipped to his Santa Ynez ranch. He had seen the giraffe while touring in Kansas City in 1988.

June 17
Michael Jackson: The Legend Continues is the number one best selling video cassette on Billboard's Top Video Cassette Sales chart, replacing Michael's own video, *Moonwalker*.

June 23
'2300 Jackson St.' (LP), the first Jackson album in five years, is released by Epic Records. The album is named after the family's home address in Gary, Indiana. The album does poorly, peaking at number 59 on the Pop albums chart. The album's first single, '2300 Jackson St.' features all of the Jacksons except LaToya and Marlon. It is the first single on which Janet and Rebbie sing with their brothers. The accompanying video shows the family enjoying 'Family Day' at Tito's home.

With the completion of the '2300 Jackson St.' album the Jackson's contract with Epic Records is fulfilled. It is not renewed.

June 27
Michael Jackson heads an American poll of stars who children would like to visit their schools. Runners-up are Debbie Gibson, Guns N' Roses, Tiffany and The Beach Boys.

July

Moonwalker is named as Favourite Musical Video by the Video Software Dealer Association.

July 4
Michael turns up at Diana Ross's Motown homecoming party with supermodel, Beverley Johnson.

July 9
Michael goes shopping for a selection of books at a book store in Santa Barbara.

July 16
'Liberian Girl' enters the Top 100 singles chart in Britain peaking at number 13 and remains on the charts for 6 weeks.

Music Week write: It is indisputable that Michael Jackson's 'Bad' has now yielded more hits than any album in chart history. As the eighth, or ninth release – depending on whether 'Leave Me Alone' is included – from an album which has sold almost three million copies, and considering that the 12" version is not extended, 'Liberian Girl' débuts remarkably high at number 18.

A Michael Jackson music laser show opens at The Laserium in London.

July 28
Michael becomes the newest claymation member of the Raisin Family by appearing in their new TV commercial called *Michael Raisin*. Michael's speaking voice is used in the ads, but his singing voice on the song, 'I Heard It Through The Grapevine' cannot be used because of his exclusive contract with Pepsi. Michael agrees to lend his image to the commercial after working with the claymation creator on his *Moonwalker* video. Michael receives $25,000 for his contribution, which he donates to charity.

1989

Opposite Page: Michael in his outfit worn for the 'Come Together' video, and a pose used on the 'Liberian Girl' picture sleeve.

1989

Paul McCartney condemns Michael's decision to allow 'All You Need Is Love' to be used in a commercial. Saatchi and Saatchi pays £150,000 to record a version of the song to promote video cameras.

July 30

Music Week write: 'Bad' becomes the third consecutive Michael Jackson album to spend a hundred or more weeks on the (British) chart following 1978's Off the Wall (173) and 1982's 'Thriller' (167). Michael joins The Beatles, Simon & Garfunkel, Phil Collins and U2 in runners-up position in this particular chart category. All trail Dire Straits, who've had no fewer than five albums on the charts for 100 weeks or more.

This Page: Michael has an Auditorium named after him at his old school in Hollywood.

September

Forbes magazine lists Michael Jackson as the number one highest-paid entertainer for the second consecutive year with two-year estimated earnings of $125 million.

A planned greatest hits album titled 'Decade' is shelved due to indecision about the tracks to be included.

September 6

At the MTV Music Video Awards, Michael Jackson's videos dominate the nominations with nine. 'Leave Me Alone' is nominated for Best Video, Best Special Effects, Best Art Direction, Best Editing, Breakthrough Video and the Viewers' Choice Award. 'Smooth Criminal' is nominated for Best Dance, Best Choreography and Best Cinematography. The only win goes to Jim Blashfield for Best Special Effects on 'Leave Me Alone.' Michael does not attend the presentations.

September 13

A press conference is held to announce Michael Jackson's new endorsement deal with LA Gear. The two-year deal calls for Michael to design and market a line of sportshoes and sportswear as well as appear in commercials. Under the special marketing campaign 'Unstoppable,' a wide range of activities was promised to promote the collection. Michael says: "I look forward to the challenge of creating and designing with this hot LA fashion leader."

September 22

The Capital Children's Museum honours Michael Jackson with the Best of Washington 1989 Humanitarian Award for his fundraising efforts for the museum and unending devotion to children and their causes. Although Michael is unable to attend, he does send a video-taped thank-you speech. The award is officially given to Michael at the 8th annual Best Of Washington Celebrity Fashion Show and Luncheon at the Sheraton Washington Hotel.

September 24

'Bad' spends its last week in the Top 100 albums chart in Britain at number 64 after enjoying 108 consecutive weeks on the chart.

Autumn

Doubleday issues the 1989 *Moonwalker* calendar, colouring book and storybook.

October

The lawsuit filed by Michael Jackson against the distributors of bootleg Beatles movies is settled. Michael is awarded $130,000 by the New York State Court Judge and further sales of the movies are prohibited.

Michael's lawyers plan to sue the toy firm, Lego, over a disrespectful advertisement using Michael's face. Over 8,000 Lego bricks are used to create Michael's image with the slogan, 'Amazing What You Can Make Out Of Plastic These Days.' It was intended to promote Lego UK in the USA.

October 10

Michael goes back to school when he visits Room 8 at the Gardner Street Elementary School in Hollywood, Los Angeles, where he attended sixth grade as a child. The school dedicate the auditorium in his honour, renaming it 'The Michael Jackson Auditorium.' Michael unveils the auditorium and listens to the children performing 'We Are The World.' Michael also gives a lengthy speech thanking his former teacher, Mrs. Gerstin, and his former tutor, Rose Fine, who also attend the dedication.

October 14

Friday Night Videos features videos by the Greatest Artists Of The Decade and declare Michael Jackson the Greatest Video Artist Of The Decade.

November 10

The Jackson family are interviewed on *Donahue* in a TV special. Michael, and LaToya do not appear.

November 13

Michael makes headline news in *New York Newsday* by meeting four-year-old leukaemia victim, Darian Pagan, through the Wishes Granted organisation.

Michael treats the youngster to a Canadian acrobatic troupe performance and gives him something we all take for granted – time.

Michael is amongst a galaxy of stars to honour and perform for Sammy Davis, Jr. at the *60th Anniversary* TV Special. Michael performs, 'You Were There,' a song especially written for Sammy by Michael and Buz Kohan and only ever performed on this one occasion. The show is a UNCF benefit.

December

Michael Jackson, covering his face with a huge scarf, attends the world class boxing fight between Sugar Ray Leonard and Roberto Duran. Sugar Ray Leonard enters the ring to Michael's hit, 'Leave Me Alone,' and wins the fight.

Bo Jackson of the LA Raiders gives Michael an autographed football and baseball during a visit to a Los Angeles studio.

Michael is on the cover of *Vanity Fair* magazine, which focuses on the 'Media Stars Of The Decade.' This is the first time Michael has posed for a magazine cover since 1984. Celebrated photographer Annie Leibovitz says of the photo session: "Before I took it, I wanted a dance photograph, but he was reluctant until I asked everyone to leave the room. Then he danced for 45 minutes. It was unbelievable. I sweated right through my clothes. Looking in the mirror he became – excuse the pun – very reflective, in a way he hadn't been when he looked into the camera. He got much more involved."

MTV count down the Top 100 Videos of the '80s. Michael Jackson has four entries with 'Man In The Mirror' at number 40, 'Billie Jean' at number 27, 'Beat It' at number 13 and 'Thriller' as the number one video of the '80s.

Entertainment Tonight names Michael Jackson as the Most Important Entertainer Of The Decade.

USA Today music critics choose 'Leave Me Alone' as the number one Best Video of 1989. They vote Janet's 'Miss You Much' as the fifth best video of the year.

'Leave Me Alone' is honoured with a Teddy Award, a Canadian Music Award.

Jim Blashfield wins a Golden Lion Award at the Cannes Film Festival for his work on the special effects on the 'Leave Me Alone' video.

Billboard commemorates Quincy Jones' 30 years in show business. A full-page drawing of Michael Jackson with a glove and fedora reads, 'Q – Congratulations – Michael Jackson.'

December 6

MTV airs a special, *Rate The '80s*, in which viewers vote for their favourites in several categories. Michael Jackson has the most nominations, with three. 'Thriller' is voted The Greatest Video In The History Of The World, with 35% of the vote, 'Thriller' comes in at number three for Really Big Album, with 14% of the vote, and Michael Jackson is rated the number four Mega Artist Of The '80s with 15% of the vote.

Michael's award for the 'Thriller' video is presented to him during a surprise appearance on *The Arsenio Hall Show*. Michael walks on the talk show set to present Hall's guest, Eddie Murphy, with MTV's Humour God Of The '80s Award. Murphy then presents Michael with the Award for The Greatest Video In The History Of The World.

December 12

A fire breaks out in a barn at Michael's Neverland ranch. The barn is burned down to the ground, but Michael's giraffes escape unharmed.

December 13

Current Affairs, an American TV show, airs a minute clip from a private movie filmed at Michael's ranch, showing him singing songs from *Peter

1989

This Page: Michael sings 'You Were There' at the Sammy Davis Anniversary Special.

Below: Michael leaves the Mirage Hotel after watching another great performer, Sugar Ray Leonard, defeat Roberto Duran.

1989

Pan and talking to his mother and sister, LaToya. The footage is supplied by an ex-cameraman, Steven Howell, who claims that Michael would not object to the home movie being aired, as it shows him in a different light from what the public normally see him.

December 18

Michael's lawyers contact the *Current Affairs* programme to state that, if any more of the tapes are aired, they will sue.

Reports confirm that Michael's greatest hits album, 'Decade,' is shelved due to an avalanche of new material from Michael, prompting thoughts of a brand new album instead.

December 19

Michael visits F. A. O. Schwarz toy store in Manhattan. He then goes to Radio City Music Hall, taking several children with him to the Christmas Spectacular.

December 23

Billboard magazine reviews the past year and past decade in music. Both focus heavily on Michael Jackson.

December 28-Jan. 3

Ryan White, a young haemophiliac who contracted the AIDS virus in 1984 from tainted blood products used to treat his haemophilia, spends a vacation at Michael's Neverland Valley ranch.

Banned from his local school in Kokomo, Ryan has been fighting against the discrimination that AIDS victims suffer. He

went on TV pleading for understanding and has also spoken at the White House. Michael gives his young guest a red Mustang car during this visit.

Late December

In its year end recap, *Billboard* magazine ranks *Moonwalker* as the fourth Best Selling Video Cassette of the year. Both Michael's video cassette releases are in their Top Music Video Cassettes Of The Year listing: *Moonwalker* is at number 3 with *Michael Jackson: The Legend Continues* at number 10.

Billboard's other year end charts show 'Smooth Criminal' at number 93 on the Pop Singles chart and at number 58 on the Black Singles chart for the year. Michael Jackson is ranked at number 19 on the Top Pop Singles Artist chart, and at number 83 on the Top Pop Singles Artist chart.

Rolling Stone magazine names 'Thriller' the number one album of the '80s.

December 31

Michael Aspel, one of Britain's most popular talk show hosts, presents Michael with a scroll proclaiming him Best-Selling Male Singer Of The '80s as part of the Cilla Black ITV Show, *Goodbye To The '80s.*

Casey Kasem presents a very special year end edition of *America's Top Ten* , announcing the programme as "a tribute to one of the most influential, most thrilling, most bad acts of the decade – Michael Jackson."

Kasem opens his programme by saying: "When rock historians of the future look back on the Eighties, they will see a decade filled with musical heroes; they will write about the charisma of The Boss, the showmanship of Madonna, the energy of Prince – but... mostly they will write about the most exciting phenomenon of the Eighties, the thrill known as Michaelmania."

Kasem also announces Michael as the top act of the decade saying, "The number one act of the Eighties and the most influential musician of the decade, the man who made the Eighties the Michael Jackson decade."

1990

Michael Jackson is featured on a stamp issued by the Republic of Guinea.

In response to rumours that Michael's beloved chimp, Bubbles, has died, Michael's publicist issues a statement that Bubbles is indeed alive and well.

January

Michael Jackson is presented with MTV's Video Vanguard Artist Of The Decade Award. The award presentation is followed by an evening of all Michael Jackson videos.

Friday Night Videos features videos chosen by their viewers for Favourite Videos Of The Decade. Included in their choices is 'Thriller.'

Platinum Limited Editions produce a limited edition of 1,000 numbered Michael Jackson Artist Of The Decade Awards which carry certified authentication.

Michael's *Moonwalker* is nominated for a Grammy award in the category for Best Long-Form Video.

Michael visits Disney World in Orlando to look over the new Star Wars Tours ride. The following day Michael is spotted skating at the Rockin' Rollerdome.

Reports appear that Michael has opened his private ice skating rink to disadvantaged children, allowing them to skate free of charge.

January 6

Michael invites eighty-two abused and neglected children from Childhelp USA to Neverland Valley ranch. The two busloads of children are treated to games, a barbecue and a private screening of *The Little Mermaid* and *Back To The Future Part II* in Michael's Theatre.

January 19

USA Today carry a full-page ad from CBS proclaiming Michael Jackson 'The Artist Of Our Time' for selling 100 million records during the Eighties.

January 26

Michael Jackson is at the Beverly Hilton Hotel for the unveiling of a painting of himself, titled *The Book*. *The Book* has been sold to Hiromichi Saeki, Corp., a Japanese international investment and development firm for a record $2.1 million, making it the most expensive painting in the world of a subject still living. The work by Australian artist, Brett-Livingstone Strong, a descendant of the famous explorer, shows Michael holding an unidentified book. The title of the mysterious tome is a highly-guarded secret but

Jackson's spokeswoman, Maureen O'Connor, revealed at a press conference in Los Angeles that it has significantly influenced the singer's life.

January 27

Michael receives the Entertainer Of The Decade award at the 7th Annual American Cinema Awards held at the Beverly Hilton Hotel. Hosted by Kirk and Anne Douglas, Michael receives his award from his guest, Sophia Loren. Judges choose Michael as showman of the Eighties for his multi-million selling albums 'Thriller' and 'Bad' and his sell-out world tour in 1988. Michael gives a three-minute thankyou speech.

February 3

Michael receives a Role Model Award from Japan, which he accepts via satellite.

February 4

The tribute to Sammy Davis Jr.'s 60th year in show business, filmed in November, is aired by ABC with all the proceeds from the show, some $250,000, going to the United Negro College Fund. It will win the Emmy for Outstanding Musical Special.

February 20

Michael attends a sit-down breakfast at the Regent Beverly Wilshire Hotel. The party is organised by CBS Records for unprecedented record sales of 110 million records throughout the 1980s making Michael the Top Selling Artist of the Decade. Michael says: "I have to say now, no album sells itself, it's up to the people to buy it."

This Page: Michael is accompanied by Sophia Loren to the American Cinema Awards.

Michael is honoured by the Broadcasting Music Industry, and CBS celebrate Michael selling over 100 million records.

1990

February 21

Michael wins the Best Short Music Video award for 'Leave Me Alone' at the 32nd Annual Grammy Awards Show.

February 27

A bogus press release is issued to the media announcing a new multi-million dollar deal between Walt Disney Studio and Michael Jackson. The deal involves movies, albums and theme rides, but the release – which looks like it did come from Disney – is denied by them as being totally false.

March

The British tabloids report that Michael is to 'go public' this summer, saying he has teamed up with his family to launch £60 million worth of shares on the world's markets. Cash from the family's shares are to be used to build a new Jackson Theme Park in Las Vegas and to launch their own record company called Jackson Records. The flotation is to be masterminded by three top Wall Street underwriters and a new company, Jackson Entertainment Corp., has been formed to handle it.

Michael receives The Silver Award at the 4th annual Soul Train Awards as part of of his recognition as the 1980's Artist Of The Decade.

March 20

Adrian Grant, Editor of *Off The Wall* magazine, the official Michael Jackson fanzine in Britain, presents Michael with the 'Off the Wall Appreciation Award,' a montage of images of Michael throughout his career captured on canvas by artist, Vincent McKoy. After the presentation, Adrian spends the day in the Recording Studio where Michael is recording new songs for his next album. Michael poses for exclusive photographs for the magazine and writes a note to all the readers.

March 26

Adrian Grant visits Michael at his Neverland ranch and becomes the first journalist ever to be allowed to write a cover story about the experience. During the day's visit, Adrian plays on all the amusements, watches a film, and sees many of Michael's treasured accolades which are kept safely in a special exhibition room. In his report on the visit Adrian states, "The scenery was quite breathtaking – never before had I seen land and property so beautiful. The lakes, the bridges all set amongst the sweetest flower gardens from which classical music rose out into the summer air."

Spring

Movie theatres begin airing commercials for LA Gear using Michael Jackson's music, 'Wanna Be Startin' Somethin'', but Michael himself does not appear in the ads. The teaser ads are later aired on TV.

Wade Robson, a seven-year-old Australian boy from Brisbane, flies to America with his parents to study singing and dancing with Michael Jackson. Wade met Michael when he was five after winning a dance competition. Wade's mother, Joy, says her son learned to dance by watching Michael's videos and considers him a perfect role model for her son.

April 2

Ryan White, the young AIDS victim, slips into a coma.

April 4

Michael visits the Capital Children's Museum in Washington DC for 90 minutes, where he is taken on a general tour by Ann Lewin, Executive Director of the Natural Learning Center. He is surrounded by children and stops to play with several of the hands-on exhibits.

Michael also spends a few minutes at the Smithsonian Museum of American History where he views the Star Spangled Banner.

April 5

Michael Jackson meets with President Bush at the White House Rose Garden ceremony to be honoured as 'Entertainer Of The Decade' by the Capital Children's Museum, Washington DC. Michael, who has long been devoted to children's causes receives the award for his philanthropic activities for children. President Bush tells the gathered press that Michael did what he called 'Points of Light' good work on humanitarian issues.

The Friends of the Capital

Children's Museum hold a fund-raising evening as part of their special ceremony to honour Michael. The guests pay $5,000 for tickets to the exclusive collar and tie event at the historic Merrywood Estate in McLean.

At some time during this very eventful day, Michael telephones to check on Ryan White's condition. A speaker phone is used in an attempt to provoke some response from Ryan, who has now been in a coma for four days.

April 7
Michael arrives as one of the first guests at the Taj Mahal Casino as a special guest of millionaire, Donald Trump.

April 8
At the age of 18, Ryan White loses his fight against the deadly disease, AIDS, after being comatosed for six days. Michael, who had become a close friend of Ryan's, hears of the tragic loss whilst at the Taj Mahal Casino. He leaves immediately with Donald Trump to travel to Ryan's home in Indiana. Michael spends four hours inside the family home consoling Ryan's mother, Jeanne.

April 11
Michael comforts Ryan White's mother, Jeanne, as he attends the funeral service held in Indiana along with 1,500 other mourners including Barbara Bush, Elton John, Phil Donahue and football star, Howie Long of Ryan's favourite team, the Los Angeles Raiders.

May
Fans force Michael to retreat while visiting F. A. O. Schwartz Toy Store with two young girls as companions. Store assistants take him to the executive rooms to escape autograph hunters and he eventually leaves through a safety door.

John Brown, a 14-year-old cancer sufferer from Wakefield, West Yorkshire has his ultimate wish granted by Michael. As part of the 'Make A Wish Foundation Charity' John is invited to Michael's Neverland ranch to meet his idol in person.

May 8
In recognition of his enormous contribution to American culture, The Broadcast Music Industry presents its first ever BMI Michael Jackson Award to Michael himself in a ceremony held at the Regent Beverly Wilshire Hotel. The award honours a songwriter or composer whose work encompasses important contributions to such creative disciplines as recording, film, dance and video. The Michael Jackson Award won't be handed out on a yearly basis, instead the BMI says it will occur only when artists have attained similar creditable heights as Michael regarding record sales, humanitarian efforts, business attributes, etc. President Frances Peterson says, "In the past we have awarded Michael Jackson for his songs and sales. This is an award for Michael Jackson the man."

May 16
Sammy Davis Jr., a long-time idol and inspiration to Michael Jackson, dies of throat cancer. Michael Jackson is named as an honorary pallbearer along with Frank Sinatra, Dean Martin and Bill Cosby.

May 26
The African Republic of Tanzania releases a collection of stamps featuring ten great African and Afro-American performing artists in the series 'Famous Black Entertainers.' Michael Jackson is issued on the most expensive one with Bill Cosby.

June 3
Michael arrives at St. John's Hospital and Health Center emergency room complaining of severe chest pains. The incident occurred whilst he was rehearsing at his Encino home and sparks rumours that Michael has suffered a heart attack.

June 4
Thousands of Michael's fans stream into the hospital grounds carrying flowers and get-well messages to begin a vigil outside St. John's Hospital. Bob Jones, Vice President of Communications for MJJ Productions says, "He's undergoing several important tests. I don't think it was a heart attack. He just experienced some discomfort. He had been feeling bad the past two or three days."

June 5
Michael suffers more chest pains and tests are carried out. Throughout the day, Jackson family members visit their brother in hospital while his sister, LaToya, sends him a dozen black

On May 26, *Billboard* magazine publishes its Readers' Poll for favourites of the 1980s. Michael Jackson dominates the poll, with eleven placings in eight categories for:

#2 Pop Artist Of The Decade
#4 Dance Artist Of The Decade
#1 Black Artist Of The Decade
#1 Favourite Pop Album Of The Decade – 'Thriller'
#2 Favourite Black Album Of The Decade – 'Thriller'
#2 Favourite Pop Single Of The Decade – 'We Are The World' 'Billie Jean' (#4)
#1 Favourite Black Single Of The Decade – 'Billie Jean' (1) 'Beat It' (5)
#2 Favourite Dance Single Of The Decade – 'Billie Jean' 'Beat It' (4)

This Page: Michael is honoured as Entertainer Of The Decade by President George Bush.

Page Opposite: The hand written note Michael gave *Off The Wall* magazine for his fans.

1990

roses. The suspected heart attack is now thought to have been a nervous attack brought on by the star's heavy workload, which includes an overdue new album. Bob Jones tells the press, "Michael has been under a lot of pressure lately. His friend Sammy Davis, Jr. passed away, his grandmother passed away about a month ago and his friend, Ryan White died of AIDS last month."

June 6
Michael Jackson is confirmed as suffering from costochondritis, inflammation of the cartilage on the front of the rib cage, which has been caused by over-exertion and stress. Michael leaves the hospital 48 hours later.

Summer
Michael is on the cover of *Music World*.

Michael is honoured with one of the first Broccoli Awards issued by the American magazine, *Alive And Well*. The awards are presented for efforts towards promoting good health through diet.

A bootleg of Michael's 'Human Nature' coupled with Snap's 'The Power' circulates on the British club scene under the title, 'The Power Of Human Nature.'

July
Michael attends the wedding of Berry Gordy to Grace Eaton in Santa Barbara.

Forty-five children from Los Angeles' Dream Street, a programme for children

Page Opposite: Michael, honoured with the first ever 'Michael Jackson Good Scout Award Humanitarian Award,' salutes peace, hope and goodwill with Boy Scouts.

with life-threatening diseases, are invited to Michael's Neverland Valley ranch. The children come from all parts of the world.

The first publicity pictures of Michael Jackson's LA Gear campaign begin to circulate in magazines. His eight year old niece, Brandi, daughter of elder brother Jackie, is featured in the promotion and appears in the TV ads. Michael's first TV commercial in nearly four years is heralded a 'creative breakthrough' by the industry.

A leather stage outfit worn by Michael on the 'Bad' tour is sold at Philips auctions in London. It is bought by the US Hard Rock Café for £16,500.

August
Walter Yetnikoff refuses permission for any Michael Jackson songs to appear on the soundtrack to *Days Of Thunder*. Yetnikoff had, at one stage, refused permission for Michael to appear on the *Listen Up – The Lives Of Quincy Jones* documentary.

Sega/Genesis releases a new video game cartridge depicting Michael Jackson, *Moonwalker*. The game, based on 'Smooth Criminal' is designed by Michael. Arcade-size versions of the game are also available in video arcades.

Commercials for LA Gear with Michael Jackson begin airing in movie theatres.

August 8
An up-dated wax figure of Michael Jackson is unveiled in the 'Superstars' area at

Madame Tussaud's in London.

August 18
Michael invites 130 children from the YMCA's Summer Programme in Los Angeles and Santa Barbara to his ranch. The children show their appreciation by making a banner, 'We Love You Michael.' Michael is made an honorary member of the 28th Street YMCA in Los Angeles.

It is announced that Michael Jackson has hired Sandy Gallin as his new personal manager.

September
Listen Up! The Lives Of Quincy Jones, a documentary film, is released. The film includes an off-camera interview with Michael Jackson, who had agreed to answer questions if the lights were turned off.

September 12
Michael attends a City of Hope gala in honour of CBS Records Division President, Tommy Mottola.

September 14
The Los Angeles Council Of The Boy Scouts Of America honour Michael with the first ever 'Michael Jackson Good Scout Humanitarian Award.' The award is in recognition of his humanitarian efforts for all mankind through fund-raising efforts for the Make A Wish Foundation, The Prince's Trust, The United Negro College Fund and Childhelp USA. The award is presented to Michael by Disney Chairman, Michael Eisner, at the Century Plaza Towers in Century City, Los Angeles.

September 28

Billboard magazine includes a special section commemorating the tenth anniversary of Black Entertainment Television, BET. Among the congratulatory messages is one from Michael Jackson, 'I am extremely appreciative of BET's support of my efforts. They have always provided a welcome home for my music.'

October

Michael Jackson is included in *Entertainment Weekly* magazine's list of the 101 Most Influential Power People in Entertainment.

Reports start circulating regarding Michael's threat to leave CBS in favour of a better contract elsewhere.

October 23

Michael Jackson and Elton John are named as the first recipients of the Ryan White Memorial Awards scheduled for 1991.

My Family, The Jacksons by Katherine Jackson is published.

A Michael Jackson chocolate bar is distributed worldwide by Starchoc SA in Geneva, Switzerland.

A lawsuit filed against Michael Jackson by George Mollases and John Griffen claiming the 'Man In The Mirror' video infringes on their 1986 video 'All Over The World' is rejected by the judge.

December

A Tribute To John Lennon is broadcast and includes Michael's performance of 'Come Together' taken from *Moonwalker*.

1991

January

Michael Jackson's new album, due out this month, is put back until the beginning of the summer.

MTV counts down The 100 Greatest Video Hits, with Michael's 'Thriller' at number one.

January 21

Michael cancels a proposed trip to Africa following the outbreak of the Gulf War.

January 26

'Do The Bart Man' by The Simpsons, from the cartoon series of the same name, enters the Top 75 singles chart in Britain. Rumours run high that Michael Jackson is involved on vocals. Bryan Loren, who is working with Michael on his new album, wrote the song.

Michael Jackson gives permission for his name and image to be used in a series of holograms reproducing his face in three lifelike dimensions. A limited edition hologram sized 22"x32" retailing at $20,000 is displayed in galleries and museums. Smaller versions of the holograms are later distributed to leading stores.

The Story of Michael Jackson published by Cosmo is introduced into Japanese high schools to aid students with English grammar and vocabulary. Takako Yasuo adapts Michael's *Moonwalk* autobiography into a 47-page illustrated textbook complete with multiple choice questions and exercises.

February

'Bad' is certified platinum for the tenth time in Britain, having sold 3 million copies to date. The sales of 'Bad' now equal those of 'Thriller' in Britain.

March 18

Michael is seen out with Madonna enjoying a candlelit dinner at the Ivy restaurant in Los Angeles.

March 20

In New York City the biggest deal in music history is announced between Michael Jackson and Sony Software, who bought CBS Records in 1988. The Japanese-owned multinational corporation signs Michael to a fifteen year, six-album record and film contract. The record, film and TV projects, to be effected through Sony Music, Columbia Picture Entertainment and Sony Electronic Publishing, could be worth a potential $1 billion. Michael receives an $18 million cash advance for the forthcoming album, plus a $5 million bonus for this and each of his next five albums.

Michael Jackson is now the highest-paid entertainer in the music industry, receiving a royalty rate of 25% on each album sold. He is also CEO of his own record label, Nation Records, for which he will receive $1 million per annum. The lucrative deal is reported in the press as setting new standards for cost and scope.

It is rumoured that Michael's first full-length film for Columbia Picture Entertainment is a musical action adventure motion picture based on one of Michael's ideas. The scriptwriter is said to be Caroline Thompson of *Edward Scissorhands* and Larry Wilson, co-author of *Beetlejuice,* with sets by *Batman's* Anton Furst.

March 25

All eyes are on Michael Jackson and Madonna when they show up together for the 63rd annual Academy Awards ceremony. *People Weekly* reports that 'Michael looked positively legendary in gold-tipped cowboy boots, a blinding diamond brooch and – in a dramatic sartorial departure – two gloves.'

The title of Michael Jackson's new LP is revealed to be 'Dangerous.'

April

Michael is sued for £21 million by Hugo Zuccarelli, who claims that although his breakthrough Holophonic Sound System was used on the first two million copies of the 'Bad' album, he did not receive any royalties. The next 18 million copies did not feature the Holophonic Sound System but the album cover failed to stipulate this.

Zuccarelli claims his business suffered because, when potential customers heard later copies of 'Bad' with an inferior sound system, they thought they were listening to Holophonics.

Reports circulate that Michael made a loss of some £9 million on the *Moonwalker* video. Information taken from Fredrick Dannen's book,

Hitmen, states that it was a well-known fact that Michael fired Frank Dileo because of his failure to get *Moonwalker* a theatrical release in the US.

April 8

Michael organises a £500-a-seat chimps' tea party to raise money for Jane Goodall's ape research institute.

April 9

For the fourth time in two weeks, Michael and Madonna are spotted at the Spago Restaurant in Los Angeles. After a three hour meal, they leave the restaurant 'arm-in-arm,' sending rumours of a romance buzzing around Hollywood. It will soon emerge that the King and Queen of Pop are discussing ideas for a possible duet on Michael's new album.

April 15

Michael and Madonna are on the cover of *People.*

April 17

A tiny Indie dance label, Nation Records, threatens to see Michael in court if he uses their name for his own record label. Katherine Canoville says that they have been trading under the name for three years and have developed an international reputation.

April 29

The press report on Madonna's statements to the media regarding the proposed collaboration with Michael, in which she says: "I have this whole vision about Michael. We're considering working on a song together. I would like to completely

re-do his whole image, give him a Caesar – you know, that really short haircut – and I want to get him out of those buckly boots and all that stuff. What I want him to do is go to New York and hang out for a week with the House of Extravaganza (a group of voguers). They could give him a new style. I said, 'Could you give this guy a make-over for me?' because I think that's really what he needs."

May

Michael Jackson: The Magic And The Madness by J. Randy Taraborrelli is published.

Michael's manager, Sandy Gallen, invites top designers Jean-Paul Gaultier and Azzendine Alai to submit ideas for Michael's proposed new image.

Sir Richard Attenborough is approached by Michael to direct one of his videos from 'Dangerous.'

May 4

A group of dedicated Michael Jackson fans turn up at Vision Trax Studio in Nottingham to sing a tribute song 'Look What You Have Done' written by British megafan Denise Pfeiffer with music by Nigel Rutherford Young.

May 6

Michael Jackson is invited to the Jane Goodall International Tribute Benefit. Michael has been supporting Goodall, the ethologist who has spent over thirty years researching chimpanzees in Gombe, Nigeria. Their press release states that Michael had 'assumed the honorary chair.'

This Page: Michael on an evening out with Madonna.

1991

Milk chocolate with broken hazelnuts · chocolate con leche y avellanas

This Page: Michael with Macauley Culkin in Bermuda.

The Michael Jackson chocolate bar.

Due to other commitments, Michael does not attend.

June

'Dangerous' is postponed once again because Michael, it is reported, is not happy with some of the tracks.

Stevie Wonder is presented with the Nelson Mandella Award. Michael Jackson serves as co-chairman of the event with Quincy Jones, Harry Belafonte, Eddie Murphy, Lionel Richie, Denzel Washington and Oprah Winfrey.

A new Michael Jackson chocolate bar is launched in America, estimated to earn him £1m per month.

June 1

David Ruffin, a member of The Temptations, dies of a drug overdose. Upon learning that the former Motowner was broke, Michael pays approximately £3,000 for the funeral costs and sends flowers.

Michael does not attend the funeral for fear of turning it into a media circus.

Reports appear in the press that Madonna has flatly rejected to duet with Michael.

It is reported that Michael is trying out a new look under the camera-eye of Herb Ritts. *The Sun* newspaper prints exclusive pictures of Michael's proposed new look, which shows him in Gianni Versace's leathers with a slicked-back hair style.

Michael enlists the help of top Los Angeles producers,

Babyface and L. A. Reid to work on ideas for his new album. The collaboration is said to have upset brother Jermaine, who is also working with the duo.

Jermaine is quoted in the tabloids as saying: "I could have been Michael. It's all a matter of timing, a matter of luck."

Michael appears on the cover of *The Wire* magazine in Britain.

June 15

Off The Wall magazine, holds the UK's first ever Michael Jackson Day. The party held at London's Hammersmith Palais attracts over 1500 fans who dance to Michael's music and videos, raise money for charity and are given the chance to actually meet Michael Jackson in person!

June 19

Michael visits the island of Bermuda with *Home Alone* star, Macauley Culkin for a short holiday and to look for possible video shooting sites. Macauley's parents, three of Michael's aides and the two stars check in to the city of Hamilton's £600-a-day Princess Hotel where Michael occupies the penthouse, and Macauley's parents are located on the sixth floor, immediately below. The pair spend most of the time playing games, swimming, diving and shopping.

June 21

Michael and Macauley drop water-filled balloons on passing tourists seven floors below, laughing hysterically as their water-bombs hit the unsuspecting targets. Later in the day, Michael organises a private performance of a musical at the hotel for Macauley and his parents.

June 22
Michael and Macauley go scuba diving before taking in another musical in the evening.

June 23
Michael and Macauley spend a day visiting Disney World near Orlando.

July

'Monkey Business' is reported to be one of the hot new tracks from Michael's forthcoming LP. However with over 70 songs recorded, it never makes the final 14.

News surfaces of Michael's first project for Columbia Picture Entertainment, *MidKnight*. It is described as a science fiction musical extravaganza and is scheduled for release in early 1992.

The Hollywood Arts Council announce their intention to construct a mural of Michael Jackson's image on the El Capitan Theater near Hollywood. It is to include a 3-D extension of Michael's arm lit by strobe lights to give the illusion of movement.

July 23
MC Hammer challenges Michael to a dance contest, saying that he could easily "dance the pants off anyone who moonwalks." On *Evening Magazine*, an American TV talk show, he talks about how the publicity from the contest could promote both his and Michael's new albums.

July 24
Michael's PR aide says, "Michael invented most of the steps Hammer uses. He has nothing to prove." The challenge is ignored.

July 26
Michael Jackson visits the Community Youth Sports and Arts Foundation Center in Los Angeles. The center assists parents and families of gang members in developing ways of dealing with, and deterring, gang involvement and drug-related problems. Michael, who is accompanied by Emmanuel Lewis (17), mingles with the children and, before leaving, presents the Foundation with a Sony Wide-Screen TV, a *Moonwalker* video tape and a large undisclosed cheque.

The Los Angeles Times reports that Steven Spielberg has invited Michael to make a cameo appearance in his new film *Hook*, which is based on the book, *Peter Pan*.

August

Michael is one of several celebrities pictured on the cover of *Ebony* magazine as part of their focus on 'How Black Creativity Is Changing America.' The article centres on 'The Biggest Brother-Sister Stars In Show Business History,' which features the impact of Michael and Janet Jackson.

Michael is on the cover of *Upscale* magazine.

Michael and Janet attend a birthday party for Joseph Jackson at Spago's in Los Angeles.

LaToya: Growing Up In The Jackson Family by LaToya Jackson is published by Dutton.

Billboard magazine reports that Michael has agreed to lend his image and three songs: 'Billie Jean,' 'Man In The Mirror' and 'The Way You Make Me Feel' to a Sony mini disc demo, which will début at the end of 1992.

Michael donates an autographed LP for an auction hosted by the Artists And Musicians Protecting The Tomorrow organisation, with the proceeds going to the Rain Forest Action Network.

A UK-based video company, River First, release a video containing a compilation of news reports on Michael called *The Mad Bad World Of Michael Jackson*. Michael is said to be furious and demands that Sony make a full investigation.

August 7
Staff at Disneyland fail to recognise Michael when he turns up in disguise, wearing a wig, blue contact lenses, false teeth and light make-up. A cashier becomes suspicious when Michael's friend presents his (Jackson's) credit card. In the end, Michael has to prove his identity by demonstrating some of his famous dancesteps, including the moonwalk. Disneyland politely request that Michael rings up first in future, before visiting.

August 26
Macauley Culkin spends his 11th birthday at Neverland Valley.

1991

This Page: Visuals taken from David Lynch's storyboard for the forthcoming 'Dangerous' teaser adverts.

September

At the MTV Music Video Awards show it is announced that their Video Vanguard Award has been renamed The Michael Jackson Video Vanguard Award. Bon Jovi are the first recipients.

Hardliners in Pakistan threaten to hold huge demonstrations against proposed concerts due to be staged by Michael and Madonna. The militant religious party, Jamaat, threatens to mobilise the people and throw out the government. However, Culture Minister Shaikh Rasbill intends to ignore the threats and proceed with the proposed concerts.

September 19

The autumn début of the animated third TV series of the American cartoon, *The Simpsons*, features a huge, White, mental patient who thinks he is Michael Jackson. Michael provides the voice for the character, who sings sections of 'Billie Jean' and 'Ben' – using Homer's name – and duets with Bart Simpson on 'Happy Birthday Lisa.' Michael's representatives deny his involvement and the performance is credited to John Jay Smith.

October

Michael pays £9,732 for two seats on Concorde for bodyguards Raymond Thomas and Cooper Jones to bring over the master tape of his new single, 'Black Or White.' Michael fears that bootleggers may get hold of the tapes and orders his guards not to let go of them until security staff are met in London.

Michael Jackson's sequined glove, donated to the Motown Museum in 1988, is stolen from the museum. It is recovered two days later.

It is reported that a mystery woman has paid over £30,000 to hold her child's birthday party at Michael's Neverland Ranch. Michael, it is said, offered the unique opportunity for bids in a celebrity AIDS charity auction.

October 6

Elizabeth Taylor marries for the eighth time to Larry Fortensky at Michael's Neverland Valley Ranch. Michael gives the bride away in the ceremony. There is mass media attention and the ceremony is almost interrupted when a photographer, imitating the Rocket Man, jet-packs into Michael's ranch in an attempt to get exclusive photographs.

October 21

Michael together with Elizabeth Taylor and Larry Fortensky are on the cover of *People* magazine, 'Liz and Larry's Wedding Album.' *Hello!* magazine in England also print the 'exclusive' pictures

Jean-Paul Gaultier, Vivienne Westwood, John Galliani and Helen Storey appear in *Sky* magazine with designs illustrating how they would restyle Michael's new look.

November

Thirty second ads directed by David Lynch begin airing on TV to promote the forthcoming release of Michael Jackson's 'Dangerous' album.

November 2

PLJ-FM, a New York radio station, begin airing Michael's new single 'Black Or White.' Within hours, Sony Records are besieged by other radio stations, asking for copies of the song, which is not scheduled for airing until 6 November.

In Los Angeles, KPWR-FM also begin airing their copy of the song, but are 'rapped' by Sony for doing so, and pull it off their playlist until a rival station, KIIS-FM begin airing their copy on 4 November.

Top 40 WPLJ (Mojo Radio) in New York City play Michael's 'Black Or White' for ninety minutes straight. Other radio stations complain bitterly to Sony/Epic, who are quickly forced to bring forward the scheduled radio airing date from 6 to 5 November.

Michael is on the cover of *TV Guide* promoting the forthcoming release of the 'Black Or White' video.

Riding on the back of his brother's publicity blast, an unofficial version of Jermaine's 'Word To The Badd' is aired on KPWR radio station in Los Angeles. This version, which is a 'no-holds barred' attack on Michael, carries different lyrics to the original featured on his 'You Said, You Said' album, produced by L. A. and Babyface. Jermaine denies having supplied the radio station with the single, saying it had been stolen.

Pertinent lines from Jermaine's ode to his brother, are: 'Once you were made, You changed your shade, Was your colour wrong? Could not turn back, It's a known fact, You were too far gone.'

November 4
Michael Jackson's Thriller video is inducted into the Music Video Producers' 'Hall Of Fame.'

November 6
'Black Or White' is premièred on British radio during Simon Mayo's Radio One show, just a few minutes before sixty other regional stations receive it via satellite. It is the first time a simultaneous broadcast of this type has been attempted.

November 7
Publicity for the airing of Michael's first video release from his new album begins on British TV with David Lynch's 30-second commercial.

Retail stores in twenty American cities hear the first full airing of the 'Dangerous' album.

November 8
'Black Or White' is released in some shops in America.

November 11
'Black Or White' is released in Britain. It also receives its official release in America and sets a new record when it is added to 96% of 237 of the top forty radio stations on its first day of release.

'Black Or White,' which features Guns N' Roses guitarist, Slash, is developed from a track which was intended for the 'Bad' album. In 1989, when Michael began work on 'Dangerous', he asked Bill

Bottrell, who wrote the rap lyrics and co-produced the track, to dig it out of the vault. The 'Black Or White' video features Macauley Culkin, Michael's niece, Brandi, Bart Simpson, George Wendt, who plays 'Norm' in Cheers, and rapper, Heavy D. Movie director, John Landis, who directed 'Thriller,' also directs 'Black Or White.'

November 14
Top Of The Pops TV programme premières the 'Black Or White' mini-feature and, in so doing, swells their average viewing figures from 6.5 million to 10.8 million. TV commercials have been running all week advertising the première, and there is mass media coverage in the national press on the day of the airing. However, BBC decide to cut several seconds from Michael's 'masturbation' scene in the second half. MTV première the full 11-minute 'uncut' version less than one hour later at 8.25 p.m.

Fox Network, BET and MTV simultaneously première the video for 'Black Or White.' BET airs the video at the conclusion of a Michael Jackson special, *Live And Dangerous*, while Fox air the video directly following *The Simpsons*. MTV, who declare it 'Michael Jackson Week,' air the video twice, back to back. The music video channel give the video the highest airplay to date and features Michael Jackson videos and specials the entire week. *Black Or White* is Fox's highest-rated show with 14.4 million viewers in the US tuning in for the

première and it is also the first video to be aired on German National TV news. The video, costing an estimated £3.5 million, is seen in 27 countries around the world by approximately 500 million people.

Fox Broadcasting Company have gained the rights to première each of Michael's music video films from 'Dangerous.' They expect to air a new Michael Jackson video each quarter and ask for two months' notice to organise their TV schedules around the premières.

1991

"It upsets me to think that 'Black Or White' could influence any child or adult to destructive behaviour, either sexual or violent. I've always tried to be a good role model and, therefore, have made these changes to avoid any possibility of adversely affecting any individual's behaviour. I deeply regret any pain or hurt that the final segment of 'Black Or White' has caused children, their parents or other viewers."

Michael Jackson, November 15,1991

November 15
24 hours after the première, TV stations around the world, but especially in America, receive complaints regarding the video's somewhat violent

four-minute conclusion, which causes widespread controversy. Parents in particular are disturbed by the violence and sex enacted by Michael breaking windows and simulating masturbation. The BBC's switchboards are buzzing with calls both of delight and dismay. Michael's publicist says that Michael's dance sequence is meant to portray Jackson's interpretation of the panther's wild and animalistic behaviour. Michael succumbs to public pressure by agreeing to edit out the final four minutes of the video, and issues a statement.

November 15-16
Michael tapes two songs for MTV's 10th Anniversary Special to be aired on 27 November. Slash, from Guns N' Roses, appears with him on 'Black Or White.' Michael also performs 'Will You Be There' from the new album. Filming for the special takes place at Santa Monica Airport in Los Angeles.

November 16
American reporter Janis Da Silva is called upon to present Michael Jackson with his second *Off The Wall* Appreciation Award, after publisher, Adrian Grant, survives the fright of engine failure during his flight to Los Angeles from London.

November 17
'Black Or White' enters the Top 75 singles chart in Britain at number 1, holding its position for two weeks and remains on the charts for ten weeks. Although this is the 26th single to enter the British charts at number one, it is the first by an American artist since 1969 when Elvis Presley did it for the second and last time with 'It's Now Or Never.'

'Black Or White' will become Michael's highest-ever débuting single of any of his previous albums.

The single is also a 'high flyer' in Australia – a comparatively rare occurrence – débuting at number 5.

'Black Or White' débuts on the Pop singles chart as the highest new entry at number 35.

Dangerous, a TV special, airs on Fox and MTV showing clips of Michael's career and concluding with the now edited version of the 'Black Or White' video.

November 18
Michael takes his friend, Brooke Shields, out for dinner at the Inn Of The Seventh Ray Restaurant in Malibu to celebrate his latest hit.

November 20
Radio One's Mark Goodier airs exclusive tracks from Michael's 'Dangerous' album, much to the dismay of Sony Records.

30,000 copies of the 'Dangerous' album are stolen from a Los Angeles air terminal, by three men brandishing shotguns. The albums are valued at $400,000.

Sony Records hold the official launch party for Michael's 'Dangerous' album at the Savoy Hotel in London. Jackie Hyde, Sony Music's artist liaison manager, who set up the lavish affair, started planning the event in early October. The elaborate decoration includes massive recreations of the 'Dangerous' album sleeve and guests have to walk through a bizarre 'time-tunnel' of a corridor of howling wind, fairytale images and twinkling star-lit walls. The invites are pressed onto gold cards and each person attending receives a copy of the album. Michael sends a video-taped message.

Over one million copies of 'Dangerous,' which contains fourteen tracks, are reserved in advance. The album features the music industry's hottest producers and technical innovators: Teddy Riley, Bryan Loren and Bruce Swedien.

November 21
For the first time in twenty years, an album is released on a Thursday instead of the traditional Monday. Threats of parallel imports lead to the decision for a Thursday release date, after

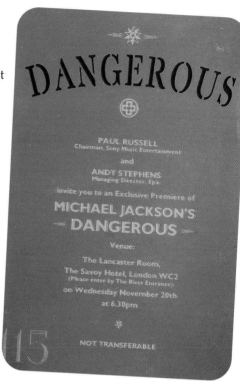

1991

This Page: The gold invite from Sony for the launch of 'Dangerous.'

Michael treats good friend Brooke Shields to an evening out.

Michael receives his second *Off The Wall* Appreciation Award.

Page Opposite: Michael in action from the 'Black Or White' video.

1991

DANGEROUS

Michael Jackson

Epic E2 45400
EPC 465802-1

Side One
1. Jam
2. Why You Wanna
   Trip On Me
3. In The Closet

Side Two
1. She Drives Me Wild
2. Remember The Time
3. Can't Let Her Get Away
4. Heal The World

Side Three
1. Black Or White
2. Who Is It
3. Give In To Me

Side Four
1. Will You Be There
2. Keep The Faith
3. Gone Too Soon
4. Dangerous

Page Opposite: Michael's famous white glove, one of which was bought for £16,500 by The Hard Rock Café.

it is learned that US rack-jobbers and wholesalers are to receive copies of 'Dangerous' on 21 November, five days before the scheduled official release date.

Radio play of 'Dangerous' is restricted to 15 minutes in any one hour period to protect the album from copyright infringement.

'Bad' is certified platinum for the eleventh time for sales of more than 3.3 million in Britain, which means that it has now out-paced 'Thriller,' which has sold 3 million copies to date.

Michael is on the cover of Germany's *Stern* magazine – a serious news and political journal – with a ten-page report.

November 22
Michael's 'Dangerous' album hits the streets of Japan – three days before the official release date.

November 24
'Dangerous' (LP) enters the Top 75 albums chart in Britain at number one holding its position for one week and remains on the charts for ninety-six weeks. 'Dangerous' is the fastest selling number one album of all-time and makes history by entering the charts at number one just three shopping days after its release. Sony estimate it sold more than 200,000 copies in hectic trading.

In America, Tower Records on Sunset Boulevard opens at midnight to sell copies of 'Dangerous' and also unveil a giant 25-foot, roof-top display.

Loew's Theatre chain have been showing a 30-second teaser for the album directed by David Lynch, which features Michael dancing to 'Black Or White' in the desert.

'Dangerous' (LP) is released in Japan and Canada.

'Black Or White' jumps from number 35 to number 3 on the Pop singles chart and becomes the highest-climbing single since The Beatles' 'Let It Be' rose to number 2 in 1970.

The 'Dangerous' sleeve, which took six months to complete, is the creation of Mark Ryden who worked with both Sony Music Senior Art Director, Nancy Donald, and Michael to develop the very symbolic, acrylic glaze painting. Michael wanted the cover to be mysterious and for people to interpret the images for themselves.

Bubbles, Michael's chimpanzee co-stars with Bob Newhart in the TV movie, *The Entertainers*.

November 26
'Dangerous' (LP) is released by Epic Records in the US.

November 27
MTV 10 airs, celebrating the tenth anniversary of the music video network. Michael performs 'Black Or White' and 'Will You Be There.' He is the only performer on the special to sing two songs.

November 29
Michael appears on the cover of *Entertainment Weekly*.

November 30
To celebrate the release of Michael's new album, 'Dangerous,' *Off The Wall* magazine hold a second MJ Day party at London's Hammersmith Palais.

December

MJJ Productions, Michael's company, provides over 200 turkey dinners for families in Los Angeles.

One of Michael's sequined gloves is auctioned at Christie's in London. It is purchased by Robert Earl of Hard Rock Café restaurants for £16,500 and will be displayed in a new Dublin branch.

TV Guide chooses the Black Or White video as one of the '12 Most Mesmerising TV Moments From The Last 12 Months.'

December 1
'Black Or White' reaches number 1 on the Pop singles chart holding its position for 7 weeks and remains on the charts for twenty weeks. This equals Michael's record for weeks at number one achieved with 'Billie Jean.'

'Black Or White' sells more than 500,000 copies in a three-week period whilst climbing to the top of the US singles chart. The last record to reach number one that quickly was The Beatles 'Get Back' in 1969.

Michael now holds the record for being the first artist to have had number one hits in the '70s, '80s and '90s. 'Black Or White' is also Michael's first solo number one record without the collaboration of Quincy Jones since 'Ben' in 1970.

'Black Or White' is a number one record in the following countries: USA, UK, Australia, Italy, Spain, Mexico, Sweden, Denmark, Norway, Switzerland, Finland, Israel, New Zealand, Cuba, Canada, France, Zimbabwe. It also reaches number 1 on the Euro Hot 100 Singles Chart.

'Black Or White' enters the Black singles chart peaking at number 3 and remains on the charts for fourteen weeks.

'Dangerous' in only its second week on the British charts is already certified double-platinum but through the untimely, and sad death of Freddy Mercury, after only one week at number 1, it is replaced by Queen's 'Greatest Hits II' album.

December 2
Michael appears on the cover of *Jet* magazine.

December 3
Sony Music issue a statement that sales of 'Dangerous' outside the US have reached 5 million. 4.1 million (2.5m CDs, 1.1m cassettes and 400,000 vinyl albums) were shipped for its first week release as follows: 705,000 UK, 560,000 France, 500,000 Germany, 450,000 Italy, 300,000 Spain and 250,000 Sweden. In Germany, 'Dangerous' is the first album ever to achieve advance orders of 50,000. In the former East Germany, Mike Heisel, Senior Product Manager – International Product says that 624,000 copies were sold in the first three days of trading. Virgin Records in France reports that

'Dangerous' is their fastest-selling album ever.

Michael pulls out of a tour of Pakistan proposed for 12 April, 1992 following threats of demonstrations and riots by the militant leader of the Jamaat party, Kazi Hussain Ahmad who feels that American singers will come over to his country and just 'spread obscenity.'

December 8
'Dangerous' (LP) débuts on the Pop albums chart at number 1 holding its position for six weeks. 'Dangerous' débuts at number 11 on the Black albums chart, reaching number one in its fourth week and holding its position for twelve weeks.

'Dangerous' debuts at number one in several countries around the world: USA, Britain, Australia, Spain, Switzerland, Finland and France. The album enters the albums chart at number two in Sweden and Germany, number three in Italy, number five in Japan and the Netherlands and it enters the European chart at number fourteen.

'Dangerous' turns triple platinum in Britain in only its third week on the charts.

'Black Or White' is certified Silver in its fourth week on the Top 75 singles chart in Britain.

December 11
Several days before The Guinness World of Records Museum officially opens, Michael is given a private viewing during which he

also examines his own special exhibit.

Michael is on the cover of *Rennbahn Express*, an Austrian pop magazine, with an account of Adrian Grant's visit to Michael's ranch.

Michael appears on the cover of *WOM Journal* in Germany.

December 29
'Dangerous' is the best-selling album over the Christmas period in America when, between November 26 and December 29, it sells 1.8 million copies. 'Dangerous' has now sold 4 million copies in the US and 10 million copies worldwide.

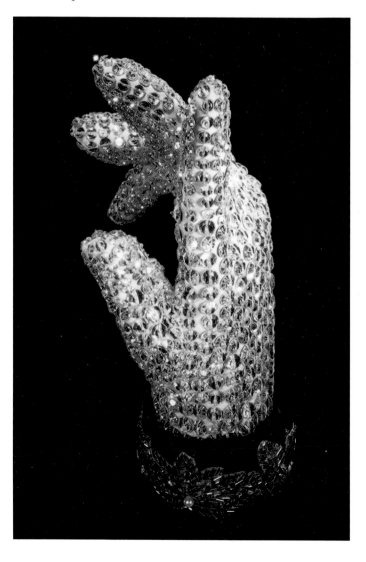

1992

1992

The Guinness Book Of World Records lists Michael Jackson's deal with Sony as the largest entertainment contract ever at $890 million.

The Caribbean islands of St. Vincent and Grenada both issue sets of stamps honouring entertainers including Michael Jackson.

January

'Black Or White' is certified platinum.

'Black Or White' reaches number 1 in Cuba, a weekly music poll by government-run Radio Progreso.

Michael is on the cover of *Rolling Stone* magazine.

On a UK network TV programme, *Rapido*, Jermaine explains why he wrote the song 'Word To The Badd': "I tried to put some phone calls to him and I didn't get a reply... it's a number of things but it's nothing that we couldn't work out, had we spoken, but I wasn't granted an opportunity from his people to speak to him... the overall message is an older brother telling his younger brother to get back to reality... you have

This Page: Michael is honoured by the National Association of Black-Owned Broadcasters. Jesse Jackson presents the award.

Eddie Murphy and Iman star with Michael in his video for the single 'Remember The Time.'

done it to the ultimate level, but you're still a person..."

Anton Furst, the director of *MidKnight*, commits suicide. Later, the film's producer, Jon Peters, says, "We have been unable to find a suitable replacement and, until we do, the film is on ice."

January 1

Moonwalker airs for the first time on UK network TV. As it is broadcast by BBC1 early in the evening, a few seconds of the violent scenes are cut.

January 4

'Dangerous,' which débuted at number 11 on the Black albums chart on December 8, reaches number 1 and holds its position for twelve weeks.

January 12

'Black Or White – The Clivillés & Cole Remixes,' released in Britain on January 6, enters the Top 75 singles chart peaking at number 14 and remains on the charts for four weeks.

January 19

'Remember The Time,' released on January 14, enters the Pop singles chart at number 53 peaking at number 3 and remains on the charts for twenty weeks.

January 27

Michael is on the cover of *People* magazine.

February

The Pro-Set Los Angeles Music Awards honour Michael Jackson as the Best Pop Male Vocalist and 'Black Or White' is hon-

oured as the Video Of The Year.

Michael helps organise Elizabeth Taylor's 60th birthday at Disneyland.

February 2

Fox, BET and MTV simultaneously première the 9-minute short film for 'Remember The Time,' the second single released from 'Dangerous.' The video features model Iman, comedian Eddie Murphy and basketball star, Magic Johnson, and shows Michael's first on-screen kiss. The video is directed by John Singleton, who directed the film *Boyz In The Hood*.

'Remember The Time' peaks at number 1 on the Black singles chart.

February 3

Michael holds a press conference at Radio City Music Hall in New York to announce plans for a new world tour to raise funds for his newly-formed Heal The World Foundation. The Foundation contributes to Paediatric AIDS in memory of Ryan White, Camp Ronald McDonald, Make A Wish Foundation, Juvenile Diabetes, and the Minority AIDS Foundation.

Michael signs a Pepsi endorsement deal in front of the media, after which the St. Thomas Boys' Choir sing 'Heal The World,' almost reducing him to tears.

February 5

Michael is in Washington DC to receive a Lifetime Achievement Award by the National Association of Black-Owned Broadcasters.

issues a special postage stamp bearing Michael's image. Michael travels 30,000 miles in eleven days, but his excursions to hospitals, orphanages,

The event is attended by Jesse Jackson, Stevie Wonder, Muhammad Ali and Spike Lee.

February 6
'Remember The Time' video premieres on *Top Of The Pops* and also airs on MTV Europe.

February 8
Over 300 people attend an auction at Oxnard in California to bid for articles belonging to Michael and The Jackson 5. Amongst the memorabilia are instruments, music storage cases and a black sequined glove, which is bought by Thomas Boe for $1,000.

MTV launch their 'Dinner With Michael Contest.'

February 9
'Remember The Time,' released on February 3 in Britain, enters the Top 75 singles chart as the Highest New Entry at number 6, peaking at number 3 and remains on the charts for eight weeks. The single features 'Come Together' from *Moonwalker* on the B-side.

February 10
'Remember The Time' remixes are released in Britain.

Michael Jackson departs from Los Angeles International Airport for a two-week visit to Africa. He will visit the Republic

of Gabon and be escorted on a tour of Abidjan on the Ivory Coast, Dar-Es-Salaam in Tanzania, Nairobi and Egypt. He is said to be making a film for his own private collection, *Return To Africa.*

February 11
Michael is welcomed by 100,000 people when he arrives in Libreville in Gabon. President Omar Bongo presents him with a Medal of Honour at the Ambassador's Hall in the Presidential Palace.

February 12
The town of Oyen welcomes Michael with children carrying banners 'Welcome Home Michael'.
 In the West African gold-mining village of Krindjabo on the Ivory Coast, populated by the Agni tribe, Michael is crowned 'King of Sani' by tribal chief Amon N'Djafolk.
 In Dar-Es-Salaam, Michael is the guest of President Ali Hassan Mwinyi and Tanzania

schools, churches and institutions for mentally retarded children receive little positive coverage by the media.

February 19
Michael arrives in Britain from his African trip and at 7.45 p.m. checks in to The Dorchester hotel in London under a total news blackout.

February 20
The press converge on the Dorchester hotel to follow Michael's every move in the capital. At 1.15 p.m. Michael visits Foyles Bookstore, an antique shop and HMV, where he purchases some Doris Day LPs. Later, Michael and his cousin, Brett Barnes, visit Hamleys toy store and Rock Circus in Piccadilly.

Michael appears on the cover of *Jet* magazine with Eddie Murphy and Iman, 'Michael Jackson's New Video - Remember The Time When Blacks Were Kings And Queens.'

While Michael tours the African nations, he becomes the centre of a negative media campaign. Robert E. Johnson, publisher of *Ebony* and *Jet* magazines, one of the 26 specially invited guests accompanying him to, reports as follows on the malicious Jackson-bashing by the media:

•The trip was a 'public relations disaster for Michael.' Truth: It was a triumph in which he drew more spectators in Gabon than Nelson Mandela and more in the Ivory Coast than the Pope.

•The singer cut short an African tour after a stopover generated the wrong kind of excitement. Truth: The sponsors wanted him to extend his tour to meet the demand for his appearances everywhere.

•He held his hand to his nose because the African nations smelled. Truth: He sometimes touched his nose, an old nervous habit.

•He collapsed from the heat and he went to London for a medical appointment. Truth: He was never bothered by the heat. His personal physician, Dr. R. Chalmers, accompanied Michael on the trip.

•He refused to shake hands with Africans. Truth: He shook the hands of hundreds of people, hugged and kissed children in hospitals and institutions for the mentally retarded.

•He is 'neither Black nor White' and is not a good role model for children. Truth: After Michael read a prayer in the Basilica of Our Lady of Peace on the Ivory Coast, a 9 year-old boy exclaimed: "Michael is love, love, love! I want to be like him."

This Page: Michael in Africa.

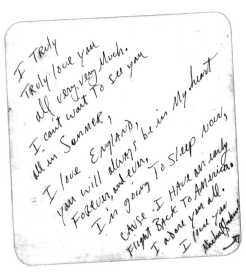

I Truly
Truly love you
all very, very Much.
I can't wait To see you
all in Summer,
I love England,
you will always be in My heart
Forever, and ever,
I'm going To sleep now,
cause I Have an early
Flight BAck To America.
I adore you all.
I love you
Michael Jackson

This Page: Naomi Campbell appears with Michael in his video for the single 'In The Closet.'

February 21

At 5.30 p.m., Michael leaves The Dorchester to visit Madam Tussaud's Wax Museum and the Disney Shop.

February 22

Probably the most eventful day of his visit to Britain, during which – unbeknown to his fans – Michael signs contracts for his British tour dates.

Michael appears on the roof of The Dorchester throwing down messages on paper planes and, evidently short of adequate writing materials, writes some on bedding (a favourite idiosyncrasy of his!).

Michael brings flowers and spends 35 minutes at Benny Hill's bedside when he visits him at the Royal Brompton Hospital in west London. Benny Hill, who has suffered a heart attack, is an artist Michael greatly admires. Sadly, Benny dies shortly afterwards.

February 23

'Motown's Greatest Hits' (LP) by Michael Jackson, released on February 10, enters the Top 75 albums chart in Britain peaking at number 53 and remains on the charts for two weeks.

Michael Jackson takes a scheduled flight home to Los Angeles from London Heathrow Airport.

March

Bubbles has a guest starring role on TV's *Father Dowling's Mysteries*.

March 16

Michael appears on the cover of *Jet* magazine.

March 29

Thirty-five winners of MTV's 'My Dinner With Michael Contest' are invited to bring a guest to dinner with Michael on the set of the video for 'In The Closet.' Michael stays at the dinner for two hours, talking and even dancing with his guests.

Spring

EuroDisney opens in Paris, France. One of its most popular attractions is reported to be 'Le Captain EO'.

April

A $7 million copyright infringement lawsuit against Michael Jackson, MJJ Productions, Epic Records and Sony Music Entertainment is filed by the Cleveland Orchestra. A performance by the orchestra of Beethoven's 9th Symphony is used as the opening 67 seconds of 'Will You Be There.'

'In The Closet' by Michael Jackson and Mystery Girl, the third single from 'Dangerous,' is released in America with a double 12" issue of mixes from Tommy Musto and Frankie Knuckles.

April 23

'In The Closet' video is premiéred on Fox TV, MTV and BET in America and on *Top Of The Pops* in Britain. Michael co-directs with Herb Ritts. Co-star for this very sensual video is British supermodel Naomi Campbell. It will later be banned by the South African government who deem it to be offensive.

The Ripley Museum in Buena Park in California open a new exhibit featuring a sculptured creation of Michael made out of pulped dollar bills.

April 24

Friday Night Videos is once again devoted entirely to Michael Jackson, titled *Live And Dangerous*.

April 26

'In The Closet' enters the Pop singles chart at number 46, peaking at number 6 and remains on the charts for twenty weeks. It becomes the album's third number 1 hit on the Black singles chart.

'In The Closet,' released on April 21 in Britain, enters the Top 75 singles chart at number 8, where it peaks, remaining on the charts for six weeks.

May

Michael is on the cover of *Ebony* magazine.

May 1

Michael is in Washington to accept a 'Point Of Light' award from President Bush, which acknowledges his efforts with disadvantaged children. While in Washington, Michael visits a little girl, Raynal Pope, who was mauled by dogs.

May 6

Michael covers the funeral costs of Ramon Sanchez who was killed by a stray bullet during the LA riots.

June

Michael and Naomi Campbell are on the cover of *Class* magazine.

Mariah Carey enjoys one week at the top of the Pop singles chart with a remake of The Jackson 5 hit, 'I'll Be There.'

A copyright infringement lawsuit is filed against Michael Jackson by Crystal Cartier, who claims that Michael's song 'Dangerous' is her composition.

June 3

Operation One To One, an organisation concerned with the betterment of youth, honours Michael with an award recognising his efforts in helping disadvantaged youth.

June 11

Michael is on the cover of Germany's *Bravo* pop magazine.

June 14

Michael is on the cover of *The News Of The World* magazine.

June 18

Dancing The Dream by Michael Jackson, a book of poetry and essays, is published by Doubleday.

June 19

'Jam,' the fourth short film from 'Dangerous,' premières on Fox, BET and MTV in America. The video features appearances by basketball star, Michael Jordan, rapper Heavy D, and rap duo Kriss Kross.

June 23

Michael touches down at London Heathrow Airport on his way to Munich to hold a press conference about his Heal The World Foundation.

June 24

The *Daily Mirror* newspaper publishes an unflattering photo of Michael on its front page with the headline, 'Scarface.'

June 25

Michael films a new video for 'Give In To Me' at 166 Landsberger Straße in Munich, Germany with Slash, from Guns N' Roses, also appearing in the video.

June 26

Michael presents a cheque for DM 40,000 to the Mayor of Munich, Georg Kronawitter, to help the City's needy children. Thousands of fans turn out to greet Michael at the capital's City Hall.

June 27

The Dangerous World Tour kicks off at the Olympic Stadium in Munich, Germany. Michael plays to a sell-out crowd of 72,000 ecstatic fans, who see him perform eighteen numbers, including four songs from his new album. The close of the show hits the headlines when 'Michael' jetpacks out of the stadium and over the heads of his fans.

'In The Closet' reaches number 1 on the Black singles chart holding its position for one week.

June 29

Daily Mirror publishes an extremely distorted photograph of Michael in concert on their front page with detrimental comments regarding Michael's face.

Michael visits Sophia Children's Hospital in Rotterdam to donate £100,000. In the evening, Michael visits Intertoys toy shop at Coolsinyel, Rotterdam, and spends 45 minutes at Blijoorp Zoo.

June 30, July 1

Michael performs in concert to an audience of 92,087 at two dates at the Feyenoord Stadium in Rotterdam, Holland.

July

Michael takes action to sue the *Daily Mirror* over Ken Lennox's distorted photograph taken during his opening concert in Munich.

Billboard announces that the Second Annual Music Video Producers' Association has added 'Beat It' and 'Billie Jean' to their 'Hall Of Fame.'

1992

"Our children are the most beautiful, most sweet, most treasured of our creations. And yet, every minute at least 28 children die. Today our children are at risk of being killed by diseases and by the violence of war, guns, abuse and neglect. Children have few rights and no-one to speak for them. They have no voice in our world. God and nature has blessed me with a voice. Now I want to use it to help children speak for themselves. I have founded the Heal The World Foundation to be the voice of the voiceless: the children."

Michael Jackson, June 23, 1992

This Page and Opposite: Michael on the Dangerous tour.

MTV counts down the Top Ten Biggest Stars of their first ten years. The special concludes with videos and concert footage of Michael Jackson.

July 4
Michael performs in concert to an audience of 35,000 at the Flaminio Stadium in Rome, Italy.

July 6-7
Michael performs in concert to an audience of 93,000 at two dates at the Brianteo Stadium in Monza, Italy.

July 11
Michael performs in concert to an audience of 65,000 at the Müngersdorfer Stadium in Cologne, Germany.

'Jam' enters the Pop singles chart peaking at number 26 and remains on the charts for fourteen weeks. This is Michael's weakest placing on Billboard's charts since 'One Day In Your Life' in 1981, which peaked at number 55. The poor chart performance is due, in part, to the late release of the CD single.

'Jam' enters the Black singles chart peaking at number 3 and remains on the charts for twelve weeks.

July 13
BBC2's *DEF II* has the world exclusive première for Michael Jackson's 'Who Is It' video which is aired during a Michael Jackson Special featuring live footage from the Munich concert.

July 14
The 'Who Is It' video is withdrawn by Michael because he is said to be unhappy with the editing and angry about its early release.

July 15
Michael performs in concert to a capacity audience of 35,000 at the Vallehovin Stadium in Oslo, Norway.

July 17-18
Michael performs in concert to an audience of 53,000 at the Olympic Stadium in Stockholm, Sweden. On the second night, despite rainy weather and advice from his doctor not to perform, Michael puts on another brilliant concert.

July 19
'Who Is It,' released on July 13 in Britain, enters the Top 75 singles chart at number 12, peaking at number 10 and remains on the charts for seven weeks.

July 20
Michael performs in concert to an audience of over 30,000 at the Gentofte Stadium in Copenhagen, Denmark.

July 22
Michael performs in concert to an audience of 40,000 at the Festival

Ground in Werchter, near Brussels, Belgium.

July 24
240 tickets are stolen from the office of promoter, Barry Clayman, in London, including the Royal VIP ticket for Prince Charles!

July 25
Michael performs in concert to an audience of 40,000 at Lansdowne Road in Dublin. It is announced that £500,000 of the 'Dangerous' tour profits will be donated by Michael to British children's charities.

July 26
Michael visits EuroDisney in France in the company of his cousin, Brett Barnes.

July 27
Michael Jackson wins a High Court injunction on the *Daily Mirror's* close-up photo of his face. Mr. Justice Millett grants Michael a fifteen-day order preventing the newspaper from republishing the unflattering photo.

July 28
The *Daily Mirror* discloses that it has received a Writ from Michael Jackson's British lawyers, Simon Olswang & Co., complaining about the description of Lennox's photo, published in their June 29 issue. However, this does not dissuade the newspaper from publishing the same photo on the front page again.

July 29
Michael flies in to Britain from Dublin and goes straight to the Queen Elizabeth Hospital for Children in London's Hackney. He is greeted by 2,000 cheering fans as he arrives by helicopter from Luton Airport. Michael brings with him an added treat for the sick children – Mickey Mouse and Minnie Mouse.

As Michael departs, the *Daily Mirror* solicitor, Martin Crudace tries to serve a Writ! Meanwhile, the *Daily Mirror* photographer responsible for the controversy over the photograph, gets his comeuppance when angry and disgruntled British fans bombard him with horse manure!

July 30
Michael opens his UK tour by performing in concert to a capacity audience of 72,000 at Wembley Stadium in London.

July 31
Eric Herminie (28), a young man obsessed with Michael, stands on a ledge on top of a 120 foot high building opposite The Dorchester hotel, where Michael is staying, and says that he will jump if he does not see him. Michael speaks to him for several minutes on the phone before appearing on his hotel suite balcony to wave and gesture to him not to jump. When Herminie finally climbs back inside, he is taken away by the police and charged with breach of the peace.

In the evening, Michael Jackson meets Prince Charles backstage before the second Wembley concert and presents him with a cheque for £200,000 for the Prince's Trust.

'Black Or White' is honoured as the music video with the best special effects at the 1992 International Monitor Awards.

'Black Or White' is voted as one of their favourite videos by the Olympic athletes competing in Barcelona, Spain.

August
Michael sells the film rights to his 'Dangerous' tour concert to America's Home Box Office (HBO) for £12 million. The deal is the highest ever paid for a live concert.

Michael buys a clock, in the shape of a monkey, from Royal jewellers, Garrard, for £40,000.

August 1
The third Wembley show is cancelled at the last minute owing to Michaels' exhaustion and re-scheduled for August 23.

August 2
Michael Jackson's US lawyer, Bertram Fields, appears via satellite from Los Angeles on LWTV's *The Richard And Judy Show* to talk about Michael's lawsuit against the *Daily Mirror*. When asked why Michael has chosen to sue now after years of speculation about his plastic surgery, Fields says, "Well, the issue is not about his plastic surgery. He's been very open about the fact that he's had plastic surgery... But the fact is the *Daily Mirror* published other things. They said that he was a 'cruelly disfigured phantom.' They said he had a 'hole in his nose' and his face was 'covered with scar tissue.' None of that is true.

1992

Finally, he decided that he had to sue."

August 5
Michael performs in concert to an audience of 50,000 at Cardiff Arms Park. Despite torrential rain, he overcomes a slippery dance floor – sometimes interrupting the show to mop the wet stage with his foot, whilst interacting and joking with his public – to give an exhilarating performance.

August 8
Michael performs in concert to an audience of 45,000 at the Weser Stadium in Bremen, Germany.

August 9
'Tour Souvenir Pack,' a 4-CD Box Set with each CD containing three tracks from each of Michael's four albums, enters the Top 75 albums chart in Britain at number 32, where it peaks, and remains on the charts for three weeks.

Michael now has five albums inside the Top 50 in Britain: 'Dangerous' at number 5 (4x platinum), 'Bad' at number 17 (13x platinum), 'Thriller' at number 20 (11x platinum), 'Tour Souvenir Pack at number 32, and 'Off The Wall' at number 48 (6x platinum).

August 10
Michael performs in concert to an audience of 51,000 at the Volkspark Stadium in Hamburg, Germany.

August 13
Michael performs in concert to a capacity audience of over 25,000 at the

Weserbergland Stadium in Hameln, Germany.

August 16
Michael performs in concert to an audience of 60,000 at Roundhay Park in Leeds, England.

Nicholas Killen, aged 6, who had lost his sight the previous month in life-saving cancer surgery, meets Michael backstage before the start of the show.

August 18
Michael performs in concert to a capacity audience of 65,000 at The Haugh in Glasgow, Scotland.

August 20
Michael performs his third Wembley concert to a capacity audience of 72,000. This concert was originally scheduled for August 21, but is rescheduled due to the rescheduling of the cancelled concert on August 1.

August 22
Michael performs his fourth Wembley concert to a capacity audience of 72,000.

Michael's concert starts late because the 'toaster,' from which he is catapulted at the start of the show, malfunctions. Due to this, the show overruns and breaches the 10.30 p.m. council curfew, causing Michael to incur a fine. The figure is reported by *The Sun* to be £60,000, which Michael will pay to a music charity.

August 23
Michael performs his fifth and final concert to a capacity audience of 72,000 at Wembley Stadium.

Michael again has all five of his recent albums in the

Top 75 albums chart in Britain with 'Dangerous' at number 2 in its fortieth week on the charts.

August 24-25
At the first Heal The World European Children's Congress at Regent's College in London, 84 children aged between 8 and 16 come together to express their views on the world's biggest problems, and the solutions, as they see them. Despite suffering from laryngitis, Michael arrives at the Congress after lunch on the second day and stays for approximately four hours. Later, Michael leaves Britain for Austria.

August 26
Michael performs in concert to an audience of over 50,000 at the Prater Stadium in Vienna, Austria.

August 28
Michael performs in concert to a capacity audience of 60,000 at the Wald Stadium in Frankfurt, Germany. Although this venue officially holds only 55,000 with fans standing in the aisles, the media report that the show is not a sell-out! Michael performs brilliantly and is in excellent spirits, with renditions of 'Happy Birthday Michael' from the crowd.

August 29
Michael, who is 34 today, spends his birthday in Regensburg at the castle of Princess Gloria Von Thurn and Taxis. The castle is closed to the public so that her son, Albert, can spend time with Michael.

August 30
Michael performs in con-

This Page: Michael on the 'Dangerous' tour.

cert to a capacity audience of over 32,000 at the Southwest Stadium in Ludwigshafen, Germany. Again, this is a rainy concert and Michael seems exhausted. Due to objections being raised by the descendants of Carl Orff, the composer of 'Carmina Burana,' Michael's opening concert music, he is prevented from using this piece tonight.

September

Sony presents Michael Jackson with an award commemorating his four albums which have all achieved sales of over ten million each.

The Hollywood Arts Council fights to get a 3-D mural of Michael Jackson displayed on the historic El Capitan Theater.

September 2
Michael performs in concert to a capacity audience of 32,000 at the Volks Stadium in Beyreuth, Germany.

Ryan White's mother, Jeanne, appears on the US TV show, *Maury Povich*, and speaks about Michael's friendship with her son. During the show, Michael phones in and reads a short poem about Ryan.

September 4
Michael performs in concert to a capacity audience of over 35,000 at the Jahn Stadium in East Berlin, Germany.

Reports appear that Michael is suffering severe throat problems each night he takes to the stage. His publicist, Bennett Kleinberg, admits that

Michael is taking painkillers to survive the dates.

September 6
The concert due to take place at the Park Stadium in Gelsenkirchen, Germany is cancelled due to Michael's ill-health.

'Jam,' released on September 6 in Britain, enters the Top 75 singles chart as the Highest New Entry at number 14 peaking at number 12. This is the fifth single released from the 'Dangerous' album.

September 8
Michael performs in concert to a capacity audience of over 47,000 at La Pontaise in Lausanne, Switzerland. Following the concert, he is taken back to the hotel in an ambulance and does not leave his hotel.

September 11
The concert due to take place at St. Jacob Stadium in Basel, Switzerland is cancelled due to Michael's ill-health.

September 12
Michael is on the cover of France's *Le Figaro* magazine

September 13
Michael performs in concert to a capacity audience of 85,000 at the Hippodrome de Vincennes in Paris, France. He is again exhausted after the show and is driven back to his hotel in an ambulance.

Michael is on the cover of Spain's *Blanco Negro* magazine.

September 16
Michael performs in con-

cert to a capacity audience of 40,000 at the Stade Municipal in Toulouse, France.

September 18
Michael performs in concert to an audience of over 42,000 at the Olympia Stadium in Barcelona, Spain.

September 21
Michael performs in concert to a capacity audience of over 25,000 at the football Stadium in Oviedo, Spain. Slash makes a special appearance and joins Michael for 'Black Or White.'

September 23
Michael performs in concert to a capacity audience of 40,000 at the Vicente Calderón in Madrid, Spain.

September 26
Michael performs in concert to a capacity audience of 64,000 at the Jose Alvalade Stadium in Lisbon, Portugal.

September 28
Armed guards are dumbfounded as 2,000 fans wait all day in the cold at Bucharest's Otopeni Airport to greet Michael on his arrival. Until this day, this kind of teenage pop hysteria and VIP treatment for a pop singer has never been seen in Romania.

September 30
An estimated 6,000 people pour onto the streets to witness the Michael Jackson procession make its way to the Leaganul Pentru Copii Sfinta Ecaterina orphanage to formally open a playground for 500 orphans funded by Michael. President Iliescu

1992

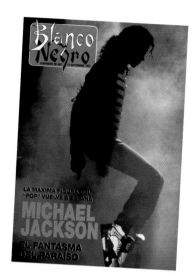

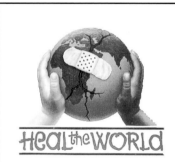

The Foundation has three main goals:

1. To make the safety, health and development of children the world's highest priority.

2. To be the voice of the voiceless by focusing worldwide attention on the needs and rights of all children and by providing children with a forum to express their unique vision for healing the world.

3. To help create a world where children will live without violence, where children will be free of disease and have healthy lives, and where each generation will have the opportunity to grow into fully participating members of the world community.

1992

and the world's press are there. Outside, Jackson is mobbed by children, on his way to the newly-restored Casino Theatre for a rare press conference to officially launch Heal The World Foundation in the presence of the Prime Minister.

October 1

Michael Jackson performs at the Complexul Sportiv National Stadium in Bucharest, Romania, before a capacity crowd of 70,000 – with an additional 20,000 police and troops in attendance! Tickets sell for half the usual price, but this is still more than a third of the average monthly salary in Romania. The country has never seen anything like it and many of the older members of the audience – used to more placid entertainment – are bewildered.

The concert, Michael's only show in a former Iron Curtain country, is attended by the Prime Minister (who presents Michael with a ceremonial uniform) and other political figures. One senate spokesman says, "This event is worth ten years of diplomacy with the West. At last the West will recognise us as a proper European country and not a strange name in an atlas."

Andy Morahan, who directed Give In To Me, uses more than 14 camera operators to tape the concert, which is broadcast live on radio and TV to 61 countries around the world, including 21 in Europe. Royalties from the TV broadcast in Europe alone are estimated at approximately £15 million.

This Page: Michael enjoys the launch of the Heal The World Foundation.

Page Opposite: The 'Dangerous' tour.

Michael chose this particular concert to be televised because the whole point of his 'Dangerous' tour was to raise funds and awareness for his Heal The World Foundation. Bucharest, with its notorious orphanages, was the ideal springboard to officially propel the Heal The World Foundation, and to point out the predicament of the Romanian babies.

October 2

Michael arrives at Ataturk Airport in Istanbul. This is Michael's first visit to a Moslem country but, more importantly, the first time the youth of modern, liberal Turkey have a chance to see a true mega-star perform live.

October 4

Five hours before Michael is due to perform at the Inonu Stadium, Istanbul, for what is billed as 'the concert of the era,' an announcement is made that, due to a vocal cord ailment, the concert has been postponed and that Michael Jackson is already on his way to London. It takes over four hours before the disappointed and disbelieving crowd disburses.

October 5

Michael consults a Harley Street specialist regarding throat problems. It is believed that nodules have developed on Michael's vocal cords, a common ailment among singers. No serious damage has been done, but Michael has to rest for several weeks.

The cancellation of concerts at the Ataturk Stadium in Izmir, Turkey, and Athens in Greece bring an untimely end to the European leg of the 'Dangerous' concert. Of the 42 concerts scheduled for Europe, Michael performed 37, with five cancellations due to ill-health.

"I am very happy to be here in Japan again. I am very lucky to see all the children and the young at heart as well. The innocence of children represents to me the source of infinitive creativity and I feel this is where all my creative source comes from. This is not an intellectual kind of intelligence but an intelligence that is full of wonder, magic, mystery and adventure. In this intelligence there is love, there is trust, there is joy and there is beauty. It's the kind of intelligence that will heal the world. That is why I am here and that is why we are here. Thank you very much. I love you."

Michael Jackson
December 10, 1992

October 6

Michael departs London Heathrow aboard a Concorde to New York for a forward journey to Los Angeles.

October 10

HBO, the American cable TV station, broadcasts the whole of the 'Dangerous' concert from Bucharest. Michael is reportedly paid $20 million for the rights to air the show, making it the largest contract ever for a one-time concert transmitted on TV. The special receives the highest TV ratings in the history of HBO (21.4% rating, 34% share). The Bucharest concert is broadcast in 21 countries around the world on different dates.

November

Off The Wall magazine launches their Michael Jackson Telephone Information Line in Britain on the number 0891-424124.

'Heal The World' enters the Pop and Black singles charts peaking at numbers 27 and 62 respectively. The single is much more successful on the Adult Contemporary charts, peaking at number 9.

Michael files a $44 million lawsuit against LA Gear, charging them with fraud and breach of contract. This is a countersuit against a $10 million suit filed by LA Gear against Michael Jackson. The company hoped to market the line of shoes to coincide with the release of a new Michael Jackson album. But the album was delayed.

A San Diego Californian-based company, The Worldwide Innovative Network, launch 'Mystique de Michael Jackson' perfume for women, and 'Legend de Michael Jackson' for men. Each bottle comes complete with an hologram of Michael.

Hundreds of Michael Jackson fans march through the streets of Bucharest demanding that The Nobel Peace Prize be awarded to Michael.

November 14

Michael is on the cover of *TV Guide*.

November 15, 18

The Jacksons – An American Dream is screened, the five-hour mini series about the career and lives of The Jacksons, is broadcast at 8.00 p.m. on ABC-TV. With 22.2% rating and 33% share it becomes the most-watched mini series of any TV station in the last three years, with 22 million households, one-third of all TV viewers, tuning in.

'The Jacksons: An American Dream,' the soundtrack album to the TV movie, is released by Motown Records. The soundtrack album performs badly on the album charts, never rising higher than number 137 on the Pop albums chart. It does not appear at all on the Black albums chart.

'Who's Lovin' You,' a special live version of the song, is released as a single. It never makes a showing on the Pop singles chart, and only reaches number 48 on the Black singles chart.

November 21

On the first anniversary of the release of 'Dangerous' in Britain, the album is now at number 45 in the Top 75 albums chart.

November 24

Inside a hangar at New York's John F. Kennedy International Airport, Michael witnesses the loading of 43 tons of medical supplies, blankets, winter clothing and shoes onto a DC-8 cargo jet bound for the children of Sarajevo in Bosnia-Herzegovina, a war zone in the former Yugoslavia.

The Heal The World Foundation teams up with AmeriCares to fly the $2.1 million worth of aid to the Croatian capital, Zagreb, and then to Sarajevo for distribution under the supervision of the UN High Command for Refugees.

November 29

'Heal The World,' released on November 23 in Britain, enters the Top 75 singles chart as the Highest New Entry at number 3 peaking at number 2 where it remains for five weeks.

December

The copyright infringement suit brought by the Cleveland Orchestra is settled. Future copies of 'Dangerous' will carry a credit to Ludwig Van Beethoven.

December 6

At the 5th annual *Smash Hits* Poll Winners Party, held in London, Michael Jackson is voted the Best Male Solo Singer by its readers.

The third annual *Off The*

Wall Michael Jackson Day is held at1 London's Hammersmith Palais.

December 9
At the Billboard Music Awards held at the Universal Amphitheater in Los Angeles and broadcast live by Fox TV, Michael receives two special honours: The 1992 Billboard World Artist Award for the Number One World Single, 'Black Or White,' and the Number One World Album, 'Dangerous.'

The second special honour is to commemorate the Tenth Anniversary of 'Thriller,' the biggest-selling album of all time. There is also a video tribute to Michael as the best-selling artist in the world.

Michael arrives at Tokyo Narita Airport and checks in to the Capitol Tokyo Hotel, where he occupies the Imperial Suite on the 10th floor.

December 10
At a press conference at the American Consulate, Michael accepts a cheque for Heal the World in the sum of $100,000 from Pepsi.

December 12
Michael performs in concert to a capacity audience of 45,000 at the Tokyo Dome, Japan.

December 13
Michael receives a phonecall from Ray Charles, who is also touring Japan at this time.

December 14
Michael performs in concert to a capacity audience of 45,000 at the Tokyo Dome, Japan.

December 15
Michael visits Sega Enterprises and discusses a new project.

December 17
Michael performs in concert to a capacity audience of 45,000 at the Tokyo Dome, Japan.

December 18
Michael visits Disneyland in Tokyo during normal opening hours.

December 19
Michael performs in concert to a capacity audience of 45,000 at the Tokyo Dome, Japan.

December 21
Michael visits Sony.

December 22
Michael performs in concert to a capacity audience of 45,000 at the Tokyo Dome, Japan.

December 23
Michael goes shopping in Akihabra wearing a black mask, glasses and hat.

December 24
Michael performs in concert to a capacity audience of 45,000 at the Tokyo Dome, Japan. Following this concert, 'Bad' and 'The Way You Make Me Feel' are dropped from the setlist.

December 26
During a TV appeal for donations in aid of the United Negro College Funds, a videotape with the following message from Michael is aired: "Black Colleges and Universities produce some of the leading personalities of our time. They are leaders in business and law, science and technology, politics and religion. I am proud to have helped over 200 young men and women to receive a quality education that has placed them closer to their dreams due to the Michael Jackson scholarship program. Tonight I encourage you to pitch in for higher education. Please support the UNCF."

December 26-28
Michael flies to Nagasaki-Ken and visits an amusement park in Huis Ten. Tito's three children, who Michael has invited to visit over Christmas, accompany him.

December 28
Michael returns to Tokyo travelling on the Superexpress train and, with his three nephews, visits the toy store, Hakuhinnan.

December 29
Michael visits Disneyland in Tokyo accompanied by Tito's three children.

December 30
Michael performs in concert to a capacity audience of 45,000 at the Tokyo Dome, Japan and Slash makes a special guest appearance for 'Black Or White.'

December 31
Michael performs in concert to a capacity audience of 45,000 at the Tokyo Dome, Japan at this Special Countdown Concert, and Slash again plays guitar during 'Black Or White.' From his changing room, Michael wishes all his fans a Happy New Year.

1992

This Page: Michael visits Sega in Tokyo.

1993

1993

Ten years after its release, 'Thriller' sells another million copies to reach a staggering 50 million copies sold worldwide, and remains far and away the biggest-selling album of all time. Worldwide sales of Michael Jackson's other albums are 'Dangerous' (20 million), 'Bad' (28m – the second biggest-selling album of all time) and 'Off The Wall' (11m).

Michael is on the cover of an issue of *Black Beat*, that is devoted entirely to him.

January 16

Michael receives the NAACP's Image Award for Best Music Video ('Black Or White') and the coveted award for Entertainer Of The Year. Following a video tribute to Michael, Patti Labelle and the Voices of Faith Choir sing 'Will You Be There' with Michael joining in the last verse.

'Heal The World' is certified Gold (400,000) in Britain.

January 18

Michael appears at the Pre-Inaugural Celebration for Bill Clinton and joins other celebrities, including Diana Ross, on the steps of the Lincoln Memorial for 'We Are The World'.

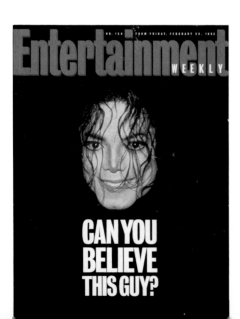

Bert Fields, Michael's lawyer, denies rumours that Michael suggested to President Clinton that he replace the ten planned Inauguration balls with a performance by him. He also denies that Michael is played by a white boy in the forthcoming Pepsi commercial, saying that Michael was "outraged and very, very hurt" by the rumours. Fields says, "Michael is going to be more receptive from now on. He was reclusive before, but the '90s demand more reality and accessibility."

January 19

Michael joins other celebrities at 'An American Reunion: The 52nd Presidential Inaugural Gala.' He is greeted with a standing ovation and, before singing 'Gone Too Soon' live, makes an appeal on behalf of AIDS sufferers, citing the case of his friend Ryan White. He also sings 'Heal The World.'

January 25

At the 20th American Music Awards ceremony held at the Shrine Auditorium in Los Angeles, Michael wins two of his five nominations for Favourite Soul/R&B Single ('Remember The Time') and Favourite Pop/Rock Album ('Dangerous'). With three awards, he becomes the evening's big winner as he accepts the first ever International Artist Award from Elizabeth Taylor. In future, the award will be known as The Michael Jackson International Artist Award. The programme is broadcast live by ABC-TV, with 20 million American households tuning in, a 32% share.

January 26

Michael attends a press conference at the Century Plaza Hotel in Century City, Los Angeles, to accept donations of $100,000 each from the NFL (National Football League) and Frito Lay, sponsor of the Super Bowl, and $500,000 from the BEST Foundation, for his Heal The World Foundation.

Heal LA, a Los Angeles based children's initiative, is launched at this event.

January 31

Michael performs a medley of 'Jam,' 'Billie Jean' and 'Black Or White' and 'Heal The World' at the Super Bowl Halftime Show in the Rose Bowl Stadium, Pasadena, California before an audience of 100,000 in the stadium and 133 million on TV. Following the show, 'Dangerous' rises to number 26 in the Pop albums chart.

February

The Jacksons: An American Dream is released on video cassette.

February 8

Michael is on the cover of *Jet* magazine with Oprah Winfrey.

February 10

The topic of Oprah Winfrey's regular daytime talk show is Michael Jackson. Her guests include Smokey Robinson, Suzanne de Passe, Gladys Knight, Iman and Jeanne White, Ryan White's mother.

Michael Jackson Talks... To Oprah is telecast live from

Neverland Valley around the world, attracting around 100 million viewers. Michael refuses to answer questions about allegations made by LaToya in her book, saying he hasn't read it, and also declines to disclose if he is a virgin, saying "I'm a gentleman." But he does reveal that he doesn't really know his father, and that he suffers from a skin disorder which destroys the pigmentation of the skin. He refutes the long-time rumours that he sleeps in an oxygen chamber, that he wanted to buy The Elephant Man's bones, that he has a shrine to Elizabeth Taylor and that he once proposed to her. The TV Special concludes with the première of the video for 'Give In To Me.'

After Michael's performance at the Super Bowl and his interview with Oprah Winfrey sales of 'Dangerous' increase dramatically. In the two weeks following the Super Bowl performance, 'Dangerous' moves up the Pop albums chart an amazing 106 places, from number 131 to number 41. The sales momentum continues after the interview when the album rises another 31 places to number 10 on the Pop albums chart, more than a year after its release. In Britain, 'Dangerous' rises to number 6 in the Top 75 albums chart.

February 24
Michael receives two nominations at the 35th Annual Grammy Awards at the Shrine Auditorium in Los Angeles for Best Pop Male Vocal ('Black Or White') and Best R&B Male Vocal

('Jam'). Although he doesn't win the categories, he is presented with the Grammy Legend Award by his sister Janet, who narrates a video tribute to her brother. Both siblings look stunning and Michael is in exceptional form as he jokes with the audience, provoking a comment from the host of the show: "When did he get so damn funny?"

Bruce Swedien receives a Grammy for Best Engineered Recording ('Dangerous').

Following the presentations, Michael and his date, Brooke Shields, attend the Polygram party at A&M Studios and later show up at the Sony Music party in Century City.

February 26
Michael is asked about his thoughts regarding Elizabeth Taylor in a video for the Arts & Entertainment Network. Cathy Griffin, the producer of the programme gives Michael a waffle-iron which makes waffles in the shape of Mickey Mouse!

Michael is on the cover of *Entertainment Weekly*.

March
It is announced that Michael has formed an independent film company, Michael Jackson Productions, which will produce uplifting movies, with a share of the profits going to his Heal The World Foundation.

March 5
US MTV broadcast another Michael Jackson Weekend.

" I hope this puts to rest, I hope this finally put to rest another rumour that has been in the press for too many years. Me and Janet really are two different people.

In the past month, I have gone from "Where is he?" to 'Here he is again!" But I must confess it feels good to be thought of as a person, not as a personality. Because... I don't read all the things written about me. I wasn't aware that the world thought I was so weird and so bizarre, but when you grow up, as I did, in front of one hundred million people since the age of 5, you're automatically different.

The last few weeks I have been cleansing myself and it's been a rebirth for myself. It's like a cleansing spirit.

My childhood was completely taken away from me. There was no Christmas, there was no birthdays... It was not a normal childhood, no normal pleasures of childhood. Those were exchanged for hard work, struggle and pain, and eventual material and professional success. But as an awful price, I cannot recreate that part of my life, nor would I change any part of my life.

However, today when I create my music, I feel like an instrument of nature. I wonder what delight nature must feel when we open our hearts and express our God-given talents. The sound of approval rose across the universe and the whole world abounds in magic. Wonder fills our hearts for we have glimpsed, for an instant, the playfulness of life.

And that's why I love children and learn so much from being around them. I realise that many of the world's problems today, from the inner city crime to large scale wars and terrorism, and our overcrowded prisons are a result of the fact that children have had their childhoods stolen from them. The magic, the wonder, the mystery and the innocence of a child's heart are the seeds of creativity that will heal the world. I really believe that. That we... I love you too...

What we need to learn from children isn't childish. Being with them connects us to the deeper wisdom of life which is ever-present and only asks to be lived. They know the way to solutions that lie waiting to be recognised within our own hearts.

Today I would like to thank all of the children of the world including the sick and deprived, I am so sensitive to your pain. I also want to thank all those who have helped me to channel my talent here on earth.

From the beginning my parents, all my brothers and sisters, especially Janet. I am so proud of her, it's incredible. I mean, I remember when we were little, I asked her to be Ginger Rogers while I was Fred Astaire.

The Motown family, my teacher Berry Gordy, Diana Ross, I love you, Suzanne de Passe, the wonderful, great Quincy Jones, Teddy Riley, my new Godson, Michael Gibb, my new Sony family, Iko Morita, Mikki Schullhall, Tommy Motolla, Dave Galub, Polly Anthony. Thanks for making one of my most creative efforts, the album Dangerous, such an incredible success. I love you all so much. Sandy Gallin, Jim Morey, all the fantastic fans around the world, I love you very much. "

**Michael Jackson
February 24, 1993**

1993

March 6-9
At the 35th Conference of the National Association of Recording Merchandisers (NARM) in Orlando, Florida, Michael wins the 1992 Best Seller Awards in the category Best Selling Urban Music Recording Male for 'Dangerous.'

March 9
Michael wins two of his three nominations at the Soul Train Awards at the Shrine Auditorium in Los Angeles for Best R&B Soul Singer, Male ('Remember The Time') and Best R&B/Soul Album, Male ('Dangerous'). He is also presented with the Humanitarian Of The Year award by Eddie Murphy. At the close of the presentations, Michael, who twisted his ankle rehearsing for the show the night before, performs 'Remember The Time' seated in an elaborate gold chair and surrounded by dancers. During the evening Michael is either helped to the podium on crutches, or in a wheelchair.

March 11
Walking on crutches, Michael attends an AFI (American Film Industry) dinner in honour of Elizabeth Taylor in the Beverly Hilton Hotel in Los Angeles.

March 15
Michael is honoured as Best International Male Artist at the Echo Awards in Berlin's Wintergarden. The ceremony is organised by the German Phono Academy, and Jochen Leuschner, the Managing Director of Sony in Germany accepts the award on Michael's behalf.

March 19
Santa Barbara County grants approval to Michael Jackson to build a 20 acre breeding ground for apes, white tigers, bears, and other animals on his ranch.

March 27
Michael makes a five-minute speech in front of 1,200 teachers and politicians at a conference in the Century Plaza Hotel in Los Angeles, which is sponsored by the Milken Family Trust.

March 31
Deadline for entries to the MTV Video Competition 'My Weekend at Michael's Neverland Valley.'

Following Michael's a cappella rendition of 'Who Is It' during the Oprah interview, US radio stations are swamped with requests for the single. Sony react quickly and decide to release 'Who Is It' instead of 'Give In To Me', as the next single from the 'Dangerous' album. In order to increase public interest in the song Sony, in collaboration with MTV, devise a competition whereby entrants are to create a video to Michael's 'Who Is It'.

April
The Hollywood Arts Council is granted permission to install a 3-D mural of Michael on the El Capitan Theater.

Michael – wearing a nun's habit – is on the cover of Spy magazine in a parody of the movie, Sister Act.

April 11
Members of the Jackson family give an interview for ABC's *Day One* programme in response to Michael's interview with Oprah.

April 15
The video to 'Whatzupwitu' by Eddie Murphy and Michael Jackson is premièred by Fox and BET.

April 26
As part of his 'Heal LA' drive, Michael visits Los Angeles South Central accompanied by Caroline Bingham of the *Los Angeles Sentinel*, and *Off The Wall* magazine publisher, Adrian Grant. Michael visits The Watts Health Foundation, the El Santo Nino after-school centre and the Horace Mann Middle School.

Michael appears on the cover of *Jet* magazine with Eddie Murphy.

May
'Who Is It,' the sixth single from 'Dangerous' in the US, peaks on the Pop and Black singles charts at numbers 14 and 6 respectively. The accompanying video in the States is a compilation of earlier video clips. The European version of the video is available in the US only on the video cassette, *Dangerous: The Short Films*.

Michael appears on the cover of *Class* magazine with sister, Janet.

First reports appear about the Jackson Family Reunion Show charity benefit scheduled for December 11 at the Convention Center in Atlantic City. Although Michael will attend the

This Page: Michael receives the 1993 Soul Train Humanitarian Award from Eddie Murphy. Below, Michael and wheelchair for a rendition of 'Remember The Time.'

Page Opposite: Michael in action at the American Superbowl.

Far Right: Michael gives a stunning performance of 'Dangerous' at the American Music Awards.

1993

event to present two awards, he will not perform.

Michael is nominated in two categories at the first American Television Awards but doesn't win.

May 5
Ex-President Jimmy Carter, co-chairman of the Heal Our Children/Heal The World initiative with Michael Jackson, invites Michael to visit Atlanta to boost the Atlanta Project Immunisation Drive.

Afterwards, Michael joins Mr. and Mrs. Carter, Ted Turner, Jane Fonda, Lisa Marie Presley and Emmanuel Lewis in the front row during the 'Kids' Celebration' at OMNI.

May 6
An American Film Institute Salute To Elizabeth Taylor, which was filmed two months earlier, airs on TV. Michael Jackson accompanies Elizabeth Taylor but does not participate in the programme.

This Page: Michael at The World Music Awards.

May 9
Michael checks in to the Winston Churchill Suite of the Hôtel de Paris in Monaco for the World Music Awards. He is accompanied by eight people: Jordi Schwarz (Chandler) and his five year old sister, Lily, an Asian Nanny, PR Bob Jones and four bodyguards.

May 10
Michael dines with Prince Albert of Monaco at the restaurant Les Folies Russes in the Hotel Loewes. They chat for about forty-five minutes, but Michael does not eat.

May 12
Michael Douglas presents the World Music Awards from the Salle Des Etoiles in the Sport Club of Monaco. Michael wins the three most important awards of the evening: Best Selling American Artist Of The Year, World's Best Selling Recording Artist Of The Year, and World's Best Selling Recording Artist Of The Era. Michael is in good spirits but a 16 year old Italian fan causes him to fall as he climbs the steps to the stage. A fight breaks out as fans and press surge forward and the inadequate security attempt to hold back the crowd trying to get to Michael.

May 13
Michael leaves Monaco by helicopter, and in Nizza transfers to a plane to Paris where he spends three days visiting EuroDisney.

May 16
Michael flies back to Los Angeles.

May 18
Michael receives two awards for 'Black Or White' and 'Remember The Time' at the 41st BMI Annual Pop Awards Dinner at the Regency Beverly Wiltshire Hotel in Los Angeles.

May 19
Michael receives the first ever Lifetime Achievement Award from Norris McWhirter, the Editor of the *Guinness Book of Records* at the Guinness Museum of World Records in Los Angeles.

May 27
ASCAP, an umbrella organisation of music publishers, presents Michael with three awards at the 1993 R&B Awards for 'In The Closet,' 'Remember The Time' and 'Jam.'

May 30
'Will You Be There,' the eighth single from 'Dangerous' released on May 24, enters the charts at number 11 peaking at number 9 and remains on the charts for eight weeks.

May 31, June 1
The World Music Awards, ABC-TV's 90-minute special, is broadcast to 70 countries around the world.

June

Michael appears on the cover of *Disney Adventures* and *Life* magazine.

Michael Jackson: The King Of Pop by Lisa D. Campbell is published by Branden Books.

One hundred children from the Challengers Boys And Girls Club visit Neverland Valley.

1993

June 5
Michael is interviewed for the Radio Station KIIS FM in Los Angeles for the Rick Dees Radio Top 40 show.

June 10
Michael makes an appearance at an afternoon rally at a middle school in Los Angeles to launch a new DARE programme designed to educate children about drugs.

June 23
Michael Jackson's 'Beat It' jacket is auctioned at Sotheby's bi-annual Rock & Roll memorabilia auction. A buyer for the Hard Rock Café purchases the jacket for $7,762.

June 26-27
'My Weekend With Michael,' the culmination of a contest in which MTV viewers were invited to make their own videos for Michael Jackson's latest single 'Who Is It,' is broadcast in America. Michael picks the winner from three finalists, who are invited to spend a weekend at Neverland Valley.

Summer
A self portrait of Michael Jackson is among several celebrity portraits on tour as part of the Image Makers Rock & Roll Art Exposition.

July
The American Friends of Hebrew University award their 1994 Scopus Award to Michael Jackson.

July 16
Free Willy, with Michael's 'Will You Be There' as its theme song, opens in cinemas in America.

August
Jack The Rapper Awards are presented. The Original 13 Award is given to Motown founder, Berry Gordy, and the Our Children, Our Hope Of Tomorrow Award is awarded to Michael Jackson, and renamed in his honour. Michael does not attend the presentation ceremony, but accepts by video-taped message.

August 15-16
Shows scheduled in Hong Kong to open the Asian leg of the 'Dangerous' tour, are cancelled so that Michael can complete other projects.

August 17
The Los Angeles Police Department officially opens a criminal investigation of Michael Jackson, based on allegations of child abuse made by Jordy Chandler, a 13 year old boy.

August 21
Michael Jackson arrives in Bangkok at 11.30 p.m. and checks in to The Oriental Hotel.

The Los Angeles Police serve search warrants on Michael Jackson's Neverland Valley ranch in Santa Barbara, California, and on his condominium in Century City, California. Boxes of photographs and video tapes are reported to be removed from each home.

August 23
Michael attends a Pepsi Tour Press Conference at The Oriental Hotel.

August 24
Michael kicks off the Asian leg of the 'Dangerous' tour in Thailand with his first concert at Bangkok's National Stadium. At 270 feet, the stage is wider than the widest American stage at New York's Radio City Music Hall, which measures 190 feet.

US Embassy officials in Seoul, Korea, appeal to the Ministry of Culture to allow Michael to perform there. The South Korean officials are concerned about the loud noise and suggestive choreography.

Reports surface in the media that Michael is under criminal investigation for child abuse by the Los Angeles Police Department. Investigator Anthony Pellicano says the accusations are the result of a failed attempt to extort money from Michael Jackson. It transpires the boy's father, Evan Chandler, a dentist in Beverly Hills, wanted Michael to fund movie projects for him, so he could become a full-time screenwriter. When his request was refused, he threatened to make child molestation allegations against his son public.

Michael's criminal lawyer, Howard Weitzman, reads a statement to the press from Michael Jackson.

The molestation story will dominate newspapers, magazines, and scandal TV shows for many months to come.

August 25
Michael's second scheduled concert in Bangkok is cancelled because Michael is suffering from acute dehydration. It is rescheduled for August 26.

"My representatives have continuously kept me aware of what is taking place in California. I appreciate the remarks of Chief Willie Williams and our Los Angeles Police Department. I am confident the department will conduct a fair and thorough investigation and its results will demonstrate that there was no wrongdoing on my part. I intend to continue with my world tour, and look forward to seeing all of you in the scheduled cities. I am grateful for the overwhelming support of my fans throughout the world. I love you all. Thank you, Michael."

Howard Weitzman on behalf of Michael Jackson August 24, 1993

1993

Sensational Michael Jackson headlines hit the front page of every British tabloid.

Elizabeth Taylor flies to Singapore to be with Michael.

Jack Gordon, manager/ husband of LaToya Jackson – an unlikely ally – tells *USA Today* that the allegations against Michael are 'totally not true.' "He really loves children. He would never harm a child," says Gordon.

August 26
The cancelled concert from August 25, rescheduled for today, is again cancelled because Michael has not fully recovered from dehydration. He releases an audio-taped message to his fans, "I promise all my fans to perform at the National Stadium in Bangkok on August 27. I will see you on Friday. I love you all."

Pepsi's rival runs ads reading, 'Dehydrated? There's Always Coke.'

Two young friends of Michael's come to his defence, telling police and the media that he never behaved inappropriately with them. However, their admissions that they shared a bed with Michael – in a friendly, slumber party spirit – only cause more damage.

August 27
Michael performs the rescheduled concert from August 25 to a capacity audience of 70,000, who chant, 'Michael, Michael' and carry banners reading 'We Love You'.

This Page: Michael becomes the focus of the world's media in Bangkok, while his family give their support.

Below: Michael is escorted to his plane for Singapore by the Thai Military School.

August 28
Michael arrives in Singapore and checks in to Raffles Hotel.

August 29
Michael is 35 today and during his first concert in Singapore, the band – and a capacity audience of 47,000 – sing 'Happy Birthday' to him.

British fans, supported by *Off The Wall* and the facility of their Telephone Information Line, organise a rally at London's Piccadilly Circus to protest about the 'Trial By Tabloid' conducted by the British gutter press, and to present a show of solidarity in support of Michael.

August 30
The second concert in Singapore is cancelled. Michael collapses backstage moments before the show is due to begin, suffering from a severe migraine.

The Jackson family go ahead with a press conference which was planned before the allegations. Jermaine reads a statement of support for his brother, before the family announce plans for a special, *The Jackson Family Honors*. The TV special is due to be filmed in December, and

televised in January. Joseph, Katherine, Rebbie, Tito and Jermaine attend the press conference.

Police search Michael Jackson's hotel room at the Mirage Hotel in Las Vegas. Nothing incriminating is found.

August 31
Michael undergoes a brain scan in hospital. A second audio-taped message is released: "I was suddenly taken ill last night and I am sorry for the cancellation of my performance and I apologise for any inconvenience it might have caused my fans in Singapore. I look forward to seeing you at the stadium tomorrow. Thank you for your continued support and understanding. I love you all. Thank you."

While in Singapore, Michael Jackson is presented with a special orchid bearing his name. The orchid accolade is normally reserved for royalty and dignitaries.

A well-known Los Angeles celebrity attorney, Gloria Allred, is retained to represent Michael Jackson's accuser. In a few days she will resign, refusing to say why she is leaving the case.

September

The Jacksons: An American Dream is nominated for an Emmy for Outstanding Mini Series, but does not win.

September 1

The rescheduled concert from August 30 takes place in Singapore today. After the show, Michael goes shopping until 2.30 a.m.

September 2

The Singapore Zoo is unable to make arrangements to close in order for Michael to visit. Instead, they truck six orang-utans to Michael's hotel!

Many attendees at the MTV Video Music Awards express well wishes for Michael Jackson.

LaToya Jackson appears on America's *Today* show, saying she feels that the press have been unfair to her brother and that, "I stand by him one thousand percent." Her support backfires when she says, "but we don't really know."

September 3

Michael arrives at the airport in Taipei, Taiwan with Elizabeth Taylor and, as usual, is greeted by cheering fans. Michael and Liz check in to the Grand Regent Formosa Hotel.

Michael's parents, Jermaine, Jackie, Randy and Rebbie arrive in Taipei to offer support to Michael and visit him at his hotel.

September 4

Michael performs in concert and electrifies 40,000 fans at the Municipal Stadium in Taipei.

A Michael Jackson jacket is stolen from the Guinness Museum Of World Records in Hollywood and sold to a second-hand clothing store, Formula Uno, for $100.00.

September 5

Michael spends two hours shopping with his nephews in the local Toys'R'Us store in Taipei and purchases video games, water pistols and other toys to the value of $4,500.

Lightwater Valley Theme Park in North Yorkshire welcomes fans and supporters to a special Heal The World Charity Day. All monies raised from the day's activities are to be donated by Heal the World UK to an airlift to Sarajevo being organised by Operation Christmas Child. *Off The Wall* co-ordinate with Heal The World UK to support the fund-raiser through their networking facilities. Michael sends a message of support.

September 6

Michael performs his second concert in Taipei.

September 7

Michael arrives in Fukuoka, Japan, then boards a bus to Huis Ten Bosch, a theme park, where he stays for two days.

September 8

Michael, accompanied by his bodyguards, boards a boat and travels along the coast of a reproduction Dutch canal to the Palace, Huis Ten Bosch Park's fanciest hotel. He also visits Bio Park, an animal park.

During his visit to Japan, Michael visits a school at a US Naval base.

September 9

Michael arrives back in Fukuoka and checks in to the Hyatt Regency Hotel.

September 10

Michael performs in concert to a capacity audience of 30,000 in Fukuoka. Fans hold banners reading, 'We Believe You' and 'We Believe You Always.'

Michael is on the cover of *Entertainment Weekly* magazine.

September 11

Michael performs his second concert to a capacity audience of 30,000 in Fukuoka.

Billboard magazine reports that the allegations made against Michael Jackson have had no effect on sales or air play of his music. His current single, 'Will You Be There' is at number 7 on the Pop singles chart, his fourth Top Ten hit from 'Dangerous.'

In Hollywood, fans march to show their support for Michael Jackson.

September 12

Michael arrives in Moscow and is greeted by hundreds of fans waving their gloved hands in the air and shouting. A banner reads, 'Siberia Loves You Michael!'

September 13

Michael is on the cover of *Jet* magazine.

Michael goes shopping in Moscow, buying a 19th Century statue, several paintings and books, and a Russian army coat. He also tours the Kremlin museum and armoury.

1993

This Page: Michael gets ready to thrill another stadium-packed audience.

September 14
Gloria Allred announces she is withdrawing from the case and is no longer representing the 13-year-old boy accusing Michael Jackson of molestation. She offers no reason for her decision. Michael Freeman, an attorney representing the boy's mother, also withdraws from the case.

A civil suit is filed in Los Angeles Superior Court accusing Michael Jackson of battery, infliction of emotional distress, and fraud. The suit asks for unspecified monetary damages.

Michael shoots a video of himself marching with Russian army soldiers.

September 15
Michael performs in concert at the Lyzhniki Olympic Stadium in Moscow.

September 17
Michael arrives in Tel Aviv, Israel and after checking in to the Hotel Dan Tel Aviv, he visits Lunar Park.

September 18
Michael visits Jerusalem on a sight-seeing trip. He is met by religious protesters at the ancient Western Wall, but is welcomed at Masada, another historic site.

September 19
Michael performs in concert to a capacity audience of 80,000 in Tel Aviv.

September 20
Michael leaves his hotel, reportedly to visit a hospital. On his return, he goes

out on to a balcony to wave and throw down pieces of memorabilia to fans.

September 21
Michael performs his second concert in Tel Aviv.

Two detectives fly to Manila to question two former housekeepers from Neverland Valley. Mark and Faye Quindoy worked at Neverland for two years and claim to have first-hand knowledge of Michael's activities. The truth is, they have nothing and are referred to as 'money hungry' by their own nephew!

September 22
Michael arrives in Istanbul, Turkey and checks in to the Mövenpick Hotel. He visits the hotel cinema and watches *Jurassic Park*.

Jeanne White Ginder, whose son, Ryan White, befriended Michael and spent time with him, tells the press that she met Michael's accuser at Neverland in July. She states the boy was completely comfortable around Michael, and was not afraid of him at all.

September 23
Michael performs in concert in Istanbul, Turkey.

Concert dates in South Africa are cancelled due to continued violence there.

September 24
Michael arrives in Tenerife and checks in to the Hotel Meliá Botánico.

The Michael Jackson jacket stolen from the Guinness Museum Of World Records is recovered. It was pur-

chased from the second-hand clothing store for $1,000 by Jackson impersonator, Audrey Ruttan. The jacket is returned and Ruttan is reimbursed.

September 26
Michael performs in concert in Tenerife.

Off The Wall magazine present Michael with this year's Appreciation Award, which is a beautiful sculpture of the star, created by Chris Rattray.

September 27
Following the cancellation of the South African concerts scheduled for September 30 and October 2, Michael takes a well-deserved break. He arrives in Switzerland and stays in Liz Taylor's chalet in Gstaad for several days. He then visits Geneva.

October

Sony Music issues a public statement expressing their 'unconditional and unwavering support' for Michael Jackson.

Tony Jackson, a cousin of Michael with whom he had a close relationship, dies in a car accident aged 35. Michael does not attend the funeral, but pays all the expenses.

October 1
A blaze in the Los Padres National Forest threatens Neverland Valley, coming within three miles of the ranch.

October 4
Firefighters enter Neverland Valley to light backfires in order to fight back the raging wildfire.

October 8
Michael performs in concert in Buenos Aires and, for the first time this year, includes 'Man In The Mirror' in the song list. He is staying at the Park Hyatt Hotel.

October 10
Michael performs his second concert in Buenos Aires where he films the audience with a camcorder.

October 11
Michael appears at his hotel window and spends a long time throwing pillows and paper planes to the crowd below.

October 12
Michael performs his third concert in Buenos Aires.

October 13
Michael arrives in Sao Paulo, Brazil and checks in to the Sheraton Moffarej Hotel, occupying rooms on the 23rd floor.

October 15
Michael performs in concert in Sao Paulo.

October 17
Michael performs his second concert in Sao Paulo.

October 18
Michael arrives in Santiago, Chile and checks in to the Hyatt Regency Hotel.

October 21
Michael's first concert in Santiago is cancelled due to a back injury.

October 22
Michael visits a hospital and a toy shop.

October 23
Michael performs in con-

1993

Page Opposite: Michael reflects while in Red Square, Moscow.

1993

cert, incorporating the rescheduled show from October 21.

October 24
Michael arrives in Mexico and checks in to the Hotel Presidente Stouffer, occupying rooms on the 42nd floor. Randy Jackson is also in Mexico and towards the end of Michael's stay, Liz Taylor arrives.

October 27
Michael meets the President of Mexico.

October 28
A letter from Bert Fields, one of Michael's attorneys, accusing the Los Angeles Police Department of lying to young friends of Michael's to coerce them into making accusations against Michael, is published in *The Los Angeles Times*.

Michael Jackson is expected to visit El Nuevo Reino Aventura amusement park in Mexico City, home of Keiko, the whale who stars in *Free Willy*. He does not arrive, but he does arrange for 5,000 underprivileged children to visit the park.

October 29
Michael performs in concert to a capacity audience of 100,000 at the Aztec Stadium, Mexico and dedicates his song, 'I'll Be There' to one of his hardcore British fans, Justin Travill.

October 31
Michael performs his second concert to a capacity audience of 100,000 at the Aztec Stadium, Mexico.

Samuel Jackson, Michael's grandfather, dies. He is reported by the media to be 100-years-old but most sources give his birth date as 1903, making him 90. Samuel lived in a nursing home in Phoenix, Arizona. Michael does not attend the funeral services.

November
The scheduled release of Michael's 'Greatest Hits' album containing three new songs is postponed because Michael has not yet finished recording them. A new release date is tentatively set for June 1994.

Pigtails & Frogs Legs, a holiday cookbook by Neiman Marcus, which includes a foreword by Michael Jackson, goes on sale.

Free Willy is released on video cassette in America. Michael Jackson's video for 'Will You Be There' is included on the cassette. The movie enters the Top Video Sales chart at number 4 before peaking at number 2, where it remains for several weeks.

November 2
Michael cancels his third Mexican concert scheduled for today due to severe toothache.

November 3
Michael visits a dentist.

November 4
Michael receives oral surgery to have an abscessed molar extracted and stays in hospital overnight.

November 5
Michael attends a party for children at the Hard Rock Café.

During his stay in Mexico City, Michael is presented with a double platinum award for sales of 'Dangerous' in excess of 500,000 copies in Mexico.

November 7
Michael performs his third concert to a capacity audience of 100,000 at the Aztec Stadium, Mexico.

November 8
As part of the ongoing criminal investigation against Michael Jackson, police search the family's home in Encino, California. Again, no incriminating evidence is found.

November 9
Michael performs his fourth concert to a capacity audience of 100,000 at the Aztec Stadium, Mexico.

Elizabeth Taylor and Larry Fortensky fly to Mexico City to join Michael.

November 8-10
Attorney Howard Manning flies to Mexico City to take a deposition from Michael Jackson for a copyright infringement suit brought by three songwriters claiming 'Thriller,' 'The Girl Is Mine' and 'We Are The World' were stolen from them.

November 11
MTV Europe continue to support the megastar by airing another 'Michael Jackson Day.' Their press release states: 'Although many allegations have been made against his private life of late, Michael Jackson remains the undisputed King of Pop and he will be strutting his famous dance routines on MTV all day today.'

Michael performs his fifth concert to a capacity audience of 100,000 in Mexico. Sadly, this concert will prove to be the last.

Despite the media's unrelenting coverage of the scandal, the concerts in Mexico City – as with all of the 'Dangerous' tour – are widely successful. In Mexico City alone, half a million people watched Michael perform live.

After the concert, Michael leaves Mexico with Liz Taylor and Larry Fortensky, stopping off in Canada and Iceland. From there he is diverted to Ireland and finally lands at Luton Airport, England. Liz Taylor flies on to Gstaad and the media hunt for Michael Jackson begins.

November 12
Michael announces that he is cancelling the rest of his tour and that he is seeking treatment for a dependency on painkillers. He explains that the stress from the false allegations made against him caused him to become dependent on the painkillers to get through the tour.

Michael's whereabouts remain unknown, leaving the media to speculate wildly. Ridiculous rumours about Michael dominate the news for several months.

Attorney Howard Manning, who took Michael's deposition for a copyright infringement case just before the cancellation of the tour, tells the media that Michael seemed fine, was articulate and was very coherent. He says he finds his addiction to painkillers hard to believe. Some time later, when the videotape of the deposition is made public, it is obvious that Michael is incoherent and has great difficulty in concentrating. At one point, the interview is stopped to enable Michael to take medication.

November 14
A spokesman for Pepsico announces their relationship with Michael Jackson

is over, causing loyal Jackson fans to stop drinking the soda. Many Michael Jackson fan clubs encourage members to boycott Pepsi and to write to the company in protest. One US fan begins distributing bumper stickers reading, 'Pepsi Dumped Michael, Now We're Dumping Pepsi.' Within two months of their announcement, Coke announces a 20% increase in sales!

November 15
Michael's attorney, Bert Fields, holds a press conference to announce that Michael is seeking treatment for dependency on painkillers. He does not reveal Michael's whereabouts.

November 16
Police obtain a strip search warrant for Michael Jackson in an effort to verify a description of his genitals, given to police by Michael's 13-year-old accuser.

November 17
Sony Music issues another statement in support of Michael Jackson: "Michael Jackson's unique position as a world class artist and humanitarian is as important to Sony Music as to the tens of millions around the globe who have been touched by his art and faith." Sony further praise Michael's courage in facing up to the pain of addiction and the uneasy path to recovery that lies ahead. They add that they will "stand by him every step of the way with all the unconditional support and encouragement that we can provide."

1993

This Page: Michael entertains children at the Hard Rock Café in Mexico.

1993

Michael declines the 1994 Scopus Award, which is scheduled to be presented to him on January 29, 1994.

November 18

Eddie Reynoza, a dancer who appeared in the 'Thriller' video, claims he received a phone call from Michael Jackson in Switzerland. Reynoza alleges that Michael says he is moving his assets to Europe and never returning to the US. As with so many statements made by Michael's former employees, it will prove to be untrue.

November 22

In response to claims in the media that Michael is in hiding or undergoing cosmetic surgery to alter his appearance, Dr. Beauchamp Colclough, the British doctor treating him for his dependency, writes to the media to "refute any suggestion that Mr. Jackson is 'hiding out' or seeking any care other than the programme for analgesia abuse."

It is reported that an additional lawsuit has been filed against Michael Jackson by five former security guards, who were employed at Hayvenhurst, claiming they were fired from their jobs, 'because they knew too much.' They admit they never witnessed any improper conduct on Michael's part, or saw a child at the house who wasn't happy.

November 23

Dangerous: The Short Films is released. It includes videos already released for the singles from the album, 'Dangerous' as well as

never before seen videos and behind the scenes footage. The video cassette is successful on the charts, entering the Top Music Video chart at number 4 in America and number 2 in Britain.

Hollywood Reporter carries on its back page an open letter to Michael Jackson from the actor, Maximilian Schell, in which he expresses his admiration for Michael and his shame for the media's handling of the situation.

November 24

The administration of Michael Jackson's music catalogue, ATV Music, moves from MCA Music to EMI Music Publishing. It is reported to be the largest deal in music publishing history, earning Michael Jackson up to $200 million with an up-front payment of $100 million.

Janet Jackson's tour in support of her latest album 'janet.' kicks off in Cincinnati, Ohio. Early in her performance, and in all subsequent shows, she asks her audience to bow their heads and say a silent prayer "for my brother, Michael."

Los Angeles Superior Court judge, David Rothman, sets March 21, 1994, as the date for the civil suit against Michael, denying a request by Michael's attorneys to delay the proceedings until the criminal investigation is completed.

November 27

It's 'Michael Jackson Day IV' in London. *Off The Wall* hold their 4th annual

Michael Jackson party at London's Hammersmith Palais, at which fans from around the world gather to pay tribute to their idol. Since the allegations broke, *Off The Wall* has constantly supported Michael. After months of depressing news, 'MJ Day IV – The Extravaganza' truly is a day of celebration and unity for Michael's fans. Dozens of media representatives are more than taken aback by the overwhelming show of solidarity and support for Michael in Britain and around the world.

November 29

People magazine features Michael Jackson on its cover with the deceptive caption, 'Michael Jackson Cracks Up.' The publication later receives many letters condemning them for trying and convicting Michael Jackson in their cover story. In *Class* magazine, Constance M. Weaver writes: 'And, finally, one of the unkindest headlines of all appeared on the cover of *People* magazine: 'Michael Jackson Cracks Up - Sex, Drugs and the Fall of the World's Biggest Star.' It is interesting to note that, though no trial had been held, this November 29 headline seemed to indicate that the jury was in, and Jackson's career was over. It was one of the most misleading and shameful attempts to capitalise on the name and persona of Michael Jackson, while simultaneously, jumping on the bandwagon of negativity created by this unfortunate affair.'

Jermaine Jackson threatens to sue the *Daily Express* for $200 million for publishing a story saying that he questioned his brother's innocence.

December

Black Beat magazine publishes an issue devoted entirely to Michael Jackson.

December 2

Katherine and Jermaine Jackson appear on CNN's *Showbiz Today*, and *Hard Copy* to defend Michael and refute remarks made by five former security guards.

December 6

Jet magazine offers support for Michael Jackson, featuring him on their cover with an article on his battle over child abuse allegations.

December 7

The copyright infringement case filed against Michael Jackson, Quincy Jones, Lionel Richie, Rod Temperton and Joseph Jackson opens.

December 8

LaToya shocks the world by holding a midnight press conference in Tel Aviv, Israel, to reveal that she 'can no longer be a silent collaborator' to her brother's crimes. While she admits she never saw Michael harm any child and has never even seen him in bed with a child, she says she feels her brother needs help for his problem.

The Jackson family immediately hold a press conference outside the gates of Hayvenhurst to refute LaToya's remarks. Katherine, Joseph, Jackie, Tito, Jermaine and Randy tell CNN that LaToya is only interested in making money from selling her story to tabloids and talk shows.

December 10

Michael Jackson proves all the sceptics wrong by returning home to the United States.

December 14

Six members of the Jackson family appear on BET live from their Encino home in support of Michael.

KEZK-FM, a radio station in St. Louis, Missouri, withdraws Michael Jackson's music from their playlist. A spokesman for KEZK says: "This community has had a lot of problems with children being molested and murdered. There is a suspected serial killer out now who has murdered children. With the holiday season and the emphasis on kids this time of year, we wanted to disassociate ourselves with the imagery surrounding Michael Jackson right now."

In a letter, Garfield Boon, President of St. Louis County's NAACP, responds: "For you to publicly condemn Mr. Jackson and his music when he is not charged with a crime smacks of a cheap publicity stunt. For you to associate Mr. Jackson's name with the terrible recent child homicides that occurred in St. Louis demonstrates bad taste and bad judgement." The letter also calls KEZK's decision, "an unsubstantiated attack on a major Black entertainer for the purpose of increased listnership."

December 15

Blanca Francia, a former maid at Neverland, gives a deposition for the civil lawsuit, but not before being paid handsomely for her story by scandal talk show, *Hard Copy*. As is the case with other 'witnesses' her story makes little sense, and raises more questions about her credibility than any that she answers in regard to the case.

December 16

Heal The World Foundation UK once again supports Operation Christmas Child in sending an airlift of toys, sweets, gifts and supplies to the children of the former Yugoslavia.

December 20

Attorney Johnnie Cochran joins Michael's legal team with Howard Weitzman. Cochran replaces Bert Fields.

The NAACP (National Association For The Advancement Of Coloured People) holds a press conference to discuss 'the media bashing of entertainer Michael Jackson and to address how other economically powerful African-Americans have been victimised by the press.'

December 22

Michael Jackson takes to the airwaves in his own defence. CNN, CBS, NBC and ABC all carry his statement broadcast live from his Neverland Valley Ranch, in which he thanks his fans for their love and support.

Following Michael's live four-minute statement on TV every poll taken by US TV and newspapers are overwhelmingly in favour of his innocence. New

Entertainment WEEKLY
NO.201 • DECEMBER 17, 1993

NOW WHAT?

As the accusations grow even more lurid, where will MICHAEL JACKSON turn? His family blasts his advisers. His friends are strangely silent. His record company has postponed his next album. And now, according to an exclusive EW poll, even his fans are deserting him.

$2.50

1993

1993

York's number one TV station has 88% of the viewers polled saying that Michael is innocent, and *Current Affair* TV poll shows 78% in favour of Michael.

December 27

People magazine lists its '25 Most Intriguing People Of The Year' and includes Michael Jackson. In reviewing the best on television throughout the year, *Michael Talks... To Oprah* is described as the TV mega event of the year.

December 28

Rap duo, Back 2 Back, nine-year-old twin brothers, release the first single from their début album. Their song, titled 'Dear Michael,' is in support of their idol and contains the line, 'Michael, we believe in you.'

Concert promoter, Marcel Avram, files a $20 million breach of contract suit against Michael Jackson, TTC Touring Corp., and MJJ Enterprises, charging them with fraud, negligent misrepresentation, and breach of fiduciary duty. They claim Michael's true condition was concealed on signing the contracts. Only two weeks earlier, Avram had published a two-page tribute and get well wishes to Michael in *Billboard* magazine!

December 30

For the first time since returning home, Michael Jackson appears in public at the Treasure Island complex in Las Vegas with the owner and his friend, Steve Wynn. He is also seen in the company of friend, Michael Milken.

This Page: Michael is beamed 'live' around the world from Neverland, to denounce allegations of child abuse.

Page Opposite: The Jackson family unite in solidarity at *The Jackson Family Honors* in Las Vegas.

Live from Neverland Valley

"I am doing well and I am strong. As you may already know, after my tour ended I remained out of the country undergoing treatment for a dependency on pain medication. This medication was initially prescribed to soothe the excruciating pain that I was suffering after recent reconstructive surgery on my scalp.

"There have been many disgusting statements made recently concerning allegations of improper conduct on my part. These statements about me are totally false. As I have maintained from the very beginning, I am hoping for a speedy end to this horrifying, horrifying experience to which I have been subjected.

"I shall not, in this statement, respond to all the false allegations being made against me, since my lawyers have advised me that this is not the proper forum in which to do that. I will say, I am particularly upset by the handling of this mass matter by the incredible, terrible mass media. At every opportunity, the media has dissected and manipulated these allegations to reach their own conclusions. I ask all of you to wait to hear the truth before you label or condemn me. Don't treat me like a criminal, because I am innocent.

"I have been forced to submit to a dehumanising and humiliating examination by the Santa Barbara County Sheriff's Department and the Los Angeles Police Department earlier this week. They served a search warrant on me which allowed them to view and photograph my body, including my penis, my buttocks, my lower torso, thighs and any other areas that they wanted. They were supposedly looking for any discoloration, spotting, blotches or other evidence of a skin colour disorder called vitiligo which I have previously spoken about.

"The warrant also directed me to co-operate in any examination of my body by their physician to determine the condition of my skin, including whether I have vitiligo or any other skin disorder. The warrant further stated that I had no right to refuse the examination or photographs and if I failed to co-operate with them, they would introduce that refusal at any trial as an indication of my guilt.

"It was the most humiliating ordeal of my life – one that no person should ever have to suffer. And even after experiencing the indignity of this search, the parties involved were still not satisfied and wanted to take even more pictures. It was a nightmare, a horrifying nightmare. But if this is what I have to endure to prove my innocence, my complete innocence, so be it.

"Throughout my life, I have only tried to help thousands upon thousands of children to live happy lives. It brings tears to my eyes when I see any child who suffers.

"I am not guilty of these allegations. But if I am guilty of anything, it is of giving all that I have to give to help children all over the world. It is of loving children, of all ages and races, it is of gaining sheer joy from seeing children with their innocent and smiling faces. It is of enjoying, through them, the childhood that I missed myself. If I am guilty of anything, it is of believing what God said about children: 'Suffer little children to come unto me and forbid them not, for such is the kingdom of heaven.' In no way do I think that I am God, but I do try to be God-like in my heart.

"I am totally innocent of any wrongdoing and I know these terrible allegations will all be proven false. Again, to my friends and fans, thank you very much for all of your support. Together we will see this through to the very end. I love you very much and may God bless you all. I love you. Goodbye."

Michael Jackson, December 22, 1993

1994
January 1

Heavily disguised, Michael spends two hours in the afternoon at the MGM Grand Hotel's theme park in Las Vegas. In the evening, Michael receives a standing ovation when he attends the New Year's Day Barbra Streisand performance at the MGM Grand Garden, receiving almost as much attention as the star herself. Michael attends the show with financier, Michael Milken.

January 3

A motion is filed by Jordy Chandler's lawyers in Santa Monica's Superior Court for Anthony Pellicano, now no longer part of MJ's defence team, to witness in court in March.

January 5

The 26th annual NAACP Image Awards are presented in Pasadena, where Michael makes a surprise appearance to present an award to Debbie Allen for outstanding choreography.

The programme for the NAACP Image Awards contains a two-page ad consisting of a picture of Michael Jackson and the words, 'Michael, I Love You. - Elizabeth.'

January 10

Michael and his parents are on the cover of *Jet* magazine.

On his 14th birthday, Jordy Chandler makes his Statement in connection with the allegations that Michael Jackson sexually abused him.

January 12

After only three hours of deliberation, a jury finds in favour of Michael Jackson, Lionel Richie, Quincy Jones, Rod Temperton and Joseph Jackson in a copyright infringement suit. They say that 'The Girl Is Mine,' 'Thriller' and 'We Are The World' were not stolen, but are, in fact, the work of Michael Jackson, and in the case of 'We Are The World,' the work of Michael Jackson and Lionel Richie.

January 17

On the weekend of Martin Luther King's birthday, Michael holds a party at his Neverland Valley Ranch for over 100 underprivileged children, all of whom have a great time in the fantasy kingdom.

January 24

Los Angeles prosecutors announce they do not have sufficient evidence to charge Evan Chandler with extortion.

January 26

After six months of hard negotiations, the lawyers representing both sides in the molestation case against Michael Jackson finally reach agreement. An out of court settlement, which both sides have been working towards, is agreed for an undisclosed sum.

January 27

Reuters News Service reports that the photos taken of Michael Jackson's genitalia do not match his accuser's description given to the police. Little coverage is given to this in the press.

February 2

Michael attends a concert by the the Temptations at the Sheraton Desert Inn in Las Vegas. His date for the evening is Elvis Presley's daughter, Lisa Marie.

February 7

Rod Stewart is presented with the Michael Jackson International Award at the American Music Awards.

Court date for the copyright infringement suit filed against Michael by Crystal Cartier, who claims he stole 'Dangerous' from

"For decades, the NAACP has stood at the forefront of the struggle for equal justice under the law for all people in our land. They have fought in the lunch rooms of the South, in the hallowed halls of the Supreme Court and the board rooms of America, for justice, equality and the very dignity of all mankind. Members of the NAACP have been jailed and even killed in noble pursuit of those ideals, upon which our country was founded. None of these goals is more meaningful to me at this time in my life, than the notion that everyone is presumed to be innocent, and totally innocent, until they are charged with a crime, and then convicted by a jury of their peers. I never really took the time to understand the importance of that ideal until now, until I became the victim of false allegations, and the willingness of others to believe and exploit the worst before they have a chance to hear the truth. Not only am I presumed innocent, I am innocent! And I know the truth will be my salvation.
You have been there to support me when others weren't around, and I thank you for that. I have been strengthened in my fight to prove my innocence by my faith in God, and by my knowledge that I am not fighting this battle alone. Together, we will see this thing through."
Michael Jackson
January 5, 1994

1994

her. She is reported, however, to be unable to locate an original demo tape of her version of the song. Michael denies ever hearing her version of the song.

February 9

A Santa Barbara Grand Jury investigation into child molestation allegations against Michael Jackson is convened to

artist the crowd most wanted to see - Michael - did not perform, causing sighs of disappointment from his fans. Liz Smith, columnist with the *New York Newsday*, writes: 'All Michael has to do to regain his place in America's heart, is perform. He was not booed because of the accusations against him; only because he wouldn't sing!

March 29

Trial date set for a lawsuit filed by Michael Jackson against Steve Howell for selling video tapes of Michael Jackson without his permission.

April 11

Attorneys for both sides are in court to meet on the matter of the naked photos taken of Michael. Michael's attorneys have been trying to get hold of the nude photographs, saying that if the wrong people get hold of them, Michael could be exploited. The judge does not make a ruling. The photos are held in a local bank in Santa Barbara.

decide whether to proceed with criminal investigations. Mike Brando, the son of Marlon Brando, is amongst the first to testify.

February 15

It takes a Denver jury only three and a half hours of deliberation to rule in Michael's favour in the copyright infringement case brought by Crystal Cartier, who claimed that 'Dangerous' was her song.

February 19

The Jackson Family Honors take place in Las Vegas at the MGM Grand Hotel. Acts appearing with the Jacksons are Celine Dyon, Smokey Robinson and Dionne Warwick but the

He is neither loved nor hated for his inner self - the public mostly couldn't care less. As long as Michael entertains, he's safe. In Las Vegas, Michael received, once again, the message that's been ingrained in him since early childhood - only your talent matters, nothing else.'

February 22

The Jackson Family Honors is aired. All profits are to be donated to the family's non-profit charity, Family Caring For Families.

March

Teen Beat publishes an issue devoted entirely to Michael, 'Michael Jackson And His Famous Family.'

April 12

Michael, who is in New York recording his next album, visits Planet Hollywood - in disguise - to check out the movie memorabilia. He also goes on a private tour of five historic mansions in Newport and buys $450 worth of books at a gift shop.

Michael attends the 2nd Annual Children's Choice Awards held at City Center in New York to accept a 'Caring For Kids' award. The Kids Award is a special category, that acknowledges a celebrity, who has devoted time to work with young people, to enhance their lives. One hundred thousand children between the ages of eight and eighteen, gave Michael their vote of confidence. The Children's Choice Awards are sponsored by Body Sculpt, a non-profit drug prevention programme for youths.

This Page: Elizabeth Taylor and Berry Gordy proudly hold their Jackson Family Honors with Michael.

April 14

Michael visits Orpheum Theater in New York where he sees *Stomp*.

April 18, 19

Michael is spotted house-hunting in Florida near Disney World.

April 25

BBC2 broadcast *The Hunt For Michael Jackson*. The documentary highlights what it calls 'the wildest media frenzy in history' as seen by US writer Richard Ben Cramer. The programme highlights the greed of newspaper editors for sales, and supposed witnesses' and agents' greed for money.

April 29

Michael books into a three-bedroomed duplex apartment at Trump Tower while working on his album in New York.

May

Stevie Wonder joins the growing list of celebrities who have decided to speak out in defence of Michael Jackson. "It seems like it's almost a witch hunt," he says. "You have the same things happening to Michael Jordan and Mike Tyson. It's almost like they're saying the person's guilty."

Michael Jackson is on the cover of *Class* magazine, 'Michael Jackson's Ordeal.'

It is confirmed that Stan Winston, the special effects wizard who worked with Michael on *The Wiz* in 1978, is involved in Michael's planned musical remake of the fantasy film, *The Seven Faces of Dr. Lao*.

May 17

Star magazine reports that Lisa Marie Presley has turned to Michael Jackson after the break up of her marriage.

May 23

On the death of Jacqueline Kennedy Onassis, Michael says: "She was my friend. Friends are few. She will be sorely missed by all who knew her."

May 25

Michael Jackson jets down to Casa de Campo, the exclusive tennis and golf resort in the Dominican Republic, reportedly checking out a nearby 6,000 seat amphitheater for a concert.

May 26

Michael Jackson is married to Lisa Marie Presley by Civil Judge, Hugo Francisco Alvarez Perez in the Dominican Republic in a ceremony which lasts twelve minutes. Eva Darling, a friend of Lisa Marie's, and Darling's husband, Thomas Keough, Lisa Marie's brother-in-law are witnesses. No members of Michael's family are present. The marriage will not become public until July 11.

June

Michael is on the cover of the first issue of *People Today*. The magazine dedicates thirty-eight of its eighty-two pages to Michael Jackson.

June 4

Michael wins MTV's Movie Award for Best Song for 'Will You Be There.'

June 5

Michael is spotted walking around Disney World in Florida with Lisa Marie Presley and her two children, Danielle and Benjamin.

June 8

USA Today reports that, according to Bob Jones Michael is taking in the Florida sun and visiting with hoop-and-rap star Shaquille O'Neal. Jones says that Michael recently spent a few days in various New York recording studios, "working on new material that will appear on a greatest hits album that is hoped will be out this Fall."

June 16

The press report that Michael is secretly planning to finish his world tour which was prematurely abandoned last November due to his addiction to pain-killers.

June 20

A long-lost song, 'Big Boy', that marked Michael's recording debut is re-released twenty-five years after it was a minor hit for the Jackson 5. Ben Brown, the owner of Steeltown Records, has recently re-mastered the song, and will initially sell it by mail order, in a limited edition package with a CD, cassette tape, and song history, for $30.

This page: Lisa-Marie Presley.

Below: Elvis Presley.

1994

June 23

Michael visits Cab Calloway, the eighty-six year old jazz legend, who is recovering from a stroke in a New York hostpial.

June 28

USA Today reports that at the VH-1 Honors, which took place on June 26, Garth Brooks, who works for Feed the Children, said: "You can beat me up for this, but who's raised more money for children than Michael Jackson has?"

July 11

In Britain, *GMTV* break the story about the marriage of Michael to Lisa Marie Presley. *CNN* report that three separate spokespeople from Michael Jackson emphatically deny that Michael has married the daughter of Elvis Presley. A spokeswoman for Presley cannot deny the report, because she is unable to reach Lisa Marie.

Daily News report they have obtained documents showing that Presley and her previous husband, Danny Keough, got a quickie divorce in the Dominican Republic on May 6.

July 26, 27

It is reported that Michael, draped in a garment that makes him resemble an Arab woman, attends Janet Jackson's two concerts at Radio City Music Hall in New York.

August 1

After weeks of rumours, it's official. Michael has married Lisa Presley. The bride, announcing that her married name is now Lisa Marie Presley-Jackson, releases a statement through MJJ Productions. In the statement, which is made in her name only, Lisa Marie says that she is very much in love with Michael and wants to dedicate her life to being his wife. The official statement gives no details of the marriage ceremony, or where it took place, saying only that the couple were married eleven weeks ago 'somewhere outside the United States.' Pleading for privacy, Michael's new wife says they are now looking forward to raising a family, and living a happy life together. The 26-year-old bride said the news was kept secret until now in the hopes of avoiding a media circus and so they could enjoy each other's company.

August 5

Michael flies to Budapest via London Heathrow with his new wife to film a trailer for his forthcoming album 'History'.

August 6

Michael, accompanied by Lisa, visits two children's hospitals where they distribute over 2,600 toys to the sick kids.

In the evening hundreds of fans gather outside his hotel, where he delights them by showering them with various signed gifts.

August 9

Michael returns to New York to complete recording of 'History'.

• • • • • • • • • • • • • • • •

This page, top: Michael and Lisa arrive in Budapest.

Michael and Lisa arrive at the Heim Pal Hospital in Budapest.

Opposite page: Michael and Lisa on the set of his 'History' trailer.

Extracts from October's Ebony Interview:

Johnson writes, 'The truth is that Michael, now 36, and Lisa Marie, 26, were just a couple of youngsters when they met in Las Vegas twenty years ago. He was 16 and she was 6. The Jackson Five appeared at the MGM Grand Hotel in 1974. Michael recalls, *"Her father used to bring her to catch our show, where all nine of us were performing. It was a real family show - the only family show in Las Vegas which allowed children to come. Elvis would bring his daughter, Lisa Marie. She would sit right in the front, and bodyguards would be right there. Afterwards, she would be escorted backstage, and I would meet her, and we would talk. This happened quite often. She would come again, again and again. It was quite an event. After that, I didn't see her for quite a while. It was like ships passing in the night - hello and goodbye."*

Johnson explains that, three years ago, when Michael started the Dangerous album, he said their relationship reached a new plateau. Michael said, *"We sort of went out together. Then we would talk on the phone... I noticed that we had come closer. We went to Las Vegas for The Jackson Family Honors in 1993. We later travelled to Atlanta for President Jimmy Carter to visit children, but no one knew that she was there with me. The brilliant thing about us, is that we were often together, but did not let anybody know about it. We got to see each other that way over the years. We were really quiet and comfortable with each other. That's pretty much how the dating started happening."*

Johnson writes that it was during this period that Michael said their relationship changed from being good friends to lovers. As a sensitive songwriter who deals with feelings that run the range of human emotions, Michael has an uncanny sense of the chemistry in writing songs. For him, that chemistry is inspiration. If you listen to the lyrics of 'Remember The Time' and 'I Can't Let Her Get Away,' you conclude that Lisa Marie could have provided the inspiration. She certainly provided the kind of support he needed in 1993, when he was going through legal trials and tribulations. Michael remembers, *"I was on tour, and it seemed like I was in Armageddon - Armageddon in the brains. All these horrible stories were going around about me. None was true. It was unbelievable. Lisa Marie would call. I could count my true friends on one hand. She was very, very supportive the whole time. That really impressed me. She would call and be crying. She was angry and really wanted to choke people. But, really, what impressed me was earthquake day in LA - June 28th, 1993. On earthquake day, my phone just happened to be working. I was terrified - almost out of my brains. I thought the world was ending. I got a phone call from her, right after the quake."*

Johnson explains that later, in London, where he underwent treatment for addiction to prescription drugs, Michael said that Lisa Marie gave him the impression that their relationship was moving them toward each other in ties that bind. Michael said, *"She would call me, but she didn't always get through to me. And that made it very frustrating for her. I got all the messages. She was very concerned."* Johnson writes that it was after these experiences that Michael says he came to that moment when he had to say 'This Girl Is Mine' and 'The Way You Make Me Feel.' Michael, chuckling at the play on words of two of his best-selling songs, said of the moment of truth, *"It kind of unfolded. We spent a lot of time on the ranch and just walked around and talked. It happened! It unfolded all natural. We could feel the feeling we had for each other, without even talking about it. It was all in the vibrations, the feelings and the look in our eyes."*

Johnson concludes that the priority the couple have agreed upon is not recording together - although Lisa Marie inherited her famous father's talent for singing, and his estate valued at over $150 million. Michael says, *"All this talk about us recording together is a complete rumour. The thing we want to do most is centred around children. I never met anybody who cared so much about children the way I do. I get real emotional about children. Lisa Marie is the exact same way. Wherever we go, we visit children's hospitals. My dream is that when we go to South Africa and India, we will aid children."*

August 20
Michael and Lisa appear on the covers of *Hello*, *National Enquirer* and *Jet* magazine.

August 27
Dolores Martez Jackson, known as Dee Dee (formerly married to Tito), is found dead at the bottom of a swimming pool by her boyfriend, Donald Bohana. Reports stated that she had superficial abrasions on her body, but an autopsy proved inconclusive. After various rumours of foul-play, police rule her death as accidental.

September 12
Michael opens the 11th annual MTV Video Music Awards with his wife. Their one hundred and twenty-second appearance 'stole the show' as Michael swept Lisa-Marie into his arms, and tenderly kissed her in public for the very first time.

September 24
On hearing that no charges of child molestation were to be brought against him, Michael issued the following statement, 'I'm grateful that the investigation has reached a conclusion. I am grateful to my family and friends, and friends who have stood by me, and believed in my innocence. Lisa Marie and I look for-

ward to getting on with our lives, raising a family, and will never forget the unending outpouring of love from all over the world. God bless you.'

October
In this months issue of *Ebony* magazine, Michael gives his first one-to-one interview since he married Lisa Marie, to Robert E. Johnson.

October 8
Michael attends the Elvis Presley tribute, at the Pyramid in Memphis, with his sister Janet, wife Lisa, and her mum Priscilla.

November
Michael is on the cover of the November issue of *GQ*.

December
Due to the wealth of media rumours circulating that Michael and Lisa are to divorce, Bob Jones makes a statement to CNN, vehemently denying both reports, saying, *"We started receiving calls that Michael Jackson had filed for an annulment against Lisa Marie. And, I am here to tell you it is absolutely unequivocally untrue. Michael Jackson is here in Chicago recording; Mrs. Jackson is in Los Angeles at her home; they are happy and we are very sad, it is very sad that these people continue to try and make problems."*

December 10
Adrian Grant visits Michael in Chicago, where he is working on the ballad 'You Are Not Alone', with R.Kelly. During a photo shoot with his nephews and cousins, Michael categorically denies all the rumours of a marriage break-up and tells Adrian to tell all the fans that he is very, very happy.

December 17
The fifth annual MJ Day is held in London. Michael sends his own film crew to tape the event and a special video message to his fans, whom he thanks for *"their unwavering support."* Two lucky fans win a trip to Neverland Valley.

1995
January 20
Michael Jackson begins a four-day visit in Los Angeles with King Nana Amon Ndoufou IV, who two years ago crowned Michael a King of his Ghana region.

February 6

Michael and Lisa attend the law office of Johnie Cochran on the opening of his new business and entertainments division. The crowd, which included many of Hollywood's best-known personalities, broke into tremendous applause as the couple walked into the lobby reception area.

Jet magazine reports on King Ndoufou's stay with Michael, including photographs of the King of Sanwi with the King of Pop and Lisa Marie.

February 23

Michael previews some new songs from his forthcoming album at The National Association of Recording Merchandisers, where he is also presented with NARM's Harry Chapin Memorial Humanitarian Award in honour of his, *'extraordinary efforts to enhance the quality of life on this planet.'*

March 2

Michael turns up unannounced at the funeral of Craig Fleming. Craig, just twenty-two months old, drowned when his mother Donna, aged 24, threw him from a bridge into Los Angeles harbour. Michael told the family he was deeply upset when he read about the tragedy.

March 30

The New York Daily News reports that a five-year-old Hungarian boy whose liver transplant operation was paid for by superstar Michael Jackson and his wife, Lisa Marie, was in satisfactory condition yesterday, the couple's

spokesman said. The operation to give Bela Farkas a new liver - as promised by the Jacksons during a visit to Budapest last August - was performed on 12th March in Brussels, said spokesman Lee Solters.

April 18-20

Michael Jackson, representing his Heal the World Foundation, and Lisa Marie welcome 46 youngsters from 17 countries to Neverland Valley for a World Children's Congress - a three-day series of seminars and workshops.

May

Michael's 'new look' is unveiled for the first time as he poses with Quincy Jones in the June edition of *Vibe* magazine and appears on the cover, styled by Jones' daughter Kidada.

May 19

'Scream' is simultaneously previewed on 80 British Radio shows at 7.45 a.m, and GMTV have to 'play it again' at the end of their show, after viewers had called in requesting to hear the song once more. One Bristol DJ got so carried away with the new release that he played the song non-stop for one whole hour.

May 25

USA Today features a photo of Michael with Sony Executives playing on their new video game system PlayStation.

Hard Copy is the first media outlet in the United States to show photos of Michael and Lisa Marie at Six Flags Amusement Park in Los Angeles.

The couple brought along Lisa's daughter, Danielle. Michael treated the six-year-old to the Mooseburger Cafe where he even sang 'The Moose Song' by placing his hands above his head and imitating the cartoon character, Bullwinkle.

May 29

'Scream', the first single from Michael's forthcoming 'History' album is released around the world.

June 4

'Scream' enters the British charts at number three.

In America it debuts at number 5, making it the highest debut in the 37-year history of the Hot 100, toping the previous record held by The Beatles with 'Let It Be' which entered the chart at number 6 in March, 1970.

June 15

Michael's 'History' album is released around the world. The double-album is made up of 15 greatest hits and 15 new songs, 150 minutes of music. Statues of Michael Jackson constructed by his record company are ceremoniously unveiled in several European cities to tie in with the Jackson bust which appears on the cover of the album.

The video for 'Scream' is aired around the world during the broadcast of ABC's live *Primetime* interview with Michael and Lisa held by Diane Sawyer.

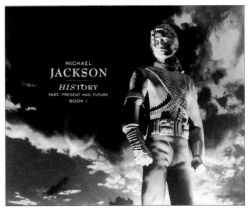

1995

HISTORY

Michael Jackson

Epic E2K 5900
EPC 474709-2

HIStory Begins
Disc One
1. Billie Jean
2. The Way You Make Me Feel
3. Black Or White
4. Rock With You
5. She's Out Of My Life
6. Bad
7. I Just Can't Stop Loving You
8. Man In The Mirror
9. Thriller
10. Beat It
11. The Girl Is Mine
12. Remember The Time
13. Don't Stop Till You Get Enough
14. Wanna Be Startin' Somethin'
15. Heal The World

HIStory Continues
Disc Two
1. Scream
2. They Don't Care About Us
3. Stranger In Moscow
4. This Time Around
5. Earth Song
6. D.S.
7. Money
8. Come Together
9. You Are Not Alone
10. Childhood
11. Tabloid Junki
12. 2 Bad
13. History
14. Little Susie
15. Smile

Page Opposite: Author of this book, Adrian Grant, with Michael, during a photo-shoot in Chicago.

1995

There is controversy over Michael's 'They Don't Care About Us' lyrics, as the media report that, 'Michael Jackson, stung by accusations of anti-Semitism, has apologised over one of his songs and promised to include a written apology on future copies of his new album. CNN report that Michael will re-record some of the controversial lyrics, replacing *"kike me"* with *"strike me"* and *"jew me"* with *"do me."*

Both *Life* and *Hello!* magazines carry the same photos by Harry Benson of Michael and Lisa together.

June 16
Michael is the subject of *Entertainment Weekly's* cover story, which reports that Michael intended to go into films before the allegations hit.

June 19-23
MTV in America affectionately called itself MJ-TV during this week, which was dedicated to Michael Jackson.

June 22
The VH-1 Awards which took place at the Shrine

This Page: Michael and Lisa appear semi-naked in the video for 'You Are Not Alone.'

Auditorium in Los Angeles paid tribute to Michael for his charitable works. Michael Jackson surprised the audience when he joined Boyz II Men on stage to sing a chorus of 'We Are The World.'

June 27
Variety magazine report that in a bid to revive his acting career, Michael Jackson has changed his agency to United Talent Agency. They stressed that so far, this is for acting only.

July 10
Michael attends the opening of The Magic Johnson Sony Theatre in Los Angeles. Afterwards, he went alone - without bodyguards - to a very busy shopping area where - in the words of a store merchant - he created 'pandemonium' in several stores.

July 25
Michael attends a packed press conference in New York to announce the 1995 MTV Video Award nominations together with Mayor Rudolph Guiliani and also to announce his only concert of the year in New York to be televised by HBO on December 10. Michael receives a record eleven nominations for 'Scream.'

July 26
ABC air a half-hour special feature called *Michael Jackson Changes History*. The video for his new single, 'You Are Not Alone' is also premiered.

August
Michael and Lisa take a week's 'break' in Paris.

August 11
The success of 'History' is widely ignored by the media despite the fact that it has sold seven-and-a-half million copies worldwide in only five weeks. Also, tucked away in an unassuming little article in the business section of the *New York Times* titled 'Sony's Group Profit Rises 91 Percent,' was the following extract, *"In the entertainment business, sales at the company's two music recording subsidiaries, in Japan and the United States, rose 2.2 percent, largely because of a hit LP by the singer Michael Jackson, 'History.'"*

August 15
'You Are Not alone', the second single from 'History' is released in America, and goes on to create chart history in America by becoming the first ever song to go straight in at number one on the Billboard's Hot 100 singles chart.

August 17
Michael 'talks' direct to his fans via the four major online carriers - America Online, Prodigy, CompuServe and the Internet, the first time they have all worked together in a simulcast. *USA Today* reported, 'There were no bombshells, but Michael Jackson was revealing in what was his first formal cyberchat, and was probably the largest ever. Jackson chatted for an hour starting at 10.p.m. ET on Prodigy, CompuServe, America On-Line and the Net, with an MTV simulcast. On AOL alone, he drew 15,000 to 18,000 more than any previous chat. Fans were able to send

whatever questions they liked to Michael, including this one, where someone asked if he wished he could go in public without being mobbed, he said, *"For this reason, I wish I could be morphed."* He also stated that Bubbles, his chimp, is still alive and likes to eat pizza. Michelangelo is the person in history he'd most like to meet. His best friend? *"The children of the world,"* he said, ignoring the implications after his recent brush with scandal.

August 21

'You Are Not Alone' is released in England, where it enters the British chart at number three, but gains top spot a week later.

September

In an unmistakable statement to those still touting Michael's album as a 'flop,' Sony Music occupy two whole pages in *Billboard* magazine for week ending September 2. Printed in white on a black background, the inside cover states simply: '5ox Platinum.' In black print on a silver background, page 3 states, quote: 'in 26 countries, and just the beginning... of HIStory.'

September 7
After giving a stunning performance at the opening of the 12th annual MTV Music Video Awards, Michael went on to pick up three awards for Best Dance Video, Best Choreography and Best Art Direction for his and Janet's video, 'Scream.' Michael's performance and the standing ovation he received proved unquestionably his continued popularity with the public in general, and his ability to excite and satisfy a live audience. Every other per-former at the show praised Michael, from alternative band Weezer to Notorious B.I.G. Chris Connely of MTV said the backstage area was filled with celebs trying to get a spot in the wings to watch Michael.

September 23
Michael attends Black Entertainment Television 15th anniversary show in Washington, where he becomes the first star to be inducted into BET's Walk of Fame. Michael then sang 'You Are Not Alone.'

● ● ● ● ● ● ● ● ● ● ● ● ● ● ● ● ●

1995

This Page: Michael, with Janet, poses for the latest promotional pictures to accompany 'History'.

1995

November 15

USA Today report on Michael's nephews, 3T: 'Taj says Michael has been strong about legal problems that have engulfed him. Adds Taryll: 'You can either back down and give up, or you can fight it. That's what he's doing,' in the court of public opinion. Their mother 'raised us to stick together,' says Taryll, who adds that the three are best friends... Uncle Michael taught them music tricks from the time they were little, Taryll says. 'A lot of our first instruments were bought by him.'

November 22

Michael was seen out shopping to buy books on photography and mentalism, a silver frame and an old photo.

November 23

Michael wins Best Male Singer at the MTV Europe Music Awards.

November 27

Jet magazine features an article detailing Michael's joint publishing venture with Sony reportedly valued at $600 million.

December 2

Adrian Grant hosts yet another successful Michael Jackson Day in London, with Michael's personal video crew once again in attendance to film the day's activities for him. For the second year running, Michael sends a special video message to the MJ Day attendees.

December 3

Michael wins the *Smash Hits* award for Best Male Solo Singer.

December 6

Michael is rushed to the Beth Israel Medical Center in New York after collapsing at rehearsals for his HBO special One Night Only. Early reports from the Center indicate that Michael is suffering from gastro-enteritis, dehydration and electrolyte imbalances. Michael was due to play before an invite-only crowd at the Beacon Theater on the 8th and 9th.

Michael was also to have attended the *Billboard* Music Awards where he was to collect a *Billboard* Hot 100 Achievement Award for having the first ever single, 'You Are Not Alone' to début at Number one on the charts. Tina Turner collected the award on his behalf, and wished him a speedy recovery.

December 11

German magazine *Bravo*, carries an interview with Bob Jones where he states that Michael was very disappointed that the HBO concert did not go through, especially for all his fans who travelled to New York from all over the world. Michael also wins four of the magazine's end of year awards including Best Male Singer and Best Album with 'History'.

December 18

Michael is resting at EuroDisney in Paris. He makes an appearance for his fans on the hotel balcony to his suite, the Sleeping Beauty Room.

1996
January

'Off The Wall' (LP) is certified seven times platinum for sales of seven million in America.

Michael wins two Danish Grammys for Best International Male Artist and Best International Album with 'History.'

January 19

USA Today reports that Lisa Marie Presley filed for divorce from Michael Jackson yesterday, ending a 19-month marriage that merged pop royalty. A statement from Jackson spokesman Lee Solters said the two 'have mutually agreed to go their separate ways. However, they remain good friends.'

January 26

The Daily News reports that Michael Jackson enjoyed a sushi dinner and the company of a mystery blonde in midtown just a week after his impending divorce was made public.

January 29

Michael Jackson wins Best Male Pop Vocal at the American Music Awards. He is not present to accept.

February 3

Michael pays tribute to Gene Kelly, who died on February 2. Michael said: 'Gene was a superb dancer, singer, choreographer, actor, director and gentleman. He is and will always remain an inspiration.'

February 5

People magazine puts MJ and Lisa on the cover with the headline, 'She's Outta There!' Lisa's attorney is quoted in the magazine as saying: 'This is a no-brainer. We wait six months. Then they're divorced.

There's really not that much to it.'

February 7

Variety carries a story about Spike Lee's opinions on the attempts to ban the filming of 'They Don't Care About Us.' Lee says, 'Michael loves Brazil and the Brazilians and he doesn't need to go half way around the world to show that shanty towns exist in Rio. This is ridiculous and pathetic. We're not trying to topple the Brazilian government. In the eyes of the world, complicating Michael Jackson's visa is making Brazil appear a ridiculous country – as if it were a banana republic.'

February 19

At the Brit Awards in London, Michael's first ever live TV performance in England for over 20 years, is interrupted by Pulp lead singer, Jarvis Cocker, who runs across the stage while Michael sings 'Earth Song' with over 60 children.

Michael went on to accept his Brit Award as Artist Of A Generation, saying, "I am humbled by this award – especially coming from my wonderful family in the UK. You have provided me with so much love and support in my career."

February 20

Epic Records issue the following statement: 'Michael Jackson respects Pulp as artists but is totally shocked by their behaviour and utterly fails to understand their complete lack of respect for fellow artists and performers. His main concern is for the people that worked for him and

the fact that children should be attacked. He feels sickened, saddened, shocked, upset, cheated, angry but is immensely proud that the cast remained professional and the show went on despite the disgusting and cowardly behaviour of the two characters that tried to disrupt it. Even though the evening ended on a sad note, he wants to thank all his fans and the media for their understanding and support.'

Michael leaves the UK and flies to Paris where he stays at Disneyland.

February 28

Michael wins a Grammy for Best Video, short form, for 'Scream.'

March

It was reported on MTV in America that Michael's 'History' album is the best-selling double album ever with three million copies sold. These figures refer to US sales only.

A 48-year-old woman who has been stalking Michael Jackson for more than ten years has been ordered by a court to stay away from the pop star. Gabriella Jamilla Jackson has been banned from coming within five hundred yards (457 metres) of Jackson's homes in Encino and Santa Barbara in California.

March 6

Michael and Janet Jackson both pick up an award at the second annual Blockbuster Music Awards. Michael won for favourite pop male and Janet for favourite pop female. The awards are voted on by

customers in Blockbuster video rental stores.

March 10

The Daily News reports: 'Michael Jackson is King of Cyberspace. His electronic chat with fans last year attracted a record 6,000 participants, and his name appears on more than 6,000 Net home pages. That means more than 6,000 users have set up sites on the Net where browsers can find information about the eccentric superstar. Bill Clinton is second, with over 5,500.

March 19

At a press conference in Paris, Michael announces plans for his new company, Kingdom Entertainment, a Paris-based multimedia corporation jointly owned with Saudi Prince, Al-Walid bin Talal bin Abdul Aziz al-Saoud.

March 25

Today is the thirteenth anniversary of Michael Jackson's first-ever public performance of the Moonwalk on *Motown 25*.

March 30

Michael's 'Earth Song' video receives the Doris Day award for music at the 10th annual Genesis Awards, which recognise concern for the plight of animals.

April

In April's edition of *Vanity Fair*, there's an eight-page article on Sandy Gallin, Michael Jackson's manager. Gallin engineered the four to five-year plan for the production of Michael Jackson's 'Dangerous,' which became one of the

This Page: Michael embraces Bob Geldof at The Brit Awards after receiving The Artirst Of A Generation Award.

Michael on Stage during his disrupted performance of 'Earth Song.'

1996

most successful albums in the world. The article states: 'Gallin has been attempting to engineer the same kind of success for Jackson's latest album, 'History', which has so far been a disappointment, selling fewer than three million copies in the US. He says the album has to be: 'viewed as a three-year project,' but admits that sales have been slow and that he expected the album would have 'jump-started much faster than it did.'

In April's issue of *Disney Adventures* magazine Michael is voted as the best male singer. Michael said he was happy, because kids are honest about who they like and don't like.

April 27
Michael's latest video, 'They Don't Care About Us,' has been pulled from the playlist of two major music channels in America, MTV and VH1, because of lingering concerns it is anti-Semitic. The song originally contained the lyrics 'Jew me' and 'kike me'.

Bob Jones of MJJ Productions, says the singer: 'is not a racist, as evidenced by his many endeavours on behalf of people of all religions.' An Epic rep agreed, registering disappointment with MTV's and VH1's actions.'

April 28
Michael attends a performance of 'Sisterella', the play he produced in Pasadena, California.

May 1
USA Today reports as follows: 'A California judge

This Page: Michael keeps grip of some of the Awards he won at the World Music Awards.

Opposite: Michael performs 'Earth Song' at the aforementioned Award ceremony.

ordered Jackson Communications Incorporated to pay $1.6 million to Smith-Hemion Productions, which claims it was hurt by the ill-fated Jackson Family Honors in 1994. The company claims it was never paid for work done on the TV special and that it lost money because Michael Jackson did not perform solo. The judge halted all proceedings in the case while the parties await the results of an identical federal case.'

May 6
Entertainment Weekly does a cover story on the biggest-selling LPs of all time. It featured an extremely positive piece on 'Thriller.' The article said everything MJ's magic feet touch turns to gold.

May 8
At the World Music Awards in Monaco Michael performs 'Earth Song' and collects five awards. Michael also makes a statement attacking critics and the tabloid press angrily denying allegations of anti-Semitism. Michael spoke out saying that he wasn't blasphemous or racist. Looking dapper in a black jacket, jeans, white T-shirt and the all-too-familiar one black glove, he spoke to *Entertainment Tonight*, "By the way, I love Jewish people," he said, while leaving the arena and juggling an armload of trophies. *Entertainment Tonight's* Mark Steines asked Michael what he was going to do with his awards, and MJ responded: "put them in a place of honour."

May 11
Michael visits Fantasialand,

near Cologne in Germany. The Colorado Roller Coaster was renamed the 'Michael Jackson Thriller Colorado Roller Coaster', and Michael went on this ride twice.

May 12
Michael Jackson pays a flying visit to Britain – to go shopping. Michael went to Dillons Book Shop in Gower Street in London.

May 15
Michael flies back to New York.

June 1
Ebony magazine lists Michael's total US sales for all of his LPs and singles at 62 million units, two million more than Garth Brooks record-breaking 60 million. Michael has sold 51 million LPs in the US and 11 million singles, which places him at the top of the list. The information comes from the Recording Industry Association of America (RIAA) which issues gold and platinum records.

'They Don't Care' débuted this week on the Pop Singles Chart at Number 30 and on the R&B Charts at Number 11.

After nine weeks, 'They Don't Care' falls out of the UK Top 40 Singles Chart this week after turning Silver last week. 'History' rose nine places to No. 28 last week, following the Music Awards Show in Monte Carlo.

June 6
Michael appears on MTV Asia's Channel V and says: "Hi, this is Michael

1996

Jackson. The first to be Number 1 entertainer of the month on Channel V, the best channel in Asia." The TV station then showed clips from 'Black or White' and the prison version of 'They Don't Care About Us.' Michael's videos will be played throughout the month on MTV Asia. Michael is also No. 1 for the third consecutive week on MTV's European Top 20 for 'They Don't Care...'

June 7

Under the heading, Jackson Faces New £40 Million Jordan Battle, the *Evening Standard* printed the following: 'Child abuse allegations against Michael Jackson are being thrust back into the spotlight despite a multi-million dollar settlement. The father of Jordan Chandler has slapped the entertainer with a $60 million lawsuit in which his son, who is now 16, will be called as a key witness. Jackson will be accused of breaking the confidential agreement of the settlement with Jordan during a television appearance with his now estranged wife, Lisa Marie Presley.

Michael Jackson issues a statement regarding the latest law suit filed against him by Jordan Chandler's father, Evan Chandler.

Chandler alleges, "Michael Jackson has developed, orchestrated, participated in and carried out a scheme to falsely accuse the minor of lying about claims that (he was) sexually assaulted and molested." Chandler names not only Michael, but also Lisa Marie, Sony Music,

Diane Sawyer and ABC Television in the suit, which claims that all of these people have breached the terms of Michael's 1994 out-of-court settlement with Chandler, by allowing MJ to maintain his innocence in the June 1995 prime time live interview.

Michael's statement is as follows: "The allegations made in the lawsuit are false, and I will vigorously challenge them. I am especially hurt that Mr. Chandler chose to involve my dear Lisa Marie in this meritless dispute. I also regret that Diane Sawyer and ABC, as well as my close friends and business associates at Sony and Warner-Tamerlane are also being sued. I am confident that we will ALL prevail in court, the proper place to put this matter to rest."

June 11

An appeals court rejects the lawsuit filed by Reynaud Jones and others in a copyright infringement case against Michael involving the songs 'Thriller,' 'We Are The World,' and 'The Girl Is Mine.'

June 21

Michael Jackson and President Clinton are just two of the famous people who lend their support to a star-studded charity event in aid of the Dunblane appeal at the Royal Oak Hotel, Sevenoaks in England. Michael donates a four-times platinum disc of his album 'History', valued at more than £5,000.

Oprah Winfrey choses Michael's 'Will You Be There' as a dedication to the memories of AIDS victims on her show, sparking

happy comments from American Jackson fans that this was Oprah's first real public acknowledgement of Michael since the allegations.

June 24

People magazine contains a photograph of Michael on the set of his new short film, entitled *Ghosts*, which includes the song '2 Bad'. Pictured with Michael on the set of the video is Steven Spielberg, quashing rumours that he had fallen out with Michael over the controversy surrounding the lyrics to 'They Don't Care...' The director of *Ghosts*, Stan Winston, who worked on *Terminator*, *Jurassic Park* and *Interview With A Vampire*, has a knack of creating living, breathing actors by combining make-up, FX, animatronics and solid acting.

July

The July edition of *Life* magazine lists the 50 most influential 'baby boomers' – people born in the US between 1946 and 1964. Michael comes in at number 42.

July 5

Adrian Grant meets Michael on the video set of 'Stranger In Moscow', where they discuss future book plans. Michael states that Jarvis Cocker's invasion of his performance at The Brit Awards, was an act of 'jealousy'.

July 15

With Michael at his side, the Sultan of Brunei celebrated his 50th Birthday a $25 million bash befitting his status as the world's richest man.

July 16
For the Sultan's birthday celebrations, Michael performs in front of 60,000 people at the Jerudong Amusement Park in Muslim Brunei, which bans the sale of alcohol, hangs drug traffickers and forbids Western practices which cause 'moral decay.' But officials said pop concerts were fine and Jackson was regarded as a 'clean' performer.

July 18
Michael arrives in South Africa, where he attends a private birthday party for President Nelson Mandela. Michael looked as if he didn't know whether to shake Mandela's hand or to hug him, but Mandela put Michael at ease by immediately embracing him, and they hugged for some time. Michael was welcomed by about 200 screaming fans at Johannesburg airport and was later mobbed by about 400 youths in the Black township of Soweto. He announced to his cheering fans that he was "glad to be back home." He went to Soweto to lay a wreath at a memorial to the hundreds of Blacks who were shot dead by police during widespread riots in 1976.

July 19
Michael addresses a news conference at Sun City, 75 miles northwest of Johannesburg, during which it was confirmed that Michael will play five dates at in the UK. The exact dates were not confirmed. During the conference, Michael makes the following speech: "First I would like to say, sincerely, from the bottom of my heart, how happy and honoured I am to be in South Africa. I would like to take this opportunity to thank President Nelson Mandela and the wonderful people of South Africa, for this gracious, really gracious, welcome to your wonderful country – I just love it, I love it so much I'm looking for a house to buy here, actually! I'm sorry that I was not able to play South Africa dates previously because... I was so much looking forward to coming here, but now I am really excited about bringing the History World Tour to South Africa."

July 20
Michael announces that he is composing a song about Nelson Mandela. "I am working on a song now... I was working on it last night," he told reporters after a brief courtesy call at the president's official Pretoria home. "This is a wonderful, lovely man. I love Nelson Mandela very much," Michael said. Shielding his face from the African sun with a cream parasol, Michael said he wanted to live in South Africa and had already begun to house-hunt. "I have had the time of my life here. I've had so much fun, I hate to leave. I'm definitely looking for a home here to buy. I would love to spend the rest of my life here."

Michael initially resisted a request from photographers to pose without his umbrella saying, "I am allergic to the sun." But he later complied, embracing Mandela with a broad smile. Mandela said, "There is really nothing I have to say except that Michael is in the country. He just paid a courtesy visit. He has made a great contribution to art, to music, and I'm very happy that he is in our country." When first emerging from the house onto a patio where the media contingent was waiting, Mandela turned towards Michael to quip, "I can see who is the world leader. I have never seen so many journalists. That shows how popular you are."

July 23
Michael Jackson and Bela, the 6-year-old Hungarian boy, whose life-saving operation Michael had financed almost two years ago, returned to the Budapest hospital that was used to treat the child. "I love being back here," Michael said to a brief news conference at Bethesda Children's Hospital. "This should be a day for children."

In August 1994, Jackson promised his Heal the World Foundation would pay for a liver transplant for Bela Farkas, suffering from a life-threatening congenital liver disease that discoloured his skin. The operation was finally performed in Belgium in March last year. Bela is now well, with his skin a healthy pink hue instead of the greenish colour it had been two years ago.

This Page: Director, Stan Winston, with Michael (yes the white man in glasses is really Michael Jackson,) on the set of *Ghosts*.

1996

September 7

Michael launches his History World Tour with a high-tech spectacle in Prague playing to over 130,000 people. During his stay in the Czech capital Michael has received police escorts throughout the ancient city, and been treated like royalty. Jackson's Prague promoter, Serbe Grimaux, said the normally reclusive Jackson wanted to arrive several days before the concert to mix with the thousands who throng the bridges and palaces of the Bohemian capital 'like a normal tourist.' "He has a big interest in meeting people and doesn't want to be too incognito," Grimaux told reporters.

September 8

Michael arrives in Budapest to a welcome which outdid even the Pope's welcome. Over 4,000 fans screamed Michael's name as he descended the steps of his Boeing 747 and walked towards them. He was wearing a long black overcoat to protect him from the extreme cold. "I love it here," he told reporters as he strolled across the tarmac. "I love these people." Fans swarmed over the smoked glass windows of his car as

This Page and Opposite: Michael on the History World Tour.

Gloria Haydock, my good friend, editor of MJ News International, and a key researcher on this book, meets Michael in Bucharest.

it inched its way out of the airport to his hotel, where hundreds more waiting fans were rewarded minutes after his arrival with an appearance and a wave from his open top-floor window.

Later, Michael has dinner with 100 lucky Hungarian children.

September 9

Michael begs his fans to move back after they smash a record shop window in Budapest as they try to get close to him. Jackson was coming out of the shop after spending an hour inside buying CDs when the window gave way in the crush. Michael, clearly alarmed, climbed on his car and gestured to his screaming fans to get away from the glass, pieces of which continued to fall onto the pavement. No-one was hurt.

September 10

The concert is a big success with Michael continuing to be in a very relaxed and happy mood. Press sources reported that the Budapest concert was not a sell-out but, in fact, the 60,000 tickets sold represent a record number for Hungary.

September 12

Michael arrives in Romania. Hundreds of fans wait outside the small Baneasa Airport for him, with anti-riot troops and police with armour-plated cars standing guard.

Michael went on a post-revolutionary tour of monuments and orphanages. Traffic in Bucharest was disrupted as Michael knelt and laid flowers at a cross in University Square,

where protesters died from police bullets in Romania's violent 1989 revolution. Later in the day, he visited a state orphanage and watched a children's show staged for him in the giant marble-walled palace built for late dictator Ceausescu. "I wish all the world was here to see this, instead of sending our brothers to the killing fields," Jackson said. "This is our future, children. I love you all so much."

'Stranger In Moscow' is now on release throughout Europe. The UK release date has been postponed from September 23 to November 4 due to the speed of the British charts compared to the rest of Europe. The release of the single will coincide with a new promotional drive for the album for the Christmas period in the UK and throughout Europe.

September 16

Michael's arrival in Russia is such a success that MJJ Productions issue the following press release: "Calling it a 'great gift to Moscovites for him to be here,' Moscow Mayor, Yuri Luzhkov, officially welcomed Michael Jackson to the city with a ceremonial reception at the city government's White Hall. Flanked by other government officials, Luzhkov called Jackson 'a great talent and an outstanding artist' before presenting him with a replica of an official Russian plate from which he said, 'the people's predecessors took their food.' 'Michael Jackson gives himself to all people,' said Luzhkov, 'you can sense the warmth. We love classic music and modern music and Michael Jackson is the best as far as modern music is concerned'."

September 20

Under the heading Bee Gees, Jackson 5 Among Rock Inductees, the *New Jersey Herald & News* reports as follows, "The Bee Gees, the kings of disco, are headed to the Rock and Roll Hall of Fame along with another successful brother group from the 1970s, the Jackson 5. The May 15 induction ceremony will take place at the Rock and Roll Hall and Museum, a first for the year-old Ohio facility."

Polish newspapers hail Michael Jackson's first concert in Poland, which drew a record 100,000 to 120,000 fans to an unused air base near Warsaw. The best-selling daily *Gazeta Wyborcza* said, 'Michael is Beautiful,' while top tabloid Super Express said, 'Music in a Crowd, Jackson in Great Form.'

September 23

Forbes magazine ranks MJ as the 4th highest-paid entertainer of 1995-96. Based on estimated gross income, MJ ranks 4th with earnings of $90 million. The top five are: 1. Oprah Winfrey ($171m), 2. Steven Spielberg ($150m), 3. Beatles ($130m), 5. Rolling Stones ($77m).

October

'Thriller' has been voted the best ever music video of all time: "A panel of music video experts said 'Thriller' is a musical masterpiece and will probably

never ever be beaten unless it is by Michael!" said the *Guardian* newspaper, who asked the opinion of Kevin Godley, from rock group 10cc, film directors Julian Temple and Tim Pope, MTV Europe Executive and Owner Bret Hansen, and *Top Of The Pops* producer Ric Blaxill.

October 1

Prior to Michael's concert in Tunisia on October 7, a press release from Kingdom Entertainment includes a statement from Jackson in which he says, "This concert will be of special significance for me because it will be my first in Africa and the Arab World. The people and nations of both regions have always held a special place in my heart and I always wanted to perform for them. I am particularly delighted that this concert will be in Tunisia, a peaceful and tolerant nation which cares equally for men, women and children. Proceeds from my concert will go to a national charity helping the needy and that's an extra source of satisfaction for me."

Michael Jackson's concert will benefit 'The National Solidarity Fund,' a Tunisian charity dedicated to fighting poverty called 26-26 and promoted by the Tunisian President.

The King of Pop was cheered by thousands of fans at Tunis airport and his hotel in central Tunis. Tunisian media said that hundreds of fans also flew to Tunisia from neighbouring Algeria, and also from Italy, France and Spain aboard 23 charter flights to attend the concert.

October 2

In Holland, a new official Michael Jackson product – a soft drink – is launched. The drink, called Mystery, comes in a 250ml gold can bearing an image of the 'History' statue in grey with print in red and white. The fizzy fruit drink carrying the byline 'fresh – cool – magic' is expected to be sold on the tour and to retail outlets. Mystery is described as an 'energy' drink made from fruit and plant extracts and vitamins and minerals.

October 3

Michael Jackson flies into Stansted Airport for a surprise short stay in England. Michael travelled in a plane which bore the logo of his newly-founded entertainment company, Kingdom Entertainment. Michael stays at the Lanesborough Hotel, and during his short stay in London, completes work on his soundtrack for his forthcoming movie, *Ghosts*.

October 4

Michael attends a performance of one of his favourite musicals, Lionel Bart's 'Oliver' at the London Palladium.

October 29

The Hollywood Reporter contains the headline, ' Theme Park Would Be Landmark For Italian', stating that, "Michael Jackson is leading a group of US investors in talks with Italian authorities about building a new, mega budgeted – $700m reportedly raised to date – amusement park only 18 miles north of Rome, in the town of Civitavecchia. Now we've discovered that

1996

2,000-acre extravaganza will almost certainly feature a major design involvement by theme park entrepreneur Gary Goddard."

Kingdom Entertainment, the company owned by Michael Jackson and Saudi Prince al-Waleed bin Talal, bought 50 percent of Goddard's Landmark Entertainment Group. "With Kingdom's involvement, Landmark Entertainment Group will immediately expand its motion picture, television, and live entertainment activities, while at the same time building its theme park and attraction division into an even greater force," said in a statement issued by the Prince's Riyadh office.

November 5

Michael Jackson's 35-minute short film, *Ghosts*, is premièred in eleven selected Sony cinemas in America.

November 6

Liz Smith reports in her column in the *San Francisco Chronicle* as follows, "Congratulations and good luck to Michael Jackson and Debbie Rowe, the woman who is reported to be carrying his first child."

November 7

Jeannie Williams reports in her column in *USA Today* as follows, "The LA-based, British-run, Splash news agency is very smug about breaking the Michael Jackson baby story with London's *News of the World* under the noses of us Yanks. 'We've been working on the story for two-and-a-half months. Our

source told us originally that Debbie Rowe is having his baby, but it was us who established it was true,' says Splash partner Kevin Smith."

November 10

Michael gives an interview to VH1, an American Music Channel, by answering selected questions sent in by VH1's viewers.

November 11

'Sisterella', the musical stage production of a black version of Cinderella which Michael Jackson co-produced, wins an incredible eight NAACP Theatre Awards at the Hollywood Roosevelt Hotel. The show was a huge success in the Pasadena Playhouse earlier this year, and is in preparation for New York showings.

November 15

Hotel publicist, Brian Walsh, tells the media that Michael has married again saying that Jackson, 38, married Rowe, 37, before a handful of friends in the Sheraton-on-the-Park Hotel only hours after kicking off the Australian leg of his History World Tour.

Jackson married Rowe, a former nurse, in a civil ceremony in his presidential suite, said Walsh. He did not know whether the couple exchanged any special wedding vows. "The ceremony was attended by a

few friends and people from the tour entourage. Debbie has known Michael for a long time and has been with the entourage for a while and they have a lot of friends in common." he said.

In a written statement distributed on the Internet global computer network, Michael said, "Please respect our privacy and let us enjoy this wonderful and exciting time." The wedding took place only ten days after Jackson announced Rowe, who nursed him while he was being treated for a rare skin disorder, was to give birth to his child early next year. Jackson denied news reports that Rowe had been artificially inseminated and that he paid her $500,000 to carry his child.

November 25

Michael Jackson completes

This Page: Michael with new wife, Debbie Rowe.

Michael in a scene from his short-film, *Ghosts*.

his 5-day History World Tour stop in Melbourne, with a surprise visit to the Royal Children's Hospital. He visited with sick children in the hospital, delivered toys to them, signed autographs, and had pictures taken with them. He made a special point to see cancer patients and children suffering from cystic-fibrosis. A nurse commented later about Michael's special gift, when she witnessed a very ill little girl smile for the first time when Michael visited with her.

November 28

The *New York Times* publishes an article declaring Michael Jackson's 'History' ablum a global success. Neil Strauss points out that 'History' may even realize Sony Music's goal of selling 20 million 2-CD boxed sets of 'History' worldwide, and may exceed Sony's prediction that 'History' will be a hot item two Christmases after it was released.

Today, the marketing campaign is still in full gear and is, in fact, outlasting Sony's 18-month plan. Now, 17 months and two Christmases since the release of 'History,' the album is actually climbing the charts in Malaysia, Australia, France, and elsewhere, and remains a top seller in dozens of European and Asian countries. Sony is shipping as many as 100,000 copies of 'History' overseas every week. Considering that the 2-CD sets are priced as double albums, this would make 'History' almost as big a source of revenue as 'Thriller,' which sold 46 million worldwide.

November 30

Adrian Grant holds his seventh MJ Day in London. The event is the most popular ever, with over 2,000 people attending. The show includes a special performance from Michael's nephews 3T, and a phone message to the fans from Michael in Australia.

December 5

Entertainment Wire reports that, 'The King of Pop, Michael Jackson, performed the last of his three sell-out shows in Perth, ending his three-week stint 'Down Under.' A total of 54,000 (18,000 per night) fans filled Burswood Dome to watch the magic that is the superstar. The concerts were met with rave reviews in local publications. His performance in Perth was called 'stunning' and he was marked a 'musical wizard.'

December 5

Associated Press reports that, 'Hundreds of screaming fans lined the street from the Manila airport to the historic Manila Hotel as Michael Jackson arrived Thursday evening for the Philippine leg of his History World Tour. Jo Ramos-Samartino, a daughter of President Fidel Ramos, welcomed Jackson at the Manila airport, putting on a lei of Sampaquita, the Philippine national flower.

December 12

Michael nearly caused a riot when he made an appearance at Tokyo's Tower Records to set his hand and signature in plaster for a plaque to be displayed permanently in the store.

December 19

Michael attends the Tokyo premiere of his short-film *Ghosts*.

Later that evening, Michael also receives a platinum disc award from Sony Music Japan Chairman Shugo Matsuo, representing 600,000 unit sales in Japan of the 'History' album.

December 22

Michael Jackson was a nominee for the annual Sour Apple award, given to "the least cooperative entertainment figure of the year or the person who has brought dishonor to the industry," by the Hollywood Women's Press Club's. The winners were Dennis Rodman and Howard Stern, but Michael handled the dubious honor with a sense of humor. He sent a message explaining why he could not attend the awards ceremony: "I am sorry cannot be here in person, as I am currently in Japan for my History World Tour and am hosting a holiday party for the employees of Star magazine tonight. Thank you very much for this award, and I wish all of you a very happy holiday season. I love you." *The Star*, a newspaper, has been reporting false stories on Michael unmercifully for years.

December 29

Michael Jackson ended his 18-day stay in Japan today, when he left for Brunei. During the Japan leg of his History World Tour, Michael performed in 6 concerts: 4 in Tokyo at the Tokyo Dome on December

HISTORY Tour Dates (First Leg)	
September 7	Prague
September 10	Budapest
September 14	Bucharest
September 17	Moscow
September 19	Warsaw
September 24	Zaragoza
September 28	Amsterdam
September 30	Amsterdam
October 2	Amsterdam
October 7	Tunisia
October 11	Seoul
October 13	Seoul
October 18	Taipei
October	Kaoshung
October 22	Taipei
October 25	Singapore
October 27	Kuala Lumpur
October 29	Kuala Lumpur
November 1	Bombay
November 5	Bangkok
November 9	Auckland
November 11	Auckland
November 14	Sydney
November 16	Sydney
November 19	Brisbane
November 22	Melbourne
November 24	Melbourne
November 26	Adelaide
November 30	Perth
December 2	Perth
December 4	Perth
December 8	Philippines
December 10	Philippines
December 13	Tokyo
December 15	Tokyo
December 17	Tokyo
December 20	Tokyo
December 26	Fukuoka
December 28	Fukuoka
December 31	Brunei
January 3	Honolulu
January 4	Honolulu

13, 15, 17, and 20; and 2 concerts in Fukuoka on December 26 and 28

December 30
Michael spends about one and half hours at Jerudong Park in Brunei, enjoying roller coaster rides and other attractions including Formula One, Ranger, Gokart, and Aladdin. Between rides he waved to fans, signed autographs, kissed children, and shook hands.

December 31
Michael Jackson was in Brunei today, welcoming the New Year with a special concert held in Jerudong Park, a world renowned amusement park. The concert was organized by the Sultan of Brunei for 4,000 specially invited guests, but the public was also invited.

1997
January 2
Michael Jackson arrives in Hawaii where he is greeted by a keiki hula troupe of 150 dancers, two dozen Tahitian dancers, and about 200 fans.

January 6
Michael Jackson performs to record crowds in Honolulu, Hawaii - his first U.S. tour stop since 1989. The two concerts held on January 3rd and 4th at the 35,000-seat Aloha Stadium made history - no other musical act ever sold out the stadium, and Michael sold out 2 shows in less than 24 hours, a record time. Hawaii promoter, Tom Moffatt said: "I've never seen anything like it, ...there's been nothing even close to this - the Rolling Stones, Elton John, Julio Iglesias, the Eagles. . ."

January 20
Michael Jackson is voted as the Most Memorable Male Performer and a 'legend of live entertainment,' by readers of *Live!* magazine.

January 25
A Michael Jackson Memorabilia Auction is held in Bombay, India. Diamond merchant, Bharat Shah, paid $10,081 for a pillow case on which Michael wrote, ``India, all my life I have longed to see you....'' Another businessman paid $5,500 for a mirror on which Jackson scrawled "I love you India. I have seen the face of God in your children..." The money raised was given to a charity, which helps educate children living in slums. Micheal Jackson had also waived his personal fee for the Bombay appearance and donated $1.1 million to charity.

February 1
The *New York Post* reports as follows, 'The music industry - as well as the Velvet Mafia - is agog that Michael Jackson has severed ties with his personal manager Sandy Gallin, who has seen him through the release of his History album and associated tours and scandals. Sources in Jackson's camp confirmed that his career will be handled by Kingdom Entertainment, the management company jointly owned by Jackson and Prince Waleed Bin Talal of Saudi Arabia. '

February 3
A federal judge dismisses fraud claims in a lawsuit filed against eight members of Michael Jackson's family over the failed 1994 *Jackson Family Honours* TV special.

February 4
Michael Jackson flies to Rome where he denies charges that he copied 'Will You Be There' in his 1991 'Dangerous' album from a song by Italian singer Al Bano. "I have never taken or stolen anything in my life," Jackson told the court. Bano accused Jackson of plagiarising his 1987 song 'I Cigni di Balaka (The Swans of Balaka).'

February 13
Michael Jackson's wife, Debbie Rowe, gives birth to a healthy baby boy, at Cedars-Sinai Medical Center in Los Angeles. Michael is present at his son's birth.

February 14
Following the birth of his new son, Michael Jackson issues this statement, "Words can't describe how I feel...I have been blessed beyond comprehension and I will work tirelessly at being the best father that I can possibly be. I appreciate that my fans are elated, but I hope that everyone respects the privacy that Debbie and I want and need for our son. I grew up in a fish bowl and will not allow that to happen to my child. Please respect our wishes and give my son his privacy."

February 16
Elizabeth Taylor, who is facing surgery soon for a benign brain tumour, celebrated her 65th birthday in

"Words can't describe how I feel...I have been blessed beyond comprehension and I will work tirelessly at being the best father that I can possibly be. I appreciate that my fans are elated, but I hope that everyone respects the privacy that Debbie and I want and need for our son. I grew up in a fish bowl and will not allow that to happen to my child. Please respect our wishes and give my son his privacy."

Michael Jackson, February 14, 1997

Page Opposite: Michael with his new son, Prince Michael Jr. Photograph by JK Issac © OK! Magazine and Triumph International Ltd 1997

her characteristic glamour at a black-tie gala in Hollywood Sunday night with a star-studded cast of well-wishers.

Michael Jackson, arrived as Taylor's escort for the evening and sat by her side throughout. Michael was making his first appearance since the recent birth of his first son, whose godmother is Taylor. Jackson sang, 'Elizabeth,' which he wrote especially for the occasion.

Michael gave a markedly sparce performance without his usual pyrotechnics, props or supporting cast, with the exception of a child actress appearing at the beginning of the number who was representing Taylor as a girl. Jackson's lyrics proclaimed: 'They wanted you to fall / It's very sad / People can be very bad... / But you were the victor...'

February 18
Michael has donated his seven year-old pet African elephant, Ali, to the Jacksonville, Florida zoo. Michael had originally planned a breeding program at his Neverland Valley Ranch, but contruction of the breeding area was delayed.

This Page: Michael escorts Elizabeth Taylor on her 65th birthday.

Page Opposite: Michael with his new born son.
Photograph by JK Issac © OK! Magazine and Triumph International Ltd 1997

February 25
A Superior Court judge dismisses most of a lawsuit that held Michael Jackson responsible for production loses from the failed 1994 Jackson Family Honours show. Judge Sherman Smith Jr. threw out two of three claims brought against Jackson by Smith-Hemion Productions. The judge found that Jackson did not commit a breach of contract or break implied contractual indemnity. "It is undisputed that Mr. Jackson made a written promise to appear on the show, and that gave the big greenlight to go ahead with production," Smith-Hemion attorney William Briggs said. "His failure to appear caused all the hurt and damages." The lawsuit seeks to have Jackson pay most or all of a $1.7 million judgment brought against Jackson Communications Inc. The company claimed it had no assets and was unable to pay. Smith-Hemion also has sued in federal court to have the judgment enforced.

March 7
Soul Train Music Awards rename their video award in Michael's honour to the "Michael Jackson Award for Best R&B/Soul or Rap Music Video." Recording star Brandy read the following dedication at the awards ceremony, "As of this year, the Soul Train Music Award for Best R&B/Soul or Rap Music Video is named in honour of Michael Jackson for his unique contributions as a pioneer in the creation of sophisticated, high quality music videos, as well as his contributions to the overall development of major music video media worldwide, through his liberal use of his image."

March 18
After a 6-month long civil trial that began in Sept. '96, a 12 member jury in Santa Maria, California, sided with Michael Jackson and six other defendants, and ruled that he did not wrongfully terminate, harass, or threaten five former employees at his Neverland Valley Ranch. One of the jurors, Lorie Durnin, said the plaintiffs "lost their credibility when they went to the tabloids" and sold their stories. Jackson's lawyer, Zia Modabber, said the evidence proved the plaintiffs were nothing more than "people trying to capitalize on Michael's fame." Michael's other attorney for the case, Steve Cochrane, added, "We're happy to be finally and fully vindicated."

March 20
A judge annuls a previous decision and decides to allow copies of 'Dangerous' (LP) to be sold in Italy, and that Michael Jackson can perform 'Will You Be There'. Previously, the judge decided that Michael's song sounded too similar to the Italian songwriter Al Bano's 'I Cigni de Balaka'. The judge announces that there was no evidence that Michael had plagerized the song. Al Bano's song was written in Italian and only played in Italy.

March 21
Sony Music present Michael with a special award to signify sales of 100 million singles and albums outside of the United States, since his first solo album for Epic Records in 1979, 'Off The Wall'. The accolade recognizes the popularity of the LP's, 'Off the Wall,' 'Thriller,' 'Bad,' 'Dangerous,' and 'History.' The special presentation takes place at a Sony International meeting in Marbella, Spain.

OK!

1997

This Page: Michael in the video, 'Blood On The Dance Floor.'

Michael applauds Marcel Marceau at the unveiling of his waxwork at the Grevin Museum, Paris.

March 25

OK! magazine publish the worldwide exclusive pictures of Michael Jackson's new son, whom Michael has called, Prince Michael Jackson Junior. The British publication also carries an exclusive interview in which Michael states, "My grandfather and great-grandfather were both named Prince, so we have carried on the tradition and now we have a third Prince in the family...Debbie and I love each other for all the things you'll never see on stage or in pictures. I fell for the beautiful, unpretentious, giving person that she is, and she fell for me just being me. "

April 2

Michael's new video, 'Blood on the Dance Floor' is premiéred on VH1 in the U.S.

April 11

Michael wins 'Best Male Singer' and 'Best Live Act' at the annual Music Factory Awards in Holland. The awards were based on votes submitted by viewers of The Music Factory (a Dutch music TV channel) and the readers of *Hitkrant* magazine. Michael's father, Joseph Jackson, accepted the awards on Michael's behalf, expressing his pride in Michael's achievements and thanking the audience for their support of the entire Jackson family.

April 20

Michael Jackson attends the unveiling of a special waxwork of his likeness at the Grevin Museum in Paris, France. Over 2,000 fans are there to greet him.
  Michael is surprised by the appearance of his idol, Marcel Marceau.

April 27

Michael Jackson debuts at number one in the U.K. with his single 'Blood On The Dance Floor.'

May 2

Michael arrives in Munich, Germany, where he is presented with a plaque from soccer club 1860 Munich, aswell as a blue & white soccer-shirt saying 'Jackson' on the back. Michael then takes part in a news conference, organized by Mama Concerts, in the stadium. Most German TV stations carry live coverage of the conference, which centers on Michael's connection with imprissoned Marcel Avram and his company, Mama Concerts.

May 3

Michael visits his tour promoter, Marcel Avram, in a Munich jail today, spending over half an hour with him. Avram, was arrested in April on suspicions of tax evasion.

May 5
Michael Jackson arrives at Linate Airport close to Milan, in Italy. Hundreds of fans greet him at the airport and follow him to his hotel, the Hotel Principe di Savoia.

Later, Michael is the star guest for the annual awards of Italian TV show, *Gran Premio Internazionale della Televisione*. He presents the award for best TV programme of the year and is introduced by Luciano Pavarotti, whom embraces him as he comes on to the stage. The two stars say they plan to do a record together and donate the proceeds to helping the needy children of the world.

May 6
The Jackson 5 are inducted into the Rock and Roll Hall of Fame. Michael flies into Cleveland, Ohio from Italy so he can be present at the induction ceremony. He is joined on stage by his brothers and Diana Ross who presents the awards to the Jackson 5. Michael pays much respect to his parents and Berry Gordy.

May 8
Michael's short film *Ghosts* is shown at the 50th Cannes Film Festival. Michael attends the screening which takes place at midnight in the main auditorium. The film is also attended by many celebrities and hundreds of screaming fans.

May 14
Michael Jackson's new album, 'Blood On The Dancefloor - History In The Mix,' is released in the U.K. It storms straight in at number one.

The album contains 13 tracks, with 5 new songs and 8 previously unreleased re-mix versions of songs from the 'History' album. According to Epic, the album was initially intended as a promotional item for Michael's forthcoming European summer tour, but the project soon blossomed due to dance club's continued unwavering support of Michael Jackson. Work on the album has taken place all around the world as Michael has been touring, and the remixes have been done by many of the leading producers and creators in this field.

The following day, *Ghosts* receives its U.K premiere.

May 31
Michael starts the second-leg of his History World Tour with a sold-out performance in Bremen, Germany.

1997

**BLOOD ON THE DANCE FLOOR -
History in the Mix**

Michael Jackson
**EK 68000
EPC 487500-2**

1. **Blood on the Dance Floor**
2. **Morphine**
3. **Superfly Sister**
4. **Ghost**
5. **Is It Scary**
6. **Scream**
7. **Money**
8. **2Bad**
9. **Stranger in Moscow**
10. **This Time Around**
11. **Earth Song**
12. **You Are Not Alone**
13. **HIStory**

This Page: Michael in a scene from his short-film, *Ghosts*.

The second leg of the 'History' World Tour becomes the 2nd Biggest Tour of 1997. This does not include the first leg, these 40 shows were seen by over two million people with a total gross income of $83,514,126.

HISTORY Tour Dates
(Second Leg)

May 31st	Bremen	Germany
June 3rd	Cologne	Germany
June 6th	Bremen	Germany
June 8th	Amsterdam	Holland
June 10th	Amsterdam	Holland
June 13th	Kiel	Germany
June 15th	Gelsenkirchen	Germany
June 18th	Milan	Italy
June 20th	Lausanne	Switzerland
June 22nd	Luxembourg	Luxembourg
June 25th	Lyon	France
June 27th	Paris	France
June 29th	Paris	France
July 2nd	Vienna	Austria
July 4th	Munich	Germany
July 6th	Munich	Germany
July 9th	Sheffield	England
July 12th	London	England
July 15th	London	England
July 17th	London	England
July 19th	Dublin	Ireland
July 25th	Basel	Switzerland
July 27th	Nice	France
August 1st	Berlin	Germany
August 3rd	Leipzig	Germany
August 10th	Hockenheim	Germany
August 14th	Copenhagen	Denmark
August 16th	Gothenburg	Sweden
August 19th	Oslo	Norway
August 22nd	Tallinn	Estonia
August 24th	Helsinki	Finland
August 26th	Helsinki	Finland
August 29th	Copenhagen	Denmark
September 3rd	Ostend	Belgium
September 6th	Valladolid	Spain
October 4th	Cape Town	South Africa
October 6th	Cape Town	South Africa
October 10th	Johannesburg	South Africa
October 12th	Johannesburg	South Africa
October 15th	Durban	South Africa

Page Opposite: Michael performs 'The Way You Make Me Feel' during the start of the second leg of the 'History' World Tour. This song however was replaced by 'Blood On The Dance Floor' from June 18th onwards.

1997

June 6
Michael Jackson signs a three-year contract to promote the new video compact disc player - Esonic Video Discbaby.

June 16
Michael's 'Blood On The Dance Floor' album receives a Platinum Award in Europe for selling over a million copies.

June 18
Michael attends the 30th Anniversary of 'Phantasialand' celebrations in Bruhl, Germany. He signs the 'Children in Need' book which was later auctioned by the charity UNESCO, and tried out one of the latest rides in the theme park - 'Colorado Adventure -

The Michael Jackson Thrill.'

June 25
After selling more than 554,000 tickets, Michael Jackson's 'History' tour breaks all previous German box office records for open-air concerts.

July 17

Michael Jackson and Wembley Stadium make history as ticket 'one million' is sold to a Michael Jackson concert. Michael, who also performed at the stadium with his 'Bad' and 'Dangerous' Tours, made this piece of history with the tour of the same name.

August 1

Tickets go on sale for the South African leg of the 'History' Tour. Over 40,000

tickets are sold within the first 90 minutes. This is the first time Michael will perform in South Africa.

August 8
Michael's short film *Ghosts* premieres at the 1997 Palm Springs International Film Festival.

August 29
Michael celebrates his 39th birthday by performing at the Parken Stadium, Copenhagen, Denmark. A three-tier cake is presented to him on stage. The 52,000 strong crowd, backing singers and dancers all sing 'Happy Birthday'. Shortly afterwards a gigantic firework display lit up the entire stadium, spelling out the words 'King of Pop'. "I can't believe it," he says. "It's incredible... this is a complete surprise!"

This Page and Opposite: Michael in action during the second leg of the 'History' World tour.

Above: Michael promotes the Esonic Video Discbaby.

1997

September 1

Michael Jackson cancels his scheduled concert in Ostend, Belgium due to the death of his friend Diana, Princess of Wales. His prepared statement reads: "The sudden loss of Diana, Princess of Wales, is one of the greatest tragedies of the millennium. She was a friend to the world. As one who has been under scrutiny the majority of my life, I speak with authority when I say that I am horrified that the paparazzi, supported by the tabloids' animalistic behaviour, may be acceptable to the public. It is totally unwarranted in a civilised society. The world's acceptance of the practise if continued will accelerate tragedies of this magnitude."

September 3

Michael dedicates his rescheduled concert in Ostend, Belgium to Princess Diana. Michael's song 'Smile' is played during the show while two large images of the Princess wearing a tiara were displayed either side of the stage.

September 13

Michael is interviewed by Barbara Walters in Paris, France. During this interview for ABC's *20/20*, Michael talks about Princess Diana, the paparazzi and the media, stating: "I'm not a Jacko, I'm Jackson!" Asked about what it was like to be a father Michael says: "I love it! When he's crying, to keep him from crying I have to do one thing. I have to stand in front of him and dance!" Michael laughs with delight as he explains that this quietens Prince and he admits that he does a lot of dancing! Asked what he would do if Prince wanted to follow in his footsteps, Michael says that he would point out all the pitfalls and adds if he still wanted to do it then: "Go, but do it better than I do!"

September 13

Michael is one of the 800 attending a memorial service for Princess Diana at St James' Episcopal Church in Los Angeles.

October 6

Nelson Mandela attends Michael Jackson's concert in Cape Town, South Africa. Prior to the show Mr Mandela is reported to have had "snacks with the star".

October 11

Michael is made an honorary member of the Bafokeng Ka Bakwena Tribe in Africa. Michael's ex-wife Lisa Marie Presley also attends the ceremony which takes place in Phokeng, Africa. Michael's parents, Katherine and Joseph Jackson also receive tribal certificates prior to the ceremony.

October 15

Michael performs his last concert on the 'History' Tour at the King's Park Rugby Stadium, Durban, South Africa

November 9

Michael Jackson, LaVelle Smith, Travis Payne and Barry Lather are awarded the 'Bob Fosse Award' for best choreography in 'Ghosts', at a gala dinner at The Palace in Hollywood. The 'Bob Fosse Awards' are only awarded to those in the music and film industry who are considered to be the top of their fields in choreographic excellence.

November 25

Debbie Rowe-Jackson is interviewed by Chuck Henry of KNBC TV Channel 4 at Neverland Valley Ranch. Michael is present with their son Prince during the interview, although he did not speak.

Debbie announces that she and Michael are expecting another baby, a girl to be named Paris Michael Katherine. "I wanted to name her after Michael, but Michael said 'no', so we decided Paris because that's where she was conceived. Michael because I really want Michael's name in her name and Katherine after his mum."

November 30

Adrian Grant holds his eighth MJ Day at the Cambridge Theatre in London. The event sells out its seated capacity of 1300, so an additional show is held in the evening which attracts another 500 fans.

December

A 36-track CD 'Diana Princess of Wales', including Michael's song 'Gone Too Soon', is released in honour of Princess Diana. All proceeds raised will be donated to 'The Princess Diana Memorial Fund'.

December 1

Michael's 'Ghosts' Deluxe Collector Box Set - Limited Edition is released by Sony Music. The Box Set comprises of *Ghosts* - The

Page Opposite: The death of Princess Diana is described by Michael as "one of the greatest tragedies of the millennium."

1997

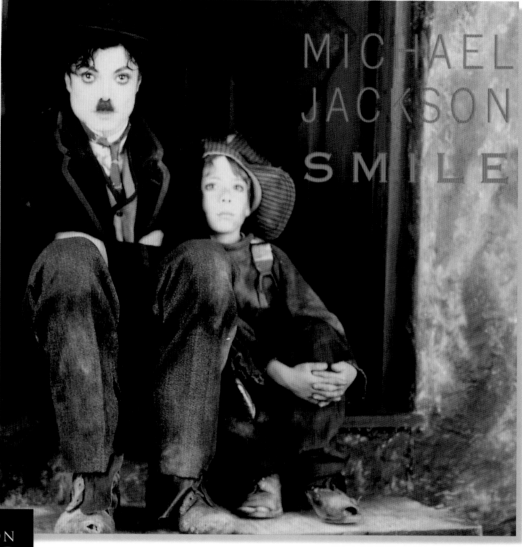

MICHAEL JACKSON SMILE

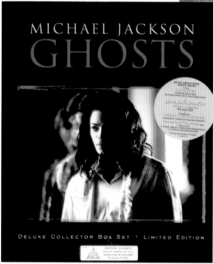

This Page: The front cover from the unreleased 'Smile' CD.

Above: The Limited Edition 'Ghosts' Box Set.

Page Opposite: Michael announces his plans for concerts to benefit the World Peace Foundation for Children.

Vincent McKoy chats to Michael and Adrian Grant about his work.

Home Video, 'Blood On The Dance Floor' - The Album, *Ghosts* - The Programme and 'Ghosts' - The Mini`max CD Single, which includes the previously unreleased track - 'On The Line' (taken from the Spike Lee movie of the same name.)

December 3
The release of 'Smile' the last single to be taken from the 'History' album is cancelled. Some CDs and 12" promos are issued with a picture on the front of Michael dressed as Charlie Chaplin.

December 17
Michael visits English boxer Prince Naseem at a New York City gym prior to his fight with Kevin Kelly at Madison Square Garden.

December 22
In a 'Most Cherished Celebrity' Poll put together by NBC TV in America, Princess Diana takes first place with Michael Jackson second.

December 23
The second leg of the 'History' World Tour becomes the 2nd Biggest Tour of 1997. Remembering this does not include the first leg, these 40 shows were seen by over two million people with a total gross income of $83,514,126.

1998
January 18
Michael Jackson wins his fourth consecutive copyright infringement case against Al Bano Carrisi, an Italian artist. Al Bano is ordered to pay all legal costs after the court refutes his claims that Michael copied and released parts of Al Bano's song 'I Cigne de Balaika' ('The Swans of Balaika'), in his song 'Will You Be There.'

February 9
Michael's short film *Ghosts* hits number 1 on the UK music video charts.

February 13

Adrian Grant holds an exclusive interview with Michael, for his forthcoming book, *Making History* During the interview, he presents Michael with a beautiful oil painting by Vincent McKoy.

February 20

During the second Annual World Animation Celebrations in California, Matt Groening known for his creation of the *The Simpsons*, confirms that not only did Michael write the song 'Do The Bartman' but also lent his voice to the character Michael Jackson on the episode entitled *Stark Raving Dad*. Michael was credited at the end of the episode under pseudonym John Jay Smith

March 26

During a visit to Munich, Germany, with his son Prince, Michael is serenaded outside his hotel by a group of Bavarian musicians. Hundreds of fans gather outside Michael's hotel - The Bayerischer Hof. Michael later holds up a sign from his bedroom window that simply reads - 'STOP FILTHY PRESS'.

April 3

Michael's wife Debbie Rowe gives birth to a healthy baby girl - Paris Michael Katherine Jackson.

Paris is born at 6.26 a.m. and weighs in at 7lb 7oz.

May 15

At a press conference at the Beverley Hills Hotel in LA, Michael announces his plans to stage concerts to benefit the World Peace Foundation for Children.

May 19

Michael and President Larent Kabila of the Democratic Republic of Congo have a 20-minute private meeting at the World Economic Forum Summit in Namibia, South Africa.

1998

"I am very excited to be organising and performing the first of what I hope to be a series of concert appearances, to benefit the World Peace Foundation for Children.

In 1985, I joined with many others in the music industry to create 'We Are the World', a song which led to the USA for Africa concert. That event brought millions of dollars in aid to hungry families and children throughout Africa, and the United States.

Following that experience it was my dream to create a world-wide series of concerts, which would raise funds to bring aid to suffering people around the globe. Today with the help of many friends we are taking the first step towards realising that dream.

I am delighted to be working with my good friends Luciano Pavarotti and Elizabeth Taylor, to perform the first of these concerts at Chamsil Stadium in Korea, a country I have grown to love very, very much.

We are also working on plans to have a special performance in the de-militarised zone, which separates North and South Korea.

Elizabeth Taylor has supported this endeavour since its inception and I'm very excited that she will join me at this very important event. It is my sincere hope that through my efforts and through the support of Cheil Communications and the Korea Peace Foundation for Children, we can bring an end to famine in this troubled part of the world.

In the years ahead it is my intention to create similar events which will bring together musicians from around the world to raise additional funds for the World Peace Foundation for Children.

Thank you very much."

**Michael Jackson
May 15, 1998**

1998

July 19

Michael is one of the 2,000 invited guests at Nelson Mandela's 80th birthday banquet and wedding.

July 26

The Jackson 5 are inducted into the KISS FM Classic Soul Legends Hall of Fame. KISS FM radio station is based in New York, USA.

July 27

Michael establishes a new Japanese company - Michael Jackson Japan Company. The company has been encouraged by the Japanese government to build two theme parks in Japan. Michael would also like to use the company to launch a new toy shop chain entitled - Wonder World - Land of Toys.

August 4

Michael Jackson and Stevie Wonder make an unannounced visit to the Motown Museum in Detroit, USA. Berry Gordy's sister, Ester Edwards, is on hand to show the superstars around.

August 16

Michael's *Captain Eo* has its last showing at Disneyland, Paris, France.

August 29

TV and Radio specials are today broadcast throughout the world in celebration of Michael Jackson's 40th Birthday.

At the tenth annual 'Michaelfest' in Denver, Colorado, a quilt designed and created by Deborah Danelly is auctioned in aid of Michael's Heal the World Foundation (USA). The quilt, which has been signed by Michael, contains 45 squares, each featuring a part of Michael's history.

September 18

In celebration of *Billboard* magazines 40th anniversary, a breakdown from their Hot 100 chart over the past 40 years is published. Michael is voted number one in the 'Most Hits By A Male Artist' catagory with 13 entries.

October 20

Motown Records release an album of Frank Sinatra songs covered by Motown artists. The album - 'Motown Celebrates Sinatra' includes a track from Michael Jackson singing 'All The Things You Are'.

November 9

London's *Daily Mirror* newspaper apologise to Michael Jackson for false statements published by them in 1992. In a statement they say: "Back in 1992 prior to Michael Jackson's then world tour we published some photos of Michael Jackson, particularly close-up photos of his nose and face. We suggested that they showed him to be hideously disfigured and scarred. He immediately issued legal proceedings against us strongly denying the allegations. During the course of the proceedings we recently went to Los Angles together with an eminent expert in plastic surgery to view his face close up. The inspection showed that, in fact, his face is not disfigured or scarred. We saw for ourselves this was not the case." Kevin Bays one of the *Mirror's* solicitors adds: "We are glad this matter has been resolved so amicably, it has gone on long enough and hopefully we can now put it behind us."

December 16

Michael attends the grand opening of Royal Towers of Atlantis resort in the Bahamas. He performs along with Stevie Wonder and other invited guests.

1999
January 13

The Japanese pop group J-Friends releases a single and album which features a song written, composed, produced and arranged by Michael Jackson entitled 'People of the World'.

January 16

CNN Internet Poll lists Michael's Thriller short film as being the Best Music Video Of All Time. In the same category at number 3 is 'Black Or White'.

January 26

Michael is taken to the Cedars Medical Centre in Miami, Florida for x-rays and treatment to a minor fracture to his wrist. Michael was on a flight returning from a visit to South Africa when he stopped at Miami for treatment on the way back to Los Angeles. Michael's Vice President of Communications, Mr Bob Jones said, "He's fine. He checked in and checked out. He was treated for a small fracture to his right wrist, and it won't hamper his activities."

February 5

A Denver federal judge awards Michael Jackson $200,000 in attorney's fees in a copyright infringement case brought by Crystal Cartier. The award comes five years after a Denver federal jury ruled that Michael did not steal the hit song 'Dangerous'. The federal judge found that the plaintiff's case was "implausible and objectively unreasonable."

February 7

Adrian Grant holds his ninth MJ Day at London's Astoria Theatre. LaVelle Smith, Michael's personal choreographer, attends the show and receives an accolade for his lifetime achievements and outstanding work on the short-film, *Ghosts*.

March 20

Michael appears on the German TV Show *Wetten Das* to announce his plans to stage two concerts in Korea and Germany to raise funds for The Nelson Mandela Children's Fund, the Red Cross and UNESCO.

April 6

In the 'CD First' poll for the Greatest Pop Artist of the Nineties, Michael Jackson takes a staggering 90% of the votes.

April 10

After attending an English league football match at Fulham's Craven Cottage, Michael Jackson makes a surprise visit to Liberty Radio in London, a station owned by Mohammed Al Fayed. Michael gave an impromptu interview and spoke of attending the football match earlier. "I've never been to one before. I thought it was really exciting. I thought it was great!" Asked what he thought of the game compared to American football he says: "I think this is tougher, because in our football we are all padded, we have all the protection and it looks tougher, but I think yours is really, really tough."

April 11

Michael spends over an hour speaking to his fans outside Mohammed Al Fayed's apartment on Park Lane in London. During this 'fans question time' Michael talks about the "immortalising work" that he wants to do in films and explains that he is now channelling his efforts more towards this type of project. Asked what his favourite piece of music is he says: "You won't laugh will you?" and states it is a classical piece by Claude Debussy entitled 'Afternoon Of The Faun'. Michael adds that 'Stranger In Moscow' and 'Earth Song' were his two current favourites out of all the hundreds of songs that he'd written.

May 1

Michael Jackson receives a 'Bollywood' Award from the Indian Film Industry for World Humanity. The award is presented at the Nassau Veterans Memorial Coliseum in New York.

1999

This Page: Michael sits next to Mohammed Al Fayed (left) at Craven Cottage, home of Fulham Football Club.

May 10
Michael attends a private screening of the special effects movie, *The Matrix*, at a Manhattan theatre in New York.

June 1
Jonathan Morrish of Sony Music issues a statement informing the media, that Michael will not be performing at today's 'Pavarotti & Friends' Concert in Modena, due to the illness of his son Prince. Mr. Morrish said, "Prince suffered a seizure early Saturday due to a high temperature. This is the third seizure over the last year." He added that the concert meant so much to Michael but, "he is an artist like the others, but also a parent."

June 10
The first Michael Jackson Dance Studio is opened today in Tokyo, Japan.

June 25
Michael performs at the first 'Michael Jackson And His Friends' concert at the Olympic Stadium in Seoul in Korea. This date is chosen to mark the 49th anniversary of the Korean War.

June 27
Michael performs at the second 'Michael Jackson And His Friends' concert in Munich, Germany. Due to a technical problem part of the set, the central section of 'The Bridge Of No Return' collapses, leaving Michael to climb back on to the stage. Michael continues to perform as planned and is taken to hospital for a check-up after the show.

July 1
Billboard reports that the 'Michael Jackson And His Friends' concerts have raised $3.3 million dollars for the following charities: UNESCO, Nelson Mandela Children's Fund and the International Federation of Red Cross and the Red Crescent Societies. Proceeds will also go to the victims of Kosovo.

July 5
Sony Music re-release the album 'Off the Wall' as a Limited Edition Digipac CD. The album is issued as a gatefold and includes colour pictures and booklet with lyrics.

July 30
MCY.com announce that they have made history by receiving over ten million hits in one day for their live broadcast of the 'Michael Jackson And His Friends' concert from Munich on June 27.

August 2
Michael Jackson is amongst the invited wedding guests at the wedding of Rory Kennedy (daughter of Senator Robert F. Kennedy). Michael also sends a message of sympathy on hearing the tragic news of the plane crash in which John F. Kennedy, his wife, and her sister, were killed in the plane that was to take them to the wedding ceremony.

August 16
Michael is awarded with the 'New Millennium Visionary Award' during 'An Intimate Evening with Whitney Houston' held by the American Cinema Awards Foundation.

September 4
Michael receives a Lifetime Achievement Award from ex-president Nelson Mandela at the Kora All African Music Awards held at Sun City in South Africa. During the show Michael hands over a cheque for one million South African rand to Nelson Mandela for the 'Nelson Mandela Children's Fund'. They money was raised at the 'Michael Jackson And His Friends' concerts.

September 9
Elizabeth Taylor and Michael Jackson speak of their close friendship in *Talk* magazine. Elizabeth describes Michael as "magic, loving, sweet, true" and adds that their friendship has lasted longer than any of her marriages. "He is part of my heart. We would do anything for each other." Speaking of Elizabeth, Michael states: "She's a warm cuddly blanket that I love to snuggle up to and cover myself with. I can confide in her and trust her. She's Mother Teresa, Princess Diana, the Queen of England and Wendy."

Page Opposite: Michael in action during the 'Michael Jackson And His Friends' concert in Munich.

This Page: The stage for 'Michael Jackson And His Friends' is adorned by two massive banners, promoting 'What More Can I Give'. It was thought to be the anthem for the show but Michael never performed the song.

1999

October 8

Michael and his wife Debbie Rowe agree to end their marriage. The couple's spokesman Howard Rubenstein said: "Michael and Debbie remain friends and they ask that the public respect their desire not to further comment or speculate upon the reasons for their decision."

October 18

'Thriller' is re-released as a Limited Millennium Edition CD by Sony Music. The gatefold album which has the CD in it's own separate sleeve, also includes a fold out lyric sheet.

October 27

MJJ Communications issue a press release stating that videos have been stolen from Michael's hotel suite at Disneyland Paris. The videos, all of which were personal to Michael, contain footage of him and his family at Michael's ranch, Neverland Valley, over the Christmas and New Year holiday period. Shortly after the theft an anonymous phone call was made demanding $100,000.

The press release added that "Jackson is the sole and exclusive owner of the copyright in and to the stolen videos and any photographs made therefrom."

November 11

Sony Music Media release 'Pop Songs' a limited edition promotional CD for McDonalds in Germany (Cat No: SMM 986129 2). This double CD contains 24 tracks which includes The Jacksons' hit 'Blame it on the Boogie'. With the CD booklet comes an advertisement for Michael Jackson's forthcoming album. Written in German the advertisement reads:

'Finally: The new Michael Jackson album.

Four years after his sensational album 'HIStory' a new studio album by Michael Jackson will be released. Already, you can be sure that the King of Pop *will deliver a firework of emotional ballads and great pop songs. COMING SOON'*

November 12

The Hollywood Reporter reports that Michael plans to star as the lead actor in a film based on Edgar Allan Poe's life story - *The Nightmare of Edgar Allan Poe.*

November 15

In the 2000 Edition of the *Guinness Book Of World Records* Michael Jackson is listed as having supported more charitable organisations - 39 - than any other individual, including monetary donations through sponsorships or other participation. The charities involved include AIDS Project LA, American Cancer Society, BMI Foundation Inc., Childhelp USA, United Negro College Fund (UNCF), YMCA - 28th Street Crenshaw, The Sickle Cell Research Foundations and Volunteers of America.

November 16

A 4 CD Box Set entitled - 'The Ultimate Grammy Box' is released in the United States. The compilation covers the 40 year history of the Grammy's. Michael's 'Beat It' is one of 73 songs included.

November 29

MTV in conjunction with *TV Guide* (US) vote *Thriller* the Greatest Video Ever. MTV have shown 19,000 videos over the past 18 years and *Thriller* is chosen because it was the most "innovative and ambitious for its time". Michael also appears on the cover of this special issue of *TV Guide* with a new look which includes designer stubble.

December 4

Michael attends Whitney Houston's Fund Raising Event at the Marriott Marquis hotel in New York.

December 11

During MTV USA's '100 Greatest Videos Ever Made' Michael's 'Thriller' video was voted - The Greatest Video Of All Time. An exclusive interview with Michael is also aired during the show, in which he speaks about some of his videos.

December 31

In Times Square, New York, a special 'Millennium Mix' is played to the thousands of people who gather to celebrate the dawn of the new millennium. The 'Millennium Mix' is a compilation of ten songs which were selected by internet poll. Included in the top ten tracks chosen is Michael's eighties classic 'Beat it.'

2000
January 8

Michael Jackson is among the stars who contribute performances to 'An Evening of Stars: A Celebration of Educational Excellence'. Michael's performance of 'Earth Song' from Seoul, Korea, was used as part of this annual fundraiser for United Negro College Foundation. The four-hour telethon was broadcast live in the US on over 70 television stations.

January 20

VH1 Viewers vote 'Billie Jean' as their number 1 song of the Eighties.

March 11

In the latest edition of *The Oxford Dictionary of 20th Century Quotations* Michael is listed with the following entry, "Before you judge me, try hard to love me, look within your heart then ask - have you seen my childhood?" taken from the lyrics of 'Childhood.'

May 8

Michael visits the Circus Knie in Germany with Prince and Paris. Circus owner Freddie Knie at first thought the visit was a hoax, but soon realised how wrong he was when the real Michael Jackson turned up with his bodyguards and children.

May 10

Michael receives the 'Millennium Artist Award' from Prince Albert at the 2000 World Music Awards in Monaco.

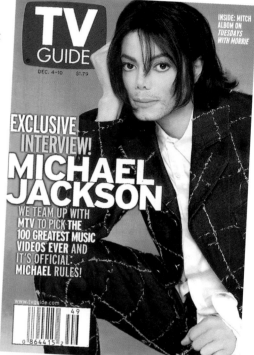

2000

2000

May 22
In the latest issue of *Ebony* magazine Michael's *Thriller* short film is listed as one of the 25 most important events in black music history. *Thriller* is chosen because it not only changed the way videos are made, but also the way that they are marketed.

May 26
Michael Jackson escorts Dame Elizabeth Taylor to 'A Musical Celebration - A Tribute to Elizabeth Taylor' at the Royal Albert Hall in London. Michael, dressed in a long black tailored coat, does not perform, though he presents Dame Elizabeth with a large bouquet of flowers at the end of the show.

May 30
Michael's 'Dangerous' album is certified Multi-Platinum. Billboard Online report "the 'Dangerous' album has just been certified 7 times Platinum by the Recording Industry Association of America (RIAA)."

Michael becomes a key investor and partner of HollywoodTicket.com Inc.

HollywoodTicket.com is an interactive promotional and marketing entertainment web site, which covers movies, television, music, Internet, sports, merchandise and books.

Michael will play a major role in securing the participation of important people from show business. Michael said of the venture, "Through Holly-

This Page: Michael escorts Elizabeth Taylor to 'A Musical Celebration - A Tribute to Elizabeth Taylor' at the Royal Albert Hall.

woodTicket.com talent professionals have a business and artistic opportunity to get involved on a much more active level, in the creation and distribution of innovative entertainment for our fans. The Internet allows us to bring fans together with top talent in creative new forms of entertainment that provide fun, adventure and meaningful interactive experiences for everyone."

July 18
Africanwatch magazine publishes the results of a poll in which the top ten African musicians of the 20th century were chosen.

The selection of the ten musicians, all of whom had to be be of African ancestry, included Michael Jackson, Stevie Wonder, James Brown and Aretha Franklin.

July 24
Music channel VH1 and *Entertainment Weekly* Magazine team up to create a list of 'Rock and Roll's Top 100 TV Moments.'

Michael appears on the list five times including his first 'Moonwalk' on stage during *Motown 25* and the first screening of the 'Thriller' video on MTV.

July 29
Motown Records and Universal MCA Music release a Jackson 5 compilation CD in the UK. The CD entitled 'Ripples and Waves - An Introduction To The Jackson Five' contains 17 tracks, but what sets this apart from other recent releases is that this compilation includes two songs never before released on CD

which have been taken from the 'Joyful Jukebox' album. The two songs are listed as 'Pride And Joy' and 'The Eternal Light.'

July 31
Geraldine Hughes, the former legal secretary representing the child who accused Michael of child molestation, announces she can prove Michael's innocence in a new book soon to be released entitled - 'The Set Up - The Truth Behind the Child Molestation Allegations'. Hughes stated: "So much about the case never came to the public's attention. I was there, and I know!"

August 9
The Daily Variety reported today that Michael Jackson has invested in WebEl, an Internet company which will be an online production studio, intended to aid not only established filmmakers and studios but also those looking to get started in the industry.

August 18
Yaboom Ltd. release a new Michael Jackson MCD and singing locker poster aimed at the 'back-to-school' market in the US. The new MCD's (Mini CD's) are available on collectable key chains that play high quality music. The locker poster not only features a picture of Michael but at the touch of a button also plays one of Michael's greatest hits.

September 6
British Newspaper *The Times* reports that Michael may deliver his first public speech on child welfare, at Oxford University in February 2001.

Rabbi Shmuley Boteach, whom Michael met through Israeli magician Uri Geller is said to be jointly addressing the Oxford Union Debating Society with Michael. Rabbi Boteach insists that Michael is widely misunderstood and, in fact, dedicates his time to helping and caring for sick and underprivileged children. He added: "I have never witnessed anything like Michael's work with children. The time he gives to children and his commitment to them is incredibly inspiring."

September 7
The Hard Rock Café in Orlando, Florida displays the latest items in their collection - A 'Thriller' Jacket, two photographs from the 'Thriller' era and Michael Jackson 'Beat It' doll created by LJN Toys in 1984.

September 21
Michael Jackson is asked to use his talent as a creative artist, to design and underwrite an 'African' Theme Park near the city of Manzini in Swaziland. Mathwes Phosa, the former Mpumalanga Premier added: "It would be great if Michael Jackson agrees to design or underwrite the proposed Millennium Park theme resort. My company is currently engaged in talks with the leading people on this issue."

October 18
It was announced that Michael Jackson has been the 'Most Requested Artist of the Year' - October 10th 1999 - October 10th 2000 in Voice Of America's (VOA) Border Crossings show, with the most requested songs being 'Heal the World' and 'You Are Not Alone'.

October 28
The US TV Programme 'Entertainment Tonight' announces that over it's 16 seasons, Michael Jackson is the person that they have most reported on, during their exclusive interviews, movie premieres, award ceremonies and Hollywood Walk of Fame accolades.

Michael makes a guest appearance at the 'Carousel of Hope Ball' in Beverley Hills, California. Michael, received a warm reception as he accompanied Dame Elizabeth Taylor to the world's premier charity event, benefiting childhood diabetes research. Michael took to the stage at the end of the evening congratulating Ricky Martin on his live performance, and was also one of the 50 celebrities who had painted a plate previously to be auctioned for the charity.

This Page: Michael on stage at the conclusion of the 'Carousel of Hope Ball'.

2000

This Page: Michael makes a speech after receiving an award from the G&P Foundation for his work in helping to fight cancer.

October 30
Michael's 'Thriller' album is certified Multi-Platinum for sales in excess of 26 million.

'Blood On The Dance Floor: History In The Mix' is certified Platinum for sales of one million copies in the USA.

November 9
In a recent interview on boy-band Westlife's web site Mae Filan, mother of Shane said; "He (Shane) was singing before he could talk and would happily gurgle a tune in his pram. At 5 he could sing Billy Joel's song 'Uptown Girl', but it is his Michael Jackson impersonations that we remember vividly! At home he would wear the full outfit with the sunglasses, hat. He adored Michael and not only dressed like him, but danced and sang like him too."

November 17
MTV and *Rolling Stone* have teamed up to compile a list of the 100 Greatest Pop Songs ever. Michael appears on the list four times: 'Billie Jean' – 5, 'I Want You Back' – 9, 'Beat It' – 22 and 'Rock With You' - 82.

November 23
In a private news conference held for approximately 30 people, Michael talked about his new album: "My new album should be out in March (2002)," he said, crossing his fingers. "I played six songs for Sony Music today and they were walking on air. They applauded. They really loved them. Now I just have to come up with five more."

Michael also said that the album is still untitled and that the songs are written and produced by him with Teddy Riley, R. Kelly and Rodney Jerkins. He ended by saying (whilst laughing): "But you know I'm in charge!"

November 30
Michael is in New York to receive an award for his work helping the fight against cancer from the G&P Foundation founded by songwriter and philanthropist Denise Rich.

As Michael recieved his award he said, "I'm extremely honoured and moved by this gracious award, and first and foremost, I'd like to thank our hostess and my date tonight, Denise (Rich), who, with her beautiful spirit and abundant kindness, has quickly found a special place in my heart."

Michael also thanked President Bill Clinton who was present, "I'm honoured Mr. President to receive this award in your presence, and I want to thank you, for the years of dedication and service that you've rendered to the American people, you've been an incredible president and I love you.

"Cancer is the number one killer of children and it is only when we join together on evenings like this, that we can summon the courage and determination to stop it from ever robbing another child of the precious gift of life, or a parent of the joy of watching their child grow."

December 2
Michael is one of 1,200 guests who attend the wedding of Mexican singer and actress Thalia (Ariadna Thalia Sodi Miranda) and Tommy Mottola, president of Sony Music.

Other celebrities present at the ceremony that took place at St Patrick's Cathedral in New York, include Jennifer Lopez, Ricky Martin, Gloria Estefan and Robert de Niro.

December 10
Ebony magazine celebrates its 55th Anniversary this month and Michael is included in their list of the '55 Most Beautiful People' of 2000.

December 12
Following the announcement that Michael will be inducted into the Rock and Roll Hall of Fame as a solo performer, Michael said: "I am thrilled and humbled to receive this great honour. I could not ask to be in better company than the list of fellow inductees. Each and every one is a master from whom I have learned. My sincere thanks to the rock and roll historians and experts who have chosen me."

December 19
Michael appears on stage at the 'Miracle On 34th Street' charity concert organised by radio station KTU 103.5 FM at Madison Square Gardens in New York. He joined other artists, including Ricky Martin, Christina Aguilera, Toni Braxton, and Destiny's Child, for the finale but did not perform.

2001
February 5
The Smithsonian Institution National Portrait Gallery will be showing painted images of 75 Americans who they feel shaped our culture. Paintings of Benjamin Franklin, Mark Twain and Davy Crockett are amongst the collection, along with a painting of Michael by Andy Warhol.

February 14
Hundreds of fans gather inside Carnegie Hall in New York to welcome Michael to a pre-launch event for his new charity 'Heal The Kids'. The charities main initiative is to help restore a child's birthright to nurturing care.

March 4
Michael arrives in London, England on crutches after injuring his foot. "It's painful," he told reporters at Heathrow Airport. "I've broken two bones in my foot and it hurts!"

March 5

Michael goes shopping in one of London's HMV stores along with his friend, actor Macaulay Culkin. An HMV spokesman described Michael as being "incredibly approachable" as he chatted to staff and signed autographs.

Michael attends the launch party for a book written by Rabbi Shmuley Boteach and Uri Geller entitled *Confessions Of A Rabbi And A Psychic* at the Royal Institute of British Architects in London.

March 7

Michael is best man today at a traditional Jewish wedding for Uri Geller and his wife Hanna as they renew their wedding vows at Uri Geller's home, in Sonning, Berkshire. Other guests include political interviewer Sir David Frost, Barry Gibb and Nigel Mansell. When asked why he'd chosen Michael as his best man Uri Geller replied: "I chose Michael because he is a good friend and I wanted him to experience a Jewish wedding."

March 6

With over 20,000 people requesting tickets to attend the launch of Michael's 'Heal The Kids' charity at the Oxford Union, the few hundred who managed to gain entry to the 178-year-old debating society were thrilled as they listened to Michael speak for over 35 minutes as he called for a Children's Universal Bill of Rights.

Specifically, Michael's bill included:
• The right to be loved, without having to earn it
• The right to be protected, without having to deserve it
• The right to feel valuable, even if you came into the world with nothing
• The right to be listened to without having to be interesting
• The right to be read a bedtime story without having to compete with the evening news or *EastEnders*
• The right to an education without having to dodge bullets at schools
• The right to be thought of as adorable (even if you have a face that only a mother could love).

And in concluding he stated: "From this day forward, may a new song be heard. Let that new song be the sound of children laughing. Let that new song be the sound of children playing. Let that new song be the sound of children singing. And let that new song be the sound of parents listening

"Together, let us create a symphony of hearts, marvelling at the miracle of our children and basking in the beauty of love. Let us heal the world and blight its pain. And may we all make beautiful music together. God bless you, and I love you."

Later in the day, over 3,000 very excited and extremely vocal Michael Jackson fans gather in London for the 10th Annual Michael Jackson Day, held at the Hammersmith Apollo Theatre. It is the first time that Michael has ever appeared live at an MJ Day. At the end of the show, Michael (on crutches) takes centre stage, receiving thunderous applause, and a five-minute standing ovation. He tells fans that his new album will be out in two months, before graciously accepting an award presented to him by the show's producer, Adrian Grant, on behalf of Michael's fans the world over. Michael describes the show (which included over 100 performers and was directed by Kerys Nathan) and Adrian Grant as, "Incredible!"

March 9

Michael gives GMTV exclusive permission to broadcast his speech from MJ Day 10 for their breakfast show. Adrian Grant appears on the programme, and talks about his work with Michael.

March 11

The Recording Industry Association of America (RIAA) and The National Endowment for the Arts (NEA) announce 365 recordings that make up their 'Songs of the Century'. Michael is featured three times with his songs divided by era: The Rock Era (1970-1980): 'I Want You Back', The Eighties (1980-1990): 'Beat It' and 'We Are the World' (co-written by Michael Jackson with Lionel Richie).

March 15

German TV show *Wetten, dass* is celebrating its 20th Anniversary this year. Several celebrities, including Michael have sent messages to congratulate the popular programme which airs on the channel ZDF.

2001

This Page: (inset) Michael gives the peace sign to fans after his speech at the Oxford Union. (Top): Michael leaving the Lanesborough Hotel in London. (Below): Michael tells fans his album will be two more months in production, after attending his first ever fan party - MJ Day 10.

2001

March 15

A Rome Appeals Court overturns a lower court's decision, clearing Michael of plagiarism allegations.

In May of 1999 a court in Rome found Michael guilty of plagiarism in his song *Will You Be There* but now the court suspends their decision. Al Bano had filed the lawsuit against Michael for plagiarism, alleging that *Will You Be There* was partly taken from Bano's *I Cigni di Balaka.*

March 16

A tribute to Janet Jackson aired on MTV tonight features a pre-recorded message from her brother Michael: "Janet, I am so thrilled that you are being honored tonight. No one deserves this more than you. You have achieved so much and you will only keep climbing higher and higher. Your talent knows no boundaries. I am honored and proud to be your brother. I love you."

Above: Michael poses with members of N'Sync, after being inducted into the Rock and Roll Hall of Fame.

March 19

Michael arrives at the Waldorf Astoria in New York, to be inducted into the Rock and Roll Hall of Fame.

Lance Bass of N'Sync, who had the honor of inducting Michael into the Hall of Fame, says: "Michael was always a man who inspired more questions than answers. Michael became the youngest inductee in the history of the Hall of Fame. In 1997, he also became the youngest artist to be inducted as part of a music group, namely the Jackson 5."

March 21

After meeting with President Bush and U.S. Secretary of State Colin Powell, Israeli Prime Minister Ariel Sharon ends his United States trip by meeting Michael. They discuss the possibility of Michael traveling to Israel this summer at a reception for Sharon at the home of Israel businessman Benny Shabtai.

March 25

Today Michael was hard at work promoting literacy by handing out books to young people at a Newark, NJ, theatre. The event, which helped to launch the Michael Jackson International Book Club, part of his new 'Heal the Kids' charity, aims to promote childhood reading and encourage parents to return to reading bedtime stories.

March 26

During an interview with *Planet Jackson* Janet Jackson spoke of her main influence as a dancer: "Michael is definitely my biggest influence. I don't think I dance like him though, and if I do to some extent, I can only say that we are brother and sister so the same blood does flow through us, plus we were so close growing up, and we did dance together growing up. But he's an amazing dancer and I don't think I dance anywhere near his ability."

April 20

The BBC reports that Michael will travel to the east African country of Sudan to campaign for an end to child slavery.

Michael will use his new charity 'Heal the Kids' to try and help these victims.

Interviewed by the *New York Post* about this project, Michael said: "I want this slavery to end, now and forever. I mean this from the bottom of my heart. The existence of child slavery shakes me to my very core. Children need a childhood. They need to play and run and have fun. They can't be forced to work. Childhood is the greatest gift of life that must be preserved. I think this is something that we can't turn a blind eye to."

May 1

VH1 (USA) announces their list of 'The 100 Greatest Videos of All Time', which have been selected by a panel of experts from VH1. Michael was included on the list five times, only to be beaten by Madonna with six entries. Nevertheless 'Thriller' came out top as 'The Greatest Video of All Time', beating Madonna's 'Like A Prayer' which came second.

Michael's listings were: 1 – 'Thriller'; 9 – 'Scream'; 21 – 'Beat It'; 34 - 'Billie Jean'; 38 - 'Black Or White'.

May 9

Michael denies worldwide press reports claiming he wants to sell the Beatles song catalogue: "I want to clarify a silly rumour. The Beatles catalogue is not for sale, has not been for sale and will never be for sale."

May 15

A life-sized porcelain sculpture of Michael on a bed of roses holding Bubbles was auctioned in New York today for $5,615,750 (US). The sculpture, made by artist Jeff Koons in 1988, went under the hammer at Sotheby's Spring Contemporary Art Auction.

May 20

The current issue of the American magazine *Teen Vogue* features an interview with the all girl group Destiny's Child in which they all praise Michael Jackson as their idol.

Michelle said, "We had the pleasure of meeting Michael Jackson at a Christmas concert, and he came onstage for the finale. I was very nervous because he's the biggest male artist in history and you have to be careful not to do or say something stupid!"

May 22

Released to radio today is a brand new version of 'Smooth Criminal' by US rock band Alien Ant Farm.

Frontman for the group Dryden Mitchell said: "We're all big fans of Michael Jackson. We were messing with it in the garage one day, and the riff screamed out to be heavy."

June 4

Ready 2 Rumble Boxing: Round 2 is released for the Game Boy Advance.

The game features 11 characters, including two hidden celebrity boxers: NBA star Shaquille O'Neal and Michael Jackson.

June 19

MJ Net Entertainment AG, a company based in Frankfurt, Germany is launched. It has a twenty-year exclusive worldwide right to license the use of Michael Jackson's name, character, image and the 'thematic' from his songs.

The company announces that the first in a line of Michael Jackson products to be released will be MJ5, a unique state-of-the-art three-piece flat-panel multimedia speaker system. The front panel of the speakers has high-quality photographs of Michael performing 'Billie Jean' live.

June 28

Michael makes a surprise appearance at the 'Summer Jam 2001' in Long Island, USA. Festival headliner Jay-Z brings Michael onstage during a break in his performance, to the delight of the sold-out audience, and although Michael doesn't perform, his presence is enough to elicit the loudest welcome of the evening from a crowd that had seen performances by Eve, Nelly, R. Kelly, Outkast and Destiny's Child.

July 6

The famous African-American music magazine *Right On!* is celebrating its 30th anniversary in its August issue. Michael is amongst the many celebrities congratulating the editor Cynthia Horner.

Michael said: "Congratulations, *Right On!* on turning 30. It seems like only yesterday we were both infants getting started. Love always, M.J."

Right On! magazine was launched in 1971 and since that time the Jackson family have featured many times, so to mark this special occasion they include an old action pin-up poster of the Jackson 5 and four reprinted articles: 'The Monarchs of Pop 'n Rock' (Michael Jackson and Prince), 'What's Next for the J-5… Hollywood?', 'Jackson Tattle-tales!' and 'Six Secrets about Michael Jackson'.

August 7

Motown Records re-release the following Jackson 5 albums on CD: 'Diana Ross Presents the Jackson 5' (the first time this has been released by itself onto CD), plus the following double albums on single CDs; 'Third Album'/'Maybe Tomorrow', 'Skywriter'/'Get It Together', 'Looking Through The Windows'/'Goin' Back To Indiana', and 'Dancing Machine/Moving Violation'.

August 17

In a recent interview with the *Daily Record*, pop star Britney Spears said of Michael: "I love him because he's not only a singer, but he's a performer as well. He is a genius. When he gets up on stage, he just takes over. I've always really looked up to him."

August 18

New York radio station KTU premieres Michael's brand new song 'You Rock My World' taken from Michael's forthcoming album 'Invincible'.

August 24

Today at 7.45 am Michael's new single 'You Rock My World' is delivered to radio station Capital FM in London for its UK premier.

August 29

Michael celebrates his 43rd Birthday.

August 30

This morning at 9.30am at the MarketSite Tower in New York, Michael rang the famous NASDAQ bell to signify the start of trading in New York.

The NASDAQ is the world's first electronic stock market and is the fastest growing major stock market in the world.

NASDAQ officials present Michael with a glass trophy, a 1934 Shirley Temple poster and a vanilla birthday cake lined with strawberries.

In a statement a NASDAQ executive said that they had invited Michael because of his "extraordinary vision and commitment to excellence in the entertainment industry".

September 6

At the MTV Video Music Awards in New York, Michael joins N'Sync towards the end of their single *Pop* performance. The surprised audience gives him a standing ovation.

This Page: Michael at the Market-Site Tower in New York with a NASDAQ official.

2001

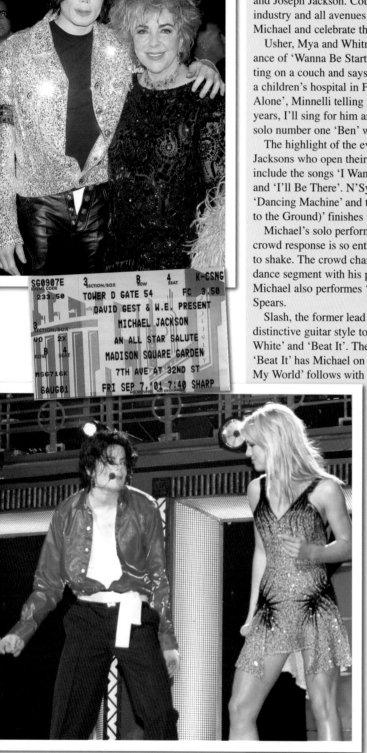

September 7

As Michael approaches Madison Square Garden for his sold out tribute show with Elizabeth Taylor by his side, a reporter asks him about the evenings entertainment. Michael replies: "It's a reunion! I'm honoured! I'm honoured that the world appreciates my art! I'm very honoured."

Wearing a loose, white, sequinned jacket and black leather trousers, Michael begins the evening seated on the front row along with Elizabeth Taylor, Macauley Culkin and his parents Katherine and Joseph Jackson. Countless celebrities from the entertainment industry and all avenues of entertainment have turned out to honour Michael and celebrate the 30th anniversary of his solo career.

Usher, Mya and Whitney Houston begin the show with a performance of 'Wanna Be Startin' Somethin'. Marlon Brando appears, sitting on a couch and says that Michael was donating money to build a children's hospital in Florida. Liza Minnelli sings 'You Are Not Alone', Minnelli telling the audience: "He's sang for me for so many years, I'll sing for him anytime!" Billy Gilman sings Michael's first solo number one 'Ben' which is well received by the audience.

The highlight of the evening for many fans is the reunion of the Jacksons who open their segment with 'Can You Feel It' and also include the songs 'I Want You Back', 'ABC', 'The Love You Save' and 'I'll Be There'. N'Sync join the Jackson brothers on stage during 'Dancing Machine' and the Jacksons' hit 'Shake Your Body (Down to the Ground)' finishes the brothers' reunion for the evening.

Michael's solo performances includes 'Billie Jean' to which the crowd response is so enthusiastic that his video screen image begins to shake. The crowd chant along spontaneously during his extended dance segment with his patented moonwalk and robotic moves. Michael also performes 'The Way You Make Me Feel' with Britney Spears.

Slash, the former lead guitarist of Guns N' Roses, brings his distinctive guitar style to rock-influenced Michael songs 'Black Or White' and 'Beat It'. The extended Slash guitar solo at the end of 'Beat It' has Michael on his knees and flat on his back. 'You Rock My World' follows with Michael singing on stage with a 48-piece orchestra behind him. Other performers during the evening are Ray Charles, Gladys Knight, Destiny's Child, Yoko Ono, Marc Anthony, Jill Scott, Alicia Keys, Shaquille O'Neal, Chris Tucker and Samuel Jackson.

The concert ends with an all-star 'We Are The World' finale at 12.25 am.

The official programme for Michael's tribute concerts, a 94 page A4 in size and costing $25.00, is a must have for all MJ Collectors.

Inside the programme begins with the event's Producer, David Gest, reminiscing of his childhood, growing up with Michael and his brothers, concluding with their rise to stardom. It includes photos of all the star-guest performers, including Michael and a congratulations message to Michael from many in the entertainment business, including The Hit Factory, Artista Records, Gloria Estefan, Stevie Wonder and Gloria Gaynor. Also included are messages from American Airlines, Epic Records and Amazon.com.

This Page & Opposite: Images from Michael Jackson's amazing 30th Anniversary Concert.

September 10

Michael performs at Madison Square Gardens for the second sell-out tribute show.

After the concert MJWN spoke with Rodney Jerkins who said: "I haven't been to Michael's concerts before. I ain't seen nothing like it! He should change his title from King of Pop to King of Music!"

September 11

Thousands of Michael Jackson fans are left stranded in New York as the terrible events of 9/11 unfold.

September 16

Michael calls on those he knows in the entertainment business to come together to record a song that will hopefully raise $50 million for the survivors and the families of victims of 9/11. The song, 'What More Can I Give', will be produced by Michael and all proceeds will go to a relief fund for the victims' families and survivors.

Michael says: "I believe in my heart that the music community will come together as one and rally to the aid of thousands of innocent victims. There is a tremendous need for relief dollars right now and through this effort each one of us can play an immediate role in helping comfort so many people. We have demonstrated time and again that music can touch our souls. It is time we used that power to help us begin the process of healing immediately."

On this week's US *Billboard* music video charts, Michael's *History On Film: Volume II* has turned platinum and placed at number 7 after 105 weeks on the chart.

2001

"Join hands and reach to the heavens... Don't do it because I'm asking you to, do it because it's the right thing to do. Now I ask you for a moment of love and silence...

"And tonight we all stand united and ask 'What More Can I Give?' and when we leave here tonight let us take this love and give it to all the people everywhere in every corner of the Earth... To the families of the victims of September 11 that are here with us tonight, 'You Are Not Alone'. You are in our hearts, you are in our thoughts and you are in our prayers!"

Michael Jackson, October 21, 2001

September 21

The new video for 'You Rock My World' premiers across Europe.

The short film, directed by Paul Hunter, features Michael and Chris Tucker pursuing a girl who happens to be dating a mobster. The Don of all fictional mob bosses, Marlon Brando, appears in the video, as does Michael Madsen of *Reservoir Dogs*.

September 30

Concert gross figures reported for the week ending September 25th show Michael's Tribute Concerts at Madison Square Gardens in top place with grossing sales of $10,072,105. The Backstreet Boys were in second and third place.

October 1

In the current issue of *TV Hits* magazine, pop star Usher, talks about how much he has been influenced by Michael.

October 5

'You Rock My World' is released in UK record stores.

October 7

In a recent interview with *Smash Hits* magazine, Justin Timberlake spoke of his memorable moments of meeting Michael.

Timberlake says: "We've met a few times but he was one of my childhood heroes... Performing with him at his tribute concert was an awesome experience that I won't ever forget."

October 12

Tickets go on sale for Michael's all-star music festival in Washington D.C. on October 21, 2001 at the RFK Stadium. The concert, which is being called 'United We Stand - What More Can I Give', will benefit the American Red Cross Liberty Relief Fund, the Salvation Army Relief Fund and the Pentagon Relief Fund which will help with the recovery efforts in Washington and New York City.

All 54,000 tickets priced between $25 and $75 are sold out within an hour.

October 14

'You Rock My World' enters the UK charts at number 2.

October 15

Epic Records release the re-mastered CDs of 'Off The Wall', 'Thriller', 'Bad' and 'Dangerous'. All of the CDs feature previously unreleased bonus songs.

The Seattle Mariners, an American League baseball team, have played the entire Michael Jackson 'Off The Wall' album in their clubhouse locker room following any game they've won.

After their win against the Cleveland Indians today someone asks why Michael's music is missing. DJ Mike Cameron stops his interview, runs across the room and puts on the 'Off The Wall' CD. "You got to have Michael," he explains.

Producer Quincy Jones is guest on the *The Oprah Show*. During the show Michael calls in to pay tribute to him. Oprah asked Michael what he had learned from Quincy, "I learned a lot. He once said, 'You don't write the music. You let the music write itself. Let it create itself. It's like we're just the source through which it comes'."

October 16

'You Rock My World' reaches number 1 on the R&B charts.

October 17

Sony hold a playback session today of Michael's forthcoming album 'Invincible' at their offices in London, which the media and fan clubs attend.

October 19

Director Barry Sonnenfeld tells MTV that he has recently recruited Michael for his upcoming science fiction film *Men In Black 2*, which stars Will Smith and Tommy Lee Jones. Michael will have a small part as an agent called 'Agent M'.

October 20

In France 'You Rock My World' enters the national singles charts at number 1, a feat that only four other artists have ever achieved.

October 21

More than 25 artists gather at Washington DC's RFK Stadium for Michael's eight-hour marathon 'United We Stand – What More Can I Give' show. The Backstreet Boys who lost a crew member in the September 11 attacks began the evening's entertainment with a rendition of 'The Star-Spangled Banner'. "We can't let them defeat us," band member Kevin Richardson tells the sold-out audience of 54,000 people. "We have to get up, get out and live our lives every day."

Much later in the evening Michael's takes to the stage with a performance that begins with 'We Are The World' followed by 'Man In The Mirror' during which he is lifted high above the crowd on a hydraulic lift.

For the finale Michael welcomed back all of the assembled performers including Usher, Rod Stewart, Al Green, Backstreet Boys, N'Sync, Mariah Carey, Carole King, James Brown, P. Diddy, MC Hammer, Pink, Bette Midler and Michael, as they sang 'What More Can I Give'.

October 22

Michael, Britney Spears, N'Sync, Celine Dion and Mariah Carey participate in an all-star, Spanish recording of 'What More Can I Give'.

The Spanish title for the song is: 'Todo Para Ti', and it will also include vocals by Destiny's Child, Gloria Estefan, Ricky Martin, Boyz II Men, Jon Secada, Julio Iglesias, Ruben Blades, Brian McKnight, Nick Carter of The Backstreet Boys, Luis Miguel, Shakira and Luther Vandross.

October 27

Today Michael participates in an online/audio chat hosted by Yahoo and Get Music. During the chat Michael answers questions from his worldwide fans and openly talks about his plans for the future and his new album.

October 27

Michael and his fellow artists have raised over 3 million dollars from the Washington concert 'United We Stand: What More Can I Give'. The money wll be donated to charities helping the victims of 9/11.

October 29

Today Michael's latest album 'Invincible' is released. It comes in a choice of four different colours; red, blue, green and gold.

November 1

Tonight USA television network ABC air a two-hour special of footage taped from Michael's benefit concert 'United We Stand - What More Can I Give' that took place on October 21.

November 2

The video for Michael's new single 'Cry' is airs in the UK on BBC's *Top Of The Pops*.

Nick Brandt who has previously worked on three other Michael Jackson short films, 'Earth Song', 'Childhood' and 'Stranger in Moscow', directs the 'Cry' short-film.

November 2

Within five days (four within the USA) Michael's new album 'Invincible' has already sold three million copies worldwide. In France, Switzerland, Norway, Italy and Spain, the album has even broken Michael's previous records and has become his fastest-selling album ever.

November 4

'Invincible' tops the album charts in the UK, making it Michael's seventh consecutive number one album in the UK. Every solo album released in the UK since Michael has been with Epic Records has gone to number one.

November 7

Michael makes a special appearance at MTV's *Total Request Live* show with VJ Carson Daly, which is filmed live from the MTV studio's in New York City.

After being interviewed by MTV, Michael, for the first time ever in his career, makes an appearance at the Virgin Megastore in New York City's Times Square, to promote and sign copies of his new album 'Invincible'. Wearing a blue silk shirt and blue trousers, he steps onto a podium in front of the store to acknowledge the huge crowd that has gathered to see him.

November 7

'Invincible' has now debuted at number 1 in several countries apart from the UK. These countries include the USA, Australia, Belgium, Denmark, France, Germany, Holland, Hungary, Norway, Sweden, Switzerland and Turkey. In the USA alone 'Invincible' has sold 366,300 copies in its first week.

November 9

'Butterflies', which has yet to be released from the

This Page: Michael waves to hundreds of fans in front of the Virgin Megastore, New York.

'Invincible' album as a commercial single, has jumped to number 15 (up from 32) on the *Billboard* Hot R&B/Hip-Hop Singles chart. The chart placements are based solely on radio airplay in the US.

November 12

TV Guide, an American television magazine, has Michael featured on two different covers this week. The collector's covers are to commemorate Michael's 30th Anniversary concerts which are being aired on November 13 by CBS. The magazine also features a great exclusive interview with Michael.

American television show *Entertainment Tonight* features a behind-the-scenes look at Michael and many others from the recording of *What More Can I Give*.

'Michael Jackson Greatest Hits, History Volume 1', catalogue number 5018692, is released today as a single CD.

INVINCIBLE

Michael Jackson
EPC 495174

1. **Unbreakable**
2. **Heartbreaker**
3. **Invincible**
4. **Break of Dawn**
5. **Heaven Can Wait**
6. **You Rock My World**
7. **Butterflies**
8. **Speechless**
9. **2000 Watts**
10. **You Are My Life**
11. **Privacy**
12. **Don't Walk Away**
13. **Cry**
14. **The Lost Children**
15. **Whatever Happens**
16. **Threatened**

2001

November 13

Sony release *Video Greatest Hits - History* (originally released in 1995 on VHS) and *Dangerous – The Short Films* on DVD.

Tonight American TV Network CBS broadcast Michael's 30th Anniversary concert from Madison Square Garden in a two-hour special. An average of 25.73 million viewers in the US tune in, making the broadcast the largest audience for a music special on any network since ABC's two-part *Beatles Anthology* in 1995.

November 13

Epic Germany announce that the 'Invincible' album has sold more than 300,000 units in their country meaning it has already gone Platinum.

This Page: Michael receives 'Artist Of The Century' at the American Music Awards.

Page Opposite: Michael poses for a promotion picture taken for MJJ Productions by Jonathan Exley.

December 3

Michael speaks today of the death of Beatle George Harrison who passed away on December 1. "The world has lost a great spirit in George Harrison; a great musician, songwriter, and friend. He was an inspiration to me, and I will miss him a great deal."

December 5

'Cry', the second single from Michael's latest album 'Invincible', has been released in several countries worldwide.

December 6

The Recording Industry Association of America (RIAA) announces that *Invincible* has sold just over 1 million copies in the United States, which means that the album is now officially platinum. In Europe, where it has sold almost twice as many as the USA, sales are already multi-platinum.

December 14

Michael gives an interview to *USA Today* newspaper.

December 19

Michael attends the KIIS-FM Jingle Ball concert at Los Angeles' Staples Center where Radio host Rick Dees and basketball legend Magic Johnson present Michael with the KIIS-FM L.A. Legend Award.

2002
January 4

In Australia Michael's latest album 'Invincible' has been certified 2x Platinum, selling over 140,000 units. In Australia singles and albums are certified Gold at 350,00 units and Platinum at 700,00 units.

January 6

Epic records today announce on their web site that Michael's 'Invincible' album has reached sales in excess of 5.2 million worldwide.

January 9

Tonight at the 29th annual American Music Awards at the Shrine Auditorium, Los Angeles, Michael is awarded the 'Artist Of The Century Award', presented to him by good friend, Chris Tucker.

January 10

In the latest edition of *Q* magazine, Ali Campbell of British pop group UB40 praises Michael's new album 'Invincible'. "I think this album is fantastic. The production is something else, he's taken the best producers in the world and whittled those tracks down from about 100. He's gone back to singing R&B and there are some nice ballads... I think it's a great album."

January 20

Michael receives the award as 'Best International Male Singer' at the NRJ Awards 2002, in Cannes (France). Michael does not attend the award show.

January 23

'Cry' is released on CD in Japan. The Japanese version includes the lyrics to the song 'Cry' and 'Shout', with the Japanese translation of the lyrics.

January 25

Michael's 'Invincible' album goes Multi Platinum in the USA with sales of over 2 million.

February

In the March edition of *Vibe* magazine, Michael is featured on the front cover and inside there is an exclusive interview.

February 5

The computer animated film *Final Fantasy*, is released today on DVD. Amongst the special features are a *Final Fantasy* 'Thriller' music video, showing the 'cast' of this dancing along to Michael's pioneering 'Thriller' video.

2002

This Page: Michael attends the wedding of Liza Minnelli and David Gest, accompanied by good friends, Elizabeth Taylor and Diana Ross.

February 9
Michael and Dame Elizabeth Taylor are featured guests at a major fund-raiser - 'Art for AIDS: A Tribute to Rock Hudson', at the Laguna Art Museum in Laguna Beach, California, Orange County, USA.

Later in the evening Michael and Dame Elizabeth attend a $2,500 per plate private dinner at Dana Point, California.

February 18
During their 'free dance' routine Skaters Shae-Lynn Bourne and Victor Kraatz of Canada use Michael's music during the Winter Olympics in Salt Lake City. They begin their routine with 'Billie Jean', followed by 'In The Closet', 'Smile', ending with 'Don't Stop 'til You Get Enough'.

They come in fourth in the competition.

Russian ice skater Evgeni Plushenko, who has dominated men's skating for the past three years, finishing first or second in nearly every major competition, always performs to Michael's music.

After 17 weeks on the US *Billboard* charts and still not released, 'Butterflies' is at number two on the R&B/Hip Hop Singles Chart. The single still has not been released.

February 19
American DJ Steve Harvey interviews Michael for 20 minutes over the phone for his morning radio station The Beat 100.3.

February 23
Although not present for the ceremony, Michael wins three NAACP (National Association for the Advancement of Colored People) Image Awards at this 33rd annual event: Outstanding Variety Series/Special for 'Michael Jackson: 30th Anniversary Special; Outstanding Performance in a Variety Series/Special: 'Michael Jackson: 30th Anniversary Special; and Outstanding Music Video: *You Rock My World*.

Founded more than 30 years ago during a meeting at the home of Sammy Davis Jr., the NAACP Image Awards honour projects and individuals of all races who have helped promote "positive images of people of colour."

February 25
A press release is issued stating that Neverland Entertainment, headed by Michael Jackson and film producer Raju Sharad Patel, have signed an agreement in principal with Mark Damon's MDP Worldwide Entertainment Inc. to enter into an investment and partnership for all of MDP's film production.

With the investment by Neverland Entertainment, MDP will operate a new division called Neverland Pictures, which will be the production arm of MDP, and all feature films produced will carry the Neverland Pictures banner.

Michael states: "Both Raju and I love the way classic stories can be reinvented for the screen. My favorite movies such as Raju's *Jungle Book* and *Pinocchio* were re-imagined as major features, and were produced outside the traditional studio system. Films have always been a passion for me as a fan and as an artist and there is nothing in the world like the magic captured forever in a time capsule like motion picture images."

February 27

At this years Grammy Awards singer Missy Elliot wins 'The Michael Jackson Award For Best R&B/Soul Or Rap Music Video' for her album *Get Ur Freak On*. On winning Elliot said: "This is big. I won two Grammys, but (winning) the Michael Jackson award is major - especially for somebody who always wanted... videos to come across on a different level, like Michael."

March 1

To celebrate Lionel Richie's twenty years in the music industry, *Billboard* magazine includes a special section dedicated to Richie. 'The 20th Anniversary *Billboard* Salute' includes a full page advertisement from Michael that reads: "Congratulations on your 20th. Love, Michael".

March 16

Liza Minnelli and David Gest are married in New York. Michael, who is best man, arrives with Liz Taylor and Diana Ross.

As Liza Minnelli walks down the aisle to the altar, Michael picks up the train of her wedding dress and carries it until one of the bridesmaids take over. Later during the reception Michael makes a brief speech: "I am a man of few words… but please raise your glasses to the bride and groom".

March 20

The current issue of *Life* magazine features a list of their 'Top 100 Rock & Rollers' of all time. Michael is listed at

number nine on their chart. The list includes: 1. Elvis Presley, 2. The Beatles, 3. Bob Dylan, 4. James Brown, 5. The Rolling Stones, 6. Madonna, 7. Stevie Wonder, 8. Chuck Berry, 9. Michael Jackson, 10. Kurt Cobain.

They also add: "When Jackson moonwalked to the gritty disco-pop classic 'Billie Jean' on *Motown's 25th Anniversary* TV special in 1983, he created a sensation - people were gushing about it the next day at school and work. Jackson's early videos led to must-watch MTV. His fame was global to a degree not seen since The Beatles."

March 22

Today's issue of *OK* magazine features part one of 25 pages of photographs and reportage from Liza Minnelli and David Gest's wedding celebration. The article includes many photographs of Michael who will also feature in part two which will available in next week's issue.

April 2

People Weekly magazine (April 8, 2002) is a special double issue that contains an article on celebrities, their various inventions and patents for these ideas and devices.

Some of the inventions listed are Steven Spielberg (patent No.D401,951) for an ornamental switch for camera equipment; Eddie Van Halen (patent No. 4,656,917), for a hands free guitar support; and Michael's (patent No. 5,255,452), for shoes that slip into a hitch attached to the stage, allowing the wearer to lean far forward and appear to defy gravity.

Each celebrity sent a drawing of their idea to the U.S. Patent and Trademark Office, paid a fee and were granted exclusive rights for 14-20 years.

The article includes a photograph of Michael in dance mode, wearing the shoes, and also a diagram he submitted for obtaining the patent.

April 20

At the Pasadena Civic Auditorium, the very same venue which Michael performed his very first moonwalk during *Motown 25*, Michael performs 'Dangerous' in front of a live audience, at the taping of a special for Dick Clark's 50th Anniversary of *American Bandstand*.

The show, hosted by Dick Clark, is due to be screened on US TV on May 3.

April 24

Michael performs 'Dangerous', 'Black or White' and 'Heal The World' during a charity fundraiser for the Democratic National Committee's 'Every Vote Counts' campaign.

'A Night At The Apollo' held at the famed Harlem Theatre, is expected to raise $2.5 million for the charity. Tony Bennett and K.D. Lang also perform for the 1, 400 strong crowd, some of which have paid $1,000 per head.

This Page: Michael performing 'Dangerous' at the 50th Anniversary of *American Bandstand*.

Below: Michael on stage with Diana Ross at the Apollo Theatre.

2002

April 29

AOL Music and Tonos Entertainment announce an alliance to benefit musicians and songwriters in a worldwide agreement that includes an exclusive Michael Jackson Songwriting Contest where one lucky AOL member will have their lyrics recorded by the King of Pop.

The contest provides AOL members with the chance to co-write a song with three musical legends: Michael Jackson, 14-time Grammy-winning producer David Foster and Oscar winner/Songwriting Hall of Fame inductee Carole Bayer Sager.

May 4

EMP's newest exhibition, '(Un)Common Objects', runs from today until October 20 and gathers together a wide range of memorabilia and trademark items from the world of pop. Among the memorabilia that is on show is Michael's sparkly jacket and glove that he uses in his performance of 'Billie Jean'.

Other items on show are the famous gold bustier worn by Madonna and a plaid shirt worn by Bruce Springsteen.

May 13

In a recent interview with MTV, US rapper Eminem says he thought Michael Jackson's album 'Invincible' was by far the best album of 2001.

May 22

In a recent interview for the Australian TV show *A Current Affair*, film star Will Smith spoke of Michael's role in the forthcoming film *Men In Black II*.

"Listen," Smith said. "Michael Jackson is really funny. To have time to spend with him and actually be around him, he's not what... people think he is. Michael Jackson's like a black belt too,

so he will kick your ass if you say somethin' about him."

In disbelief the interviewer replied "No, really?" to which Will said, "Yes, Michael Jackson kicked over my head"

June 6

At a press conference in New York, Michael lends his voice to a coalition demanding 'justice' for recording artists. The recently formed New-York based National Action Network (NAN) has been set up to investigate artist exploitation by major record labels. NAN has drawn support from lawyer Johnnie Cochran and

civil rights campaigner the Reverend Al Sharpton.

Michael releases the following statement explaining his reasons for joining the coalition. "Record companies have to start treating artists with respect, honor and financial justice. Therefore I am proud to join this coalition which represents all artists.

"For Sony to make a false claim that I owe them $200 million is outrageous and offensive," he adds.

In response to Michael's comments, Sony releases the following statement, "We have never issued any statement, verbally or in writing, claiming that Michael Jackson owes us $200 million. As a result, we are baffled by the comments issued today by his press representatives."

June 10
Michael arrives in London and checks into the Marriott Renaissance Hotel in High Holborn at around 10.20pm. Later in the evening he issues a brief message to the fans which Uri Geller reads out to them. The message reads: "To all my fans, I can't wait to see you all. Love, Michael".

June 11
Michael leaves his hotel at around 8.20pm for dinner with Uri Geller and his family.

June 12
Michael goes shopping at the world famous toy store, Hamleys, which opens at 9.30pm especially for him.

June 13
In the late afternoon Michael spends just under an hour at an HMV store in London, but finds it difficult to leave as so many fans gather outside. Unfortunately an elderly lady is knocked over in the chaos. On seeing this, Michael gestures to the fans to calm down, helps the lady to her feet and gives her a lift home.

Michael is inducted into the National Academy of Popular Music/Songwriters Hall Of Fame at the Sheraton Hotel in New York. Although he is not there to collect his plaque, Liza Minnelli and David Gest received it on his behalf.

Minnelli says: "You write the songs that make the whole world dance."

June 14
In London, Michael visits the Houses of Parliament accompanied by Uri Geller and

magician David Blaine. On arrival he is met by Labour Party Peer Lord Janner who has invited him to come along and join in the birthday celebration for Chief Secretary to the Treasury, Paul Boateng, the first black minister in the Cabinet.

The House of Lords is Michael's favourite room. He points at the gold throne and says: "I want that." However, he was less impressed by the seats in the Commons chamber, sitting on one and asking: "Are they comfortable after hours and hours?"

Boateng later says of Michael's visit, "What a fantastic birthday surprise. I can't believe it! It's the best present ever. I can't believe that I'm with the most famous musician."

June 14
Michael leaves Paddington Station, London, on a train ride to Exeter with Uri Geller, magician David Blaine and 200 fans at 12.30pm.

Reuters describes the event as bedlam, saying that the scene at the station was "Pure chaos, recalling Beatlemania back in the Sixties."

Tickets for the journey were priced at £100 each, including travel in luxury first class seats and access to the benefit concert at St James' Park, home of Exeter City Football Club, which Michael was also attending.

On his arrival in Exeter, Michael is first taken to a hotel then later to St James' Park where 10,000 had gathered for this fund raising event, organised to raise money for the football club and two charities aimed at combating Aids and malaria.

June 15
Michael leaves his hotel around 12.20pm to attend a

This Page: Michael attends a charity fundraiser at Exeter City FC organised by Uri Geller.

fan demonstration at the Sony Music offices on Great Marlborough Street in London. He arrives at 1.30pm, riding on the top deck of a London open topped bus which has been organised for him by a group of fans.

Later, at the Equinox nightclub at a fan club event, Michael speaks of his displeasure with Sony. He holds a banner reading 'Sony Kills Music' and announces that he will not release another album with the label after his box set. Michael is upset that his latest album, 'Invincible', hasn't been promoted as thoroughly as his previous releases.

Fan demonstrations around the world have been held outside Sony's offices in New York, Switzerland, Holland and Spain with another planned for the USA.

June 17
Michael leaves the Renaissance Hotel in mid-afternoon for a business meeting with Mohammed Al Fayed. After the meeting he visits Al Fayed's store, Harrods, then returns to the hotel just before seven in the evening.

Michael later meets with Adrian Grant, to sign a batch of limited edition prints, and to discuss a new book project.

June 18
Michael leaves his hotel just after 9.00am and is driven to Heathrow where he catches a plane to New York and a connecting flight to Los Angeles.

July 2
In an official press release today Gaylord Entertainment announce that Michael Jackson and Sony/ATV have agreed to purchase country music publisher Acuff-Rose. Acuff Rose's library includes 55,000 songs by music artists such as Hank Williams, Roy Orbison and the Everly Brothers.

According to the release more than 100 songs have been broadcasted on the radio at least a million times. They include 'Oh Pretty Woman', made famous by the late Roy Orbison, and 'Tennessee Waltz', by Patti Page which made number 1 in 1950.

Sony/ATV and Michael Jackson will pay Gaylord Entertainment $157 million.

July 6
Hundreds of fans gather outside Sony's Manhattan offices in New York to support Michael. The demonstration is peaceful, even when Michael arrives, as he did in London in June, on a double-decker bus. The bus drives around the block twice during which time Michael waves to fans, then he makes his way to the New York Port Authority where other fans are able to give Michael their banners and messages.

Later in the day Michael attends a fan party at Webster Hall in New York. After watching the majority of the show Michael goes down to the stage to accepts a '30th

Anniversary Fan Award' from party organisers, MJFC.

Michael speaks out against the music industry's treatment of artists, alleging that the business is rife with racism. Speaking at a civil rights meeting in New York Michael claims that there is a "conspiracy" among record companies.

"The record companies really do conspire against the artists, especially the black artists," Michael told a crowd of 350 at Reverend Al Sharpton's National Action Network headquarters in Harlem. "When you fight for me, you're fighting for all black people, dead and alive," he added.

A Sony spokesman said that Michael criticisms were "ludicrous, spiteful and hurtful".

July 9
At the Rev. Al Sharpton's National Action Network headquarters in Harlem, New York, Michael along with other musicians, producers and music executives, again speaks about corruption and conspiracy in the record industry.

Michael says: "I'm tired of the manipulation. The press has manipulated the truth. They're liars. History books are a lie. You need to know this. You must know this, that all forms of popular music, from jazz to rock to hip-hop, and dance, from the jitterbug to the Charleston, are black. But go down to the corner bookstore, and you won't see one black person on a cover. You'll see Elvis Presley. You'll see the Rolling Stones. But where are the real pioneers?"

Using Otis Blackwell as an example, Michael says that there was something missing in a system that found Blackwell dying penniless despite having written such classics as 'All Shook Up', 'Great Balls Of Fire' and 'Don't Be Cruel'.

"They didn't write one book about him that I know of, and I've searched the world over," Michael said. "And he was a prolific, phenomenal writer.

"Once I started breaking sales records, I broke Elvis Presley's record, I broke the Beatles' record, once I started doing that, overnight, they called me a freak, a homosexual, a child molester. They said I bleached my skin. They did everything they could to turn the public against me. It's a conspiracy.

"Let's not leave this building and forget what was said. Let's do something about it... And remember, we're all brothers and sisters, no matter what colour we are."

July 13

Michael continues his battle against Sony boss Tommy Mottola during a live telephone interview with *The Journal News*, saying the music establishment would "never turn the fans against me."

Now Michael's family and friends are coming forward to support him. Michael's brother Jackie Jackson said that while this is a feud between Michael Jackson and Mottola, he stands firmly behind his brother.

"Michael has his reasons for speaking out like this. He never speaks out, so obviously there is a good reason for it, and he knows what he's doing," says Jackie.

Jermaine Jackson adds: "The house of Sony was built by Michael Jackson and (former Sony chairman) Walter Yentnikoff, and it all started with Michael's 'Off The Wall' album. Michael saved the music industry when he made 'Thriller'. They just sabotaged him. Sony says they spent all of this money well, where did they spend it? They have the audacity to do this to him. Look what he's done for them.

Look what he's done for MTV. They are trying to do my brother the same way they did George Michael, Meatloaf and Mariah Carey. Sony tried to destroy them."

July 18

Marty Singer, a lawyer for Michael Jackson, states that a lawsuit against Sony Music for breach of contract and questionable accounting practices is being considered.

Michael claims Sony acted inappropriately in the marketing of his latest album, 'Invincible'. Sony failed to air a commercial during Michael's televised special last year at a time when his album was allegedly being promoted by Sony. There are other disputes concerning the release of videos promoting the album. Singer adds: "The 'Thriller' album did not really explode until the 'Thriller' single and video were released, which was well after the album initially came out."

July 21

UK newspaper *The People* runs an article entitled: 'Football: 20 things you didn't know about Rio'.

Rio Ferdinand, the England defender is asked who he would like to be and answered if he could be anyone, it would be Michael. "Michael Jackson is my hero," he says.

August

After severe floods cause devastation in Germany, Michael puts together a video taped condolence message for those who have been affected.

The flood, the worst in a hundred years on the river Elbe, causes damage that is estimated to run into billions. Several are killed, some are still missing and thousands of houses have been destroyed or are uninhabitable.

Michael is approached by German TV channel MDR

and asked if he is willing to take part in a charity auction to support the victims of the floods. Michael, in Las Vegas at that time, agrees and immediately goes out to a local Virgin Megastore, buys fourteen of his own CDs and videos and signs them, along with two cotton napkins for the auction.

August 29

Michael is 44 today.

In the evening, at the MTV Awards, held at the Radio City Music Hall in New York, Michael receives a huge four-tier birthday cake.

September 16

The Essential Michael Jackson TV programme is screened in the UK.

October 3

'What More Can I Give', Michael's charity record for 9/11, is finally being played on radio by New York station WKTU-FM. They debuted the song last Friday and have been playing it six times a day since, without permission.

Marc Schaffel, the executive producer of the single, says at least 200 copies were sent to artists who participated and their representatives, and that the song has since surfaced on the internet. "I would hate to see it out there and not do its intended purpose, which was to raise money for the victims of September 11."

October 12

Michael plays host to more than 200 members of the US Air Force and their families at his Neverland Valley Ranch. Officials at Vandenberg Air Force Base, which is situated near Neverland, say Michael's invitation was "a gesture of appreciation" for Air Force members in the community that had served overseas.

Page Opposite: Michael speaks out against racism in the record industry, as well as his own mistreatment by Sony.

Fans show their support for Michael, and their anger towards Sony.

This Page: Michael attends the fans demonstration aboard a double-decker bus.

Michael with artist Nijel, creator of a special 30th Anniversary award presented to Michael at a MJFC tribute party, New York.

This Page: Michael attends the Bambi Awards in Germany.

Michael donates one of his jackets to an auction in aid of the 'Off-Road-Kids', supporting street kids in Germany.

October 21

Adam Hall and Ramsey Brookhart begin moonwalking the earth. Hall and Brookhart, co-founders of a non-profit organization called 'Moon-walk for Earth', have spent two years preparing for an eight-day event that includes moonwalking like Michael to help educate people about renewable energy sources, also hoping at the same time to get into the *Guinness World Book Of Records*.

October 26

The Making Of Ghosts featuring never before seen footage taken from behind the scenes of the 1997 short film, aired tonight on VH1 in the USA. After the half hour special, *Ghosts* short film also aired.

November 2

Michael is awarded the 'World Arts Award' at the 'World Awards For Men' event, held at the Imperial Hofburg Palace, in Vienna, Austria.

Men's World Day is a global initiative based on humanitarian, social and philanthropic objectives. Its goal is to support the cause of peace, freedom and tolerance throughout the world in order to positively influence the attitudes of men and is led by former Russian president, Mikhail Gorbachev.

November 13

Today Michael arrives, with a police motorcycle escort, at the Santa Barbara County Superior Court in Santa Maria, California, to take the stand and defend himself against a concert promoter's lawsuit accusing him of fraud and breach of contract.

Marcel Avram, a German concert promoter filed the suit in June 2000, claiming Michael had cost him $21 million when he allegedly abandoned plans to perform two millennium concerts on both sides of the international date line.

Over one hundred fans are present to support Michael.

November 15

Michael turns up four hours late for the second day of the lawsuit which concert promoter Marcel Avram, after the judge granted Michael permission to postpone his testimony until the afternoon.

In the UK some of the cast of *Eastenders* perform their version of Michael's 'Thriller' short film to raise money for the BBC's annual charity television show, *Children In Need*.

November 19

Michael arrives at Berlin airport in Germany, accompanied by his three children.

Later Michael appears on the balcony of his Presidential Suite at the Adlon hotel, waving to the hundreds of fans outside. At one stage Michael also takes his children out on the balcony, including his new son Prince Michael II, whom he holds out over the railings for the fans to see, although the child has his head covered.

Later Michael releases a statement apologising for holding Prince Michael II over the balcony: "I offer no excuses for what happened. I made a terrible mistake. I got caught up in the excitement of the moment. I would never intentionally endanger the lives of my children."

November 20

There is a media backlash against Michael with many tabloids and television stations around the world reporting negatively on how he held Prince Michael II over the railings of his suite on the fourth floor of the Adlon hotel.

Wearing a dark suit and sunglasses and accompanied by his children, Michael visits the Berlin zoo.

Later in the day he travels outside Berlin to visit Potsdam's baroque Sans Souci palace.

In the evening Michael attends 'A Tribute To Bambi',

a charity gala held at a night-club on Potsdamer Platz in Berlin, to raise money for the 'Off-Road-Kids' which supports 'street kids' in Germany.

To help raise money for the event, Michael had earlier in the month donated two items that were offered up for auction by Ebay, Germany: a fedora, similar to the one worn in his 'Smooth Criminal' short film, which has his name signed inside, and one of his original stage jackets which was worn during the American Music Awards 2002.

The auction closed today with the fedora selling for 2,310 Euros (US $2,303) and the jacket going for an incredible 16,000 Euros (US $15,950). The jacket is bought by famous German composer Ralf Siegel, who attended the live event. Michael makes a brief appearance to hand over his jacket.

November 21
Michael attends the Bambi Awards where he was presented with the 'Pop Artist of the Millennium' award.

November 22
Michael shops in Berlin and visits the National Art Gallery where he signs autographs for the waiting crowd. It is also reported that he visits the Berlin zoo again, after it had been closed to the public.

November 23
Today Michael checks out of the Adlon Hotel in Berlin and makes his way to Tempelhof Airport where it is reported he will fly back to Los Angeles.

November 28
The latest issue (No. 49) of German magazine *Bunte* features an exclusive interview with Michael from his hotel room during his stay in Berlin. Michael speaks of his embarrassment at having to wear his new glasses in public for the first time during the Bambi Awards. "That was embarrassing. I wore my new reading glasses for the first time in public."

Michael also explained how his children respond to the fans. "Paris is imitating me now. When I call 'I love you' to the fans she also calls 'I love you. I love you too from the bottom of my heart.'"

Asked what his children thought of the *Spiderman* movie, Michael said, "They love the Spiderman clothes. They have seen the movie about a dozen times."

He also says: "Playstations or computers are not allowed in the house," and that he reads his children fairy tales during breakfast.

December 3
Michael arrives at Santa Barbara County Superior Court in Santa Maria, California for the continuation of the lawsuit brought against him by German promoter Marcel Avram. He is on crutches and without one shoe because his foot is swollen. Asked what had happened he says: "It's a spider bite... If I showed it to you, you'd be shocked."

In court he is asked how concerts are organised but he can't remember. "That's administrative work," he says. "That's not what I do. I'm the entertainer." Asked by Avram's lawyers if he suffers memory problems he replies: "Not that I can recall."

December 4
Michael is again at Santa Barbara County Superior Court in Santa Maria to give evidence in the lawsuit brought against him by German Concert Promoter Marcel Avram.

USA For Africa - We Are The World is released today on DVD in the USA and Japan.

December 9
Michael is presented with a *Billboard* award for his album 'Thriller', which spent 37 weeks at number 1, more than any other album in the history of the *Billboard* album chart.

Michael cannot attend the ceremony at the MGM Grand, in Las Vegas in person but is connected live via satellite from his Neverland home to the awards ceremony.

December 19
According to film producer Raju Patel, one of Michael's partners in Never Land Entertainment, Michael would like to visit India again next year.

According to Patel, he and Michael have two films planned. *Tom Thumb*, and *Wolfed* which will be based on the novel *The Wolf Leader* by Alexander Dumas.

December 20
Gold Magazine release a seven page article, photographs and interview with Michael.

December 21
Michael has recorded a Christmas message for German magazine *Bunte*. Parts of the message will also be shown on December 23, during *Leute Heute* on channel ZDF, Germany and during *Entertainment Tonight* in the USA.

2003
January 10
Reports say that Michael spoke by telephone to Maurice Gibb, who is critically ill in a Miami hospital after a suspected heart attack.

He is being comforted in hospital by his wife, Yvonne, and their two children, Adam and Samantha. His brother Barry, who had recently been working with Michael, also visited him. Michael is godfather to Barry's eldest son, also named Michael.

This Page: Michael arrives at the Santa Barbara County Superior Court, California.

2002

2003

"I trusted Martin Bashir to come into my life and that of my family because I wanted the truth to be told.

"Martin Bashir, persuaded me to trust him that his would be an honest and fair portrayal of my life and told me that he was 'the man that turned Diana's life around'. I am heartbroken that someone whom I treated as a friend could stoop so low.

"Today I feel more betrayed than perhaps ever before; that someone, who had got to know my children, my staff and me, whom I let into my heart and told the truth, could then sacrifice the trust I placed in him and produce this terrible and unfair programme.

"It breaks my heart that anyone could truly believe that I would do anything to harm or endanger my children: they are the most important thing in my life. Everyone who knows me will know the truth which is that my children come first in my life and that I would never harm any child."

Michael Jackson
February 6, 2003

January 12
Bee Gees star Maurice Gibb dies in the early hours of the morning at the Mount Sinai Medical Center in Miami.

January 14
The Globe magazine headlines today's edition with a red banner reading: "Michael Jackson's Spider Bite - Shocking Proof." The front page features a photograph of Michael holding up the leg of his trousers to show the damage a brown recluse spider did when he was bitten repeatedly as he slept one evening at his Neverland Valley Ranch.

January 15
Michael pays his respects to Maurice Gibb who died earlier in the week of a heart attack.

More than an hour after the funeral had ended, and after Maurice's twin, Robin, and other family members have left the Riverside Funeral Chapel, elder brother, Barry Gibb, arrived at the chapel with Michael.

A spokesman for the Gibb family said: "He (Barry) was too distraught to go to the funeral. He and Michael went in for private prayers."

February 3
Living With Michael Jackson, a documentary and interview by Martin Bashir airs on ITV television in the UK.

February 6
Michael releases a statement (left) pertaining to the television documentary *Living With Michael Jackson*.

Michael's lawyers send complaints to the Independent Television Commission and the Broadcasting Standards Commission, claiming he has been "unfairly treated" by the Martin Bashir programme, and that it was an infringement of his privacy.

Michael says the programme included film taken of his children which was "contrary to my express consent". Michael adds that he had not, as promised, been given the chance to view the programme before it was broadcast.

February 19
According to the BBC Michael has been told he can go ahead with two complaints against a former business manager who says Michael owes him millions.

Los Angeles judge Andria Richey, rules that Michael could pursue the allegations that Myung-Ho Lee, from South Korea, had breached contracts and did not act in good faith in giving Michael business advice.

Lee began proceedings against Michael last April, alleging that Michael had reneged on a promise to pay him $13 million in back wages in September, 2001. However, Michael filed court documents on December 20 2002 denying that he owed the money and that an unnamed person had forged his signature.

February 20
Michael Jackson - The Footage You Were Never Meant To See, is aired in the USA on the FOX network.

The programme is based on video footage, which was filmed over the period of time Martin Bashir was interviewing Michael. During the programme, many examples were shown of how in the original documentary, footage was edited to portray Michael in a negative light.

February 24
Michael Jackson - The Footage You Were Never Meant To See airs at 9pm on Sky One in the UK. After the programme Sky One asks viewers to vote on whether they thought

Michael was unfairly treated by Martin Bashir. A massive 92% of voters said they felt he had.

February 28
After out-of-court discussions today between Granada Television and Michael's legal team, it is agreed that unseen footage from the documentary *Living With Michael Jackson* would be kept under lock and key in "secure conditions" at their London headquarters.

They also agree not to release any unseen footage until the end of the full hearing in April.

March 14
Michael is ordered to pay $5.3 million to concert promoter Marcel Avram, after pulling out of two planned millennium concerts.

Michael's attorney, Zia Modabber, told Reuters: "He's (Michael) fine with it. He stood up for himself and went to trial and Mr. Avram didn't get nearly what he wanted."

April 5
Michael appears as a surprise guest at the 8th Annual Palm Beach International Film Festival Grand Gala Awards Show, at Boca Raton Resort, Palm Beach, Florida.

More than 500 guests are stunned when Michael arrives at the $1,000-a-plate dinner, joining producer Robert Evans at the centre table, where several other surprise guests were seated including Chris Tucker and director Brett Ratner.

April 24
Michael Jackson – Private Home Movies airs on the FOX network in the US.

Michael hosts this two-hour special from his cinema at Neverland. It features unseen footage from the 'Dangerous' era through to present day, his first Christmas at Neverland organised for him by Elizabeth Taylor, an Easter Egg Hunt, pushing a shopping trolley around a supermarket, visiting his grandparents, and dancing in the back seat of a car to R. Kelly's song 'Ignition' in a traffic jam, plus much more.

April 30

A pillow case signed by Michael and thrown from the balcony of his suite at he Dorchester Hotel in London on May 27, 2000, is auctioned at Christie's in London and sells for $713.00.

May 9

Michael files a lawsuit in the Los Angeles Superior Court seeking unpaid royalties for any 'Best Of 'compilations of his Motown recordings with the Jackson 5 or as a solo artist, as well as for newly issued albums of previously unreleased material.

May 17

Wearing Seventies clothes and an afro-wig, Michael attends a Seventies style themed party held at Miami's Forge nightclub to celebrate owner Al Malnik's 70th birthday.

May 20

Michael arrives in Indianapolis and checks into the Canterbury Hotel. He is in Indianapolis to give a deposition in court following a lawsuit brought by Steeltown Records boss Gordon Keith. The suits claims that the Jackson 5 had used two songs Keith had not been recognised for that appeared on the 1996 album 'Pre-History: The Lost Steeltown Recordings'.

May 21

Preceding the court appearance in Indianapolis, Michael is taken ill and visits a local hospital facility for observation and treatment. His lawyer,

Brian Oxman, "He (Michael) can become very concerned and nervous at depositions. He doesn't like lawsuits, and it makes him ill to have to cope with litigation that people seem to heap on him."

In the evening Michael flies back to Los Angeles.

May 27

Michael takes his children, Prince and Paris for a day out at Universal Studios in Los Angeles. During his stay at the amusement park, he (and his bodyguards) are followed by a huge mob of fans and curious onlookers.

May 30

Michael attends a party organised by producer Robert Evans for Brett Ratner, director of *Red Dragon* and *Rush Hour*, to celebrate the launch of his book, *Hilhaven Lodge: The Photo Booth Pictures*.

May 30

it's another late night for Michael as he attends a MTV Movie Awards post party at Ron Burkle's Beverly Hills Mansion in Los Angeles.

June 9

The *Chicago Sun-Times* reports that Michael, his brother Marlon and Chris Tucker attended the National Cable Telecommunications Association conference in Chicago today.

The report states that Michael was there to support Marlon, who is co-owner of a new cable channel, MBC (Major Broadcasting Cable).

June 10

A press release is issued detailing a new business partnership between Michael Jackson and Charles Koppelman.

Koppelman, Chairman and CEO of CAK Entertainment, will advise on a variety of new and exciting music and business ventures for Michael, including releases that may be on the market by the end of the year. Koppelman is uniquely qualified to work with Michael given his four decades of experience in the music industry and ties to the financial community.

Michael said, "I am thrilled to be working with a man like Charles Koppelman."

This Page: Michael is snapped alongside P.Diddy and Ron Burkle at a MTV Movie Awards post party.

February 6, 2003
In the wake of all of the media frenzy surrounding the 90-minute interview, *Living With Michael Jackson*, Michael's ex-wife, Debbie Rowe, gives an exclusive interview to the breakfast show GMTV.

Debbie says she was horrified by the way the media had treated Michael since the interview: "He is a wonderful, caring man," she says. "And he's not portrayed as he really is... There could be no other person that could be a better father and I resent anyone making allegations that he is not a... proper parent.

"No one has ever read more about parenting, no one has ever practised the art of parenting and parenting is an art, you earn the title parent. Because you give birth, because you impregnate someone, it does not automatically give you that title of Mother or Father. You earn the title.

"My kids don't call me mom because I don't want them to, they're not, they're Michael's children, it's not that they're not my children, but I had them because I wanted him to be a father. I believe that there are some people who should be parents and he's one of them, and he is such a fabulous man and such a good friend and he's always been there for me, always, from the day I met him."

Michael returns to court in Indianapolis for his postponed deposition and to answer questions in a lawsuit alleging copyright infringement on the 1996 album 'Pre-History: The Lost Steeltown Recordings'.

June 11
Michael arrives back in his hometown of Gary, Indiana. Outside the Gary City Hall the crowd cheers as he emerges from a black limousine at 12.30pm. Wearing a black suit and holding a umbrella, Michael climbs to the top of the steps outside City Hall and turns to wave to hundreds of people who have gathered outside to see him.

Once inside, Michael tells the invited guests that it was his first time back in Gary since the age of 9.

The mayor presents Michael with a key to the city, saying, "Now that you have the key, you don't have to be a stranger."

At a press conference for the event Mayor King announces that Michael will help with building a new Performing Arts Center in Lake County city to be known as the 'Michael J. Jackson Performing Arts Center.'

Michael then makes the short journey to his childhood home, 2300 Jackson Street. Roughly the size of a two-car garage, Michael's former home now belongs to Tim Brown, a cousin of Michael's father, Joseph Jackson.

In the living room, Michael tells Brown and other relatives: "We rehearsed, rehearsed and rehearsed all the time."

Later in the day Michael visits Roosevelt High School where he received a framed Honorary High School Diploma, and in the evening Michael attends 'Salute to the

Troops', an event held at the Baseball Stadium in Gary that was open to the public with free admission. Mayor King gives a brief speech, which is followed by a presentation to Michael from world wide fan group, MJ Unity.

According to Los Angeles Superior Court spokesman, Kyle Christopherson, the lawsuit between Myung-Ho Lee and Michael has been settled.

Myung-Ho Lee, a Korean businessman and his firm Union Finance and Investment Corp were suing Michael for breach of contract stating that Michael owed him $12 million in back pay for his services. Michael had applied to have the case dismissed. The terms of the settlement remain confidential.

June 12
Michael attends a Rainbow/ PUSH Coalition breakfast planning meeting with the Revered Jesse Jackson. During the breakfast, which was held at the First Church of Deliverance on South Wabash in Chicago, Michael signs autographs and has pictures taken with the guests.

June 16
Michael is one of nearly 3,000 people who attend a memorial service for movie legend Gregory Peck in Los Angeles.

June 24
Wearing a white frilly shirt that showed his chest, a black glove on his left hand, sparkly blue/silver trousers and a sparkly white belt, Michael makes a surprise appearance at the BET Awards in Hollywood and presents music legend James Brown with a 'Lifetime Achievement Award'.

After his speech, Michael goes into a short dance routine, which shows how the 'Godfather of Soul' had influenced his own dancing. At one point he was even showered with a long silver cloak, a trademark of James Brown's.

July 14
Michael is among forty family and friends who attend the funeral service of soul legend Barry White.

July 21
A press release is issued expressing Michael's concern over the 'Authors, Consumer and Computer Owners Protection and Security Act' of 2003 (ACCOPS Act) as introduced in the House of Representatives. The legislation, if passed, would make it a federal felony to download even one single copyrighted work, which includes music.

Michael says: "I am speechless about the idea of putting music fans in jail for downloading music. It is wrong to download, but the answer cannot be jail."

August 5
'Butterflies' taken from Michael's album 'Invincible' wins a BMI Award at the 2003 Urban Awards.

August 26
It is announced that Michael will open up Neverland Valley to public on September 13th.

For $5,000 a ticket, which will admit two people, invited guests will get the chance to tour the grounds, have access to Michael's fairground and cinema and eat lunch and dinner at the ranch.

Michael plans to donate $1,000 of each ticket to three charities: Make-A-Wish Foundation, Oneness, which promotes multiculturalism in arts and education, and E Ai Como E Que Fica, which benefits impoverished children in Rio de Janeiro, with the remainder of the money going towards the cost of the event.

August 30
The day after his 45th birthday Michael attends a party for him at the Orpheum Theatre, Los Angeles, organised by Deborah Danelly's internet fanclub MJFC, along with MJWN and TMC.

Michael arrives just before the start of the show, and is shown to a private box where he remains seated until just before the end when he takes the stage to thank everyone for organising the event and tell fans about his future plans.

September 10
Michael gives a telephone interview to DJ Rick Dees of US radio station KIIS FM. Michael was in Toronto, Canada at the time of the interview.

September 13
Michael opens up his Neverland Valley home to celebrities and members of the general pubic for a dance party.

Among the guests at Michael's ranch for this eight hour event are Patti LaBelle, Boyz II Men, Mike Tyson, Nick and Aaron Carter, Pink and Rodney Jerkins.

Michael's amusement park is open to everyone, along with his cinema and zoo. Lunch and dinner are provided and a concert features Ashanti.

Page Opposite: Michael attends the Orpheum Theatre in Los Angeles to celebrate his 45th birthday with over 2,000 fans.

This Page: Michael waves to the hundreds of fans whom had turned up to see his return to his original hometown, Gary, Indiana.

Below: The front cover of the party invitation for Michael's charity fundraiser held at Neverland on September 13.

A Once in a Lifetime Event at Michael Jackson's Neverland Valley Ranch

NEVERLAND VALLEY

NUMBER ONES

Michael Jackson
EPC 2513800

1. **Don't Stop 'Til You Get Enough**
2. **Rock With You**
3. **Billie Jean**
4. **Beat It**
5. **Thriller**
6. **Human Nature**
7. **I Just Can't Stop Loving You**
8. **Bad**
9. **The Way You Make Me Feel**
10. **Dirty Diana**
11. **Smooth Criminal**
12. **Black Or White**
13. **You Are Not Alone**
14. **Earth Song**
15. **Blood On The Dance Floor**
16. **You Rock My World**
17. **Break of Dawn**
18. **One More Chance**

September 24
Sotheby's auction the original lyrics to Michael's hit single 'Beat It', hand written and signed by Michael, for £4,320.

October 1
Michael makes an appearance at a charity event to raise funds for Lupus LA and Lupus Research at the Beverly Hills Hotel, Beverly Hills, California, and presents an award to Medical Visionary Award Recipient Dr. Alan Metzger in recognition of his work to aid Lupus patients.

At a Christie's Pop Memorabilia Auction in London, a hand-drawn picture of Charlie Chaplin, drawn and signed by Michael in 1976, sells for £4,112, more than three times its reserve price.

October 7
Michael is named as being among the 165 nominees for this years Nobel Peace Prize. The nomination was for his efforts in promoting peace via pop. Fellow nominees include Pope John Paul, Brazilian President Luiz Inacio Lula da Silva and the former Czech President Vaclav Havel.

October 25
Michael is in Las Vegas to receive the key to the city from Mayor Goodman. Three hundred fans were also present for the afternoon ceremony, which takes place at the 'Art of Music' Store at the Desert Passage Mall, Las Vegas.

Later in the evening, Michael returns to the 'Art of Music' store to attend a special sale of his memorabilia.

October 27
Michael's charity single, 'What More Can I Give' is made available as a download on the worldwide web.

The web sites, whatmore-canigive.com and musicforgiv-ing.com feature the song on their web sites at the cost of $2.00 per download. A portion of the proceeds from the download fee go to children's charities, including Oneness, Mr. Holland's Opus Foundation and the International Child Art Foundation.

In the evening, he presents the song to the audience at the Radio Music Awards in Las Vegas. Beyoncé also presents Michael with the first ever Radio Music Awards Humanitarian Award.

November 4
Reuters report that Michael is currently in talks with CBS to perform in a music special that would air on the November 26, a week after the release of the new 'Number Ones' album, and the same week as the UK release of 'One More Chance'.

November 17
The 'Number Ones' album and DVD are released today in the UK. The album comes in four different covers.

November 18
The 'Number Ones' Album and DVD were released today in the USA.

A press release is issued by Stuart Backerman, Michael's official spokesperson, in response to the Santa Barbara County Officers who earlier today conducted a search of Neverland Ranch.

It states: "We cannot comment on law enforcement's investigation because we do not yet know what it is about. We can comment on the malignant horde of media hounds claiming to speak for Michael on this and many other issues. A rogue's gallery of hucksters and self-styled 'inside sources' have dominated the airwaves since reports of a search of Neverland broke, speculating, guessing and fabricating information about an investigation they couldn't possibly know about."

November 19
It is reported by various media outlets that police have conducted a search of Michael's Neverland Valley ranch in connection to sexual abuse allegations brought by a 13-year-old boy.

Stuart Backerman releases a statement saying, "The outrageous allegations against Michael Jackson are false. Michael would never harm a child in any way. These scurrilous and totally unfounded allegations will be proven false in a courtroom.

"Naturally, the implications are distressing to everyone who hears them, which is precisely the point. Michael through his attorneys, led by Mark Geragos, has already made arrangements with the District Attorney to return to Santa Barbara to immediately confront and prove these charges unfounded."

November 20
Michael returns to Las Vegas where he is filming a video for the single 'One More Chance', following his arrest at the airport in Santa Barbara this afternoon.

Michael's lawyer, Mark Geragos confirmed, that Michael had to post $3 million bail at the Santa Barbara County main jail, posed for a mugshot, and was advised of the charges against him.

Geragos says, "Michael is greatly outraged by the bringing of these charges. He considers this to be a big lie. He understands the people who are outraged, because if these charges were true, I assure you Michael would be the first to be outraged, but I'm here to tell you today - and Michael has given me the authority to say on his behalf - these charges are categorically untrue. He looks forward to getting into a courtroom, as opposed to any other forum, and confronting these accusations head on."

November 21
The mug shot that Michael posed for at Santa Barbara County main jail is on the front page of virtually every national newspaper across Europe and the USA. TV channels also show footage of Michael arriving at the building in handcuffs.

November 22
'One More Chance' is released today in the UK.

November 23
'Number Ones' enters the UK album charts at number 1.

November 26
'Number Ones' debuts at number 13 in the US charts.

December 7
It is reported that arraignment for Michael Jackson in the child molestation case, will be held on January 9, 2004 (later moved to January 16), at the Santa Maria Courts Complex, and future criminal proceedings likely will take place in the North County. Because Neverland is in North County, the case must be heard in Santa Maria unless prosecution or defence files for it to be moved. It is unknown what judge will be hearing the case.

December 18
Prosecutors formally charge Michael Jackson with child molestation in Santa Maria.

Michael is charged with seven counts of lewd acts on a child under the age of 14 and two counts of administering an intoxicating agent to a child (in this case liquor) for the purpose of committing a crime. The charges stem for instances that allegedly took place between February 7 and March 10 for the first five counts, and between February 20 and March 10 for the last four counts.

Michael's attorney, Mark Geragos, tells reporters: "What we have here is an intersection of two things, a shakedown for money and an axe to grind. Anyone who knows the history of the accusers, anyone who knows the history of the investigator knows that the charges are driven by two things: money and revenge. There is no truth to any of this."

2003

Page Opposite: Michael makes an appearance at a charity event to raise funds for Lupus LA and Lupus Research at the Beverly Hills Hotel.

This Page: The infamous mugshot that Michael had to have taken as allegations of child abuse were brought against him.

Santa Barbara County Sheriff's Dept.

11/20/2003
Photo Image of:
NAME: JACKSON, MICHAEL
RAC: B   SEX: M
DOB: 8/29/1958   AGE: 45
HGT: 511   WGT: 120
BLD: CMP:
HAI: BLK   EYE: BRO
MKS:
BOOKING #:   621785

This Page: Surrounded by members of his family, Michael arrives at the Santa Maria Courthouse for the initial hearing in the child molestation case.

December 20

Approximately 600 friends and family gather at Neverland Valley Ranch for a private get-together, entitled 'You Are Not Alone'.

"This event is to show Michael that he has the love and support of his friends and family," Stuart Backerman told reporters outside the estate.

December 28

An interview with Michael by Ed Bradley, recorded on Christmas day is shown on CBS's *60 Minutes*. Asked about the allegations that were brought by the district attorney in Santa Barbara, that he molested a boy, Michael replies: "Totally false. Before I would hurt a child, I would slit my wrists. I would never hurt a child. It's totally false. I was outraged. I could never do something like that."

December 30

Stuart Backerman, Michael's chief spokesman, resigns over what he called "strategic differences" with other members of Michael's entourage.

December 31

The Jackson family issue a statement that reads, "What the tapes the Santa Barbara sheriff released shows is interesting but what it conceals is vital. The tapes do not address any of the allegations that Michael made but only paint a portrait of what the sheriff's men did when the cameras were on them, not what they did when no one was looking. We look forward to a further investigation when all the facts come out in due course."

The statement is in response to Michael's claims that he was injured by Police during his arrest last month.

2004
January 2

The CBS special *Michael Jackson Number Ones* airs in America.

January 4

A press release from Kevin McLin, identified in the release as Michael Jackson's publicist, states that Michael is in control of his business and those employed under him. This is in response to a news piece in the *New York Times* dated December 30, 2003 that stated that the organisation, the Nation Of Islam, is making the key decisions regarding the handling of Michael Jackson and his vast businesses.

January 10

It is announced that Michael will be featuring in the film *Miss Cast Away*, directed by Bryan Michael Stoller.

January 16

Michael arrives at the court in Santa Maria at about 8.35am local time for the initial hearing in the child molestation case. Surrounded by bodyguards and members of his family, Michael wears a smart black jacket, with a Royal Serbian medal hung around his neck from a red and white ribbon.

He is told off by the judge for arriving in court 21 minutes late. The judge schedules February 13, 2004 at 8.30am as the date for a preliminary hearing into whether there is enough evidence to hold Michael for trial.

As Michael leaves the court the noise from the hundreds of fans gathered outside reaches fever pitch, with Michael's music blasting out from various portable stereos. Not to disappoint his fans, Michael climbs on the roof of his car, smiling and waving at supporters, blowing them kisses and flashing peace signs, before being driven away.

Michael's entourage hands out invitations to the fans that read, "In the spirit of love and togetherness, Michael Jackson would like to invite his fans and supporters to his Neverland Ranch. Please join us Friday, January 16, 2004, from 11am to 2pm. Refreshments will be served. We'll see you there."

Everyone then flocks to Neverland for an 'after arraignment' party.

January 27

Michael and his support team issue a 'thank you' note to all of the fans that have shown their love and support at this difficult time.

February 13

Michael does not attend court today for the pre-trial hearing in Santa Maria, where all parties in the case agree to return to court on April 2, 2004 to set a date for the preliminary hearing.

Earlier, Charles Koppelman denies reports that Michael is having financial problems. The *New York Times* claims he owed $70m (£36m) to the Bank of America, but was unable to repay the loan.

Koppelman insists Michael's assets far exceeded his debts, saying Michael "has the ability to generate huge sums of money".

February 24

Judge Philip Simon removes Michael's name from the lawsuit brought against the Jackson 5 by Steeltown boss Gordon Keith and other musicians. The judge ruled that Michael (and his brothers) had no involvement in the disputed 1996 compilation of songs the Jackson 5 performed long ago, clearing him of any liability.

March 1

Michael launches his personal website, MJJSource.com, which becomes the official site for news and information regarding him and his projects.

Michael says, "I have become disturbed and troubled as a result of people speaking on my behalf whom I do not know. For months, I have listened to reports that are inaccurate because most have been based on hearsay, and not fact. I have also listened, with amazement, to people who have misrepresented their relationships with me. I will use this site as one of the mediums for speaking out on my own behalf."

March 9

Michael Jackson - The One DVD is released in the US. The DVD contains 44 minutes taken from the CBS Special which aired in the US.

It includes live performances from the 'Thriller' and 'Off The Wall' eras, behind the scenes footage from the 'Wanna Be Startin' Somethin' and footage from the HIStory tour. The DVD also features commentaries from Quincy Jones, Dick Clark, Missy Elliot, Pharrel Williams and Beyonce.

The 'Essential Jackson's' album is released in the USA.

March 15

Michael Jackson - The One DVD is released in the UK.

March 18

Judge Melville issues a gag order prohibiting both the prosecution and defence teams from speaking substantively about any issue relating to the child molestation criminal case involving Michael.

March 19

Michael's Personal Attorney, Steve Cochran, releases the following statement regarding a decision by the Department of Child and Family Services not to remove Michael's children from his care. "We appreciate the decision of the Department of Child and Family Services for its determination not to pursue any adverse proceedings concerning Mr. Jackson's children. That is the correct decision, because Mr. Jackson is a loving father who takes great care of his children."

March 25

Michael has filed a lawsuit in US District Court in Los Angeles to regain possessions that were sold to a European buyer by Henry Vaccaro.

Vaccaro had come into possession of the memorabilia that includes costumes, letters, financial documents, awards and other items after a tangled web of circumstances led to his acquiring the contents of a Californian warehouse filled with Jackson family memorabilia and personal property.

2004

Los Angeles lawyer, Brian Wolf, states: "Basically the lawsuit is that this guy Vaccaro has no right to any possession of property belonging to Michael Jackson."

March 30
Michael arrives in Washington D.C. to meet privately with several members of the US Congress in the office of Republican Chaka Fattah, D-Pa. During their meeting they speak of fighting AIDS in Africa. Fattah said during the meeting that Michael was, "One of the leading celebrities in the world who has actually used his celebrity status to help people."

March 31
Michael Jackson met for the second day with Washington legislators to continue his discussion on garnering more support for the fight against AIDS in Africa. A crowd of fans gather and voice their support for Michael as he enters a Capitol Hill office.

This Page: Michael at the Ethiopian Embassy in Washiongton D.C., where he was presented with an award for his work fighting AIDS.

Below: Michael is snapped ariving at the courthouse in Santa Maria.

April 1
Michael is presented with a golden elephant as an award for his work in fighting AIDS in Africa. The award ceremony is held at the Ethiopian Embassy in Washington D.C., and is presented by AASA (African Ambassadors' Spouses Association).

April 2
A further court hearing takes place in Santa Maria, as prosecutors and lawyers meet to determine whether there is enough evidence for the child molestation trial to go ahead. Michael was not required to be present during the hearing.

April 8
Michael and his children go on vacation to Orlando, Florida to visit theme parks.

April 19
Michael wins a restraining order to stop Henry V. Vaccaro from selling personal property, including his stage costumes and other memorabilia, which Vaccaro had bought from the Jackson family.

April 25
Michael dismisses Mark Geragos and Benjamin Brafman from representing him against the child molestation charges brought against him.

April 30
Michael appears in court in Santa Maria to hear the 10 charges of child molestation brought against him, after a grand jury decided there was enough evidence for him to face a trial.

Michael's new lawyer, Thomas Mesereau, enters a "not guilty to all charges" plea on behalf of Michael. After the hearing, Mr Mesereau states, "This case is about one thing only. It's about the dignity, the integrity, the decency, the honour, the charity, the innocence and the complete vindication of a wonderful human being named Michael Jackson."

May 31

A tentative date of September 13, 2004 is set for Michael's trial for alleged child molestation. Judge Melville also hears arguments on reducing Michael's bail, but does not issue an immediate ruling.

Thomas Mesereau, Michael's attorney, objects to setting the date because the prosecution had not supplied the defence with all of the evidence they hold in the case.

June 10

After 20 years at MJJ Productions, Bob Jones' position as Vice-President of communications is terminated. During his employment, Mr. Jones had been an excellent spokesman, and extremely proactive in helping to build Michael's legacy around the world.

Bob Jones was heavily involved in the original publication of this book, along with many other fan related projects.

Mr. Jones assistant, Felicia Ferris, also has her contract terminated.

June 11

Michael releases the following statement on hearing the news of the death of Ray Charles, who passed away yesterday. "I am saddened to hear of the death of my friend, Ray Charles. He was a true legend... an American Treasure. His music is timeless; his contributions to the music industry... unequalled; and his influence, unparalleled. His caring and humility spoke volumes. He paved the way for so many of us, and I will forever remember him in my heart."

June 16

Santa Barbara County Judge Rodney S. Melville refuses to lower Michael Jackson's $3 million bail. He states that Michael's wealth justified the higher-than-normal bail amount and that the bail should remain higher than what is typically imposed on defendants facing similar charges to ensure that Michael appears at future court dates.

June 16

On ebay's American website the "Most Valuable Piece of Rock Star Clothing", according to the *Guinness Book of World Records*, is being auctioned - a white sequined Michael Jackson glove.

The glove, designed by Michael in collaboration with one of his costume designers, is made with Swarovski Aurora Borealis crystals, individually hand-sewn. The assembly allows for complete flexibility and individual movement of each stone.

Michael presented this glove to the late Sammy Davis Jnr. in the Eighties and is on ebay's site with a starting price of $3 million. The money raised will benefit the SOS Fund (Support our Students).

June 28

'The Very Best Of The Jacksons' double album is released in the UK.

July 20

'The Jacksons Story', a new Jacksons' album is released in USA, on Hip-O Records

July 26

Prosecutors detail the conspiracy aspect of their case against Michael Jackson, accusing him of imprisoning his accuser and coercing him to make a videotaped statement that no molestation had occurred, all while conducting a campaign to seduce him.

During the hearing in Santa Maria, California, for which Michael was not present, Deputy District Attorney Gordon Auchincloss claims that Michael panicked after the Martin Bashir documentary *Living With Michael Jackson* aired in February 2003, because the show focused on his attachments to and behaviour with young boys, including the alleged victim. In the programme, Michael defended his decision to let children sleep in his bed.

"Michael Jackson's rationalization of his conduct on international television was his downfall," claims Auchincloss. "His reputation was completely and utterly ruined, as was his image, his empire, his career. The documentary brought Jackson's whole world crashing down."

Auchincloss argues that Jackson set about luring the boy's family to stay at his Neverland Ranch, as well as various resorts, because they could be a valuable public relations tool to "quell the outrage". During this period, Auchincloss said, Jackson decided that he needed the alleged victim to say on tape that nothing inappropriate happened. Jackson also began to entice the boy with alcohol, Auchincloss claimed — wine in soda cans called "Jesus juice".

Michael's attorney Thomas Mesereau, states: "The idea that they were imprisoned and forced to fly on private jets to Florida, to socialize with celebrities such as Chris Tucker, is absurd on its face. It would be laughed out of court by a jury."

2004

Auchincloss' arguments are a response to a defence motion to dismiss the case. Jackson's defence team also ask to delay the trial for four months. Judge Rodney Melville grants the motion, acknowledging that he had been "overly optimistic" when he originally scheduled the trial to start on September 13, 2004.

The trial is now scheduled to begin on January 31, 2005.

July 28

Accompanied by a large entourage of security guards and a female friend, Michael goes shopping at Memorial City Mall in Houston, Texas. Seemingly in good spirits, he signs autographs for by-standers.

Raymone Bain states that he was there, "on business, and just decided to drop by the mall".

August 15

Wearing a dark blue velvet jacket with a gold armband, Michael attends the First AME Church in Los Angeles for this morning's service. He is accompanied by his attorney Thomas Mesereau, brother Randy and Steve Harvey.

After the service, Michael made his way to the church's Cecil Murray Education Center, where he answers questions from Sunday school students.

August 16

Dressed in symbolic white three-piece suit, Michael returns to court to watch a showdown over key evidence with District Attorney Tom Sneddon. Michael is accompanied by his parents, Katherine and Joseph, as well as his siblings, Randy, Janet, Jackie, LaToya, and Jermaine – who also wear white as a symbol of unity and support.

August 19

The following statement, written on August 10 and approved by Judge Rodney Melville on August 16, is released to the public through Michael's official site MJJ Source: "My family and I have dedicated our lives to spreading unity and peace to the world through our music. The most recent unauthorized version of my life story, *Man In The Mirror*, in no way shape or form represents who we are as a family. It is unfortunate that for years, we have been targets of completely inaccurate and false portrayals. We have watched, as we have been vilified and humiliated. I personally, have suffered through many hurtful lies and references to me as 'Wacko Jacko' as well as the latest untruth about me fathering quadruplets.

"This is intolerable and must stop. The public depiction of us is not who we are, or what we are: we are a loving family. My success on stage can be attributed to the love and support of my family off stage. My brothers and I are 'brothers' first, we started out together and will always be together. All I can hope for is that one day, my family will be shown the same kindness and respect that we have, throughout our lives, shown to others."

August 20

MJJ Source announce that on August 16 a death threat against Michael Jackson was received via e-mail at the Santa Maria courthouse, where he was making a court appearance.

Police traced the message back to a Kitchener, Ontario address in Canada.

Adrian Poffley, 26, of Kitchener, Ontario was charged with sending the death threat and is scheduled to appear in court in September.

August 29

Michael celebrates his 46th Birthday.

September 17

Michael and his family again attend court in Santa Maria.

October 12

Michael speaks over the phone on Steve Harvey's *The Beat* radio show about the recent Eminem video which doesn't look too kindly on Michael. Within the short interview, Michael says, "I would like to thank you, Steve, Radio One, the African-American community, my fans from around the world, and some of the members of the media, for the support that you have given to me. I would also like to thank Mr. Robert Johnson, Chairman and Founder of BET for pulling the Eminem video from BET's airplay. I appreciate very much the love and support that you all have shown me. I am very angry at Eminem's depiction of me in his video. I feel that it is outrageous and disrespectful. It is one thing to spoof, but it is another to be demeaning and insensitive.

"I've admired Eminem as an artist, and was shocked by this. The video was inappropriate and disrespectful to me, my children, my family, and the community at large. It is my hope that the other networks will take BET's lead and pull it."

November 10

Michael is inducted into the UK's first Hall of Fame for Music, but is not present for the inaugural ceremony in London.

November 11

Around 300 Michael Jackson fans attend a support rally in New York City, demonstrating over MTV's refusal to stop

airing the Eminem video that demeans Michael Jackson.

In a phone call to Geraldo Rivera at the rally, Michael says: "It's demeaning and disrespectful... I also want to make it clear that it's not just about Michael Jackson... but about a pattern of disrespect that he has shown to our community. He needs to stop it, and he needs to stop it now."

November 19

'Joyful Jukebox Music/Boogie Now' is released as a double CD in the US. The 'Boogie' album also features 'Hum Along And Dance', previously unreleased, as a bonus track.

November 20

The DVD of Bryan Michael Stoller's comedy *Miss Cast Away*, which includes cameo appearances by Michael, is released on DVD.

November 21

Adrian Grant and MJWN hold an album launch party in London for Michael Jackson's new Sony releasem 'The Ultimate Collection'.

November 22

Sony releases four of Michael's albums as double CD sets, 'Off The Wall/Thriller' and 'Bad/Dangerous'.

November 23

Adrian Poffley, 26, pleads guilty to e-mailing death threats to Michael Jackson. He is given a year's probabtion and a conditional discharge.

December 3

Armed with a new search warrant, police again raid Michael's Neverland Valley Ranch.

The search comes almost a year after police officers raided the ranch in search of evidence to be used against Michael to indict him on child molestation allegations.

2004

This Page & Opposite: Michael at the courthouse in Santa Maria for the first day of jury selection

2005

The Santa Barbara County Sheriff's Department release a statement saying the search was "part of an ongoing criminal investigation."

December 4

Michael came by helicopter into Neverland Valley Ranch so that officers in the child molestation case can swab his mouth for evidence. The police requested a saliva sample from Michael for DNA testing, and he agreed to return home to give one.

December 17

Over 200 children from various organizations attend a party at Neverland Ranch. They include children with special needs from Santa Barbara as well as a group of children affiliated with the First AME Church in Los Angeles.

Michael greets the children, aged from 3 to 17 years old, wishing them, "A very Merry Christmas and a happy New Year!"

Raymone Bain, Michael's spokeswoman, says that he chose to make an unusual personal appearance as a surprise for the last group of children touring Neverland before the Christmas holidays.

2005
January 4

Michael releases a statement regarding the Tsunami Disaster: "My family and I would like to send our prayers and heartfelt sympathy to the families, friends and loved ones of those who recently perished from the horrific earthquake and tsunami… Words cannot adequately express the shock, horror and grief we've felt, while watching news reports which have captured the massive devastation and despair. It has been especially painful for me, as I have visited these areas many times and I remember the love, kindness

and warmth of the people I met there.

"I would like to encourage all of my friends, and fans, to contribute to agencies and organizations assisting in these efforts. In times like these, we need each other... we must bond together in spirit and in service. God Bless. Sincerely, Michael Jackson."

January 14

Due to a court ruling that throughout Michael's forthcoming trial no cameras will be allowed in the courtroom, Sky News in the UK announce a partnership with E! Entertainment Television in the USA to present a half hour courtroom reconstruction with actors chronicling each day. The programme will simply be entitled *The Michael Jackson Trial*.

Using reconstructions with actors of verbatim court transcripts, this series will highlight portions of the previous day's testimony and events in the courtroom.

January 30

Michael releases a video statement, approved by Judge Rodney Melville.

Michael says, "In the last few weeks, a large amount of ugly, malicious information has been released into the media about me. Apparently, this information was leaked through transcripts in a grand jury proceeding where neither my lawyers, nor I, ever appeared. The information is disgusting and false.

"Years ago, I allowed a family to visit and spend some time at Neverland.

"Neverland is my home. I allowed this family into my home because they told me their son was ill with cancer and needed my help. Through the years, I have helped thousands of children who were ill or in distress.

"These events have caused a nightmare for my family, my children and me. I never intend to place myself in so vulnerable a position again.

"I love my community and I have great faith in our justice system. Please keep an open mind and let me have my day in court. I deserve a fair trial like every other American citizen. I will be acquitted and vindicated when the truth is told. Thank you."

January 31

Michael arrives at court for the first day of jury selection, without his family and friends, who could not attend due to lack of space in the courtroom. Dressed all in white and wearing sunglasses, Michael briefly waves to his fans and gives them the peace sign, before entering the courtroom with Thomas Mesereau.

During the day more than three hundred prospective jurors are seen, with the suitable candidates going on to the second round of the selection process, by completing a questionnaire. Twenty jurors will eventually be chosen for the trial, an initial twelve, plus eight in reserve.

Throughout the day's proceedings Michael looks confident. Michael's spokesperson Raymone Bain says that he is in "good spirits" and adds: "He has the support of his family, his children, his friends. You're going to see a Michael Jackson who is going to be here today, who is very serious, very businesslike and very serious."

As expected, Santa Maria is overrun with media, many queuing five hours to receive a press pass for what they are calling "The trial of the century".

The trial is expected to go on for at least 6 months.

Afterword

Adrian Grant with Michael, on the video set of 'Stranger In Moscow', July 1996

Since the first publication of this book in 1994 it has been updated four times, and I have lost count of the number of occasions when I have had the pleasure of meeting Michael. Everyone who knows of my work always ask 'What is he (Michael) like then?'

As I said in the introduction, *The Visual Documentary* delivers only the facts behind Michael's illustrious career in the entertainment industry. I have not interviewed people Michael has met or worked with, nor sought scandalous gossip or details of his private life. Neither does the book carry my own personal opinions.

Nevertheless, I do wonder if history will portray Michael as the true musical genius he is, or as the misunderstood enigma that the media likes to ridicule.

So when people now ask me about his personality I make sure they know what a talented and kind natured gentleman he is.

Unfortunately Michael has been in the news over the last two years for reasons far removed from his music or acts of humanitarian goodwill. Accused of child molestation and kidnapping, this latest edition of *The Visual Documentary* went to press just as the trial 'of the century' began in Santa Maria, California. Michael had pleaded not guilty to 10 charges brought against him by District Attorney Tom Sneddon, based on allegations made by a teenage boy, Gavin Arvizo.

By the time this book is published and you are reading this afterword the outcome of the trial may well be known. Given a fair trial, I believe that Michael Jackson will have walked away from this case an innocent man, free to resume his life and livelihood, and putting this terrible ordeal behind him.

The Michael Jackson I know, that I have interviewed many times, played games with, dined with, visited hospitals and youth centres with, is an innocent man. The Michael Jackson that I have laughed with, watched films with, attended award ceremonies with, and seen play with and look after hundreds of kids, is an innocent man. Unfortunately for Michael it is too easy to paint a negative picture of his alternative lifestyle. It is easy to twist his motives and question his sincerity. It would be easy for me to do that, to take the trust he has put in me and do a 'Bashir', mocking him because he seems too extreme or different to your everyday guy. But I won't be joining the legions of ex-Jackson acquaintances who have 'sold-out' for a quick buck. I'd rather keep my integrity and set the record straight, where I can.

His appearance. Yes, he has had plastic surgery, but not to the extent people like to believe. He freely admits to having his nose changed a few times. Big deal. Half of Hollywood have, move on. In September 1987, during a telephone call to American chat show host Barbara Walters, Michael said his change in appearance was not only down to two nose jobs and having a cleft put in his chin, but also due to his change in diet over the years, having become a vegetarian.

But what people seem to freak out most over is his skin colour. This is where I feel most sorry for Michael, because he really does have a skin condition called vitiligo, yet most of the media still ridicule his paleness or the fact that he hides from the sun. When you see someone with skin burns do you call them names? Michael has a skin disease that cannot be cured. All he can do is control it in the most aesthetic way he feels comfortable with. When I first met Michael in 1990 he was in the very early stages of the disease, but over the years and during subsequent meetings I could see that patches were appearing across his skin. This is a common effect of vitiligo.

I also recall meeting Michael in New York, November '95, during the recording of his album, 'History'. We were having a conversation in his office, yet Michael felt so uncomfortable with the condition of his skin that he actually apologised to me. This just embarrassed me because he looked fine and I told him not to worry about it. Then there was a knock at the door. Someone had a delivery for him, but Michael felt so self-conscious that he didn't want them to come in the room. He even asked me if I should let them in, and could I lower the light dimmer. So that is what suffering from vitiligo can be like. It's an unpleasant condition to have to endure, but to be the most famous man in the world and constantly under the media microscope, makes it extremely difficult to cope with.

His home - Neverland Valley in Santa Ynez, California - is often the subject of mockery, just because he has a fun fair and a zoo. I've been there on many occasions and these things are fantastic! Who wouldn't want their own fair complete with dodgems and Ferris wheel? And who doesn't love animals? Michael has enough space (over 3,000 acres) to house and look after two zoos. Yes there are llamas, giraffes, elephants, monkeys, tigers and more, and they are all beautiful.

Yes, Michael loves the games, the rides and the animals, but it is not just for his own pleasure. These playthings are there for the enjoyment of others too. Every week Michael opens the doors of his home to hundreds of less fortunate children. Many charity organisations are granted the use of the facilities and treated by Michael's staff as special guests of honour.

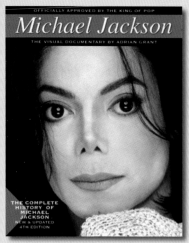

Michael has donated millions of dollars to various charities around the world, and even set-up his own, including 'Heal The Kids', an initiative that stresses the importance of parents spending quality time with their children.

Following Michael's interview with Martin Bashir and the media invasion that followed, I said to myself that the next time I met Michael I must talk with him about his public image. I had always felt that people would be more sympathetic if they knew him the way I did, if he just opened up more and said things straight – as they are. When that opportunity came I asked Michael if he was aware of all the negative media he received and couldn't he change some of his actions to help combat their slander. "I know everything that is going on. No matter what I do they'll always write something bad," Michael told me sternly.

Unfortunately for Michael this is so true. I recall a trip to Budapest in 1994. Michael, along with Lisa Marie-Presley, was visiting children's hospitals handing out various gifts and toys. I was fortunate to be the only 'journalist' allowed to accompany the couple into the hospitals, and I was delighted to help in giving the gifts to some of the sick children. However the sceptical press suggested the trip (part of Michael's 'Heal The World' campaign), was nothing more than a publicity stunt. What they didn't report was the moving moment Michael brought a smile to the face of a dying girl who had lain motionless and silent for weeks. Her mother, at her side in constant vigil, broke down in tears as her daughter reached out and touched Michael's hand. Sounds like a miracle, but I saw it with my own eyes. So why is it that people constantly deride someone who genuinely cares and who also happens to be one of the world's greatest ever entertainers to boot…

I feel the reason is a lack of understanding. People cannot relate to Michael in the way that do with other stars, especially in this day and age of reality TV. Michael is on a very high pedestal that makes him unique, but also attracts many people who want to knock him from his perch. He has been accused of all sorts, but as Michael put it, "Don't judge a man until you have walked two moons in his moccasins…" For us that would be an awful lot of moonwalking. This book emphasises how much Michael has achieved since he was a five-year old kid singing in his kindergarten. Put yourself in those shoes; imagine those achievements, the accolades, and the wealth. You could do anything you want. Give yourself three wishes. Hopefully one of them would be for peace and love in the world, but how is that going to happen? We can only do what little we can, according to the resources and knowledge we have.

While handing out the toys to the overwhelmed children, Michael turned to me, his big angelic eyes moist with sadness at the plight of some of the kids. "Nobody said healing the world would be easy," I said. He sighed and lowered his head for a second in agreement, then turned to play joyfully with a child who had received a Batman toy.

A few years later I spoke to Michael about his greatest ever achievements. During his trip to Budapest in 1994 Michael had promised to help an eight-year old Hungarian boy, Bella, who was dying from cancer. His life was saved with an operation that Michael and his 'Heal The World' foundation had paid for. "Saving Bella's life was definitely one of the most important moments in my life," said Michael honestly. Gavin Arvizo was another child, dying from cancer that Michael had innocently tried to help. Unfortunately for Michael playing the good Samaritan this time round turned into a nightmare.

I sometimes feel Michael is underrated as an artist. There is so much more to his genius than the record-breaking sales of albums such as 'Thriller', 'Bad', 'Dangerous' and 'History'. Look at the quality of his work, the videos and the live performances. I have been fortunate enough to see Michael produce songs in a recording studio on a few occasions. Here is a man who has been learning his art since the age of five, and it shows when you hear and see him. He knows the tools of his trade inside out like second nature. This allows him to channel his heart and soul into his creations, and take them a step further than most artists. Listen to tracks such as 'Wanna Be Startin' Somethin', 'Billie Jean', 'Earth Song', 'Speechless', and 'Whatever Happens' – pure pop genius.

As a perfectionist, he wants the best out of everything, especially himself. Although he is also accomplished on the keyboards and drums he would rather have the best musicians in the world do that job than receive another ego-busting credit. And even though he is an outstanding vocalist he still takes the time to train and develop his voice further. The incredible thing is that there is still so much more to come – on song, stage and film.

It means a lot to me that I have had the opportunity to document the history of one of the world's greatest ever entertainers. Indeed one of my proudest moments came one day when I was at Neverland and I saw that Michael had framed the family tree from this book, and placed it beside his grand piano where he entertained guests. He also told me how grateful he is for my work, and acknowledged *The Visual Documentary* in the 'History' album sleeve notes.

Michael - it is I who am extremely grateful to you. Your work has been a real inspiration!

Adrian Grant, January 2005

VERY SPECIAL THANKS TO:

Bob Jones for your support from the very beginning. You opened the doors to so many memorable encounters with the King of Pop. Thank you.

Jayne Ross (pictured left), you have been a tremendous support. Thank you for telling the truth when others were lying, and thank you for all the research you have done in putting this book together. Lots of love from the Special Service Department.

VINYL ALBUMS

May	1972	STML	11205	Got To Be There
Dec	1972	STML	11220	Ben
July	1973	STML	11235	Music & Me
March	1975	STMA	8022	Forever Michael
Sept	1975	STML	12005	The Best Of Michael Jackson
Oct	1978	MCA/MCSP	287	The Wiz Soundtrack
Aug	1979	EPC	83468	Off The Wall
Aug	1979	EPC	83458	Off The Wall (Picture Disc)
June	1981	STMR	9009	The Best Of Michael Jackson (Re-Issue)
July	1981	STML	12158	One Day In Your Life
Oct	1981	STMS	5007	Got To Be There
Oct	1981	STMS	5008	Ben (Re-Issue)
Oct	1982	TMS	3511	Aint No Sunshine
Dec	1982	EPC	85930	Thriller
Jan	1983	MCA	70000	ET Storybook (Box Set)
June	1983	STMS	5095	Forever Michael (Re-Issue)
July	1983	STAR	2232	18 Greatest Hits (incl. Jackson 5)
July	1983	EPC	85930	Thriller (Picture Disc)
May	1984	WL	72069	Ben (Re-Issue)
June	1984	ZL	72227	Farewell My Summer Love
Nov	1984	WL	72291	Music & Me
Nov	1984	WL	72289	Great Love Songs Of Michael Jackson
	1985	WL	72063	Best Of Michael Jackson
May	1986	WL	72424	Looking Back To Yesterday
	1986	WL	72068	Got To Be There (Re-Issue)
Sept	1987	EPC	450290-1	Bad
Oct	1987	EPC	450290-8	Bad (Casette Gift Pack)
Oct	1987	STAR	2298	Michael Jackson & Diana Ross Love Songs
Nov	1987	EPC	450290-0	Bad (Picture Disc)
Dec	1987	SMR	745	The Michael Jackson Mix
Feb	1988	ZL	72622	The Original Soul of Michael Jackson
May	1988	WL	72630	Farewell My Summer Love (Re-Issue)
Sept	1988	WD	72641	Michael Jackson & The Jackson 5 Live
Nov	1991	EPC	4658021	Dangerous
Nov	1991	EK	48900	Dangerous (Collectors Edition)
March	1992	530	014-1	Motown Greatest Hits - Michael Jackson
June	1992	EPC	658281-4	MJ4 Tour Souvenir Pack
June	1995	EPC	474709	HIStory Past Present & Future... Book 1
May	1997	EPC	4875002	Blood On The Dance Floor
Oct	2001	EPC	495174	Invincible
Nov	2003	XSS	56430	One More Chance (Promo - Double Album)

CD ALBUMS

	1985	WD	72063	Best Of Michael Jackson
Feb	1986	530	178-2	Anthology - Michael Jackson
Nov	1986	ZD	72468	Got To Be There/Ben
Jan	1987	ZD	72530	Anthology - Michael Jackson (Re-Issue)
Sept	1987	EPC	450 290-2	Bad
Oct	1987	TCD	2298	Love Songs Of Michael Jackson
Oct	1987	WD	72420	18 Greatest Hits - Command Performance
Nov	1987	EPC	450 290-9	Bad (Picture Disc)
Dec	1987	CDEPC	83468	Off The Wall
Dec	1987	CDEPC	85930	Thriller
Dec	1987	SMD	745	Michael Jackson Mix
Feb	1988	ZD	72622	The Original Soul Of Michael Jackson
July	1988	WD	72629	18 Greatest Hits (inc. Jackson 5)
Jan	1989	WD	72641	Michael Jackson & The Jackson 5 Live
June	1989	WD	72068	Got To Be There
Oct	1989	WD	72630	Farewell My Summer Love
Nov	1989	WD	72069	Ben
Feb	1990	WD	72121	Forever Michael
March	1990	WD	72891	Michael Jackson & Diana Ross Love Songs
Nov	1991	EPC	45 802-2	Dangerous
Dec	1991	EPC	465 802-9	Dangerous (Limited Edition Pop-Up Box)
March	1992		550 078-2	Motown Greatest Hits - Michael Jackson
June	1992	MJ4	658281-14	Tour Souvenir Pack (Special Ltd. Edition)
Feb	1993	EPC	465802-2D	Dangerous/Off The Wall (2 CD Set)
May	1993		550 078-2	Music & Me
Aug	1993		530 162-2	Got To Be There (Re-Issue)
Sept	1993		530 163-2	Ben (Re-Issue)
June	1995	EPC	474 709 2	HIStory - Past Present & Future...Book 1
May	1997	EPIC	4875002	Blood On The Dance Floor
Feb	1998	EFA	88902-2	The Steeltown Sessions (Jackson 5)
June	1999	CDX	83468	Off The Wall (Limited Edition Digipak)
Nov	1999	MILLEN	44952162	Thriller (Limited Millennium Edition)
July	2000	MOTOWN	157170-2	'Ripples And Waves' - An Introduction To The J5
Aug	2000	E	5304392	Forever Michael/Music & Me/Ben
Oct	2000		649792	Music & Me
Dec	2000	AA	121599172	The Millenium Collection - Michael Jackson
March	2001	E	0134912	The Universal Masters Collection: Classic Michael
Oct	2001	EPC	4951742	Invincible
Oct	2001	EPC	5044212004	Off The Wall (Special Edition with Bonus Tracks)
Oct	2001	EPC	50442212	Thriller (Special Edition with Bonus Tracks)
Oct	2001	EPC	50442326	Bad (Special Edition with Bonus Tracks)
Oct	2001	EPC	50442425	Dangerous (Special Edition with Bonus Tracks)
Oct	2001		5308042	Best of Michael Jackson/Jackson 5
Nov	2001	EPC	5018692	History (Re-mastered)
Feb	2002	MOTOWN	168192	Love Songs - Michael Jackson
Nov	2003	EPC	2513800	Number Ones
Dec	2003	EPC	5044212	Off The Wall (Re-mastered)
Dec	2003	EPC	5044222	Thriller (Re-mastered)
Dec	2003	EPC	5044232	Bad (Re-mastered)
Dec	2003	EPC	5044242	Dangerous (Re-mastered)
Dec	2003	EPC	4875002	Blood On The Dancefloor (Re-Issue)
Feb	2004	EPC	5301622	Got To Be There (Re-Issue)
June	2004		5163669	Very Best Of The Jacksons
Nov	2004		5175542	Off The Wall/Thriller (Double CD inc.Bonus Tracks)
Nov	2004		5175552	Bad/Dangerous (Double CD incl. Bonus Tracks)
Nov	2004	EPC	5177433	Ultimate Collection (incl. 4 CDs & Concert DVD)

7" SINGLES

Jan	1972	TMG	797	Got To Be There/Maria
May	1972	TMG	815	Rockin' Robin/Love Is Here And Now You're Gone
Aug	1972	TMG	826	Ain't No Sunshine/I Wanna Be Where You Are
Nov	1972	TMG	834	Ben/You Can Cry On My Shoulder
July	1973	TMG	863	Morning Glow/My Girl
May	1974	TMG	900	Music & Me/ Johnny Raven
April	1975	TMG	946	One Day In Your Life/With A Child's Heart
Oct	1975	TMG	1006	Just A Little Bit Of You/Dear Michael
Oct	1978	MCA	396	Ease On Down The Road/Poppy Girls
May	1979	EPC	7135	You Can't Win (Part 1 & 2)
Aug	1979	EPC	7763	Don't Stop 'Til You Get Enough/I Can't Help It
Nov	1979	EPC	8045	Off The Wall/Working Day and Night
Feb	1980	EPC	8206	Rock With You/Get On The Floor
April	1980	TMG	1165	Ben/Abraham,Martin & John (B side M. Gaye)
April	1980	EPC	8384	She's Out Of My Life/Push Me Away
July	1980	EPC	8782	Girlfriend/Bless His Soul
Oct	1980	TMG	973	Got To Be There (B side Mary Johnson)
April	1981	TMG	976	One Day In Your Life/Take Me Back
July	1981	TMG	977	We're Almost There/We've Got A Good Thing Goin'
Oct	1981	TMG	816 (R)	Rockin' Robin/Love Is Here And Now You're Gone
Oct	1981	TMG	826 (R)	Ain't No Sunshine/I Wanna Be Where You Are
Oct	1981	TMG	834 (R)	Ben/You Can Cry On My Shoulder
April	1982	EPC	8856	Don't Stop 'Til You Get Enough/Off The Wall
Oct	1982	EPCA	112729	The Girl Is Mine/Can't Get Outta The Rain
Nov	1982	EPC	2729	The Girl Is Mine/Can't Get Outta The Rain
Jan	1983	EPC	A3084	Billie Jean/ It's The Falling In Love
March	1983	EPC	A2906	Greatest Original Hits EP
March	1983	EPC	A3258	Beat It/Burn The Disco Out
June	1983	EPC	A3427	Wanna Be Startin' Somethin'/Rock With You Live
July	1983	TMG	986	Happy/We're Almost There (Ltd. Ed. Poster Bag)
July	1983	TMGP	986	Happy/We're Almost There
Oct	1983	R	6062	Say, Say, Say/(B Side Paul McCartney)
Nov	1983	EPC	A3643	Thriller/Things I Do For You Live
Nov	1983	EPC	3643	Thriller/Things I Do For You Live (Ltd. Edition)
Nov	1983	MJ 1	(1-9)	Thriller Singles Pack
March	1984	EPC	A4136	P.Y.T. (Pretty Young Thing)/ This Place Hotel
May	1984	TMG	1342	Farewell My Summer Love/Call On Me
May	1984	MCA	898	Ease On Down The Road/Poppy Girls (Re-Issue)
May	1984	ARISTA	12609	Tell Me I'm Not Dreamin' (Duet w. J. Jackson)
Aug	1984	TMG	1355	Girl Your'e So Together/Touch The One You Love
Feb	1985	ARIST	60 9	Do What You Do/Tell Me I'm Not Dreamin'
Aug	1985	TMG	994	Got To Be There/Rockin' Robin
July	1987	EPC	6502027	I Just Can't Stop Loving You/Baby Be Mine
July	1987	EPC	6502020	I Just Can't Stop Loving You/Baby Be Mine (LE)
Sept	1987	EPC	6511557	Bad/Bad Dance Remix Radio Edit
Nov	1987	EPC	6512757	The Way You Make Me Feel/Instrumental
Nov	1987	ZB	41655	Christmas EP
Feb	1988	EPC	6513887	Man In The Mirror/Instrumental
Feb	1988	EPC	6513889	Man In The Mirror/Instr. (Square Picture Disc)
March	1988	ZB	41913	I Want You Back Remix/Never Can Say Goodbye
May	1988	ZB	41883	Get It/Instrumental (Duet With Stevie Wonder)
July	1988	EPC	6515460	Dirty Diana/Instrumental
July	1988	EPC	6515467	Dirty Diana/Instrumental (13" Display Cut-Out)
July	1988	MJ 5		Bad Souvenir Singles Pack

Sept	1988	EPC	6528447	*Another Part Of Me/Instrumental*
Sept	1988	EPC	6528440	*Another Part Of Me/Instrumental (Poster Bag)*
Sept	1988	EPC	6528449	*Another Part Of Me/Instr. (Limited Edition)*
Nov	1988	EPC	6530267	*Smooth Criminal/Instrumental*
Nov	1988	EPC	6520260	*Smooth Criminal/Instrumental (Limited Edition)*
Feb	1989	EPC	6546727	*Leave Me Alone/Human Nature*
Feb	1989	EPC	6546720	*Leave Me Alone/Human Nature (Pop Up Sleeve)*
June	1989	ZD	41951	*Vintage Gold E.P.*
July	1989	EPC	6549470	*Liberian Girl/Girlfriend*
July	1989	EPC	6549479	*Liberian Girl/Girlfriend (Mobile Star Pack)*
Nov	1991	EPC	6575987	*Black Or White/Instrumental*
Jan	1992	EPC	6577747	*Remember The Time/Come Together*
April	1992	EPC	6580187	*In The Closet - The Mission Radio Edit*
April	1992	EPC	6580187	*In The Closet - The Mission Radio Edit (Poster Bag)*
July	1992	EPC	6581797	*Who Is It Edit/Rock With You (Remix)*
July	1992	EPC	6581797	*Who Is It Edit/Rock With You (Remix) (LE)*
Sept	1992	EPC	6584887	*Jam 7" Edit/Beat It (Remix) (Limited Edition)*
Nov	1992	EPC	6584887	*Heal The World/She Drives Me Wild (Poster Bag)*
Feb	1993	EPC	6590697	*Give In To Me/Dirty Diana (Poster Bag)*
June	1993	EPC	6592227	*Will You Be There/Girlfriend (Poster Bag)*
Dec	1993	EPC	6599767	*Gone Too Soon/Instrumental*
June	1995	662	127 7	*Scream Def Radio Edit/Single Mix (Poster Bag)*
Oct	2001		3479656	*You Rock My World*
Dec	2001		3479660	*Cry*

12" SINGLES

Oct	1978	MCAT	12-396	*Ease On Down The Road/Poppy Girls*
April	1979	12EPC	7135	*You Can't Win (Part 1 & 2)*
Aug	1989	12EPC	7763	*Don't Stop 'Til You Get Enough Ext./I Can't Help It*
Feb	1980	12EPC	8206	*Rock With You/Get On The Floor/You Can't Win*
July	1981	TMGT	977	*We're Almost There/We've Got A Good Thing Goin'*
Jan	1983	EPC	13-3084	*Billie Jean Ext./Instr./It's The Falling In Love*
March	1983	EPC	TA3258	*Beat It/Burn This Disco Out/Don't Stop 'Til You...*
June	1983	EPCT	A3427	*Wanna Be Startin Somethin/Rock With You (Live)*
July	1983	TMGT	986	*Happy/We're Almost There*
Oct	1983	12	R6062	*Say, Say, Say/Ode To A Koala Bear (P. McCartney)*
Nov	1983	EPC	TA3643	*Thriller Remix /LP Cut/Things I do For You Live*
Nov	1983	EPC	TA3643	*Thriller Remix /Things I do For You Live (LE)*
March	1984	EPC	TA4136	*P.Y.T/Thriller Instrumental/This Place Hotel (Live)*
May	1984	TMGT	1342	*Farewell My Summer Love Extended/Call On Me*
May	1984	MCAT	898	*Ease On Down The Road/Poppy Girls (Re-Issue)*
May	1984	ARISTA	22609	*Tell Me I'm Not Dreamin' (Duet w. J. Jackson)*
Aug	1984	TMGT	1355	*Girl You're So Together/Touch The One You Love*
June	1985	TMGT	994	*Got To Be There/Rockin Robin*
July	1987	EPC	6502026	*I Just Cant Stop Loving You/Baby Be Mine (PB)*
Sept	1987	EPC	6511556	*Bad Ext. Dance Mix w. False Fade/ Dub/Acapella*
Sept	1987	EPC	651100	*Bad Ext. Dance Mix w. False Fade/ 7"Mix/Dance Radio Edit/Dub/Acapella (US Vinyl in Red)*
Nov	1987	EPC	6512758	*The Way You Make Me Feel Ext./ Dub/Acapella*
Nov	1987	EPC	6512753	*The Way You...7"/ Dub/Acapella/Dance Radio Edit*
Nov	1987	ZT	41656	*Merry Christmas from Michael Jackson and The J5*
Feb	1988	EPC	6513886	*Man In The Mirror Single Mix/Album Mix*
March	1988	ZT	41914	*I Want You Back '88 Remix/Original Mix*
May	1988	ZT	41884	*Get It Extended/Inst. (Duet with Stevie Wonder)*
July	1988	EPC	6515468	*Dirty Diana/Inst./Bad Dance Mix w. False Fade*
July	1988	EPC	6528646	*Dirty Diana/Inst./Bad Mix w. False Fade (PB)*
Sept	1988	EPC	6528446	*Another Part Of Me Ext. Dance Mix/Radio Edit*
Nov	1988	EPC	6530268	*Smooth Criminal Ext.Dance Mix/ Dub/ Acapella*
Nov	1988	EPC	6546726	*Smooth Criminal Ext.Dance Mix/ Dub/ Acapella (Limited Edition - Moonwalker Advent Calender)*
Nov	1988	EPC	6530261	*Smooth Criminal Extended Dance Mix/Annie Mix*
Feb	1989	EPC	6546726	*Leave Me Alone/Don't Stop 'Til.../Human Nature*
July	1989	EPC	6549478	*Liberian Girl/Get On The Floor/Girlfriend*
July	1989	EPC	6549471	*Liberian Girl/Girlfriend/You Can't Win Ext. Mix*
Nov	1991	EPC	6575986	*Black Or White/Bad/Instr./Thriller*
Nov	1991	EPC	6577316	*Black Or White C & C House Club Mixes*
Jan	1992	EPC	6577746	*Remember The Time 12" Main Mix/(various mixes)*
April	1992	EPC	6580186	*In The Closet (Mixes Behind Door No.2)*
July	1992	EPC	6581796	*Who Is It Patience Mix/The Most Patient Mix*
Sept	1992	EPC	6583606	*Jam Roger's Club Mix/More Than Enuff Mix/ E-Smoove's Jazzy Mix/Teddy's 12" Mix/Silky 12"*
Nov	1992	EPC	6584888	*Heal The World/Wanna Be Startin'... (remix)/ Don't Stop 'Til..(remix)/Rock With You (remix)(PB)*
Dec	1993	EPC	6599766	*Gone Too Soon/Human Nature/Thriller/ She's Out...*
June	1995	EPC	662127	*Scream (Blue Sleeve) (various mixes)*
June	1995	EPC	662127	*Scream (Pink Sleeve) (various mixes)*
Nov	1996	EPC	663352-8	*Stranger In Moscow (various mixes)*
July	1997	EPC	664615-6	*History/Ghosts (various mixes)*
Dec	1997	EPC	665130-6	*Smile (unreleased)*
Oct	2001		6720292	*You Rock My World/Instrumental/Acapella*
Dec	2001		6721826	*Cry/Shout/Streetwalker*
Nov	2003		6744808	*One More Chance/Billie Jean (Limited Ed. PD)*
Dec	2003		6744806	*One More Chance/Paul Oakenfold Remixes*
Nov	2004	XPR	3829	*Cheater (Unreleased)/One More Chance (remix)*

CD SINGLES

Nov	1987	EPC	651275-9	*The Way You Make Me Feel Dance Ext.Mix/Dub*
Feb	1988	EPC	651388-2	*Man In The Mirror/Album Mix/Instrumental*
July	1988	EPC	651546-9	*Dirty Diana/Instr./Bad Dance Mix w. False Fade*
Aug	1988	EPC	652844-2	*Another Part Of Me Dance Ext. Mix/Radio Edit*
Sept	1988	EPC	653004-2	*Another Part Of Me Dance Ext. Mix/Radio Edit (Limited Edition - Picture CD)*
Nov	1988	EPC	653026-2	*Smooth Criminal Ext. Dance Mix/Annie Mix*
Feb	1989	EPC	654672-2	*Leave Me Alone/Don't Stop 'Til You Get Enough/ Human Nature/Wanna Be Startin' Somethin' Ext.*
June	1989	ZD	41951	*Vintage Gold E.P*
July	1989	EPC	654947-2	*Liberian Girl/Girlfriend/The Lady In My Life*
Nov	1991	EPC	657598-2	*Black Or White/Instrumental/Smooth Criminal*
Nov	1991	EPC	657731-2	*Black Or White C&C House Mixes*
Jan	1992	EPC	657774-2	*Remember The Time (various mixes)/Come Together*
April	1992	EPC	658018-2	*In The Closet (various mixes)*
July	1992	EPC	658179-5	*Who Is It (remix)/Don't Stop 'Til You Get Enough*
Sept	1992	EPC	658360-2	*Jam (various mixes)/Wanna Be Startin' Somethin'*
Nov	1992	EPC	658488-5	*Heal The World/She Drives Me Wild/Man In The...*
Feb	1993	EPC	659069-2	*Give In To Me/Dirty Diana/Beat It*
June	1993	EPC	659222-2	*Will You Be There/Man In The Mirror/Girlfriend*
Dec	1993	EPC	659976-2	*Gone Too Soon/Human Nature/Thriller/She's Out...*
May	1995	EPC	662022-2	*Scream CD1 (various mixes)*
June	1995	EPC	662022-5	*Scream CD2 (various mixes)*
Aug	1995	EPC	662310-2	*You Are Not Alone CD 1 (various mixes)*
Aug	1995	EPC	662310-8	*You Are Not Alone CD 2 (various mixes)*
Nov	1995	EPC	662695-2	*Earth Song CD 1 (various mixes)*
Dec	1995	EPC	662695-5	*Earth Song CD 2 (various mixes)*
April	1996	EPC	662950-2	*They Don't Care About Us CD 1 (various mixes)*
April	1996	EPC	662950-7	*They Don't Care About Us CD 2 (various mixes)*
Aug	1996	MJJ	663649-2	*Why CD 1 (duet with 3T)*
Aug	1996	MJJ	663648-5	*Why CD 2 (duet with 3T)*
Nov	1996	EPC	663787-2	*Stranger In Moscow CD 1 (various mixes)*
Nov	1996	EPC	663787-5	*Stranger In Moscow CD 2 (various mixes)*
Nov	1996	EPC	663991-2	*I Need You CD 1 (3T including vocals from MJ)*
April	1997	EPC	664462-5	*Blood On The Dance Floor CD 1 (various mixes)*
May	1997	EPC	664462-2	*Blood On The Dance Floor CD 2 (various mixes)*
July	1997	EPC	664796-5	*History/Ghosts CD 1 (various mixes)*
July	1997	EPC	664796-2	*History/Ghosts CD 2 (various mixes)*
Dec	1997	EPC	665130-2	*Smile (unreleased)*
Oct	2001		6720292	*You Rock My World (Picture CD)*
Dec	2002		6721822	*Cry/Shout/Streetwalker/The Cry Short Film*
March	2003	MRW	4277459	*Billie Jean/Beat It/Wanna Be Startin'/Thriller/PYT*
Nov	2003		67448021	*One More Chance (various mixes)*
Nov	2004	XPCD	2969	*Cheater (unreleased)*

VIDEOS

	1983	MC	2105	*The Making Of Michael Jackson's Thriller*
	1983	SMV	10302	*Motown 25 - (includes Michael & The Jacksons + Michael's legendary Billie Jean performance)*
	1985	MVP	99110062	*USA For Africa*
	1988	MJ	1000	*Michael Jackson - The Legend Continues...*
	1988	VC	416	*The Making Of Thriller/The Legend Continues... (Double Video Set)*
	1988		084248 3	*Moonwalker*
	1992	SMV	086628 3	*The Jacksons - An American Dream*
	1993	SMV	491642	*Dangerous - The Short Films*
	1995	SMV	50123	*Michael Jackson Video Greatest Hits*
May	1997	SMV	50138-2	*History On Film Volume II*
Dec	1997	SMV	200788	*Ghosts*
Dec	1997	EPC	489155-2	*Ghosts (Limited Edition Box Set)*

DVDS

Nov	2001		501239	*Video Greatest Hits - History*
Nov	2001		491649	*Dangerous The Short Films*
Dec	2002		866283	*The Jacksons - An American Dream*
Oct	2003		501389	*History on Film Volume II*
Nov	2003		2022509	*Number One's*
March	2004		2024199	*The One*
July	2004		8225120	*The Wiz*
Nov	2004	EPC	5177433	*Ultimate Collection (Box Set inc. Dangerous Tour)*
Feb	2005		82876666019	*We Are The World (20th Anniversary Special)*
Apr	2005		D000817	*Moonwalker*

Due to line space, some abbreviations have been used within this discography as follows:

Ext.	=	Extended	LE	=	Limited Edition or
R	=	Re-Issue			Special Edition
PD	=	Picture Disc	W.	=	With
Instr.	=	Instrumental	PB	=	Poster Bag/Free Poster

If you would like more information on Michael Jackson please visit www.mjworld.net